SURREALIST MASCULINITIES

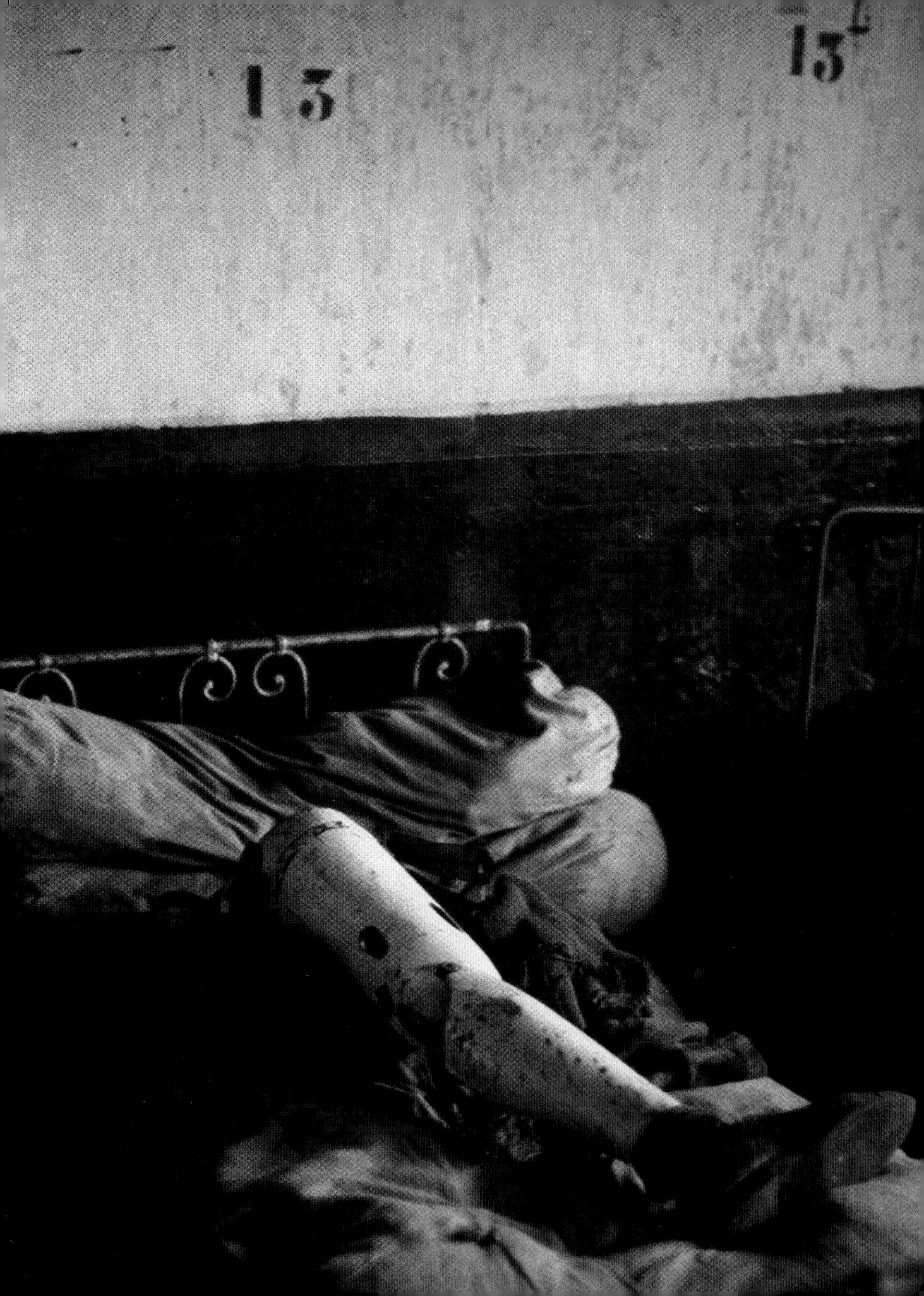
13
15

Surrealist Masculinities

Gender Anxiety and the Aesthetics of Post-World War I Reconstruction in France

AMY LYFORD

UNIVERSITY OF CALIFORNIA PRESS
Berkeley Los Angeles London

Essays based on earlier versions of some chapters have appeared in print as follows: From Chapter 2: Amy Lyford, "The Aesthetics of Dismemberment: Surrealism and the Musée du Val-de-Grâce in 1917," *Cultural Critique* 46 (Fall 2000): 45–79; from Chapter 3: Amy Lyford, "Advertising Surrealist Masculinities: André Kertész in Paris," in *Surrealism, Politics, Culture*, eds. Raymond Spiteri and Donald LaCoss (Aldershot, England: Ashgate, 2003): 73–90; from Chapter 4: Amy Lyford, "Lee Miller's Photographic Impersonations, 1930–1945," in *History of Photography* 18, no. 18 (Autumn 1994): 230–41; from Chapter 5: Amy Lyford, "Le Numéro Barbette," in *The Modern Woman Revisited*, edited by Whitney Chadwick and Tirza True Latimer (Rutgers, NJ: Rutgers University Press, 2003): 223–35.

Frontispiece: André Kertész, *Leg, Hôtel de Reveil*, 1927. See Figure 47.

University of California Press, one of the most distinguished university presses in the United States, enriches lives around the world by advancing scholarship in the humanities, social sciences, and natural sciences. Its activities are supported by the UC Press Foundation and by philanthropic contributions from individuals and institutions. For more information, visit www.ucpress.edu.

University of California Press
Berkeley and Los Angeles, California

University of California Press, Ltd.
London, England

Library of Congress Cataloging-in-Publication Data

Lyford, Amy, 1963– .
Surrealist masculinities : gender anxiety and the aesthetics of post–World War I reconstruction in France / Amy Lyford.
p. cm.
Includes bibliographical references and index.
ISBN-13: 978-0-520-24640-9 (cloth : alk. paper),
1. Masculinity in art. 2. Human figure in art. 3. Surrealism—France. 4. Arts—France—Paris. 5. World War, 1914–1918—Psychological aspects. I. Title.

NX650.M296L94 2007
709.04'063—dc22 2006016240

Manufactured in Hong Kong

16 15 14 13 12 11 10 09 08 07
10 9 8 7 6 5 4 3 2 1

The paper used in this publication meets the minimum requirements of ANSI/NISO Z39.48-1992 (R 1997) (*Permanence of Paper*).

FOR DAVE

CONTENTS

ILLUSTRATIONS

ACKNOWLEDGMENTS

This book has been a long time coming, and I could not have completed it without intellectual collaboration and financial support. I received support for research and writing from the following institutions and organizations: the Department of the History of Art and the Townsend Center for the Humanities, both at the University of California, Berkeley; the Mellon Foundation; the Samuel H. Kress Foundation; the Social Science Research Council; the National Endowment for the Humanities; and the Fulbright Fellowship program. Occidental College provided additional publication funding, and I wish to thank Kenyon Chan and Eric Frank in particular for their support of this project.

Many individuals graciously granted me access to archives and assisted my research in important ways. For their contributions to this book, I thank Thérèse Blondet-Bisch, curator of photographs at the Musée d'Histoire Contemporaine (Bibliothèque de Documentation Internationale Contemporaine), Paris, without whom I could not have found Val-de-Grâce; Mary Ann Caws; François Chapon at the Bibliothèque Littéraire Jacques Doucet, Paris; Claude Courouve; Monsieur le Colonel et Médécin-en-Chef Jean-Jacques Ferrandis and his staff at the Musée du Val-de-Grâce, Paris; Annyck Graton, Department of Photography, Musée National d'Art Moderne, Paris (Centre Georges Pompidou); Noël Bourcier and Christophe Mauberret, Fonds Kertész, Mission du Patrimoine Photographique, Paris; Danièle Maïsetti, Fonds Elsa Triolet-Aragon at the Centre National de la Recherche Scientifique, Paris; Antony Penrose, Carole Callow, and Arabella Hayes at the Lee Miller Archives, East Sussex, England; Claudia

Ponton at Art Resource New York; Lucien Treillard; Luc Vigier and François Eychart of the Société des Amis d'Elsa Triolet et Louis Aragon, France. Thanks, too, to Deb Linton for wrangling *L'Âge d'Or* stills, and especially to the intrepid John Tain, who tracked down some wayward images in Paris.

Friends' and colleagues' intellectual dialogue, support, and criticism sharpened the book. First, thanks to Stephanie Fay at the University of California Press for believing in this book from the start and to Adrienne Harris for exceptional editorial work. For posing challenging questions early on, I thank Carol Armstrong, Leo Bersani, Tim Clark, Robin Greeley, Melissa Hyde, Christina Kiaer, Bill MacGregor, Kim Sichel, and Emilie White. For their long-term scholarly collaboration, I am grateful to the following colleagues and mentors: Paula Birnbaum, Lisa Forman Cody, *Dialogica,* Stacy Garfinkel, Jennifer Shaw, Anne Wagner, and Andrés Zervigon. Finally, I thank my mother, Jean Lyford, and my husband, Dave Clegg, for the equal doses of criticism and emotional support they have given me along the way. I couldn't have done this without you.

INTRODUCTION

The Paradox of SurREalist Masculinity

Five years! Already five years! Only five years!

Murdered and mutilated, France, at the end of the horrifying drama, waited for her wounds to be healed. She had homes to rebuild, an economy to restore, suffering to assuage. She hoped to consecrate herself nonetheless, in an atmosphere of calm and security, to the work of redemption. Moreover, she believed that the sacrifice of the adult generations would spare the agony of bloody recommencements from the adolescent generations.

Alas! It is far from the armistice to peace! Treaties have been signed: they take into account none of the great problems posed by war. Conflicts loom, which, in all parts of Europe, relight the flames of discord, awaken hatred, and, little by little, recreate the atmosphere of 1914.

"Homage of Silence," *Paris-Soir,* 12 November 1923

Today, many years after the grisly events of World War I, it can be hard to grasp how deeply the conflict affected the people who survived it—such as the recovering veterans in Figure 1, lined up for a press-agency photographer at the Parisian military hospital of Val-de-Grâce. Some of the men are scarred but appear physically recovered. Bandages cover the chins, noses, and mouths of a few. One bandaged fellow in the front row sports crutches, the stump of his amputated leg balanced by the medals pinned to his woolen coat. Next to the military officer in the light-colored coat at left, who grips one veteran's arm as if to coax him back into the photograph's frame, a nurse creeps in as if to suggest that these men are still in recovery and that she is watching over them. We would like to think that these men's wounds eventually healed and that they returned to productive and fulfilling lives. Yet the photograph's crisp focus hints at another possibility: that cures were slow and not always successful. The piercing, inward gaze of the man in the center of the photograph is haunting, even though he looks away from the camera. He seems to want to avoid our gaze, even as the frozen image reveals to us his mouth's deformity. This man's injuries are visible, and although he tries to detach himself from this grouping that symbolizes wartime heroism, he must acquiesce to the wishes of his commanding officer.

This photograph's arrangement of bodies depicts more than a wounded soldier's labored recovery. Its arrangement of bodies—the nurse and officer at left, almost off frame but not quite, and the soldiers lined up in formation—underscores a power differential that perme-

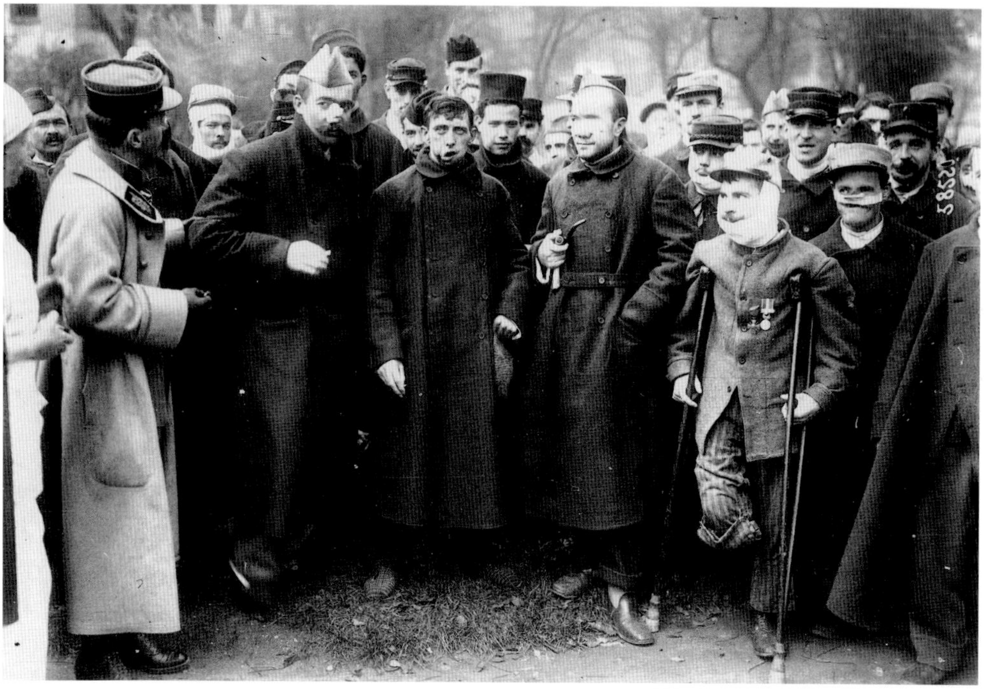

FIGURE 1 *Mutilés de guerre* at the hospital of Val-de-Grâce, Paris, October 1915. Bibliothèque Nationale de France, Department of Prints and Photographs, Collection Meurisse.

ated many aspects of French society during and after the war. Common soldiers, not officers, bore the brunt of the suffering. When men came back from the front, injured or not, their prewar lives had disappeared. Their relations with friends, family, and their communities were different and forced changes in many areas of daily life that had far-reaching consequences. How did the damage inflicted by war alter men's lives? How did it affect their experience of their masculinity? What did it mean to be a man in post–World War I France?

In this book, I suggest that ideas about masculinity and its place in the social order came under intense pressure after the war. And I look at the relationship between these shifting ideas and surrealism. Given that the texts and images and manifestos produced by the mostly male members of surrealist groups usually depict women, might surrealist artists' and writers' disturbing images of them have had a connection to the literally deformed bodies of the men who inhabited Paris and Berlin after the war? In a society such as France's that relied on well-defined ideas about sexual difference and gendered social roles, changes in the understanding of masculinity or femininity had the potential to alter the entire social order. The logic of this gendered social system permanently linked men's and women's social and cultural destinies.

Taking these ideas about postwar gender, culture, and society as my point of departure, I aim to show how surrealist artists and writers explored aspects of gender and sexuality to critique not only artistic tradition but also the economic, political, and social values for which the bourgeois republic's leaders had sacrificed an entire generation of young men.

Sources of Revolution

France has a powerful sense of history. In the modern period, it has a particularly emphatic memory of the revolution of 1789, in which the concepts of liberty, equality, and fraternity were borne on the backs of the men who destroyed the aristocracy—through the visceral yet symbolic parricide of Louis XVI—in favor of an idealized brotherhood of men. In the wake of World War I, a cataclysm whose temporal proximity to the Russian Revolution of 1917 is significant, the surrealist group paid homage to the French and Russian revolutionary moments by naming its foundational journal *The Surrealist Revolution (La Révolution surréaliste)*. Just as the French and Russian revolutions had invoked more egalitarian forms of social and economic order, the surrealists invented their own call to action on the heels of World War I's mutilation of bodies and destruction of lives. Instead of idealizing either a new brotherhood of men or a newly empowered working class, the surrealists inveighed against the corrupt global enterprise that had turned young men into cannon fodder for the world's first industrialized war. Modernity seemed not to have lived up to its promises for a better life: modern industrial warfare had left millions dead and threatened social order with the rising specters of economic disaster and political instability. Certainly, Germany suffered greatly in the war's aftermath, but France had its own problems to resolve, not the least of which was to find a way to rebuild and reconstruct the country. The concrete reminders of four years of total war—the presence of war wounded *(mutilés de guerre)* throughout the country and the physical and psychological damage evident in nearly every aspect of postwar social and economic life—undoubtedly complicated this task.[1]

In proportion to its population, France suffered the worst casualties of the war. Some 3.2 million men were killed or wounded—roughly half the number of men mobilized during the war and just over 13 percent of the male population recorded in 1913. Of these casualties, 1.1 million received pensions due to the gravity of their wounds.[2] The high mortality rate produced by modern artillery and chemical weapons had consequences other than widespread death and commonplace maiming of male soldiers. Demographic figures reveal that the ratio of women to men in France jumped significantly after the war, disrupting the numerical equilibrium between the sexes. An article in a 1920 issue of the illustrated magazine *J'ai Vu* echoed many other postwar commentators in asking, "What will happen to the 1.5 million young women of marriageable age?"[3]

Because the war had deeply disrupted family structures, agriculture, and industry, the state did everything in its power in the early 1920s to stabilize these central components of society.

After the formation of a conservative coalition government in November 1919, social and economic programs promoting a return to traditional values—particularly in the family—became familiar topics of public discourse. National regeneration depended not only on modernized industry, politicians often pointed out, but also on familial productivity. Thus, the French government gave economic incentives to families who bore multiple children, while the increasingly sophisticated advertising industry encouraged robust industrial growth.

Political support for programs to restore traditional family and community structures affected citizens' identification with the postwar nation. Although the family was only one site of state intervention after the war, it was an important one because "relations between individuals [were] . . . charged with a 'civic' function" within the context of a nation focused on "relations between the sexes," which were "aligned to procreation."[4] The postwar society in which the surrealists lived was rife with images promoting traditional social roles for men and women: images of robust manhood and female maternity cropped up everywhere as if they were antidotes to the terrible memories evoked by the sight of veterans' wounded bodies. Such images relied upon neatly defined gender roles to reassure citizens who were concerned about the effects of the war on individuals and communities. Whereas during the war men's and women's social roles blurred because of the need for women to work while men fought at the front, postwar images linked France's future to the reinstitution of traditional relations between the sexes. Women would inhabit the domestic sphere by raising children and maintaining the home (Fig. 2), and men would function as heads of household, industrial or agricultural workers, or businessmen. In a 1920 poster to solicit funds for reconstruction (Fig. 3), a robust, partially nude man appears to be France's savior as his body strains to re-create the nation's political borders brick by brick. His physical power and straining ambition underscore the crucial role that men would have to play to ensure the success of national reconstruction.

To many people in French towns and villages, the image in this poster must have seemed ironic, for the war had left reminders of its violence and destruction on so many men's bodies. Countless veterans like those in the photo at Val-de-Grâce bore visible signs of their participation in the war for years, whether scarred faces or missing limbs. Their presence posed a problem for those interested in promoting a national rebuilding campaign: their bodies reminded everyone who saw them of the horrible and ongoing physical and psychological effects of the war; the sight of mutilated bodies strained people's belief in their government's promises about social and economic progress. The palpable disconnect between official discourse and lived reality proved that national regeneration was still an ideal goal rather than a fact of life. This gap between people's experiences after the war and the national government's broad claims of social progress and reconstruction prompted the surrealists' insurrection in the early 1920s. Taking advantage of this disparity, the surrealists created images of manhood with two primary goals in mind. First, they sought to dramatize the physical and psychological trauma of a war that everyone wanted to forget so that it would not be swept away too quickly. Second, they sought to

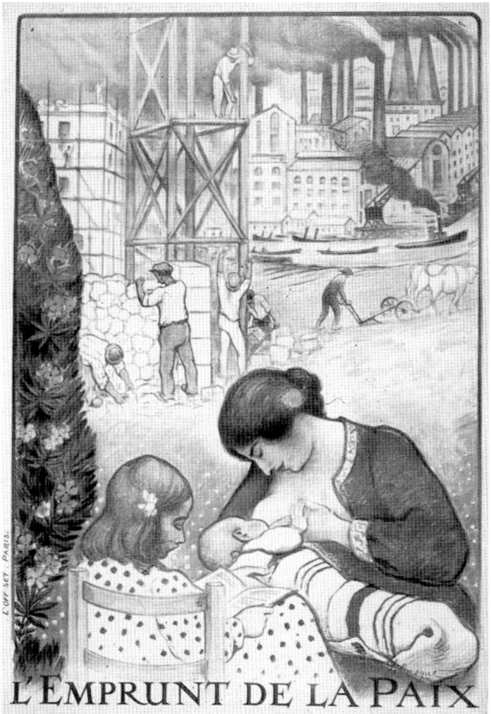

FIGURE 2 Poster, Peace Loan, 1920. Musée d'Histoire Contemporaine, Bibliothèque de Documentation Internationale Contemporaine, Paris.

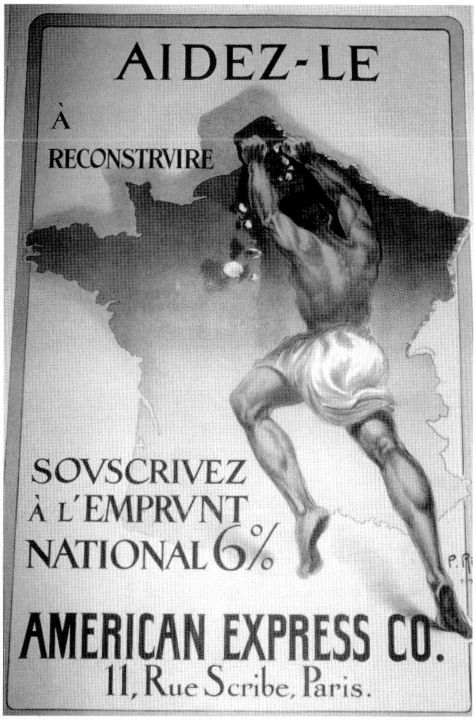

FIGURE 3 Poster, Help him to rebuild! 1920. Musée d'Histoire Contemporaine, Bibliothèque de Documentation Internationale Contemporaine, Paris.

destabilize the gender roles that had cemented traditional ideas about the family, one of the key institutional building blocks of French national identity. Thus, the surrealist approach to cultural criticism carried an implicit critique of the bourgeois sex-gender system in France, which the surrealists despised as an oppressive system of social and economic convention. What better way to derail the smooth ride of a train destined for a "return to order" than to upset the equilibrium of sexual difference by destabilizing ideas about men's and women's roles in postwar life?

In many respects the surrealist position represented a minority view. Many artists and writers in France reconsidered their practices as they looked for ways to participate in rebuilding postwar culture. As a result, the ideals of order, clarity, and rationality so central to the French classical tradition gained a number of adherents in the artistic community during the immediate postwar years.[5] Le Corbusier's 1923 text *Vers une Architecture (Towards a New Architecture)* represented one major shift in aesthetic theory toward rationalism. In this text, Le Corbusier militated for an art and an architecture that would integrate classical geometry and rational planning with the technological efficiency of contemporary industrial production. By blending postwar industry and rationalist design, Le Corbusier proposed a blueprint for a new postwar society that would be efficient, up-to-date, and stable.

Yet as much as public discourse revolved around the reorganization of society and the "return" to a familiar social and economic order, the visible changes in sexual and economic relations after the war precipitated anxiety about the status of masculinity in the 1920s. Whereas the masculine ideal of a physically and morally robust soldier was a common image during and after the war, anxiety about male weakness and a kind of self-absorbed "decadence," as some people termed the change, were among the palpable yet unintended consequences of the conflict.[6] "Shell shock," or male hysteria, was a prominent diagnosis of returning soldiers in the 1910s, suggesting a level of psychological or emotional weakness that only exacerbated worries about the health of postwar society—particularly because the returning soldiers would have to bear the brunt of the work of reconstruction.

Viewing surrealist artists and writers against the backdrop of this complicated story of cultural and political retrenchment and anxiety, this book explores how they engaged with the dominant discourses of national reconstruction by attacking the conventional ideas about masculinity and femininity that were critical to the nation's collective identity. Although we often identify surrealist work with images of female dismemberment, the surrealists' choice to target masculinity suggests a broader effort to attack the foundations of bourgeois society, from both sides of the sexual divide. By rejecting traditional imagery in their work, the surrealists sought to highlight the failure of national reconstruction. They did so by embracing images of physical dismemberment, gender ambiguity (or inversion), psychological disease, sexual deviance, or other forms of social and cultural identity that might counter the rationalist logic of the return to order. Surrealist author André Breton remembered the feeling of the immediate postwar years in this way:

> We particularly hated every concept that by convention had been granted a sacred value, first and foremost those of "family," "country," and "religion." Nor did we exclude "work," or even "honor" in the most common use of the term. For us, such flags flew over a sordid lot of goods: very present in our minds were the human sacrifices that these gods had demanded, and were still demanding. . . . We felt that an outmoded world rushing to its doom could prolong itself only by reinforcing taboos and multiplying constraints, and we were radically in favor of escaping it. . . . In a sense, for a certain time, we simply responded in kind to a world that scandalized us.[7]

Breton's manifestos of 1924 and 1929 described some strategies that artists and writers could use to counter the conservatism of the immediate postwar years. In those texts, he argued for the centrality of dreams; psychic automatism and other forms of psychological disturbance;

sexual license and the rejection of bourgeois standards of taste and social decorum; and attacks on any and all forces of "conservation" in French society, including the institutions of the family, the nation, and religion.[8] Surrealist activity in the interwar years responded to exhortations such as Breton's, often by targeting the linchpins of nation formation. Many of the surrealists had experienced the war's human sacrifices through military service, and such experiences profoundly affected their sense of place in the postwar world. André Breton and Louis Aragon met when they entered training to become military physicians at the hospital of Val-de-Grâce in 1917, where they learned firsthand about shell shock and advanced techniques of plastic surgery; Aragon was even recognized as a military hero for dragging wounded comrades out of the line of fire. Paul Eluard was a nursing orderly when he became a victim of a gas attack; Philippe Soupault was wounded as a member of the infantry; Benjamin Péret and Robert Desnos both fought abroad, Péret in Greece and Desnos in North Africa. Coming out of the war as they did, these men saw their work in the 1920s not just as a nihilistic attack on bourgeois culture but also as a protest against the state's effacement of wartime trauma. Because they had lived through the war in different yet concrete ways, their critiques of the war's aftermath—and the state's efforts to paper over the horrors that they and others had endured—were shaped by their own visceral experiences of war and its effects on individuals. The surrealists understood clearly that properly gendered and socialized individuals were crucial to the success of national retrenchment. Thus, to weaken the state's grasp on society, the surrealists developed a strategy for destabilizing traditional social life.

Drawing on the work of psychologists like Sigmund Freud (whose work was published in translation during the 1910s and 1920s in France) and Jean-Martin Charcot, the surrealists forged new models of individual and collective activity that embraced irrationality, spontaneity, and the unconscious—a notoriously sexualized structure—as harbingers of a new postwar society. Using desire as a weapon against social convention, they imagined they could create unconventional yet seductive alternatives to the tradition-bound rhetoric of the return to order.

With this wartime context in mind, I reconsider surrealist practices in the pages that follow as a concerted effort to undermine France's "return to order" through active interrogation of the concept of masculinity. Sparked by the 1990 exhibition Anxious Visions: Surrealist Art curated by Sidra Stich at the Berkeley Art Museum, this book situates surrealist art and literature within a growing body of historical scholarship that seeks to increase our understanding of the nature and effects of World War I on interwar European culture. What did surrealist artists and writers make of, or take from, their experiences of the war? Can we make more concrete connections between the strategies they used in their work and their lived experiences and the physical or psychological effects of the war itself? Perhaps most importantly, how did the war and its traumatic destruction of so many French men alter the concept of manhood? And in what ways might a range of new ideas about manhood have grown out of, or given rise to, alternative formations of femininity?

Here, I explore the idea that masculinity was a crucial element in the group's effort to dismember postwar dreams of rebuilding France around a stable and coherent sex-gender system. Although ideas of femininity, and the status of women artists more generally in the surrealist milieu, have benefited from a strong tradition of scholarly inquiry, concepts of masculinity remain largely absent from histories of surrealist art and literature. In the past few years, however, several scholars have begun to address masculinity in surrealism in compelling ways.[9] The concepts of femininity and masculinity might best be understood as linked ideas caught in an oppositional structure of sexual difference. Just as whiteness often remains a structuring absence in discourses about race and identity, masculinity's often invisible role in producing ideas about femininity affected surrealist artists' and writers' perspectives on gender and sexuality. This book describes in a fine-grained way the texture of the postwar years and expands the debate about surrealism and gender by examining historical, visual, and textual material whose overt concern is the representation of masculinity. Without losing sight of the way that representations of women served surrealism's varied aesthetic and political agendas, I ask questions about how masculinity and femininity were linked in surrealist practice. How did the actual wounded male bodies on postwar streets intersect with the surrealist penchant for fragmenting the body, usually the female body? How might postwar anxiety about the status of masculinity—who or what was a man in the 1920s—have influenced representations of both male and female bodies in surrealism? Whereas the female body was, as feminist scholarship has shown us, often the common material for male surrealist aesthetic exploration, do female bodies in surrealists' works reflect ideas about masculinity as well? Do surrealist images of women have corollaries in surrealist representations of men? If so, what might a surrealist man look like? And how would a nation populated by surrealist men and women function? Did these new surrealist characters put the brakes on the postwar juggernaut of capitalist industrialization?

I organize this book around thematic case studies that aim to answer these questions by considering surrealist representations of masculinity in light of postwar French social and cultural history. Encompassing a wide range of surrealist work, this book investigates how surrealists' sometimes contradictory images of masculinity might have encouraged the circulation of alternative ideas about manhood and, in turn, disrupted the smooth functioning of bourgeois social and economic power. I look closely at the specific ways that images of emasculated or deviant masculinity might have connected to personal and collective experiences of trauma after the war. By making visible the gaps between official rhetoric and lived experience at the time, the work I explore suggests a range of definitions for manhood in the postwar years. That only some of this work may be familiar to readers has to do partly with the state of scholarly literature on surrealism, which has just started to focus on art in which masculinity is a discrete subject.

Although masculinity is a relatively new topic for art historians, the same cannot be said about the relationships between women, femininity, and surrealist practice. This book draws upon the work of scholars such as Dawn Ades, Mary Ann Caws, Whitney Chadwick, Susan Gubar, Xavière Gauthier, Rosalind Krauss, Jane Livingston, and Susan Rubin Suleiman and extends the logic of their scholarship on femininity to masculinity. I have particularly drawn on their work in approaching gender as a category of analysis. As I analyze masculinity in the surrealist world of interwar France, then, I understand femininity and masculinity to be cultural formations that depend upon one another for their explanatory power.

Over the past thirty years, feminist criticism has taught us much about surrealism's misogynist tendencies, showing us how the predominantly male surrealists used the figure of Woman as both ground and metaphor for revolution. André Breton's text about an encounter with a woman called Nadja, for example, reveals his obsession with her *disponibilité;* Nadja gripped his attention because of her apparently innate ability to experience the city as if she were unconscious. Thus Breton's surrealist woman was a person whose being necessarily and essentially differed from that of a man, and for whom a connection to the "civilized" world was inherently less secure than a man's.[10]

Feminist critics and historians have also enabled us to see the women who were active in surrealism. We know their names now, and some of them have been the subjects of exhibitions: Meret Oppenheim, Lee Miller, *La Femme et le surréalisme.*[11] As Whitney Chadwick reminds us in *Women Artists and the Surrealist Movement,* surrealism is remarkable in that it counted more active female participants than did the other historical avant-gardes. Debates continue, however, about the role of women in surrealism, particularly because of the disturbing representations of women's bodies in the work of many surrealist men. The 1985 exhibition *L'Amour Fou:* Photography & Surrealism and Rosalind Krauss's essays from the show's catalog outlining a theory of surrealist photography catalyzed a new direction for scholarship on surrealism, particularly in analyses of the predominantly male artists' manipulations of the female body. Departing from Xavière Gauthier's account of surrealist misogyny in the pathbreaking *Surréalisme et sexualité* (1971), Krauss reads surrealist manipulations of the body as promises to dissolve categories such as gender; in their spacings, doublings, and announcements of their constructedness, surrealist photographs have the potential to deconstruct difference. For Krauss, the visibility of the surrealist photograph's ambivalence about gender inoculates it against charges of antifeminism.[12] "Within surrealist photographic practice," she writes, "woman was in construction. . . . And since the vehicle through which she is figured is itself manifestly constructed, woman and photograph become figures for each other's condition: ambivalent, blurred, indistinct, and lacking in, to use Edward Weston's word, 'authority.'"[13] For many feminist scholars, however, Krauss's words demanded a rebuttal, and a number of feminist critiques (not just of photographs) emerged in the year or two after Krauss published her text. Some responses to her argument were crafted to prove surrealism's misogyny.[14]

Hal Foster deepens Krauss's argument by describing some of Hans Bellmer's photographs of dolls (see Fig. 4 in Chapter 1) as images that the photographer specifically constructed as dismemberment—a formulation that has been integral to my thinking in this book. Like Foster, I recognize that some of the most powerful images of dismemberment are in photographs, whose inherent realism lends them visual authority at the same time that they document the existence of dismembered bodies (even if, as in the case of Hans Bellmer, the bodies were fabricated for the camera). Buoyed by the reality effect of the photograph, then, Foster sees a Bellmer *Doll* as the embodiment of both castration and fetishism; this impossible conflation reveals how a male subject can admit castration even while trying to ward it off.[15] Like Krauss, Foster intriguingly suggests that the male subject could also be ambivalent, or "lacking [in] authority," in surrealist photography, and this sense of male lack is the idea I wanted to explore as I conducted research for this book.

Foster extended his argument about the relationship between construction and dismemberment in a 1991 text about surrealism, the body, and fascism. In the introduction to that essay, he poses a question that not only draws on Krauss's reading of surrealist photography but also tests her theory's persuasiveness for feminism:

> Not only are formal conventions and idealist values subverted in these manipulated images by Brassaï and Kertész, Man Ray and Maurice Tabard, Raoul Ubac and Hans Bellmer; so too is the female body, a common ground of this subversion, often deformed, violently so, in a way that no avant-gardist claim can quite justify. Indeed, the apparent sadism of the photographs raised the specter of surrealist misogyny; but it also pointed to an adjacent issue no less difficult: are these surrealist transgressions of the body related to actual transgressions of the body during the period—from the mutilations of World War I to the atrocities of the Nazi regime? If so, why are these fantasies visited upon the female body? Do they partake in a putatively fascist imaginary, a peculiarly damaged ego that seeks a sense of corporeal stability in the very act of aggression against other bodies somehow deemed feminine by this subject (Jews, Communists, homosexuals, "the masses")?[16]

These questions about the nature and function of surrealist "transgression" cut close to the heart of my work, because they articulate gender as the connective tissue between surrealism and its approaches to cultural representation. As I pursued my research, I wondered how surrealist images of dismemberment might have resonated at the time of their production—when France struggled to return to order and linked national progress to social regeneration. How did those images tap into anxieties about the success of social reconstruction? And how did that imagery connect to the actual mutilations that the male body endured during World War I? Were the surrealists, in fact, fantasizing about "bodies somehow deemed feminine," bodies that were different from Foster's fascist subject? In their work, did surrealists consider bodies to be visually marked as social targets bearing the signs of their own destruction despite the state's desire to rebuild them? Because the French state invested heavily in the myth of a progressive modernity built on strong, legible images of masculinity and femininity, I consider the possibility that surrealist attacks on these gender-differentiated staples of interpersonal and community identities were crucial indicators of the nation's waning ability to believe its own myths of origin and renewal.

The feminist movement catalyzed new approaches to art history, and as sexual difference has become increasingly important in historical analysis, scholars have expanded the scope of their work on gender by writing about masculinity. A number of studies have historicized masculinity, paying particular attention to the history of war and its effects upon the male subject and stereotypes of masculinity.[17] This book follows the lead of these scholars and their feminist forebears by reconstructing the connections between postwar trauma, masculinity, and surrealism. In nominating World War I as a point of departure for my study of surrealism and masculinity, I propose that masculinity was implicitly the subject of the sexualized discourses of postwar reconstruction and that the surrealists manipulated dominant concepts of masculinity and femininity to question deeply held assumptions about national cultural identity. In their explorations of the immediate postwar period in France, both Mary Louise Roberts and Daniel Sherman reveal gender's important role in the symbolic and actual retrenchment of prewar power relations. The structure of postwar social and political life depended on familiar concepts of sexual difference. Yet after the war gender—in particular, the feminization of the "home front" and its workforce, coupled with anxiety about male emasculation—was a force in social disruption as well as cultural retrenchment. In this climate, masculinist politics, whether personal, civic, or national, were widely imagined to be requirements for the success of postwar reconstruction. Thus, representations of the war often contrasted the heroic masculine sacrifices of the men at the front with the decadent ingratitude of the women—and unfit men—who remained at home. Consensus about the meaning of the war emerged in varied forms of representation: picture postcards, war and peace loan posters, soldiers' memoirs, travel guides, novels, and more. And the surrealists, for their part, aimed to join the chorus of voices seeking to make sense of the war, but they approached their work from a different perspective. Instead of using clearly legible gender stereotypes to support the emerging, dominant narrative about heroic male sacrifice and its connection to the remaking of French national destiny, the surrealists explored ambiguous and deviant gender positions as a way to challenge the feasibility of a nation (a bourgeois capitalist one that the surrealists claimed to reject) whose existence depended on stable images of masculinity and femininity. Although the war actually damaged and destabilized the lives of thousands of French men, postwar messages emphasized masculine strength and heroic sacrifice as the prerequisites for national renewal. Although images of both soldiers and civilians proliferated in many formats during and after the war, everyday viewers seldom came across graphic images of the dead or wounded. Thus, most postwar representations of intact masculinity were bitterly ironic: the dominant rhetoric of the postcards, posters, and photographs circulating in the public realm was positive; yet individual men and women were living with the realities of death or terrible injury and wondering anxiously whether postwar efforts to rebuild their loved ones, their communities, and the nation itself would succeed.[18]

As Kaja Silverman argues in her work on post–World War II cinema, war often "brings a large group of male subjects into such an intimate relation with lack that they are . . . unable to sustain an imaginary relation with the phallus, and so withdraw their belief from the dominant fiction," one based on the "unity of the family and the adequacy of the male subject" in which the "affirmation of classic masculinity is . . . central to the maintenance of our governing 'reality.'"[19] Although Silverman focuses on the traumatic experiences of men returning from the battlefields of Europe during World War II, I think her logic helps illuminate the contradictions between individual experience and national consensus that World War I veterans experienced. Narratives about World War I in the 1910s and 1920s, as we have seen, often depended on strong images of masculinity to symbolize France's successful campaign of postwar national recovery. These stories about men's critical role in reconstruction have clear relevance to the status and nature of femininity, for they demand that the male subject "see himself" and that the female subject "recognize and desire him . . . through the mediation of images of an unimpaired masculinity." Such a consensus about the subject's relationship to the war and its violence "urges both the male and the female subject . . . to deny all knowledge of male castration by believing in the commensurability of penis and phallus, actual and symbolic father."[20] Within this dominant fiction, a phallus/penis equation is so central to maintaining this governing reality that when the male subject cannot recognize himself, the society suffers from a "profound sense of 'ideological fatigue.'"[21] The society depends on the image of intact masculinity for its strength; if that image falters, the society (not just the individual) may experience a crisis of confidence in the stability of the social order, the potential effect of which may be individuals' recognition of their relationship to those dominant cultural assumptions.

In contrast to official efforts to reinstate social order by redrawing boundaries between masculine and feminine, surrealist practitioners in France strained the stability of these social roles by making sexuality—and its variously gendered permutations—central to the process of social and psychological inscription. This strategy implied several outcomes, including explicit acknowledgment of gender's key role in maintaining social order. Although class figured prominently in the state's ability to maintain power, the works I focus on in this study sought primarily to make gender an axis of surrealist practice. By sowing seeds of doubt in their audiences about the health of masculinist institutions like the family, church, and state, the surrealists aimed to question the bourgeois nation that relied on these institutions for cultural and political legitimacy.

Granted, surrealist artists and writers did not refrain from using stereotypes of sexual difference in their work. Feminist scholarship reminds us that their work often reflected well-worn stereotypes about sexual difference, particularly in representing the figure of Woman. Yet if postwar rhetoric demanded that viewers believe in the image of "unimpaired masculinity," to use Silverman's words, what are we to make of the surrealist images in the 1920s that suggest the fragmentation, dismemberment, or perversion of the male body?

To answer this question, I investigate how, and in what specific (if idiosyncratic) ways, surrealist artists and writers simultaneously visualized and disavowed male trauma in the interwar years. This book finds a difficult-to-recover past in surrealism and its histories and discerns there anxiety about the status, function, and future of masculinity. It shows how surrealist artists and writers took seriously the group's goal of exposing and analyzing cultural conventions—even when this task required them to acknowledge the fictive nature and precarious status of masculinity. It exposes and problematizes received ideas about surrealist masculinity, reframing and repositioning questions about the relationship between surrealism, gender, and the cultural politics of both dismemberment and reconstruction.

Chapter 1 assesses surrealism's approach to male dismemberment, mutilation, and perversion. In this chapter, I look at a range of works: Lautréamont's *Chants de Maldoror* (1869), the confectionary images of the Exquisite Corpse, and the Buñuel/Dalí film *L'Âge d'Or* (1930), whose popular yet depraved protagonist embodies conflicting ideas about manhood. In focusing on such works, I find an anxiety about masculinity that is rarely discussed in analyses of surrealist art and literature. But I also suggest that these representations modulate between bourgeois standards of male behavior and depravity to underscore masculinity's crucial role in reproducing and securing the existing national culture.

Subsequent chapters construct an argument about the origins and stakes of surrealism's representations of contemporary masculinity. In Chapter 2, I look at the collection of visual objects—photographs, prosthetic devices, wax and plaster casts of sequential stages in cutting-edge plastic surgery—on display in the military teaching hospital of Val-de-Grâce (Paris), which led the surrealists to emphasize an aesthetics of dismemberment. Louis Aragon and André Breton, founding writers of the surrealist movement, met at Val-de-Grâce as military medical students in 1917 and probably saw this astonishing collection. The objects on view there showed the process of reconstruction and its success during and after the Great War. The surrealists saw in these displays not progress but a fragmented, mutilated masculinity, which they aestheticized—in ways that mimicked the museum displays—in order to attack the bodily rhetoric of national reconstruction. At Val-de-Grâce, Aragon and Breton saw an overtly institutional military rhetoric that championed surgical intervention as a symbol of progress and learned from it: in their hands, bodies would fail to register the progress of modern industrial society that the military establishment ghoulishly championed at Val-de-Grâce. In Chapter 3, I examine postwar efforts to efface the fragmentation of society and of male bodies by reevaluating the Parisian work of the émigré photographer André Kertész, a man not usually counted among the surrealists. I analyze a group of male distortions he made in 1929, linking them to his well-known distorted female nudes of 1933. Through careful reconstruction of the works' chronologies and a close reading of the images themselves, I aim to show that the marketability of female deformation in surrealist Paris may well have resulted from displaced anxiety about emasculation that rarely entered into public view.

In Chapter 4, I investigate the photographic practices and reputations of the surrealist couple Man Ray and Lee Miller. In the late 1920s, the period of their closest collaboration, they staged expressly surrealist models of sexual identity. The chapter focuses on both public and quasi-private representations of sex and gender in Ray and Miller's work to dramatize how these artists represented unconventional sexualities to secure their surrealist personas in the increasingly conservative cultural climate after the war. Chapter 5 describes how Man Ray and the protofascist writer (and one-time surrealist fellow traveler) Pierre Drieu la Rochelle imaged gender ambiguity in the performances of the widely acclaimed transvestite acrobat Barbette. What qualities in Barbette attracted them? To a surrealist like Man Ray, she may have represented liberation. To Drieu, she may have suggested the ideal fascist body. Their common interest in her raises the question of a connection, in the mid-1920s, between French surrealism and Drieu's gender-based critique of the bourgeois republican values of postwar France, which he would later repudiate. Even if the surrealists and Drieu relished Barbette's ambiguous gender but put the lessons they learned from her performance to radically different ends, they both made gender instability the basis of their aesthetic and political agendas in the 1930s. And key to their different ideas about the usefulness of that instability was the tendency of gender identity to imply particular forms of social—even national—organization. In examining how the destruction and reconstruction of masculinity, its subsequent conflation with femininity, and broad cultural anxiety about such gender instability offered much to both the surrealist and the fascist at the time, the chapter reveals a difficult, uncomfortable, and rarely acknowledged similarity between the two cultural patterns. Both, in their own way, understood one of the crucial organizing principles of the bourgeois nation-state: that France's institutional hierarchy could maintain power only as long as its traditional bases remained strong. The trick, then, for the surrealists (as much as for Drieu) was to weaken those bases. I argue that to destroy the social order they detested, the surrealists aimed their sights on the securely gendered subject.

CHAPTER ONE

Anxiety and Perversion in Postwar Paris

Hans Bellmer's photographs of distorted and deformed dolls from the early 1930s seem to be quintessential examples of surrealist misogyny (see Fig. 4). Their violently erotic reorganization of female body parts into awkward wholes typifies the way in which surrealist artists and writers manipulated and objectified femininity in their work. Bellmer's manipulation and reconstruction of the female form also encourage comparison with the mutilation and reconstruction that prevailed across Europe during World War I. By viewing the dolls in this context, we might see their distorted forms as a displacement of male anxiety onto the bodies of women. Thus, Bellmer's work—and the work of other male surrealists who depicted fragmented female bodies—might reflect not only misogyny but also the disavowal of emasculation through symbolic transference. The fabrication of these dolls also expresses a link to consumer society. The dolls look as if they could be surrealist mannequins made by the prosthetic industry; their deformed yet interlocking parts reflect a chilling combination of mass-market eroticism and wartime bodily trauma. These connections between misogyny and emasculation anxiety, between eroticism and the horror of war trauma, and between consumption and desire are not specific to Bellmer's idiosyncratic visual rhetoric, however. The practice of joining contradictory approaches and blurring boundaries between objects, identities, and media was more prevalent among the male surrealists than is usually acknowledged. If we open our eyes to consider these contrasts as part of a broader surrealist agenda, we can see how the surrealists aimed to destabilize their viewers' assumptions about the boundaries

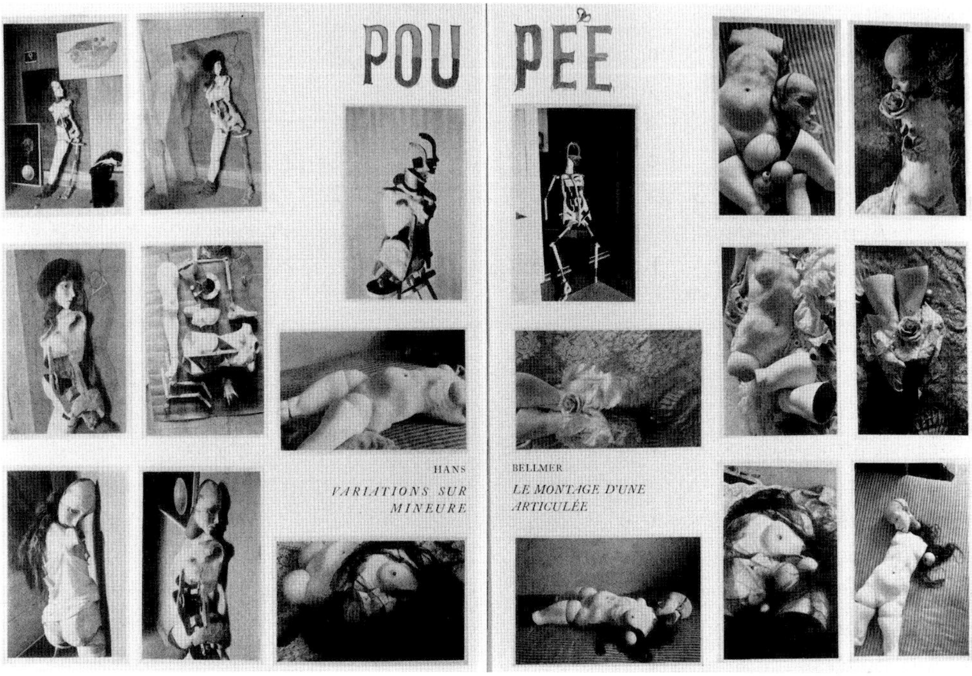

FIGURE 4 Hans Bellmer, *Poupée*, 1935. In *Minotaure* 6 (Winter 1935): 30–31. © 2006 Artists Rights Society (ARS), New York/ADAGP, Paris.

between apparently contradictory things: between conventional and "perverted" sex, between fine art and mass culture, and between men and women.

The French surrealists of the 1920s grasped the economic and political implications of the state's postwar promotion of images of a "new and improved" male populace. The French state wanted to erase signs of personal trauma and economic distress through programs promoting social regeneration—from rebuilding destroyed churches and villages to promoting high birthrates to swell the future labor pool—all in the service of securing a stable postwar social order. The surrealists, however, wanted to shake the foundations of the morally bankrupt government, which had sent young men to war and then used images of a resurgent, unimpaired masculinity to boost public confidence in the success of postwar reconstruction. Thus, men who seemed more like "typical" women—weak, hysterical, and sexually unrestrained in line with neuropsychiatric accounts of the late nineteenth and early twentieth centuries—became part of the surrealist lexicon during and after the war.[1] By creating works that dwelled upon male emasculation or confused ideas about sexual difference and gender identity, the surrealists challenged the tenets of national reconstruction that reinforced clear differences between the sexes. In their works, they regularly exploited stereotypes of femininity to undermine commonly held beliefs about the links between rationality, progress, and male creativity. Although the infusion of feminine stereotypes into their work was meant to critique French patriarchal models, the visibility of male anxiety in some works suggests that the surrealists sought to intervene in the consensus discourse about the nature and function of manhood after the war. By emphasizing hybrid subjects, male anxiety, and gender indeterminacy and by infusing their works with rhetorical and structural conventions borrowed from advertising, pornography, psychology and the mass media, the surrealists developed strategies that they hoped would upset the status quo.

◉ ⊙ ◎

The displacement of cultural anxieties from the masculine to the feminine is not new in the history of art and literature. Male artists and writers have traditionally used images of the female body to shore up their cultural capital, whether by painting languorous and available female nudes as objects of desire or by manipulating these nudes to demonstrate their mastery of their medium. In the nineteenth and twentieth centuries, avant-garde artists often claimed subversive artistic identities for themselves by incorporating stereotypically feminine elements into their work. Like their modernist predecessors, the surrealists are known for their frequent recourse to feminine stereotypes. Following the publication of Sigmund Freud's work on hysteria and psychoanalysis in France in the 1910s and 1920s, the surrealists grew increasingly interested in some of the specific psychic "effects" of femininity that Freud noted. They sought to embody the irrational and the unconscious that many psychologists of the period presumed to be the domain of women, especially women who were diagnosed as hysterics. Their familiarity with the published accounts of hysteria by the French physician Jean-Martin Charcot—work that influenced the direction of French neuropsychiatry during the war—cemented their infatuation with the idea of using hysteria as a model for artistic practice. In 1928, for example, more than ten years after they left the French military medical corps, André Breton and Louis Aragon published an homage to the female hysteric that celebrated her "passionate attitudes" as compelling aesthetic models for surrealism.[2]

Most modern psychologists presumed that hysteria was a female affliction. Although the influential Charcot recognized the existence of male hysteria in the late nineteenth century, not until World War I did the reality of hysterical men come into public view. Evidence of uncontainable war-related traumatic memories was crucial to the diagnosis of male hysteria (although sexual trauma was also noted in some cases). The diagnosis remained problematic, however, because to diagnose a man as hysterical was to emasculate him. The symptoms exhibited by the male hysteric were nearly identical to those exhibited by women, a fact that scientifically linked the disease to women. Moreover, since the 1880s, Charcot had argued that the disease in men was usually the result of an effeminate or homosexual constitution. As if to disavow this similarity between the illness in men and women, however, physicians named the affliction according to the patient's gender. Women suffered from "hysteria" (from the Greek work *hystera,* or uterus), whereas men suffered from "shell shock" in England and "neurasthenia" in France. Yet regardless of this effort to sanitize the disease in men by renaming it, the role of trauma in the production of the disease was central to its diagnosis in both men and women. As doctors began to see an increase in soldiers who returned from the front with hysterical symptoms, French neuropsychiatrists like Joseph Babinski redefined male hysteria in neurological terms to remove the threat of feminization.

André Breton and Louis Aragon learned of male hysteria during their wartime military medical training, at which time they studied the work of Charcot, Pierre Janet, and Babinski.[3] Throughout the 1920s, they wove elements of hysteria into their work, acknowledging it as a form of psychic release that rejected the rational world and its constraints in favor of irrationality and a lack of psychological or social control. Although they did so to undermine literary and artistic conventions, they also implicitly undermined traditional notions of masculine creativity by making work that courted the physical and psychological automatism associated with the hysteric. The emphasis upon automatic writing by Breton, Aragon, and Philippe Soupault in the early 1920s suggests that they wanted to parallel aspects of the hysteric's experience in their own processes of artistic production. Breton and Philippe Soupault's 1920 text *Les Champs magnétiques (The Magnetic Fields)* grew out of experiments with automatic writing, a technique by which writers jotted down thoughts as they came, without concern for organization, reason, or control. By 1924, Breton's first surrealist manifesto codified such practices by defining surrealism as "psychic automatism in its pure state."[4] According to Breton, individuals who refrained from "filtering" their thoughts became "recording instrument[s]," or receptacles, for the unconscious mind.[5] Breton's early medical training at Saint-Dizier (under a man who had himself studied with Charcot), and then at the Hôpital de la Pitié with Babinski, surely alerted him to the concept of hysteria as a kind of bodily speech emanating from the unconscious.[6] The hysteric's body externalized symptoms: tics, spasms, numbness, or partial paralysis reflected the psyche's (failed) effort to repress unconscious fears and desires. The writer practicing automatism tried to achieve a mental state approximating the hysteric's detachment from logic or reason, a "mental state characterized by subversion of the rapports established by a subject with the moral world under whose authority they [*sic*] believe themselves, practically, to be."[7] Breton and Aragon surmised that an author, like the hysteric, could subvert literary convention by fleeing the oppression of reason to court the unconscious.

In addition to modeling their own practices after the fits and starts of the hysteric, however, many of the surrealists nominated other individuals to their aesthetic pantheon. The striking aspect of the names on that list, including the Comte de Lautréamont and the Marquis de Sade, is their association with images of sexual and psychological deviance, trauma, and mutilation—a powerful concoction whose destabilizing ingredients bubbled underneath the well-publicized postwar "return to order" that many people hoped would move French society beyond the painful memories of a deadly, grueling war.

Reconsidering Lautréamont

In 1869 a young Frenchman named Isidore Ducasse wrote *Les Chants de Maldoror* using the pen name Comte de Lautréamont. As far as we can tell, however, the text did not appear in print until 1874, four years after Ducasse's death at the age of twenty-four. Chronologies of the text are sketchy at best, and although the work received intermittent attention throughout the 1880s and 1890s, it gained its greatest visibility at the end of World War I when the surrealists claimed it as a precursor to their attacks on literary and moral conventions. Populated by deformed, disreputable, and mutilated images of masculinity, *Les Chants de Maldoror* was rediscovered by Breton, Aragon, and Soupault during World War I. And with their help, the text became an important aesthetic touchstone for the surrealist movement. Surprisingly, however, most commentators on the text refrain from analyzing the work's content. The *Chants*' compulsion to rip apart male bodies and its elaborate descriptions of male devastation might seem an obvious point of contact between Lautréamont's work and that of his surrealist admirers. Yet most historians of surrealist art and literature do not discuss its literary or aesthetic parallels to the post–World War I context of surrealism, the important role that masculinity played in *Les Chants de Maldoror,* and the possible effect of its imagery of male destruction and deviance on its young surrealist readers. Instead, scholars usually quote a single phrase from the middle of the book to symbolize surrealist aesthetic theory. However, reading the book closely and holistically produces a more intensely graphic, visceral experience than analyses of the *Chants* in the literature on surrealism usually suggest. Images of bodily fragmentation, dismemberment, and psychic perversion permeate the pages of *Les Chants de Maldoror;* and importantly, the bodies being abused, emasculated, or otherwise defiled are largely those of men. We can imagine that the repeated descriptions of physically and psychologically damaged men in Lautréamont's text would have reminded postwar readers of the results of World War I. Thus, Lautréamont's text is not only a model of formal juxtaposition and fragmentation but also a work that sparks associations between past and present destructions of the male body in highly visceral, imagistic language.

The most famous phrase in *Les Chants de Maldoror*, "as beautiful as the chance meeting on a dissecting table of a sewing machine and an umbrella," is often analyzed in largely formal literary terms. Scholars focus primarily on the passage's nonsensical juxtaposition of incompatible elements in connecting the work to surrealist aesthetic theory. André Breton emphasized this position by claiming in his first surrealist manifesto of 1924 that such juxtapositions were key because they produced a spark of surrealist inspiration in their audience.[8] Today, however, the passage is nothing more than a cliché, used primarily to convey the important role of chance and spontaneity in the production of surrealist images.

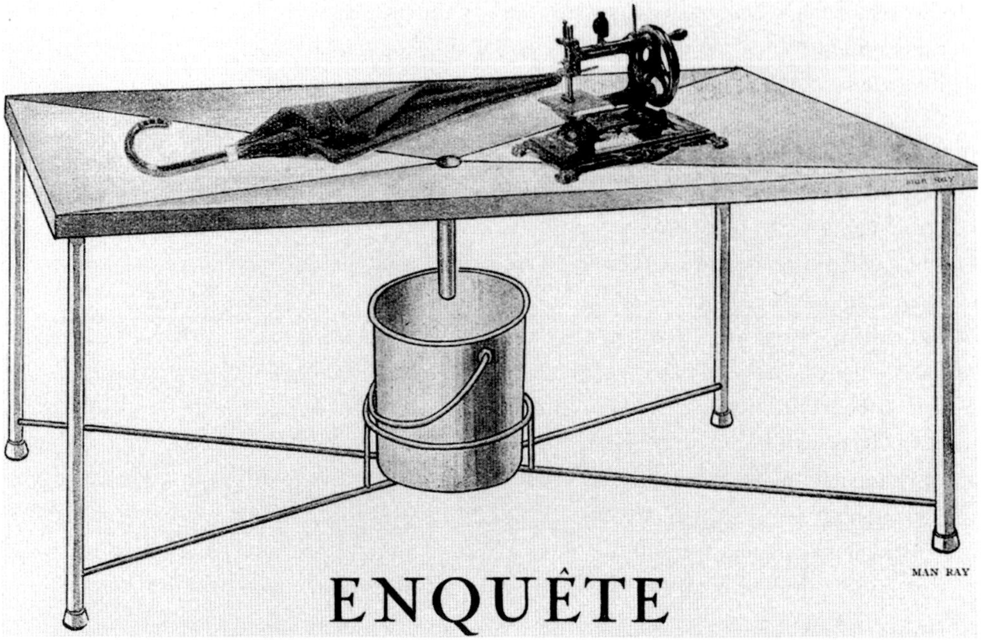

FIGURE 5 Man Ray, drawing referring to the *"beau comme"* passage in *Les Chants de Maldoror.* In *Minotaure* 3–4 (1933): 101. © 2006 Man Ray Trust/Artists Rights Society (ARS), New York/ADAGP, Paris.

Neither the imagery of this phrase nor the larger text's viscerally charged descriptions of male bodies have received sustained analysis. If we break down the image—dissecting table, umbrella, and sewing machine—and take seriously the claim that it crystallizes a surrealist approach to representation, what do we actually find? What effects do the language of forensic science, the morgue, and domestic life have upon our ability to recognize a surrealist image? How can we reconcile the medical and consumer references of the passage with the book's overarching concern with depicting mutilated and degraded men? What does the contradictory set of objects on that dissecting table tell us, exactly, about Lautréamont's appeal to young surrealist poets?

Obviously, the dissecting table at the center of the passage and at the center of Man Ray's representation of this passage (Fig. 5) symbolizes bodily death and destruction. As a site of posthumous surgery and evisceration, the dissecting table promotes an association with the scientific analysis of death. The placement of the umbrella and sewing machine on top of a table designed for efficient bloodletting—a process finely detailed in the drainage structures in Man Ray's drawing—establishes morbid continuity between the site of the image and the objects that clash within it. The gendered associations provided by this unlikely encounter of objects highlight ideas about sexual difference too. The umbrella, a pointed object that alludes to the male sex, inhabits the same space as the sewing machine, a tool associated with the feminized labor of a seamstress. By laying out both masculine and feminine objects on the table, the image unites them as objects for dissection, analysis, and scrutiny. The sewing machine, however, also echoes a surgeon's labor to suture his patient's body, making an oblique reference to reconstruction and thereby complicating our sense of the image's meaning. One could see this odd juxtaposition as nothing more than an effort to shock its audience. But the image's fragmentary quality and the specific choice of objects also suggest a connection between the grisly realities of dead and mutilated bodies, reconstruction, and an emerging surrealist aesthetic. The passage's radical juxtaposition of the three elements generates a new way of seeing the world. Moreover, those elements define the surrealist image as an unstable mixture of objects with myriad cultural associations that themselves connect to assumptions about war, productivity, and gender identity.

Throughout *Les Chants de Maldoror,* Lautréamont delights in producing images of moral and physical decay and dismemberment. Sometimes he focuses on violated female bodies, but for the most part, the text describes devilish and disturbing moments of male violation. Images of a sickening, hypocritical God; a vicious, yet violated Maldoror; and a beautiful, yet finally corrupted Mervyn populate Lautréamont's strange world. Bloated bodies float along the Seine; Maldoror cuts and licks children as they sleep in their tiny beds; men recognize their bodies as wounded, pestilent, and diseased. The repeated images of male degradation, violation, and death that permeate *Les Chants de Maldoror* demand a second look. Could the *Chants* have seduced the surrealists because of the perfection with which the Comte de Lautréamont described traumatized, wounded masculinities?

Maldoror's Body

> A nasty viper devoured my prick and took its place: it rendered me a eunuch, this villain. Oh! If I could have defended myself with my paralyzed arms; but I believe they have been changed into logs. Comte de Lautréamont, *Les Chants de Maldoror*

The male bodies described in *Les Chants de Maldoror* lack both limbs and morality; many of them are mutilated or racked with disease. Their physical inadequacies often parallel their moral laxity and thus prevent readers from seeing them as sympathetic characters. Indeed, the most attractive aspect of the *Chants* for the surrealists appeared to be the outright rejection of conventional identities and moralities. When Lautréamont created a God for his text, for example, he made him a disgusting creature with a taste for human flesh and an unparalleled moral depravity. God was an uncaring brute who, like Saturn, relished devouring his mortal brood:

> He [the Creator] held in his hand the rotting trunk of a dead man, and he raised it, alternatively, from his eyes to his nose, and from his nose to his mouth; once at his mouth, one can guess what he did with it. His feet plunged in a vast sea of boiling blood. . . . The Creator, with the first two claws of his foot, seized another swimmer by the neck . . . and raised him in the air, outside the reddish slime, exquisite sauce! . . . He devoured first the head, the legs and the arms, and lastly the trunk, until there remained almost nothing.[9]

In this section of the *Chants,* the horrific patriarchal Creator consumes men with inhuman ferocity. The sorry bodies that swim in blood-tinged pools are no more than bits of mealtime fodder, their bodies ripped apart by his hungry mouth. Like the men who fell at the western front as fuel for the machines of the Great War, the men in Lautréamont's hellish imaginary are captive supplicants to a God that is nothing more than a greedy beast. Replete as the text is with images of bodies rotting, torn apart, devoured, and emasculated, the *Chants* likely resonated with the experience of the trenches that so many of the young surrealist poets had had. Maldoror's wounded body, as well as the bodies he sees or creates throughout the text, not only rewrites the image of the *grand homme* but also displays the male body as a site of cultural violence and decay.

The Comte de Lautréamont, as Philippe Soupault would write in 1946, would remain forever outside the confines of conventional literary and moral histories—a position the surrealists also courted.[10] The "odor of death and the stench of corpses" prowled around Lautréamont's "crib," according to Soupault, like a thick haze of gloomy smoke.[11] Soupault's words conjure up not only the pacing and tenor of Lautréamont's own text but also focus the reader's attention. Whiffs of rotting bodies, the chalky smell of the muddy coffinlike trenches we might recall at the sound of the word "crib"—these words project Lautréamont's world onto the recent history of World War I. Soupault, who read the *Chants* while recovering from war wounds, was overwhelmed by the book's visceral language and violent content. "Since that day," he recalled a few years later, "no one . . . recognized me. I myself no longer know if I have a heart."[12]

The *Chants* juxtapose Maldoror's pestilent figure with a beautiful flaxen-haired young man named Mervyn, a character with whom Maldoror eventually has a subtly erotic friendship. The contrast between the profligate, disreputable Maldoror and the idealized, naïve Mervyn underscores a choice between diseased and healthy masculinity in Lautréamont's text. And as Maldoror pursues a friendship with Mervyn, the reader soon understands that Mervyn's freshness will not last long. Spying Mervyn near the corner of the Rue Colbert and the Rue Vivienne, Maldoror describes his young friend as follows:

> He is fair as the retractility of the claws of birds of prey; or again, as the uncertainty of the muscular movements in wounds in the soft parts of the lower cervical region;

> or rather, as that perpetual rat-trap always present by the trapped animal, which by itself can catch rodents indefinitely and work even when hidden under straw; and above all, as the chance meeting on a dissecting table of a sewing machine and an umbrella![13]

In an inversion of the logic of the return to order—decay and degradation restored to beauty through reconstruction—Maldoror likens Mervyn's beauty to sharpened talons, pulsating muscle, or the metaphorical bodies displayed on a dissecting table. This juxtaposition of conventional definitions of beauty and horror, purity and corruption, is key to the unresolved conflicts that permeate *Les Chants de Maldoror.*

The shifts between Maldoror's descriptions of his own body and the violent beauty he sees in Mervyn impede the reader's ability to settle on a coherent, idealized concept of masculinity. The text forces the reader to oscillate between possibilities. For this reason, we can consider the text an endorsement of juxtaposition as a protosurrealist form; but we might also come away with the idea that the beauty the surrealists saw in Lautréamont's text was the product of conflict, trauma, and perversion. Maldoror is a filthy eunuch in persistent pain, yet the moment he sees Mervyn, his fantasies turn to the beautiful youth's corruption. The unsuspecting young Mervyn (Maldoror tell us that he is only sixteen) is no match for Maldoror's wily depravity. And nowhere is this disjunction between concepts of masculinity more evident than in a section of the *Chants* that reveals Maldoror's plan to seduce and then murder his youthful prey. Escaping one attempt on his life, Mervyn is eventually killed by Maldoror. The book ends with Mervyn hanging dead from the roof of the Pantheon in Paris—the tomb of some of France's most illustrious male citizens—after Maldoror catapulted him there, having completed his slow torture of the golden-haired man's young body.[14]

If a conflict between healthy and diseased forms of manhood structures much of the narrative about Mervyn and Maldoror's relationship, a second important theme of the book is male passivity and impotence. The postwar environment, in which many soldiers faced physical and psychological traumas that made them either physically or sexually impotent, gave the text's articulation of impotence an added rhetorical charge. One of the text's more disturbing images of a violated male body—in which the body is penetrated and defiled by a host of unwelcome guests—recalls the rat- and mud-filled trenches of the war:

> I am filthy. Lice gnaw me. Swine, when they look at me, vomit. The scabs and sores of leprosy have scaled off my skin, which is coated with yellowish pus. . . . From my nape, as from a dungheap, an enormous toadstool with umbelliferous peduncles sprouts. Seated on a shapeless chunk of furniture, I have not moved a limb for four centuries. . . . A nasty viper has devoured my prick and taken its place. It rendered me a eunuch, this villain. Oh! If only I could have defended myself with my paralyzed arms, but I believe they had been changed into logs. . . . Two small full-grown hedgehogs flung to a dog—which did not decline them—the contents of my testicles; inside the scrupulously

scrubbed scrotal sac they lodged. My anus has been blocked by a crab. Encouraged by my inertia, it guards the entrance with its pincers and causes me considerable pain![15]

Maldoror's body has been mutilated, invaded, and paralyzed. He is a eunuch, emasculated by a snake and a pair of hedgehogs who have taken up residence in the hollow sac that once enshrouded his sexual organs. Unable to move or fight back because of paralysis, his body is a passive host for a gang of pain-inflicting parasites. In this passage—singled out by Soupault in his book on Lautréamont—the male body is impotent and lacks the will and energy to fight the invading creatures. The language of this passage focuses the reader on the physical body and its pain rather than on the mind and its reason. Horrifically, it details things from which a reader is likely to recoil. Yet its visual character also creates a fascinating space for imagining Maldoror's victimized flesh. A haunting reminder of the passivity imposed on so many soldiers during the war, and of their anxieties about returning home with arms and legs missing, this passage exquisitely bridges the gap between Lautréamont's time and that of the immediate postwar years.

A third theme in *Les Chants de Maldoror* highlights a deviant, perverse strain of male sexuality. Given anxieties about male impotence and the prevalence of postwar psychological and sexual illness, this theme likely resonated with cultural anxieties about war's potential to exacerbate male sexual deviance. Maldoror, for example, has "congenitally" deformed sexual organs; he admires pederasty and other forms of sexual depravity. Homosexual conduct is at once a "great degradation" and a sublime form of intelligence.[16] And for the surrealists, the celebration of such perversity not only represented an attack on conventional sexual habits but linked Lautréamont to another perennial surrealist favorite, the infamous Marquis de Sade.[17]

Maldoror also reveals an interest in ambiguous sexual identity in a section in which he describes a hermaphrodite. The hermaphrodite incorporates aspects of both masculinity and femininity, yet deep ambivalence about "his" own desires creates a visceral experience of the splitting of the self, presenting sexual identification as a difficult, even traumatic experience:

> When he [the hermaphrodite] sees a man and a woman who walk in several alleys of plane-trees, he feels his body cleave in two from bottom to top, and each new part strain to clasp one or other of the strollers; but it is only a hallucination and reason is not slow to regain her sway. This is why he mingles neither with men nor women: his excessive modesty, which dawned on him because of this idea of being but a monster, prevents his bestowing his glowing compassion upon any man.[18]

In Lautréamont's text, the hermaphrodite's attraction to each member of the heterosexual couple causes him to fantasize about his body's splitting in two. Fearful that he is a monster whose identification morphs from one gender to the other, the hermaphrodite insures social and sexual decorum only by avoiding contact with the objects of his desire, thus protecting himself from the anxiety and pain of his conflicting desires. The hermaphrodite's ambiguous sexual identity foregrounds both physical and psychological fragmentation in ways that parallel the themes that the surrealists were exploring in the 1920s and 1930s, including the heterogeneous bodily forms resulting from the game of "exquisite corpse."

André Breton defined an exquisite corpse as a text or image assembled simultaneously by several individuals, with each participant furnishing "a single element (subject, verb or predicate, head, belly, or legs)." This single work made collectively was thus the textual or visual representation of a fragmentary but unified body.[19] Breton's definition compared body parts to parts of speech, emphasizing that the body could be a form of representation just as a sentence is. Breton also made clear that he considered the exquisite corpse's visible fragmentation to be a key surrealist model, one that echoed the stylized forms of contemporary advertising that juxtaposed bodily fragments in surprising combinations to enhance their visual power.

Salvador Dalí's work reveals his ongoing interest in the *Chants'* graphic investigation of bodily dismemberment and sexual ambiguity. The illustrations he made for a 1934 edition of *Les Chants de Maldoror* (edited by Albert Skira) recall both the texture of Lautréamont's visceral prose and the structure of the exquisite corpse. Interestingly, the first published example of an exquisite corpse, which appeared in *La Révolution surréaliste,* was resolutely masculine (Fig. 6).[20] A dark jacket and white shirt signify the figure's contemporary bourgeois status. His body, however, contradicts such conventionality. He lacks a head and shoulders—apparently just eaten by a spider—and his juglike feet seem to have immobilized him. Like a descendant of Maldoror, he is a passive victim, his petrified legs and disappearing head rendering him a helpless target of the hungry insect.

Dalí's illustrations for *Les Chants de Maldoror* were popular enough to warrant publication in the surrealist-friendly journal *Minotaure* in advance of the book's release (Fig. 7).[21] Of the four figures reproduced in *Minotaure,* the one in the lower right transforms the exquisite corpse into a Maldororian image: the figure appears to be at war with itself, grasping and violating its own flesh while struggling to maintain a sense of corporeal unity. Etched with thick hatchings suggestive of tree bark, the figure recalls the moment in the *Chants* when Maldoror's arms become logs. The body also seems sexually ambiguous in ways that mirror Lautréamont's anxious hermaphrodite. The breastlike forms at the top of the figure imply femininity, whereas the wooden limbs at left look vaguely phallic. This body attests to a deep and deliberate confusion about gender: it is split and conjoined simultaneously by symbols of male and female.

The hybrid structures of Dalí's figure and the exquisite corpse reflect a surrealist understanding of the body as a construction of disparate pieces. These images emphasize the body as a liminal object caught in a place where it is neither part nor whole. By emphasizing discontinuity, Dalí's representation mirrors Lautréamont's linguistic descriptions of bodily violence and confusion. Because the exquisite corpse's hybridity called into question ideas of unity and

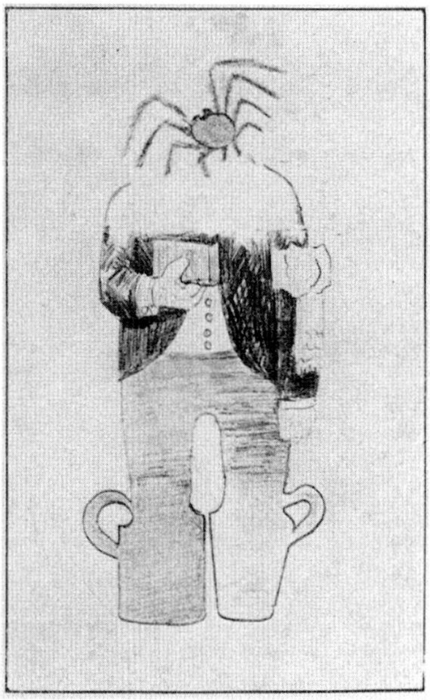

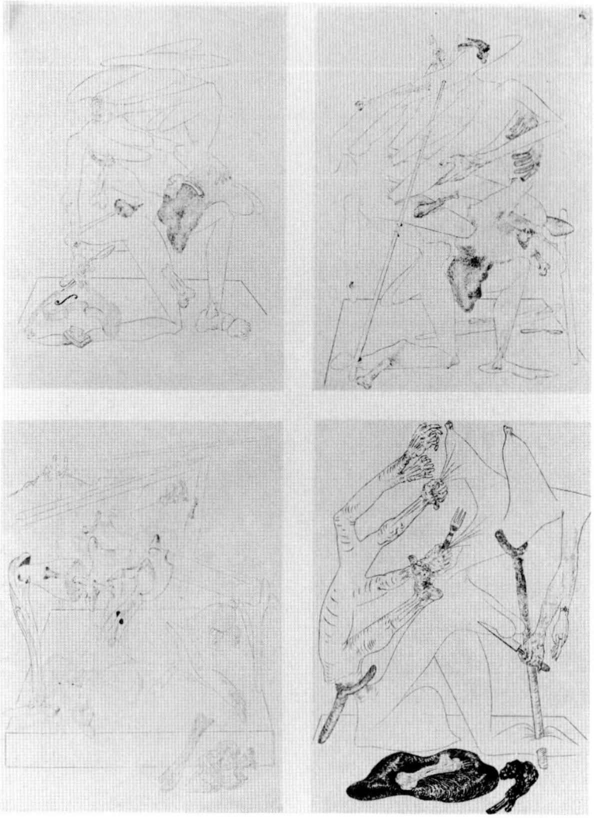

FIGURE 6 Exquisite Corpse, 1927. In *La Révolution surréaliste* 9–10 (1 October 1927): 8.
FIGURE 7 Salvador Dalí, etchings for *Les Chants de Maldoror.* In *Minotaure* 3–4 (1933): 37. © 2006 Salvador Dalí, Gala–Salvador Dalí Foundation, Figueras, Spain/Artists Rights Society (ARS), New York.

coherence, it was a powerful model for surrealism, delineating a new body riddled with instability and incoherence. Pitted against conventional images that played to people's desire for a return to order, the exquisite corpse and its offspring celebrated the discontinuous body as a symbol of cultural confusion and decay.[22] Armed with models like Lautréamont's scandalous world and the exquisite corpse, surrealist artists and writers created images of masculinity that deviated in varying degrees from bourgeois cultural norms as they perceived them. Such images complicated viewers' efforts to grasp an essential image of postwar manhood because they created a range of competing masculinities. And many of them, particularly those of damaged or deviant masculinity, made postwar stabilization seem like a distant goal.

Sexuality, Perversion, and Cultural Politics: *L'Âge d'Or.*

L'Âge d'Or, the 1930 film by Luis Buñuel and Salvador Dalí, remains one of the most compelling examples of surrealism because it still has the capacity to surprise viewers with its antiestablishment, anticlerical message. Depicting a modern world in which sexual desire rules the lives of its two main characters, it promotes deviant social and sexual behavior as a way to reject the forces that André Breton named as the most important elements of social conservation at the time: family, nation, and religion.[23] The film is both a direct critique of these fundamental institutions within French society and a précis of the ways in which surrealist images could catalyze subversive behavior. As films go, it was quite effective at creating outrage when it first screened: Studio 28, the theater where it had its first public showing, was attacked, and the surrealists seemed to have expected as much, for they laid out the group's thinking about the film in the program. For the film to have the greatest cinematic and political impact, they believed it had to be viewed in the context of bourgeois cinema.[24]

L'Âge d'Or signals this desire to attack the social bases of French society from its first scene: it begins with two scorpions locked in mortal combat and quickly shifts to a single scorpion battling a rat. Although the rat is much larger than the scorpion, the scorpion slays the rat with his tiny yet powerful stinger. Using the metaphor of a small yet deadly scorpion whose venom can kill its larger opponent on contact, Buñuel and Dalí saw their film as an opportunity to attack the powerful forces of social, cultural, and political convention that they and their surrealist friends despised.[25] Soon after the rat's untimely death, in fact, the film proceeds to attack bourgeois sexual mores as well as the institutions of family, church, military, and state. The film both revels in images that produce antiestablishment behavior and lays down images that are explicitly antifascist: a blind war veteran is kicked to the ground, and a note taped to the window of St. Peter's references the 1929 Lateran treaties between Mussolini and the pope. Such vehicles point to the state's complicity with fascism and are essential to the film's biting wit.[26]

According to Dalí, the film also sought to "present the straight and pure line of 'conduct' of a being who pursued love across the ignoble humanitarian ideals, patriotic and . . . miserable mechanisms of reality."[27] And in many respects, the central characters in the film live for love, often in direct conflict with patriotic, social, or moral ethics. Their disruptive, erratic behavior parallels the film's antiestablishment message, whereas their individual exploits exemplify surrealism's agenda, as Dalí saw it: to attack social and ethical propriety.

> Being quite on the fringes of plastic investigations and other kinds of "bullshit," the new images of Surrealism will more and more take on the forms and colors of demoralization and confusion. . . . The new images, as a functional form of thought, will adopt the free disposition of desire while being violently repressed. The lethal activity of these new images, simultaneously with other Surrealist activities, may also contribute to the collapse of reality, to the benefit of everything which, through and beyond the base and

> abominable ideals of any kind, aesthetic, humanitarian, philosophical, and so on, brings us back to the clear sources of masturbation, of exhibitionism, of crime, of love.[28]

Although the handpicked, opening-night audience appreciated this bohemian critique of bourgeois conservatism, the film's inflammatory content (particularly its antipatriotic and antireligious passages) drew hostile words from some press and political organizations. A letter in the conservative newspaper *Le Figaro* in early December 1930, just a few days after the first screening of the film, illustrates the hostility with which the film was received: "*L'Âge d'Or,* in which I defy any authorized technician to find the least artistic value, multiplies into public spectacle the most obscene, repugnant and poor episodes. The Fatherland, the Family, and Religion are dragged through filth."[29]

By tarnishing the institutions of nation, family, and church upon which the authority of contemporary bourgeois society depended, Buñuel and Dalí's film achieved its disruptive aims. At an early screening on December 3, for example, members of the ultranationalist League of Patriots and the Anti-Jewish League started a riot inside the theater. Shouting "We will see if there are any more Christians in France!" and "Death to Jews!" members of these two groups hurled purple ink at the screen and destroyed the exhibition of surrealist art on view in the theater lobby. The rioters were particularly upset about the film's depiction of religion: near the end of the film, a man dressed in a simple robe with a rope belt who looks suspiciously like Jesus Christ emerges from a mountaintop chateau along with several men dressed in revolutionary-era costumes. The film's intertitles identify this Christlike figure as the Duke of Blangis, the devious ringleader of the Marquis de Sade's pornographic novel *The 120 Days of Sodom*. By linking the image of Christ with the Duke of Blangis, *L'Âge d'Or* viciously attacked the church's morality and tormented those members of the audience who put their faith in Christ's beneficence. This scene was not the only instance of cultural heresy in the film, but this particular scene could well have been the spark that lit the fire under the rioters. The police who came to squelch the riot prohibited future screenings pending an investigation. Incensed by this turn of events, the surrealists made hay from the incident by publishing their own account of the riot, including a photograph of the iconoclastic attack on the artwork on view in the lobby (Fig. 8).[30] In response to accusations that extra footage had been added to the film after it received the censor board's approval, the police confiscated the film.[31] In early January 1931, nearly a year later, the group pushed the film back into public view with a text on "the affair" of *L'Âge d'Or* that detailed the film's seizure by the police and asked readers if that suppression was not a "sign of fascisization" in France.[32] In some respects, the riot, the film's suppression by the state, and the surrealists' counterattacks all worked to ensure the film's surrealist credentials.

Even today we can see why the film might have shocked some viewers in 1930. The film's central male character, played by Gaston Modot, is a pervert and a menace to society (though

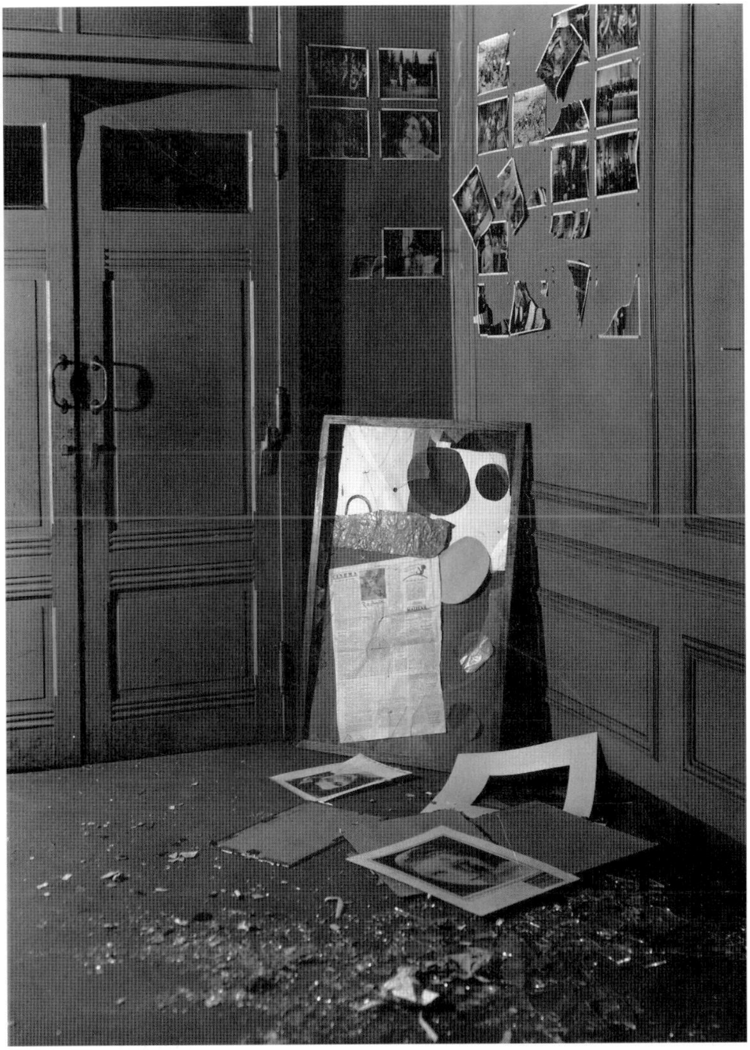

FIGURE 8 Lobby of Studio 28 the day after the 3 December 1930 screening of *L'Âge d'Or*. Courtesy of the Salvador Dalí, Gala–Salvador Dalí Foundation, Figueras, Spain.

we learn that Modot was once an upstanding citizen in the employ of the French state). Modot drives the film's narrative, taking the viewer on a tour of his corrupt activities. Coprophilia, sadomasochism, and murder are just a few of his more sensational crimes. The female object of his desire, played by Lya Lys, lives an aberrant life herself. She partakes of autoerotic pleasures, laughs at her mother's humiliation, and daydreams about infanticide. Lys and Modot's unconventional desires push them to antisocial acts, effectively tearing at the fabric of bour-

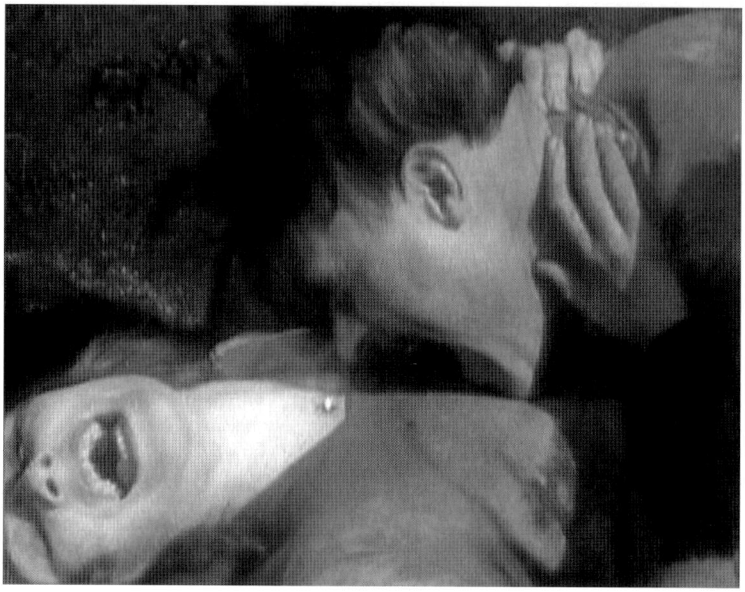

FIGURE 9
Still from Luis Buñuel and Salvador Dalí, *L'Âge d'Or,* 1930. © 2006 Salvador Dalí, Gala–Salvador Dalí Foundation, Figueras, Spain/ Artists Rights Society (ARS), New York. © Herederos de Luis Buñuel.

geois social convention. The couple rejects conformism to fulfill their most immediate desires, thereby revealing a culture in conflict—between so-called normality and perversion and between buttoned-up respectability and pulsating desire.

An early sequence in the film in which viewers first meet Lys and Modot cements the film's antiestablishment position. Both Lys and Modot are offscreen, during a scene in which the keystone of a religious monument is being dedicated. The only clue to their presence is the sound of Lys's voice emitting cries of pain or ecstasy. The camera moves to find the source of those cries, and we soon see Lys and Modot entwined on a muddy patch of earth, writhing with erotic pleasure (Fig. 9). The camera pans outward, and we suddenly see that they are lying just a few feet away from the monument.

Shocked onlookers separate them immediately. Lys is escorted away by two nuns, while Modot remains on the muddy ground, his hands compulsively squeezing the mud between his fingers as if to hold onto his lover's body through tactile association. Then, in a juxtaposition of images that exaggerates the perversity of Modot's hand gestures, the film presents Lys astride a toilet (the location implied by a pull chain and plumbing visible behind her). A second cut shifts from her face to an image of roiling, shitlike mud whose status as excrement is confirmed by the sound of a flushing toilet. Modot's erotic desire emerges in this initial sequence as both compulsive and abjectly perverse. He is out of control both physically and psychologically: he rejects social convention by engaging in sexual play during an official pub-

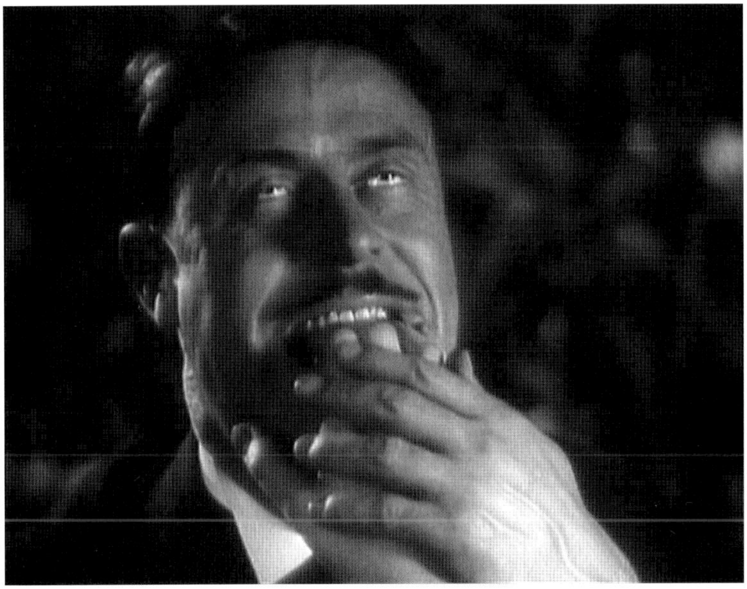

FIGURE 10
Still from Luis Buñuel and Dalí, *L'Âge d'Or,* 1930. © 2006 Salvador Dalí, Gala–Salvador Dalí Foundation, Figueras, Spain/ Artists Rights Society (ARS), New York. © Herederos de Luis Buñuel.

lic ceremony, and he reveals a perversity of mind in the pleasure he takes in the thought of coprophilia.

Modot's deviant manhood surfaces in different ways throughout the film as if to illustrate the wide variety of perversions that could taint the image of conventional bourgeois masculinity. He kicks a small white dog; he squashes bugs with pleasure; he knocks a blind man to the ground to steal his cab; he slaps his lover's mother; he marvels at seeing a father shoot his son dead with a rifle; he languorously sucks his lover's fingers (and encourages her to do the same) (Fig. 10). Although these incidents solidify Modot's reputation as a man without much of a social conscience, we learn toward the end of the film that he was once an upstanding member of the bourgeois political class whose work on behalf of the government saved the lives of hundreds of women and children. He is a man who has rejected a life of state service and social respectability to pursue his innermost fantasies and desires. Once a lionized member of the political and social elite, he has become an antisocial deviant and sexual pervert by the end of the film.

In a sequence toward the end of the film in which Modot is finally alone with Lys, the introduction of male trauma suggests that the intimacy he wants with his female lover may be both exciting and dangerous. While Modot caresses his lover's face , his hand almost imperceptibly turns into a fingerless, mutilated stump (Fig. 11). The effect is twofold: the scene underscores a moment of tender intimacy and then transforms that tenderness in a way that illuminates

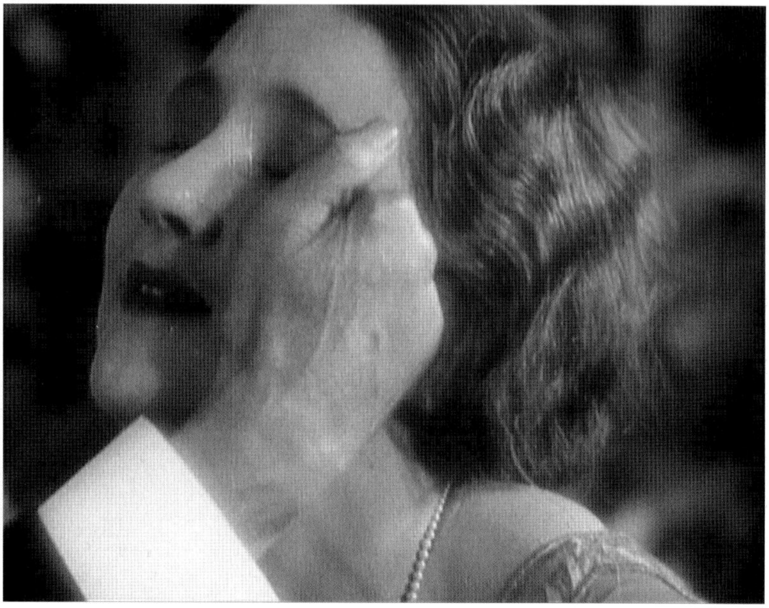

FIGURE 11 Still from Luis Buñuel and Salvador Dalí, *L'Âge d'Or,* 1930. © 2006 Salvador Dalí, Gala–Salvador Dalí Foundation, Figueras, Spain/ Artists Rights Society (ARS), New York. © Herederos de Luis Buñuel.

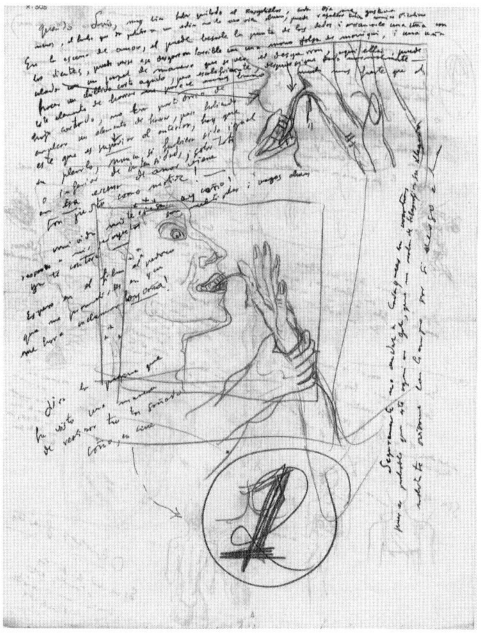

FIGURE 12 Drawing by Salvador Dalí in an undated letter to Luis Buñuel. Courtesy of the Filmoteca Española, Madrid, Fondo especial Buñuel, R.305. © 2006 Salvador Dalí, Gala–Salvador Dalí Foundation, Figueras, Spain/ Artists Rights Society (ARS), New York.

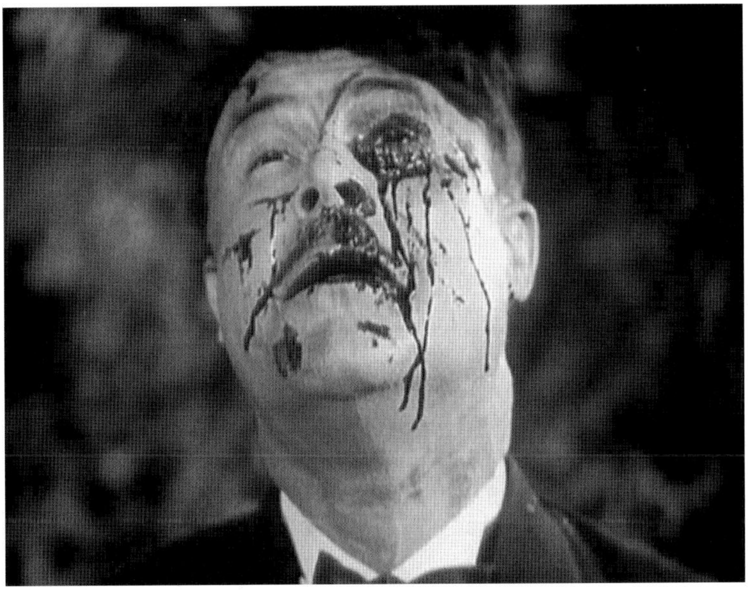

FIGURE 13
Still from Luis Buñuel and Salvador Dalí, *L'Âge d'Or,* 1930. Copyright 2006 Salvador Dalí, Gala–Salvador Dalí Foundation, Figueras, Spain / Artists Rights Society (ARS), New York. © Herederos de Luis Buñuel.

the trauma embedded deep within such moments of intimacy. At this point in the lovers' story, Modot changes from a citizen with a defective moral compass into an erotically obsessed yet emasculated man. His weakened sense of patriotism, familial duty, and social responsibility cinematically appear to be the result of his mutilated body's uncontrolled yet unfulfilled desires.

Intriguingly, a letter from the Dalí-Buñuel archives suggests that Dalí initially envisioned this sequence differently. Dalí had imagined that before Modot stroked Lys's cheek, he would kiss her fingertips. Then, as if gripped by passion, he would grasp her fingers with his teeth and rip off her fingernail and a piece of flesh in plain view of the audience.[33] In the letter, Dalí laid out how he and Buñuel could achieve this grisly effect. He suggested that they use a mannequin hand and attach a nail to it with a bit of paper trailing behind so that they could mimic the dramatic tearing of flesh and fingernail from Lys's hand.[34]

Two drawings in the letter show how he envisioned the scene (Fig. 12). Especially when juxtaposed with the film's final scenes of mutual finger sucking, the drawings' violence (complete with drops of blood from the torn-away finger, detailed in the upper right) prefigures the structure eventually chosen for this final sequence. Instead of showing Lys's finger being torn, the final version of the scene sequentially depicts two mutilated images of Modot's body: his fingerless hand caressing Lys's face (see Fig. 11) and his trembling, wounded face mouthing the words, "mon amour, mon amour, mon amour" as blood trickles down his cheeks and his neck, pinched by his formal attire, becomes a distended, blood-engorged muscle (Fig. 13).

Dalí's initial idea about violating Lys's hand changed to the image of Modot's fleshy, fingerless one. The image of violence to the female body that Dalí initially envisioned gave way to one that perpetrated violence on the male body, conjuring associations with the wounds of veterans in the recent world war.[35] Indeed, in a letter Dalí wrote to Buñuel about the use of a bloody male face in the film, he described two alternate scenarios: a horribly bloody man walking among a group of pedestrians or a split-second image of the man's bloody face.[36] Although the final choice in the film was a long shot of Modot's bleeding face, the wounds afflicting his body provide visual cues for the audience's fantasies. The wounding of Modot's body at this point in the film—his hand a fingerless stump, his face lacerated and dripping blood while he repeats the words "my love, my love, my love"—suggests that Modot finds sexual release in his own wounds and presumes that the audience will have its own visceral attachment to the pleasures and pains of Modot's experience.

These images of Modot's mutilated hand and bloodied face at the end of the film suggest that the strange mix of pleasure and pain in his desire might be an outgrowth of the wounded male body. The image of his bloodied face above his tightly bound neck suggests a phallic shape, further asserting a potential connection between his facial wound and attacks on male (phallic) power. Modot and Lys are a disconcerting if fascinating pair of lovers whose unconventional approaches to erotic satisfaction—the sucking of toes and fingers, pleasure in pain, the trauma of intimacy—in *L'Âge d'Or* demonstrate that desire could become a useful means of undermining not just sexual but social convention. Although the film's characters grovel in the mud, kick a small dog and a blind man, dream of masturbation and the murder of their own children, the film was more than a shocking catalog of social taboos or perverse sexual pleasures to viewers at the time. *L'Âge d'Or* showed that desire wouldn't be controlled easily and that it might crash the gates of restraint protecting the bourgeois subject from the workings of his or her unconscious. And the film did so by visualizing the power of advertising posters and photographs to elicit unconventional acts from unsuspecting viewers.

Advertising Surrealist Desire

L'Âge d'Or not only tried to destabilize audience assumptions about appropriate behavior and proper sexuality, but it also promoted the idea that advertising images had exceptional potential to awaken strange new desires in the viewer. Buñuel and Dalí apparently believed that contemporary pictorial advertisements could successfully jump-start a surrealist aesthetic experience by using images to evoke a chain of associations. Dalí wrote of the fabulous "antiartistic world of advertisements!, magnificent invitations to the senses and to the voyage of discovery of unknown objects."[37] Like the "double images" he believed were necessary to provoke "mental crisis" in their viewers, these advertisements could entice viewers to see and experience the world in entirely new ways.[38] Thus, in two key sequences, the film methodically illustrates how cutting-edge advertising posters and photographs can first arrest the viewer's attention and then plunge him or her into a landscape teeming with fragmentary images. These fragments retained the power to create new associations, which in turn produced new forms of desire, pleasure, or perversity in viewers.

To make their point as effectively as possible, Buñuel and Dalí worked with the well-known photographer and advertising designer André Vigneau to produce several posters and a photograph especially for *L'Âge d'Or.*[39] Using Vigneau's images in ways that paralleled the actual deployment of posters in and around the city of Paris (Figs. 14 and 15)—on a fence next to a sidewalk, on a sandwich man, or in a shop window—the film showed exactly how mass-marketed images could trigger powerful, psychologically dense associations. The first advertising sequence shows Modot, immediately after being arrested for his mud-spattered indiscretion with Lys, escorted through a city by two policemen. The three men walk by a wooden fence plastered with Vigneau's posters. One of the posters, an ad for Leda facial powder, attracts Modot's attention (Figs. 15 and 16). A series of rapid cuts between the poster and Modot's face suggest that the poster impresses itself on Modot's subconscious. Soon, a cinematic dissolve suggests Modot's mind at work: the female hand and powder puff in the poster have turned into oscillating objects in Modot's mind (Fig. 17). With the box of powder supplanted by a mound of dark hair and the female hand now moving in rapid circles at hair's edge, the film at this juncture baldly suggests female masturbation.[40]

A second advertising image that soon crosses Modot's path reiterates how advertising posters arrest their viewers' attention with careful yet strange and unexpected juxtapositions. After shaking himself out of his masturbatory fantasy about the Leda poster, Modot focuses on a pair of inverted female legs attached to a man's sandwich board that advertises hosiery. As Modot whips around to follow the man, whose body has become a living billboard, his face registers his surprise at the mixture of signs: a man who is also a pair of woman's legs. Quickly, however, Modot's escorts get him moving again. A few moments later Modot notices a third image, this time in a shop window: a photograph of a woman's tipped-back head. Once again, the visual effects grab his attention; they also forge an associative link to his earlier fantasy of female masturbation. A rapid dissolve overtakes his sight of the photograph and turns the woman in the picture into an image of his girlfriend lying on a couch with her hand in her lap and her neck arched back in a suggestion of autoerotic pleasure.

In Modot's eyes, the poster, the sandwich man, and the photograph each generate an erotic fantasy or at least, a visual shock. But the film also shows how one image's effects lead to other experiences as the viewer makes visual links between the varied, often fragmentary images Modot sees as he walks along the city's streets. The images accrue power because they suggest chains of associations that in turn create new webs of desire—unplanned and previously unimagined. Vigneau's advertisements do not sell products; they trigger narrative fantasies that may create desire for a product but may also irritate the mind to generate other, more

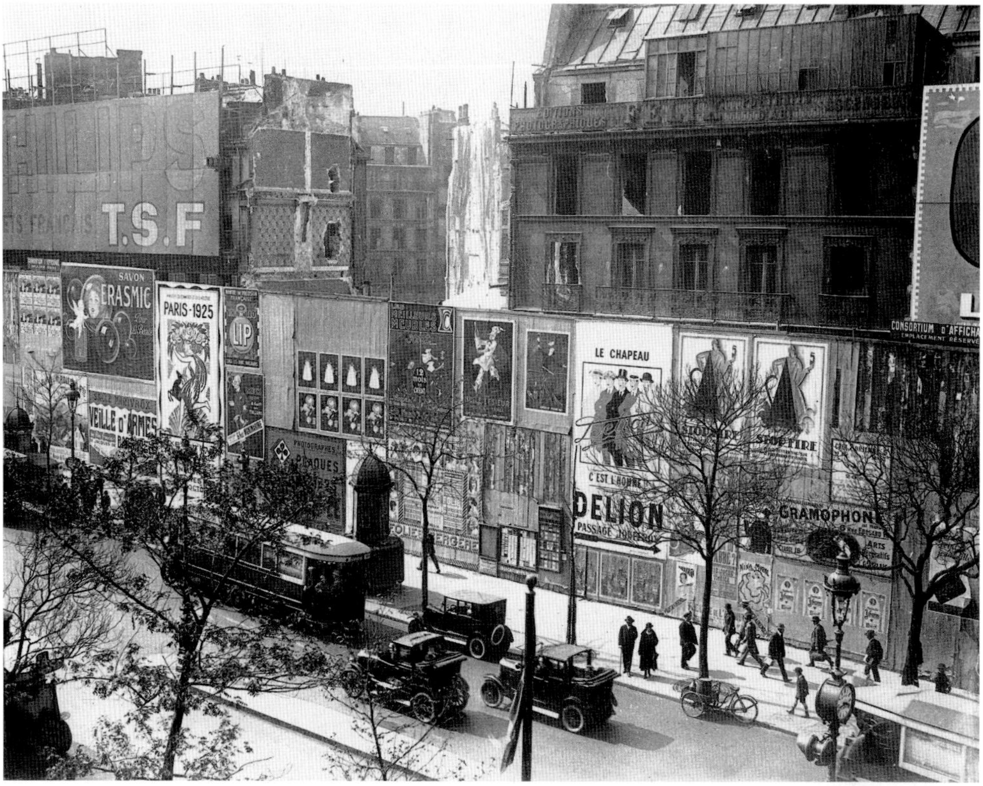

FIGURE 14
Boulevard Haussmann, Paris, 1925. Bibliothèque Nationale de France, Department of Prints and Photographs, Collection Meurisse.

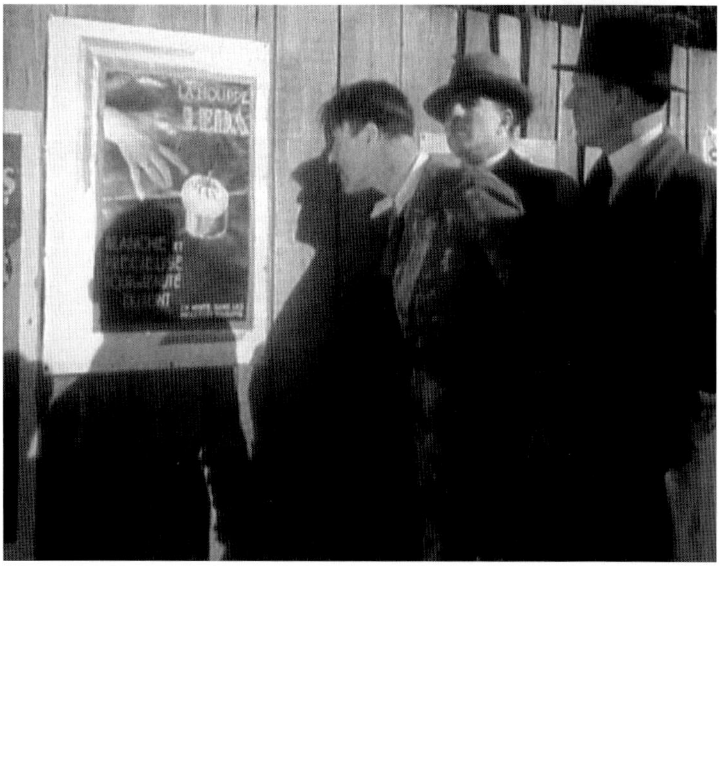

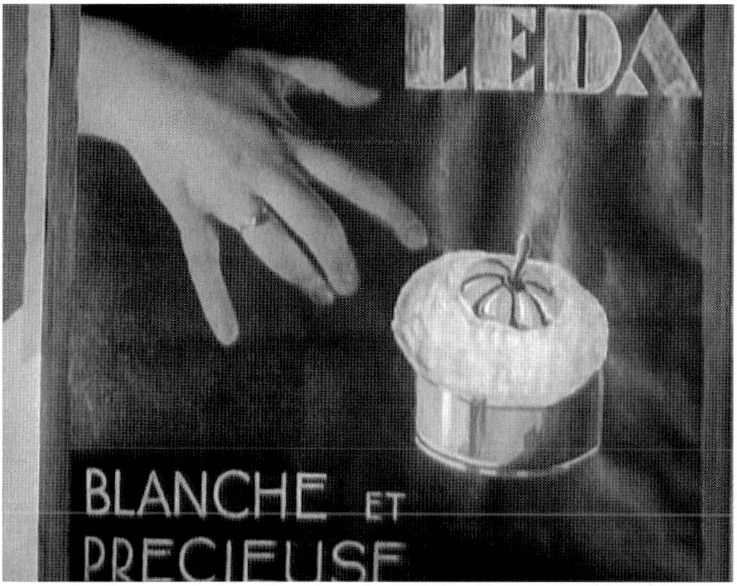

FIGURE 16
Still from Luis Buñuel and Salvador Dalí, *L'Âge d'Or,* 1930. © 2006 Salvador Dalí, Gala–Salvador Dalí Foundation, Figueras, Spain/Artists Rights Society (ARS), New York. © Herederos de Luis Buñuel.

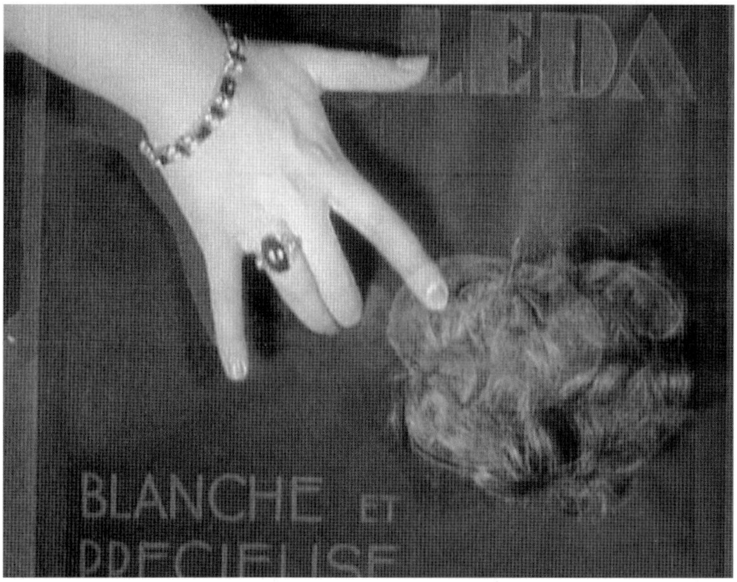

FIGURE 17
Still from Luis Buñuel and Salvador Dalí, *L'Âge d'Or,* 1930. © 2006 Salvador Dalí, Gala–Salvador Dalí Foundation, Figueras, Spain/Artists Rights Society (ARS), New York. © Herederos de Luis Buñuel.

FIGURE 15
Still from Luis Buñuel and Salvador Dalí, *L'Âge d'Or,* 1930. © 2006 Salvador Dalí, Gala–Salvador Dalí Foundation, Figueras, Spain/Artists Rights Society (ARS), New York. © Herederos de Luis Buñuel.

visceral forms of desire with the potential to destroy the vestiges of the bourgeois social order.[41] Thus, by using Vigneau's advertising, Buñuel and Dalí imagine a world of images that teach their audiences to desire a new way of being in which love can conquer the brittle, sacrificial "religions" of bourgeois society. *L'Âge d'Or* dramatized how individual experience could catalyze political transformation, and Vigneau's posters, as channeled through the eyes of Gaston Modot, sought to create a longing for both personal, erotic satisfaction and a newly desirous surrealist society.

Dreaming the Surrealist City

Although recent work on surrealism has begun to ask questions about surrealism's relationship to popular culture—cinema, pulp fiction, public exhibitions, even wax museums—scholars often shy away from analyzing how advertising theory and practice might have informed surrealist work, particularly surrealist visual representations, in the 1920s.[42] In the years preceding *L'Âge d'Or,* writers like Louis Aragon and Robert Desnos had already begun to imagine advertising's potential to produce a surrealist experience of the city, and in their novels, they seem to have laid the groundwork for Buñuel and Dalí's surrealist flâneur to contemplate the posters that dominated many Parisian boulevards. Aragon remarked on the city's potential as the site of advertising-created revelations in his 1929 essay "Introduction to 1930": "a poem . . . if it were written on the walls, would it stop the crowd? would they read it? would they hold on to it?"[43] His comments alluded to the phenomenon that *L'Âge d'Or* was to envision a year later. Perhaps, the surrealists thought, visual images that used the strategies of visual fragmentation and juxtaposition so familiar in contemporary publicity could prepare the passing crowds to see the world differently. Perhaps these images could help consumers see the largely invisible ideological and psychological structures that were so central to surrealism's interpretation of modern life. How could one make advertisements that would create a surrealist individual? What would the advertising images look like, and to whom would they be pitched? Robert Desnos' work, as reflected in his 1927 book *La Liberté ou L'Amour,* may well have been the textual precursor to the practical, associational applications that Buñuel and Dalí imagined for advertising in *L'Âge d'Or.* Desnos' text explores how a surrealist city could provoke its inhabitants to experience the city differently and, subsequently, to succumb to their repressed desires. Lying in wait for the unsuspecting viewer, the billboards that populate Desnos' vision of Paris become living beings: at one moment, these beings lie flat and still, plastered against the city's walls; in the next, they come to life and jump into the streets so that they can unleash their audience's wildest dreams. Desnos' city—not unlike the cities of *L'Âge d'Or* and Aragon's *Paysan de Paris*—feels like a dream.

Desnos mounts his surrealist ad campaign at the beginning of *La Liberté ou L'Amour.* A well-known contemporary advertising image—the giant face of the Bébé Cadum, a "logo" that

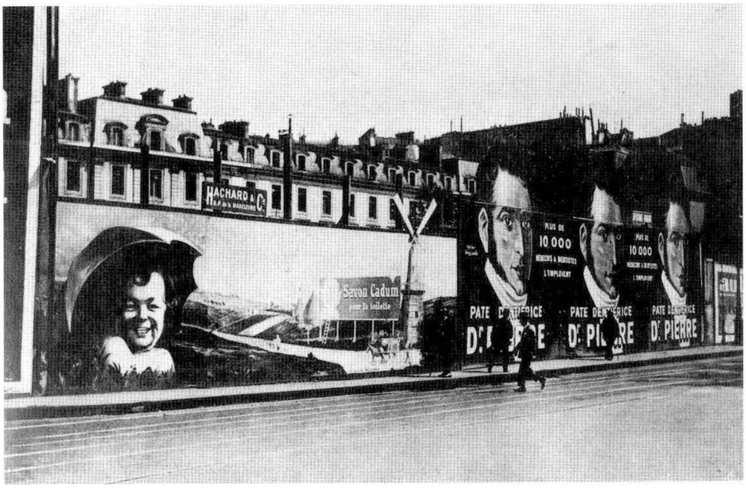

FIGURE 18
Bébé Cadum billboard in Paris, 1926. In *L'Art Vivant* (15 August 1926): 619.

sought to represent Cadum soap's purity (Fig. 18)—leaps from its two-dimensional surface and is transformed, through Desnos' prose, into a living, breathing inhabitant of a dreamlike urban landscape in which the Michelin man, Bibendum, also lived:

> Bébé Cadum was born without the aid of parents, spontaneously. On the horizon, a somber giant stretched his limbs and yawned. Bibendum Michelin introduced him to a terrible battle of which the author of these lines will be the historian. At the age of twenty-one years, Bébé Cadum was big enough to fight with Bibendum. . . . A policeman who was strolling foolishly along the Avenue des Champs-Élysées heard suddenly great clamors in the sky. The sky was obscured and, with thunder, lightning, and wind, a soapy rain fell upon the city. In an instant the landscape was ghostly. The roofs were covered with a light mousse which the wind picked up by flakes. . . . A multitude of rainbows emerged. . . . Passersby walked in an odiferous snow that rose up to their knees. . . . Then a charming madness moved into the city. The inhabitants removed their clothing and ran around the streets, rolling on the soapy carpet.[44]

Desnos conjures an image of Paris in which streets turn into strange theaters and billboards, and posters and marketing symbols come to life to battle for market share. Their antics encourage others to behave erratically: people begin to shed their clothes and to follow their desires rather than their good sense—all at the behest of these strange new residents. Desnos imagines that the poetic potential of the advertising icon is real in this text. Thus, the beholder's experience of the city shifts from one of passive consumption to one of active participation—mimicking the trajectory of the iconic corporate logos' newfound embodiments. Bébé Cadum doesn't simply want to sell soap; he aims to change the world into a place of his own making. He will blanket the city in a sudsy snow, and he will entice the city's residents to rip off their clothes and roll shamelessly in the streets.

Walter Benjamin, in his writing on surrealism, echoes the ideas in these two surrealist texts about the potential effect of advertising on contemporary culture. In a passage from his unpublished "Arcades Project" on advertising, he notes that "publicity [is] the ruse that permits the dream to impose itself on industry."[45] Surrealist poems use words that are "like the names of commercial firms," and "their texts are at bottom prospectuses for businesses which have not yet been created."[46] Benjamin noticed that surrealism's appropriation of advertising language encouraged the development of imagery with widespread commercial power. Thus, he likened surrealist works to proposals for surrealist businesses whose products would not be commodities but a new society shaped by the unconscious desires made manifest by these advertising images. Interestingly, by the mid-1920s many prominent advertising theorists and practitioners had already begun to codify the crucial relationship between unconscious desire and the success of visual advertisements, and Desnos, Buñuel, and Dalí were apparently at least somewhat aware of these developments.

Advertising-industry publications were full of discussions about how best to develop new visual languages that would attract a customer's attention just long enough to lodge desire for a product in his or her mind. Most advertising professionals at the time understood that co-opting the viewer's sense of sight was crucial to this process. Through visual suggestion, an advertisement should capture and then modify the viewer's consciousness through an associational chain of psychological attachment or identification with the depicted object, eventually leading to action: purchase of the desired consumer product. In this way, advertisements could create a set of lasting, if unfocused, experiences of desire in the beholder. According to a 1927 essay in the high-end advertising and design journal *Arts et Métiers Graphiques,*

> The advertisement, when it is simply "seen," does not have the same value for immediately creating the desire for the purchase; it is even frequently seen by passersby without their knowledge. Because publicity, like any thing which falls under the senses, may be perceived in the state of waking, or on the contrary in the state of sleeping—during the hours where the spirit is passive, available for the impressions that are indifferent to it in appearance.—An idea is going to lodge itself in one of the folds of the brain, in one of its mysterious pockets, in the subconscious!—The seed is sown; and external influence will make it germinate. The need for a product or an article will happen unexpectedly one day, and this need, impersonal at first, will make itself more concrete and will take for its object the brand read everywhere.[47]

Visual advertisements not only generate desire, but they also push their viewers to act upon a potentially endless, and individualized, series of psychological and emotional experiences. This advertising principle is strikingly close to the formula at work in the publicity sequences in

L'Âge d'Or. Where the film's account of publicity diverges from this textual account, however, is in the final product: rather than working to create desire for a commodity, the posters in *L'Âge d'Or* release Modot's desires without a discernible commodity, or purpose, in view. His emerging desires push him to become a social pariah instead of going shopping.

In advertising, surrealist artists and writers found a means to turn the rhetoric of mass culture—whose most potent form is publicity, as I have suggested—into a tool to develop new and potentially subversive surrealist messages. Working on its audience's subconscious, the surrealist text, image, or object had potential to alter the social order by luring people's desires away from assembly-line products and toward new forms of individual and collective expression. *L'Âge d'Or* dramatized the way in which a visual language of juxtaposition and decontextualization could achieve both the publicists' and the surrealists' goals: to produce and consolidate desire in the consumer. But *L'Âge d'Or*—and to an extent, Desnos' *La Liberté ou L'Amour*—sought to produce desire for a surrealist experience, and this "product" was unconventional, antiestablishment conduct.

Reconstruction and the Promise of the Postwar Body

From the *grands magasins* to the walls of Parisian streets plastered high with visually arresting advertisements (see Fig. 14), consumer culture was dependent on fragmentary images whose primary purpose was to generate visual shock through the use of a properly aestheticized visual fragment. Many of the images by advertising professionals like André Vigneau, the poster artist for *L'Âge d'Or,* effectively used body parts to sell consumer products. Yet many modern publicists also promoted the reconstructed male body as a sign of the nation's increasing economic and industrial stability in the 1920s. And nowhere was this thrust more evident than at the 1925 Exposition Internationale des Arts Décoratifs et Industriels Modernes, an exhibition designed to signal France's increasingly important role as an international leader in advertising, design, and industrial arts. As a result, some of the imagery of the exposition's publicity campaign linked national power and industrial productivity not to the derealized bodies produced by the avant-garde but to an idealized image of masculinity.

An official advertisement for the 1925 exposition (which ran from April through October) exemplifies this embodiment of productivity (Fig. 19). With robust male bodies piled high in the foreground and factories belching smoke at the rear, this advertisement heroizes industrial labor and presents pictorial evidence that reconstruction depends not just on the cooperation of man and machine but on the use of the powerful male body as an engine of national rebirth. The exposition also showcased the latest in mannequin design, which favored idealized images of postwar masculinity and femininity. These new standards of beauty and potential marketing power attracted attention not only in professional advertising journals but also in the surrealist journal *La Révolution surréaliste.*

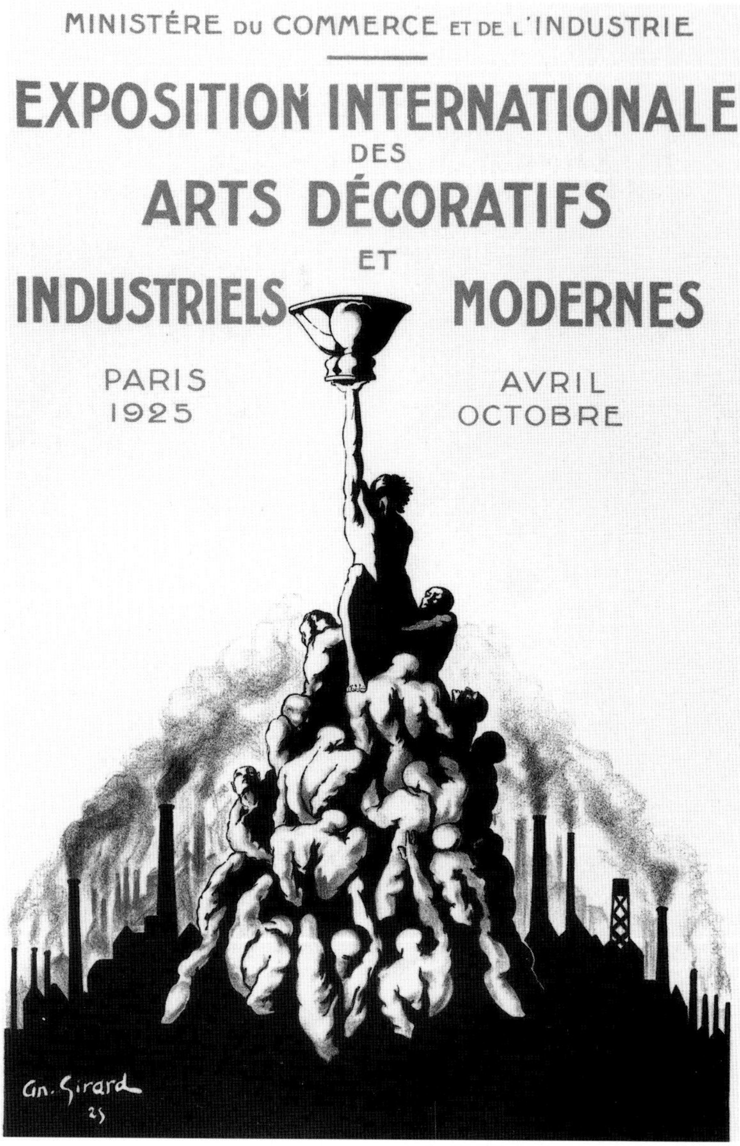

FIGURE 19
Poster, International Exposition of Modern Industrial and Decorative Arts, Paris, 1925. Bibliothèque Nationale de France, Department of Prints and Photographs.

FIGURE 20 Man Ray, Siégel mannequin, 1925. Cover of *La Révolution surréaliste* 4 (15 July 1925). © 2006 Man Ray Trust/Artists Rights Society (ARS), New York/ADAGP, Paris.

N° 4 — Première année 15 Juillet 1925

LA RÉVOLUTION SURRÉALISTE

ET GUERRE

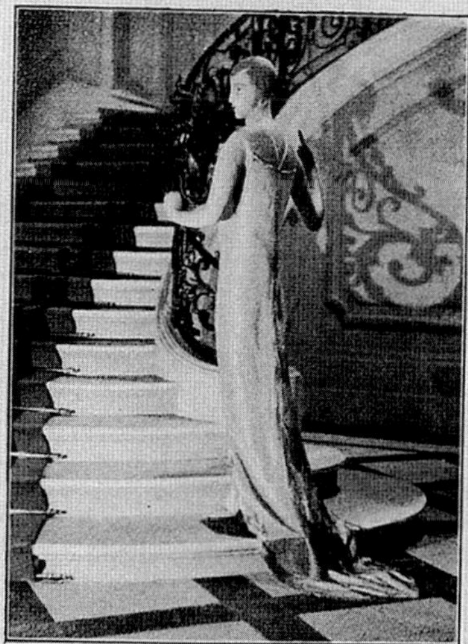

AU TRAVAIL

SOMMAIRE

ABONNEMENT, les 12 Numéros : France : 45 francs Etranger : 55 francs

Dépositaire général : Librairie GALLIMARD
15, Boulevard Raspail, 15
PARIS (VIIe)

LE NUMÉRO : France : 4 francs Étranger : 5 francs

A l'Exposition Internatio

Pour la défense des Manne

Nous avons déjà parlé (numéro de juillet, page 397) de l'évolution des mannequins de mode, à propos de l'Exposition Internationale des Arts Décoratifs : il faut y revenir. Ne cite-t-on pas telle maison qui pour cette manifestation a créé jusqu'à six cents modèles!! Ce très gros effort mérite attention puisque demain, pour nos étalages, nous serons appelés à choisir celui-ci ou celui-là, qui doit plaire à la clientèle et au passant. Le mannequin étant un élément publicitaire important, il n'est pas superflu de revenir sur ce sujet, — très vaste d'ailleurs.

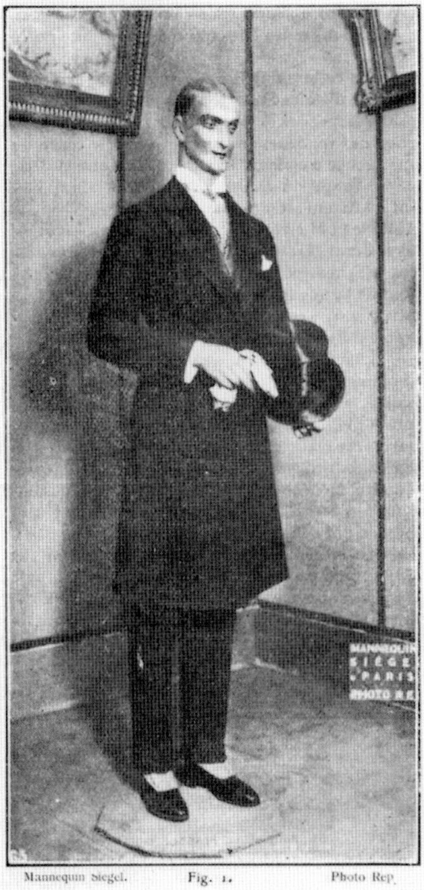

Mannequin Siegel. Fig. 1. Photo Rep.

M. André de Fouquières lui-même, dans une de ses chroniques du *Figaro*, n'a pas craint de citer ces « personnages de cire », auxquels de nombreux journaux et de nombreuses revues ont déjà consacré de nombreux articles et de nombreuses reproductions.

A notre point de vue commercial, reprenons la critique ou l'éloge qu'on en a faits au point de vue artistique.

Ne trouvez-vous pas qu'il était nécessaire de bousculer un peu, en cette matière, nos vieilles habitudes? Nous avions accoutumé de voir de mignonnes figures sans caractère, qui posaient devant nous comme chez le photographe : pas de naturel, des gestes faux, précieux et toujours semblables. Les perruques, les cils, les sourcils étaient véritables et personne n'imaginait qu'il en pût être autrement... Et, pourtant, en l'espèce, à quoi cela sert-il ?

Le mannequin n'est qu'un support, un « portemanteau », qui doit mettre en valeur une étoffe, un vêtement ou une partie du vêtement; il n'est que cela. Au fond, on ne devrait pas le voir, ou, tout au moins, il ne devrait rester dans notre souvenir qu'à l'état de second plan.

Les fabricants — mais ne sont-ils pas orfèvres, comme M. Josse? — parlent autrement : « Si vos yeux conservent l'image du mannequin, disent-ils, vous vous rappellerez la robe et le manteau qu'il porte. De plus, pour ne pas compliquer vos souvenirs, nous stylisons, nous revenons à la ligne. »

L'erreur du bon public est de croire que le mannequin doit être obligatoirement une statue de cire « ressemblante ». Il veut pouvoir se tromper et dire comme le cicerone de l'abbaye de Hautecombe en montrant une statue : « Regardez cette main; on dirait qu'elle va parler. » Il veut comme au Musée Grévin pouvoir enlever son chapeau devant M. Rostand ou Mme Dieulafoy. Faut-il le contenter, même aux dépens de l'art et de la publicité? Nous ne le croyons pas.

D'ailleurs, et peu à peu, les yeux s'habituent à

Although the surrealists' work did not receive direct recognition in the exposition, the surrealists understood the implications of the exposition's glitzy presentation of a new commercial culture. Both intrigued by and disdainful of the exposition and its commercial goals (indeed, Louis Aragon wrote a rather scathing review of the exposition in October 1925), the surrealists' decision to publish a Man Ray photograph of one of the mannequins at the exhibition on its July 1925 cover (Fig. 20) indicated their willingness to explore the increasing power of simulated bodies as marketing tools.[48] This female mannequin, a product of the Siégel design firm, whose mannequin division was led by André Vigneau, would presumably stimulate consumer desire for the clothes that she wore or for the personality she seemed to embody. One can imagine that the same held true for her male counterparts, such as the mannequin that appeared in a 1925 issue of the trade journal *Publicité* (Fig. 21).

The presence of the Siégel-Vigneau mannequins at the exposition, with their seductive, uncannily lifelike bodies, underscores the importance in 1925 of creating images of a vibrant, healthy consumer society that would attest to the success of social and cultural reconstruction. Instead of simply marketing paintings to go with chairs or promoting the rebuilt veteran as a more productive version of the old, Vigneau's Siégel mannequins created desire for those commodities or social results by encouraging viewer identification with the perfected images of well-crafted, conventionally gendered mannequins. Like streamlined descendants of the rebuilt male veteran, perhaps Vigneau's male mannequins helped erase the gap between the reality of postwar trauma and the promise of regeneration. Men and women could interact with these humanoid symbols of postwar progress through corporeal identification and desire. Perhaps these embodied ideals held the key to a newly minted, blemish-free social body.

Throughout the 1920s, the surrealists co-opted the images of contemporary publicity for their own purposes. Using techniques of juxtaposition and comparison that mirrored those popular with designers in the 1920s, the surrealists labored to reveal the slippages in meaning that most images of postwar reconstruction tried to avoid. They sought to show that the ideology of regeneration was in large part a fantasy, concocted as a balm for the traumatized national psyche, and that the promised changes of reconstruction had not yet taken place. By producing images that emphasized dismemberment instead of seamless reconstruction, surrealist writers and artists launched a movement that I think of as an ad campaign for a surrealist future. The surrealists borrowed the visual and rhetorical structures that the establishment was using to promote national progress and used them to emphasize anxiety, trauma, and uncertainty. And because their images seemed poised to trigger unconscious desires and, by

FIGURE 21 Male mannequin (Siégel), 1925. In *Publicité* 213 (November 1925): 676. Courtesy of the Bibliothèque Nationale de France.

implication, to evoke the very feelings about the war that postwar rhetoric sought to repress, the surrealists believed that their work had the potential to undermine the state's rosy predictions of a return to order. Whether or not they realized that potential is another story, particularly because visual shock and mental fantasy continue to be hallmarks of the most successful marketing campaigns of our time.

CHAPTER TWO

The Aesthetics of Dismemberment

There are pieces of flesh and clothing held within the strange branches above my head. . . .
"Do you see the cutlets in the tree?"

JEAN PAULHAN, *Le Guérrier appliqué*, 1919

The end of the gallery is occupied by an orthopedist-bandagist. . . . Next to the champagne merchant, see how he displays beautiful articulated wooden hands, some made of a single piece. And canes, crutches, nozzles, anti-migraine chalks. And then again, so as to explain this crime of passion, two cut-off hands in a bidet.

LOUIS ARAGON, *Le Paysan de Paris*, 1926

Surreality will be in any case a function of our willingness to completely defamiliarize everything . . . right up to the point of defamiliarizing a hand by isolating it from an arm.

ANDRÉ BRETON, preface to *La Femme 100 Têtes* by Max Ernst, 1929

Before Louis Aragon and André Breton became surrealists, they worked in a hospital ward packed with mutilated, shell-shocked veterans of World War I. Both had enrolled as physicians in training at the Parisian military hospital of Val-de-Grâce in September 1917, and there they learned about the newest ideas in French psychiatry.[1] They also read the *Chants de Maldoror* aloud to one another while watching over their suffering patients late at night.[2] Val-de-Grâce was a military teaching hospital that collected and displayed images of male bodily trauma and reconstruction for contemporary viewers. By creating painstakingly accurate displays of the surgical repairs of soldiers' bodies, the Musée du Val-de-Grâce framed France's reconstruction in bodily terms—the very terms that surrealist artists and writers would put to use throughout the 1920s. For this reason, Val-de-Grâce ought to figure prominently in the history of surrealism.

Although histories of surrealism mention Val-de-Grâce as the cutting-edge teaching hospital where Aragon and Breton first met, they largely overlook the fact that it housed a museum of medical iconography (including human bones, preserved body parts, prostheses, sculptural casts, photographs, surgical instruments, as well as drawings, paintings, and sculptures) that documented in concrete form the military's wartime medical activities.[3] Although museum policy had always limited access to physicians and trained military personnel, in the fall of 1916 the head of the Health Service opened the museum to the public amid a blitz of publicity.[4] A crew from Gaumont newsreels captured the crush of the opening on film, as a capacity crowd packed the galleries in an effort to see what the state was doing to help the war's most severely injured soldiers *(mutilés de guerre)*.[5] By 1917, then, Val-de-Grâce played both a political and an aesthetic role in the state's public-relations program to deflect criticism about the huge numbers of casualties occurring along the western front.

Not only have scholars overlooked Val-de-Grâce's importance as a collection of provocative visual objects, but they have also paid little attention to the institution's significance in altering ideals of masculinity. As we have seen, by 1920 the heroic male body was central to the visual rhetoric of postwar reconstruction; instead of Marianne, the revolutionary-era heroine, muscular young men would rebuild France this time around (see Fig. 3 in the introduction). Yet the streets were populated with wounded veterans, and the state was working hard to counter anxiety about a weakened male citizenry by promoting images of healthy masculinity. The Val-de-Grâce collection was important because it appropriated male mutilation to demonstrate the promise of bodily reconstruction.

A careful look at the collections of Val-de-Grâce reveals that the surrealists were not the first to aestheticize trauma. The French state had done the same at the Musée du Val-de-Grâce by creating physical examples that narrated national regeneration for the public. The museum's collection of moulages (wax and plaster casts) demonstrated that the surgical repair of mutilated soldiers' bodies was a key component of national reconstruction. Jean Bonnerot, head archivist of the Musée du Val-de-Grâce at the time of its reopening in 1916, underscored this agenda by describing the collection as material traces of the military's devotion to the French state. For Bonnerot and many other commentators, the collection bore witness to the physical—and by extension the psychological—progress enabled by wartime medical advances.[6] Through tragic displays of bodily injury and subsequent repair, the collections symbolized not only physical rebirth but also the meshing of science and aesthetics within therapeutic practice. Study of the museum's archival holdings show that the hospital also used the moulages (Figs. 22 and 23)—along with colored-pencil drawings (Fig. 24), sculptures and moulages of mutilated hands and feet (Fig. 25), and photographic records of serial treatment (Fig. 26)—as evidence of its important scientific innovations.[7]

How did the moulages articulate progress through the injured body? And in what concrete ways might we consider the museum's version of bodily progress a catalyst for the well-known surrealist penchant for dismemberment? A military photograph of one of the museum's vitrines (see Fig. 22) shows how the aestheticization of the wounded soldier's body could be tied to reconstruction. Sculpturally accurate casts of mutilated men's faces illustrated the war's evolution—by showing the progress from traumatic injury to reconstructed face. To engage the viewer more directly, the moulages were often painted to simulate the look of bloodied flesh, yellow fat, and exposed white bone (see Fig. 23).[8] Although these realistic approximations of the process of reconstruction were compelling to look at, the museum staff realized that they might seem "too real" for civilian viewers. For some viewers, the lurid paint might look like

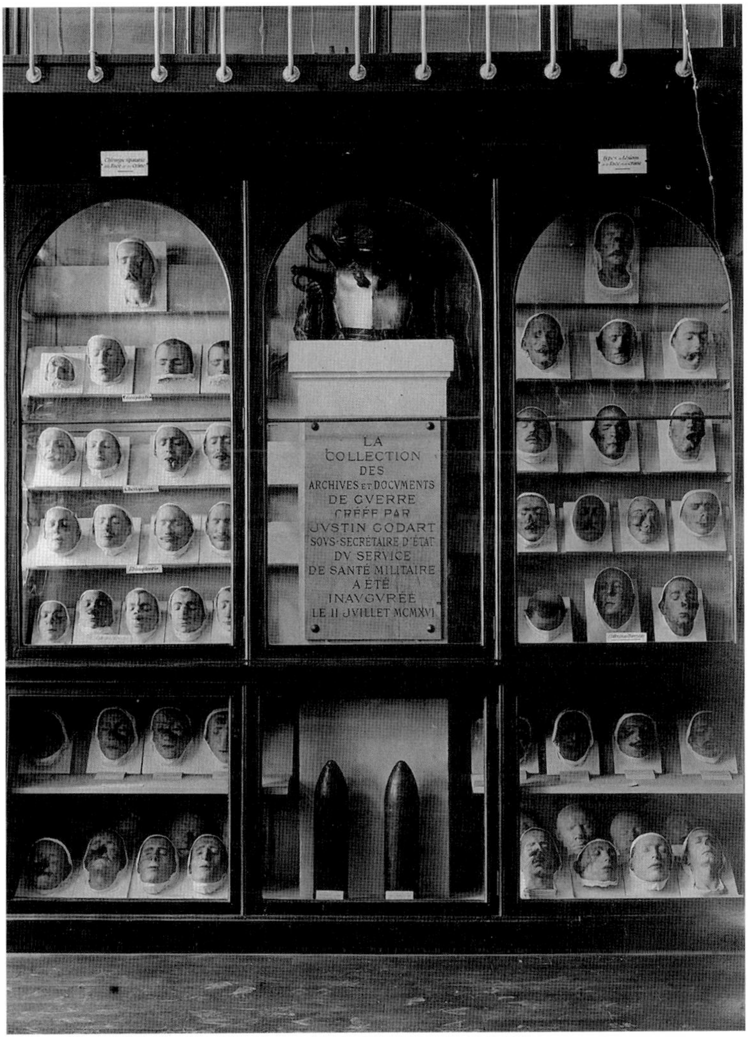

FIGURE 22 Vitrine housing surgical moulages, Salle Morestin, Musée du Val-de-Grâce, Paris, after 1916. Courtesy of the Musée d'Histoire Contemporaine, Bibliothèque de Documentation Internationale Contemporaine, Paris.

theatrical makeup. For others, however, the moulages might produce nausea or disgust. As if to evade either of these misreadings, the exhibit situated the individual masks in a structure that taught viewers how to look at them. Art historians from the national museums organized the moulages according to an evolutionary model, using a before-and-after visual logic to transform the traumas endured by individual soldiers into examples of collective therapy.[9]

The aestheticizing impulse of the collection was not lost on its first civilian viewers. Many commentators who wrote about the opening of the collection recognized the evolutionary and

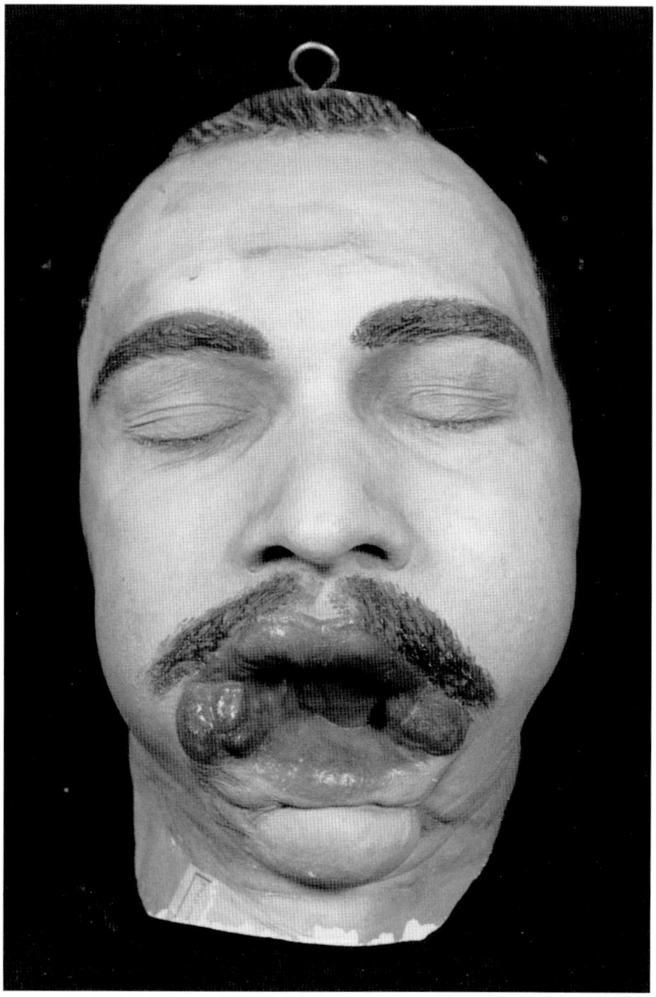

FIGURE 23
Moulage (painted plaster), Musée du Val-de-Grâce, Paris, ca. 1916. Courtesy of the Musée du Val-de-Grâce, Paris (Archives du Musée/Service de Santé des Armées, Ministère de la Défense, France).

aesthetic aspects of the displays, and many of them likened the surgeons at Val-de-Grâce to sculptors or artists. In a piece in the newspaper *Le Figaro* in July 1916, a writer who had attended the collection's opening reception noticed that although the objects could cause distress (particularly those recording facial injuries), the works by a "sculptor" were effective precisely because of their heightened realism. Although the moulages documented the soldiers' terrible wounds, their sequential organization suggested that those wounds would be healed. "One gets used to looking at them and one follows, with interest, the diverse phases of the . . . graft that marvelously remakes the faces of men who appeared to have none."[10] Léo Clarétie,

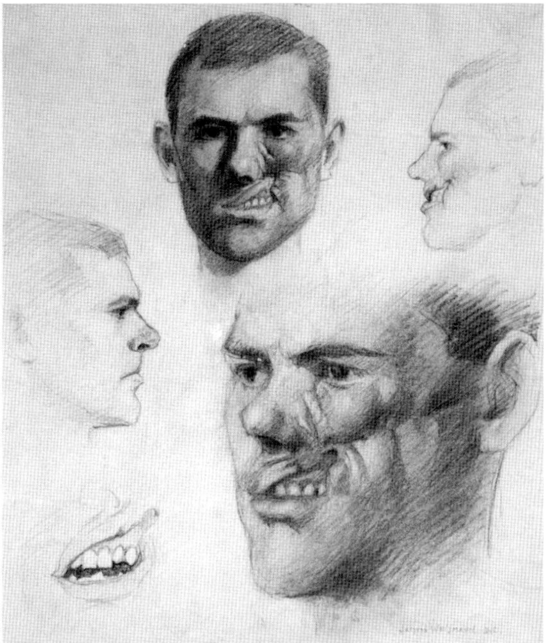

FIGURE 24
Drawings (colored pencil) of surgical patients and techniques, ca. 1917. Weissmann Collection, Musée du Val-de-Grâce, Paris. Courtesy of the Musée du Val-de-Grâce, Paris (Archives du Musée/ Service de Santé des Armées, Ministère de la Défense, France).

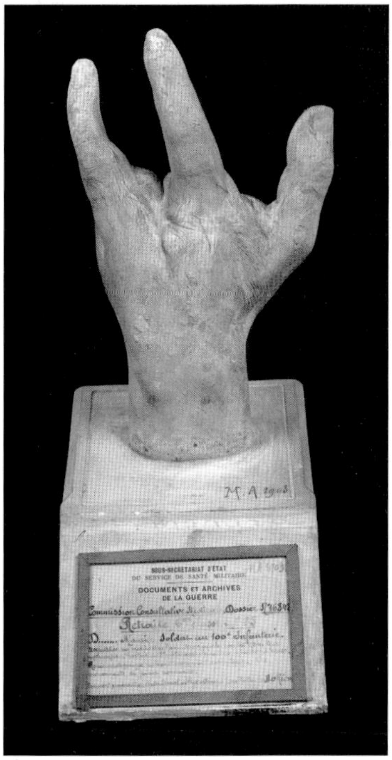

FIGURE 25
Moulage of a hand, Musée du Val-de-Grâce, Paris, ca. 1916. Courtesy of the Musée du Val-de-Grâce, Paris (Archives du Musée/ Service de Santé des Armées, Ministère de la Défense, France).

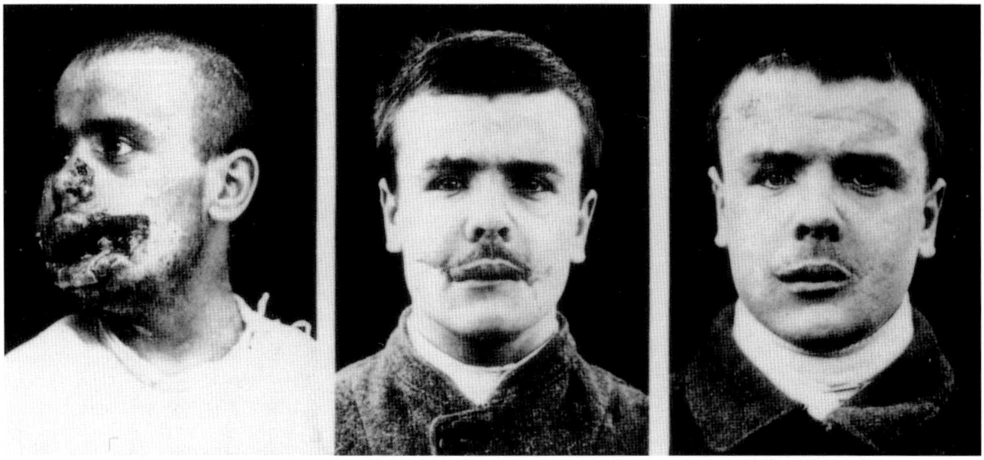

FIGURE 26 Facial reconstruction on a *mutilé de guerre,* 1916. In *Science et Dévouement* (Paris: Aristide Quillet, 1918): 144.

writing in the widely read *L'Évènement,* described the museum as a place where viewers could learn about the war's history of "suffering and remedy" and see how the surgical objects "modeled in wax by great artists" revealed the "spectacle of a smashed-in face and a face repaired." Emphasizing the successive phases of treatment in his comments, Clarétie surmised that the collections would demand "a certain respect . . . [and] admiration for science and human generosity, such that the horror of the wounds disappears."[11]

Clarétie's equation of the moulages' medical functions and their cultural ones—they both show traces of surgical treatment and are markers of historical change—reveals how palpable the museum's public-relations agenda was to the people who went to see the new exhibition. The museum's careful arrangement of the grisly artifacts dramatized the facts of mutilation for the French public, but only within a larger context that presented war injuries as unfortunate stages in a long-term process of national reconstruction. By placing the moulages into a therapeutic narrative, the collection commended military medicine while defusing the explosive political situation that loomed after France's slaughter at Verdun and the Somme that summer.

The moulages were arranged in sets—usually in pairs but sometimes in groups of three or more—that illustrated successive stages of surgical treatment. Discrete sets of moulages were then arranged in rows corresponding to types of surgical intervention. Each set thus represented a different kind of cure, and seen as a unit, the overall display functioned like a visual archive of collective regeneration, achieved on a case-by-case basis.[12] Looking at a moulage

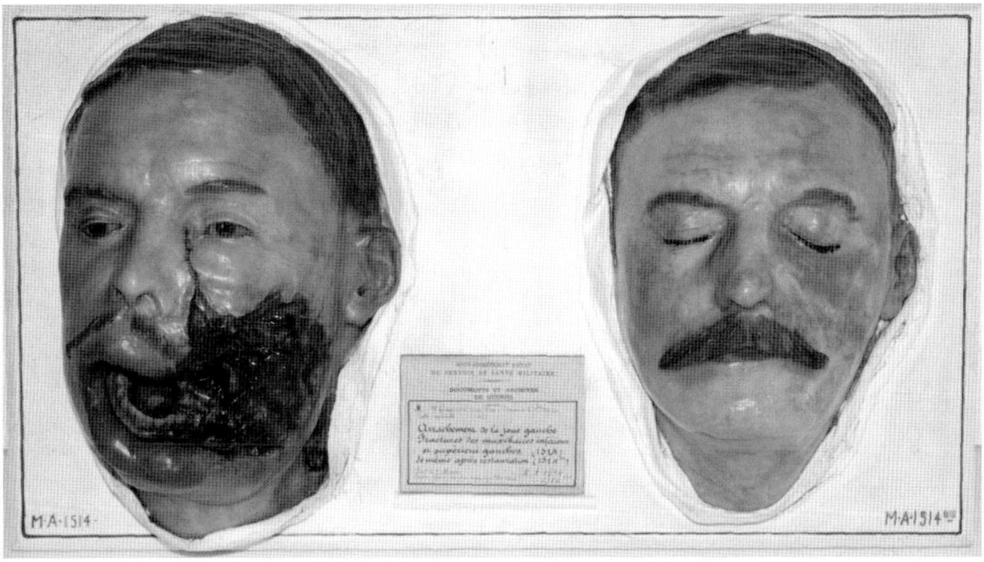

FIGURE 27 Serial moulages (painted wax), Musée du Val-de-Grâce, Paris, ca. 1916. Courtesy of the Musée du Val-de-Grâce, Paris (Archives du Musée/Service de Santé des Armées, Ministère de la Défense, France).

alone, a viewer sees the trauma as permanent, static, and without end (see Fig. 23). Seeing the same moulage within a visual narrative of therapeutic reconstruction, however, the viewer is likely to see the moulage as a stage in recovery rather than a fact of physical trauma (Fig. 27). Viewed from left to right—from before to after—the moulages appear to erase their own violations: the violence embodied in the individual moulage is repressed by its sequential positioning. Placed within this process-oriented structure, the fragmented remains of wounded soldiers functioned like words in a narrative chain whose meaning was meant to be grasped as a whole: although the war had brutalized these men, the medical establishment had found spectacular ways to bring them back. The moulages conformed to aesthetic rules that placed a positive spin on the work of the military medical establishment, thereby confirming the promise of postwar reconstruction via scientific innovation. Individual loss and suffering were depicted as prerequisites for national rebirth. The lives of individual soldiers, and the violent injuries they sustained, many of which would mark the men for life, were secondary to the collection's emphasis on the soldiers' sacrifice on behalf of the nation. Rather than functioning solely as evidence of the war's horrific, brutal violence, the moulages became a way of showcasing advanced medical technology and the nation's compassion for its wounded citizens. Yet the difference between the mutilation the soldiers endured and the record of its subsequent rehabilitation makes visible the process of ideological construction (what we might call today state-sponsored political "spin" to turn bad news into good) at the heart of the museum's displays.

The museum's consolidation of a dominant rhetoric about physical loss and subsequent rebirth was probably not lost on savvy viewers like Aragon and Breton. Because Aragon and Breton were probably some of the first viewers of the new collection in 1917, the Musée du Val-de-Grâce may have been where they started to *see* as surrealists.[13] The aestheticization of dismemberment at the museum seems to have given them a rich source of imagery to mine for their own purposes in the 1920s. After seeing how the museum transformed the mutilated body into a positive image of national rebirth, Aragon, Breton, and their friends began to showcase fragmentation and dismemberment in ways they hoped would highlight a *lack* of social or cultural progress or coherence. In the years after the war, surrealist work would often expose the gaps between things—between words, concepts, bodies, or rhetoric—in ways anticipated by the Val-de-Grâce collections. By emphasizing dismemberment, the surrealists translated the state's rhetoric of reconstruction into a language that reasserted the carnal horror of war and dismissed the idea that trauma was a necessary step in France's social and industrial evolution.

Failure did not seem to be an option at the museum. Indeed, the exhibit suggested that the process of repair would enhance the aesthetic beauty of the soldier's disfigured faces. This positive outlook made the moulages visually palatable and urged viewers to move beyond their initial horror at the sight of the soldiers' ragged, gaping wounds.[14] Civilian viewers were taught to read male dismemberment as a necessary element of the French nation's rebirth at Val-de-Grâce. The bodily losses sustained during the war were brushed aside by the museum's visual rhetoric: from the ruins of war, new bodies would spring, in some cases becoming more efficient and productive than before. But how would the nation create these new men, exactly? Would the effort to repair their injuries and reintegrate them into postwar society succeed—with the military's diligent efforts to valorize the soldiers' new, improved, and often prosthetically augmented bodies? Although the collections at Val-de-Grâce honored the work and sacrifice of both surgeons and soldiers, they also revealed uneasiness about whether reconstruction would take hold, especially in rebuilding French domestic, familial, and industrial life.

The Politics of the Prosthetic

The Musée du Val-de-Grace did more than document the process of reconstructive surgery. It exhibited photographs and prosthetic devices alongside the moulages (in an adjoining room) that showed how the rebuilt soldier could rejoin French society with the support of a wide range of new prosthetic technologies.[15] Modeled by full-size wax mannequins, the prosthetics on display suggested that a wounded soldier could fairly easily learn how to lead a productive

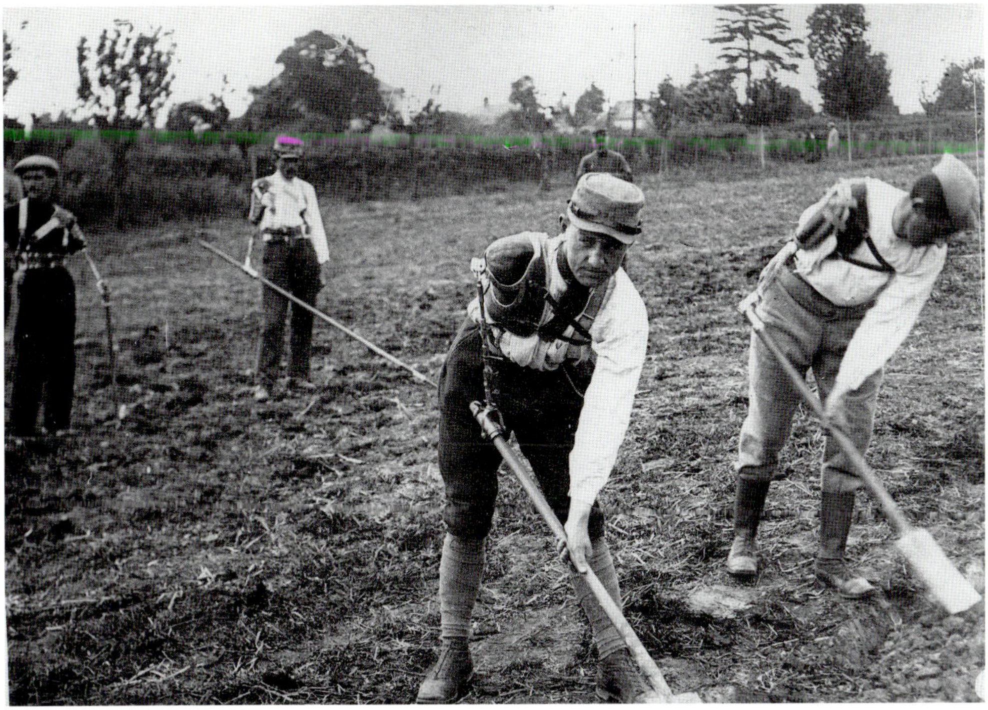

FIGURE 28 Reeducation of *mutilés de guerres* at the Maison Blanche reeducation camp for agricultural workers, 8 January 1919. Musée d'Histoire Contemporaine, Bibliothèque de Documentation Internationale Contemporaine, Paris.

postwar life. He could learn to perform everyday tasks quite effortlessly because of the wide range of attachments that were newly available, including those for eating, personal hygiene, and agricultural and industrial labor.[16] Prosthetic devices were often made specifically for "work" or for "dress," although some were suitable for a variety of circumstances. The dress arm, or *bras de parade,* was a simulated limb that was appropriate for a variety of domestic and recreational situations; the work arm, or *bras de travail,* in contrast, tied the soldier's body more directly to a specific type of labor like digging, raking, or hoeing (Figs. 28, 29, and 30). Although these devices were promoted as vast improvements on earlier prototypes, they were also chilling reminders of the soldier's role as a cog in the war machine (now translated into the role of workhorse in industrial and agricultural labor), for they quite literally turned his body into a tool. When he went to work, for example, a well-fitted *mutilé de guerre* could simply remove his dress or domestic arm (as in Fig. 30) and replace it with a prosthetic trowel or hoe that would be less aesthetically pleasing, of course, but much more efficient.

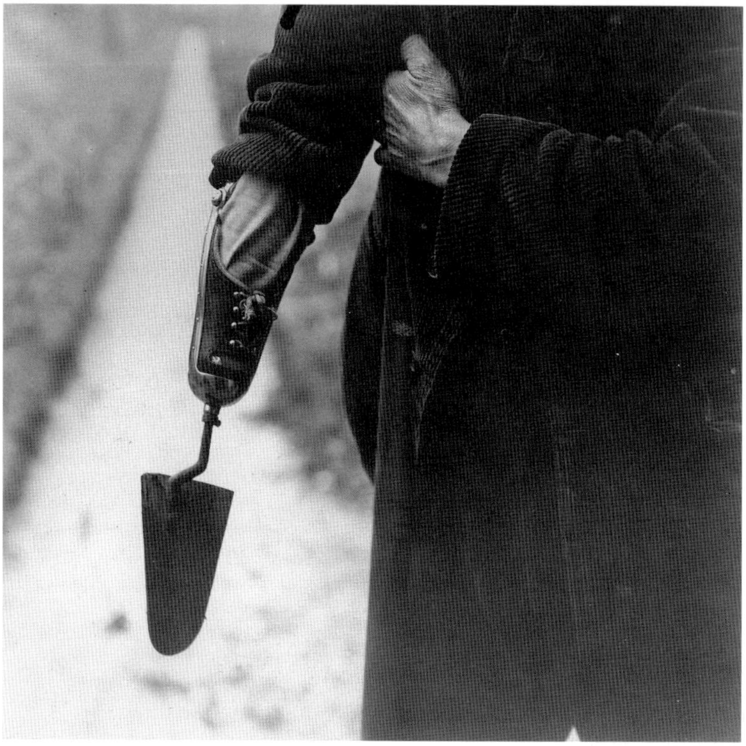

FIGURE 29
Amputee with trowel attachment, Maison Blanche reeducation camp for agricultural workers, 8 January 1919. Musée d'Histoire Contemporaine, Bibliothèque de Documentation Internationale Contemporaine, Paris.

Once they learned to use their bodies again, reeducated veterans could begin the arduous task of rebuilding their wounded nation by working in field or factory. Because of this significant link between the condition of ex-soldiers and the stability of French society, government reeducation centers became essential to postwar rehabilitation. A month after the Musée du Val-de-Grâce opened, for example, the reeducation center of Maison Blanche opened its doors to recovering Val-de-Grâce patients. The two institutions were complementary in many people's eyes, because reeducation of the reconstructed body was the last step in the veteran's recovery and subsequent reintegration into society. Indeed, a speaker at the Maison Blanche hospital's opening, Madame Bayliès, suggested that the soldiers who had once been fighting for French territory would begin a new fight for economic power once the war was over: "Soldiers of France, this work is for you! At the victorious end of the war, more than ever France will need your labor and your support. I have great confidence in your perseverance and I assure you that in learning a new skill *(métier)*, you will work not only for yourselves, but for the future of your dear country."[17]

The implications of the state's varied efforts to reindustrialize after the war were probably

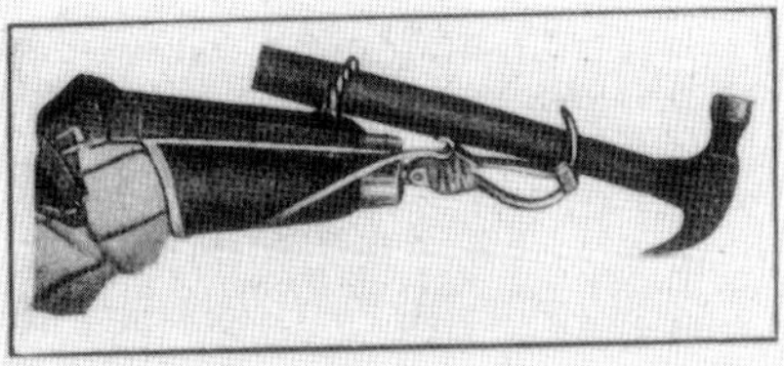

FIG. 410

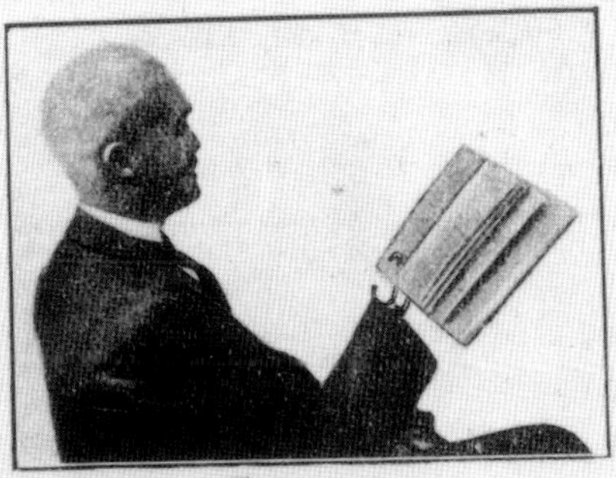

FIG. 411

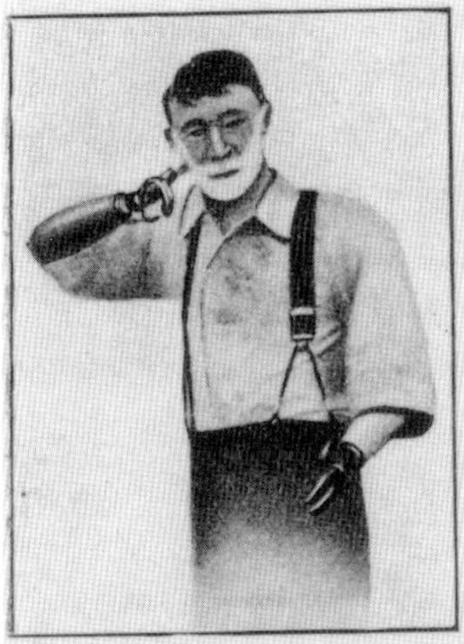

FIG. 412

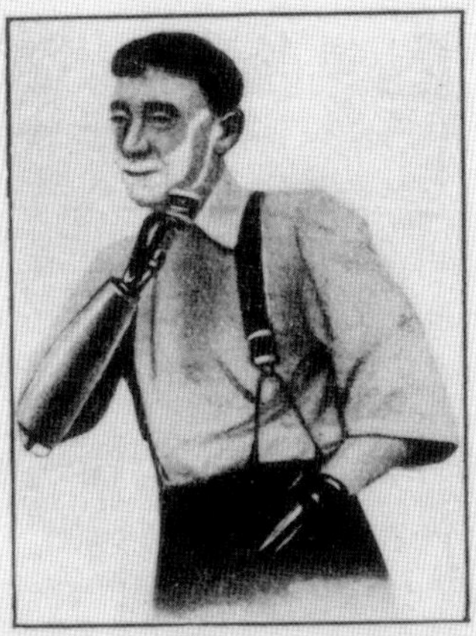

FIG. 413

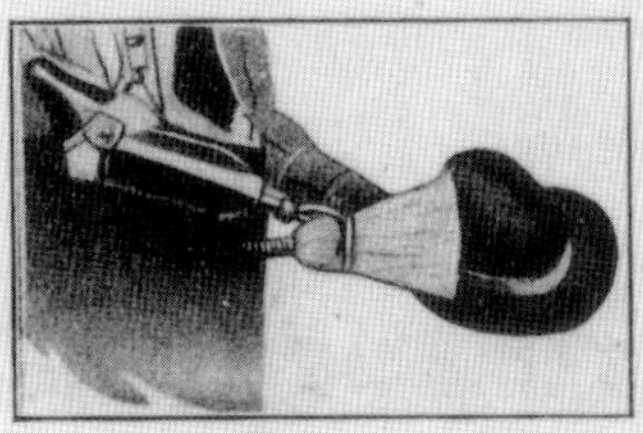

FIG. 414

FIGURE 30
Specialized prosthetic attachments. In Dr. Florent Martin, *Les mutilations et les appareils de prothèse* (Liège, Belgium: Imprimerie Georges Thone, 1924), 247. Courtesy of the Bibliothèque Nationale de France.

not lost on the *mutilés de guerre* themselves. After having been fodder for trench warfare, the veterans must have found the idea ironic that they would realize their potential as workers by being outfitted with specialized, task-specific prosthetic devices. But with the facts of their damaged bodies also came their realization of the fragility of their positions in postwar society. In poignant testimony, a veteran named Carlier made clear that although he knew he was needed to rebuild his country after the war, his state pension would not be enough to support him and his family. He made the following comments after Madame Baylìès's speech at the Maison Blanche dedication: "Certainly . . . we know well that the pension allotted to us by the State will not entirely suffice to support us and those persons in our charge. But we feel also that tomorrow, when peace will have sanctioned the victory of our troops, France will need a new army, that of workers, and we want to serve with as much devotion in this as we have on the battle field."[18]

As a soldier participating in the government's reeducation program for wounded veterans, Carlier obviously recognized the link that government officials were making between France's economic and political future and his body's future physical recovery. His new duty after leaving the front was to recover as quickly as possible and become a productive member of the nation's new industrial army. Ironically, however, his debilitated condition was a direct result of national policy; the reeducation program being touted as the nation's new savior was in effect the result of a military policy that relied on lavish use of soldiers in trench warfare.

For returning veterans, economic instability and their uncertain relation to the national economy were two of many postwar anxieties they faced. These men also required physical and emotional assistance from their families, and many of them had to rely on wives, sisters, and mothers as never before. Published testimony of some returning soldiers reveals that many men were anxious about their postwar personal relationships, particularly their interactions with women. Often unable to perform the most basic domestic tasks on their own, many men had to remake their personal lives while they also learned new *métiers*. The fact that many women had assumed traditionally male jobs and family responsibilities during the war only compounded men's anxiety about postwar social integration. Thus, not only did physical afflictions and the visible disparity between the numbers of men and women complicate relations between the sexes but so did the psychological problems that men experienced as they tried to repossess their prewar lives.[19]

The military apparently acknowledged these problems (although for the most part, only within the protected channels of military documentation) and worked hard to find ways to help veterans return to civilian life. Military photographers at the reeducation centers documented men's efforts to learn how to use their new prosthetic limbs (as in Figs. 28 and 29), although their cameras also captured the less visible problem of how to help men recover their social status as husbands and fathers. Because the national birthrate was falling at the same time that men were being slaughtered at the front, the reinforcement of conventional social and domestic roles for men and women became a priority for the French government.[20] A startling group of photographs taken by a military photographer on 28 June 1916 reflects the depth of official interest in the postwar social rehabilitation of the *mutilés de guerre*—although these images were withheld from publication at the time due to stringent policies of military censorship (Figs. 31 through 34).[21] Featuring a ritualized representation of courtship between a damaged soldier named Bravais and his female nurse, these photographs provide a compelling picture of the war's effects on both the male body and its relationship to the dominant social order.

The first photograph of the series depicts Bravais, dressed in military garb, smoking a cigarette (Fig. 31). Initially, Bravais' prosthetic arms are hard to make out, save for the strangely rigid quality of the hand at his side. In the next image in the sequence, Bravais appears without his shirt, his naked torso enabling us to see that both arms are missing and that he has been outfitted with prosthetic limbs of the "dress" variety (Fig. 32). This photograph does not simply investigate the technology of his bodily augmentation, however. It also captures the effects of his mutilation upon his experience of heterosexual courtship. Flexing his mechanical arm to offer a flower to a female nurse, Bravais makes a gentlemanly gesture that highlights the sexualized undertone of the familiar social ritual. The fact that the photographs show other female nurses watching the pair's interaction underscores the fact that rediscovering how to engage with other people was as important to a soldier's rehabilitation as was learning a new trade.

In a third photograph, the female nurse's posture reveals the photographer's interest in documenting the social effects of bodily reconstruction (Fig. 33). Somewhat nervously, she has turned to face the camera. She presses one arm to her side as if willing it to disappear and folds the arm closest to Bravais' bare chest away from him in order to avoid physical contact—a contact alluded to by the flower at the collar of her uniform. Hiding her arm in this way, she enacts his mutilation across her own body. Her desire to erase her own arm from Bravais' line of sight suggests that she, too, is anxious about how men and women ought to interact. Will he be hurt when he recognizes his own lack in the face of her bodily plenitude?

The final image in the series poignantly reminds the viewer that even with the best prosthetic technology, the mutilated soldier will never quite be the same (Fig. 34). Holding his stumps out to the camera while another man stands next to him holding his prosthetic arms *for* him, Bravais openly acknowledges his loss. Instead of offering the nurse a delicate flower this time around, he presents his mutilated body to the camera. When juxtaposed with a male counterpart in this way, Bravais' pitiable (if still reasonably well-muscled) body announces its inadequacies. Looking at this photograph, one begins to wonder how Bravais completes the most banal of tasks: How did he light the cigarette he now smokes? How will he flick the ash? The photograph elicits other, more ominous questions as well: How will he work if he has no arms? What woman will have him if he cannot hold her? By showing him without his prosthetic limbs, the photographer illuminates the fragility of Bravais' position in postwar society. Without his arms, he will forever have to depend on other people. Helpless to light a cigarette

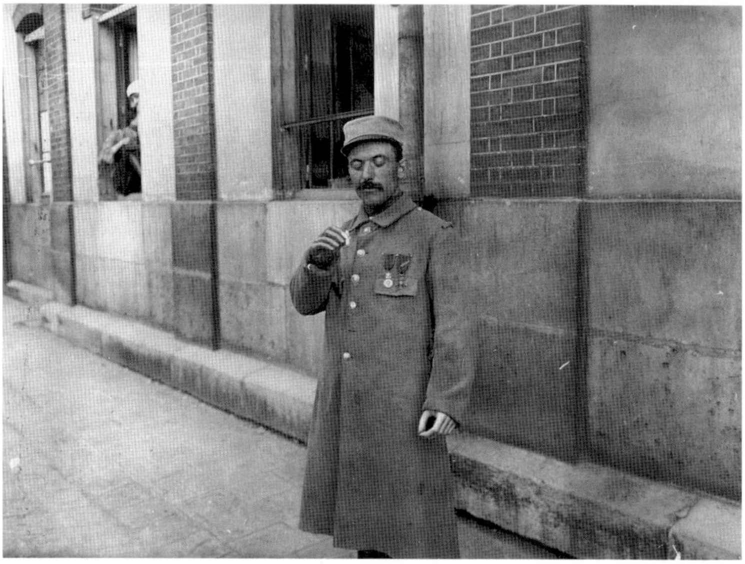

FIGURE 31
A double amputee (Mr. Bravais) at the Hôpital St. Maurice, 28 June 1916. Musée d'Histoire Contemporaine, Bibliothèque de Documentation Internationale Contemporaine, Paris.

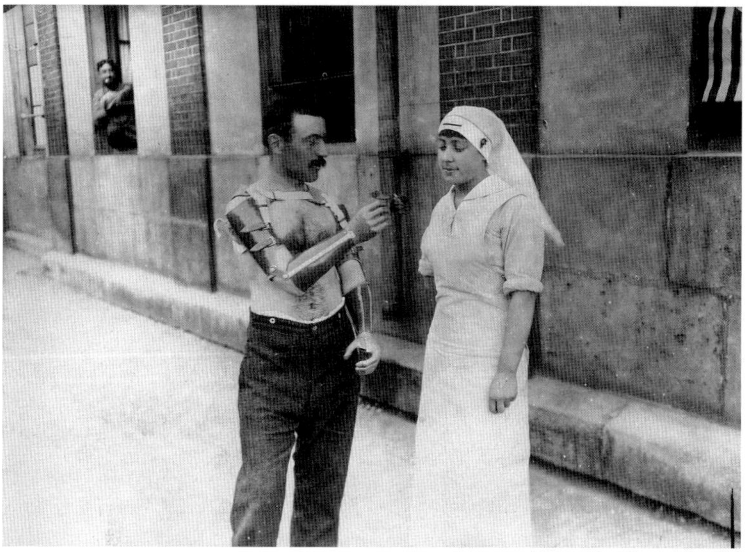

FIGURE 32
Mr. Bravais at the Hôpital St. Maurice, 28 June 1916. Musée d'Histoire Contemporaine, Bibliothèque de Documentation Internationale Contemporaine, Paris.

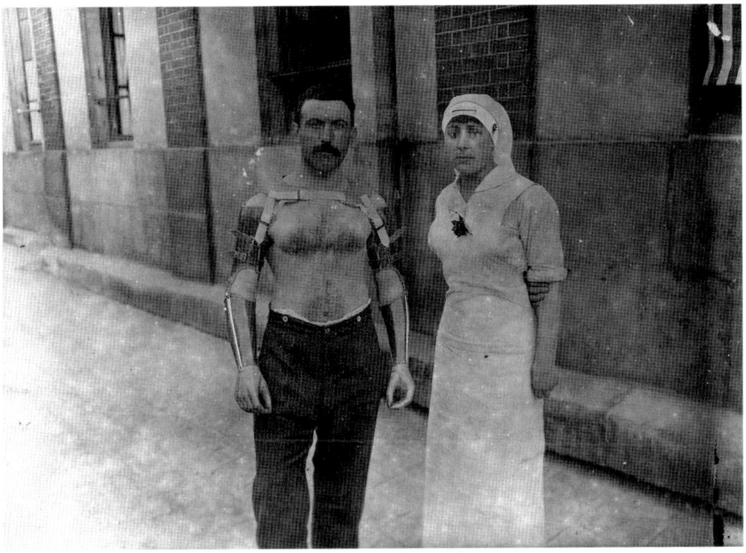

FIGURE 33
Mr. Bravais at the Hôpital St. Maurice, 28 June 1916. Musée d'Histoire Contemporaine, Bibliothèque de Documentation Internationale Contemporaine, Paris.

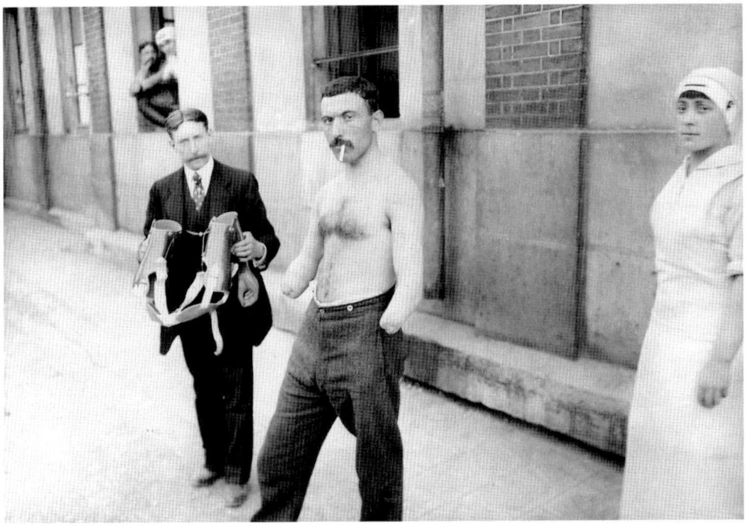

FIGURE 34
Mr. Bravais at the Hôpital St. Maurice, 28 June 1916. Musée d'Histoire Contemporaine, Bibliothèque de Documentation Internationale Contemporaine, Paris.

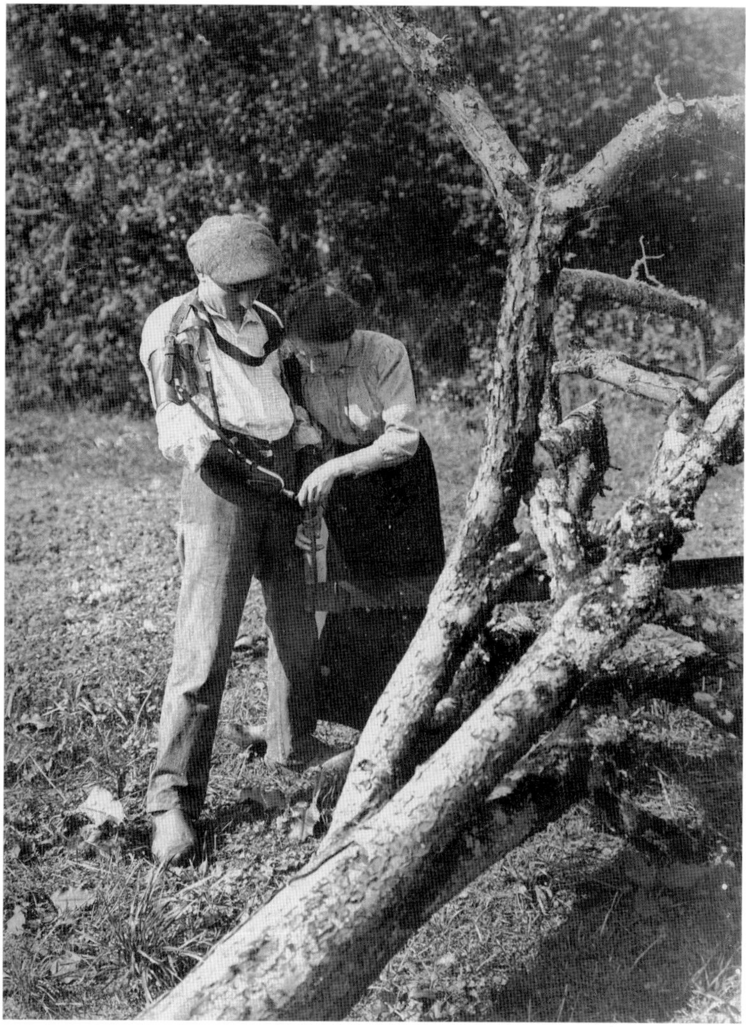

FIGURE 35
"Les deux maris" (the married couple), 5 October 1917. Musée d'Histoire Contemporaine, Bibliothèque de Documentation Internationale Contemporaine, Paris.

without his prosthetic limbs, Bravais appears forever tied to a technology created by the war that mutilated him. In a chilling way, the photograph shows that his injuries are both the consequence of, and the catalyst for, modern industrial achievement. Man has truly become more intricately tied to the realm of the machine in this image; however, the photograph does not show us the implications of this fact for the individual soldier's sense of his masculinity. Is Bravais less of a man now that he is part machine?

A military photograph depicting a married couple (according to the label on the reverse) offers an equally blunt assessment of the difficult transition that awaited injured veterans upon their return to domestic life (Fig. 35). The female member of this couple has responsibility for helping her male partner regain control over his newly mechanized body.[22] Instead of taking her husband's job (as many women had during the war), this wife helps him learn how to use his mechanical arm. Although this man's mutilation could have made him a permanent cripple who is unable to work, the photograph avoids this possibility by showing his wife (like the prosthetic limb) as a helper rather than a usurper. In this way, the image avoids exacerbating the anxiety that clearly existed about the ability of returning soldiers to return to the postwar labor pool.

The photographs we have seen confirm that the rebuilt veteran tried to take up his old social and economic roles, although he was forced to do so in ways that hammered home that his life was never going to be the same as it had been before the war. Such photographs seem to ask whether men and women would be able to return to their prewar identities if men needed such extensive physical and psychological help. Bravais' awkward attempts at courtship imply that the military recognized that its plans to rebuild society might fail. Unlike the models of progress and rehabilitation promoted at Val-de-Grâce, the photographs of Bravais show postwar masculinity under duress. Because these photographs show how difficult and disquieting recovery was for the returning soldier, they help us see how important the images of a strong and resilient masculinity were at that time. Although the military clearly wanted to document the facts of male anxiety for its own purposes, the fact that these photographs were inaccessible to the contemporary public underscores the danger that these images of male debility posed to postwar stability.

In contrast to such efforts to hide male weakness, surrealist writers and artists stressed the dislocations of war by depicting physical and psychological disruption, anxiety, and trauma in their work. Rather than pretending that the trauma did not exist, or that it had been erased by national efforts at reconstruction, the surrealists created an aesthetics of dismemberment that emphasized social decay and destruction. And they did so by embedding references to disfigured, dismembered, and emasculated male bodies in their work.

Surrealist Method: A Précis

André Breton's first account of surrealist methodology, "Manifesto of Surrealism," poetically echoes the traumatized representations of manhood on view at Val-de-Grâce. In one crucial section that analyzes an apparitional image that Breton claimed he saw as he fell asleep—the image of a "man cut in two by a window"—the manifesto locates male dismemberment at the core of Breton's aesthetic practice:

> One night, before falling asleep, I perceived, clearly articulated to the point where it was impossible to change one word, but distracted nonetheless by the sound of many voices, a rather bizarre phrase . . . [a] phrase that seemed to me insistent, a phrase dare I say it that was tapping at the window. . . . In truth this phrase surprised me . . . it was something like "There is a man cut in two by the window," but it could not suffer from any ambivalence, accompanied as it was by the weak visual representation of a man walking and truncated half-way up by a window perpendicular to the axis of his body. No doubt it was about the simple standing up in space of a man who stood leaning toward the window. But this window having followed the movement of the man, I understood that I had had to deal with a rather rare type of image and that I had quickly no other idea than to incorporate it into my material for poetic construction.[23]

The phrase "a man cut in two by the window" surprised Breton. And because a visual image accompanied this phrase, it seemed to him an exceptionally concrete example of how surrealism worked. The window that bisected the man in Breton's vision persisted, with the result that he saw a male body in a state of perpetual fragmentation. In the wake of the war's actual brutality, it seems important that the body Breton saw cut in two was a man's. The fact that he included this vision in his manifesto as a prime example of surrealist imagery suggests that he recognized the potential power of the image of the fragmented male body in particular, because it would subtly echo the brutalities he and others had experienced during the war. We are thus encouraged to consider a causal link between the actuality of the war's destruction and the violent imagery of surrealist literature and art. Moreover, by promoting an image of a body perpetually split in two, Breton encouraged his readers to mentally compare that image to the idealization of corporeal unity being promoted in the 1920s. Instead of supporting the ideological use of the injured male body as a sign of reconstruction, Breton's image heightened the reader's awareness that official rhetoric papered over the reality of physical reconstruction. Because Breton's man cut in two would never heal, the image also alluded to the gaps between the medical treatments that were necessary to achieve recovery. The moulages' organization implied the existence of spaces between treatments, and in those absences, the soldier was suspended between the horror of injury and the fantasy of cure. He, like the man cut in two, was in a state of perpetual disfiguration.

Louis Aragon also meditated on the role that a mangled body could play within artistic practice. In one intriguing instance, Aragon recalls writing an early prose poem on the viscerally suggestive surface of a "gray envelope open like a belly." With this imagery, Aragon suggested that writing was an activity that used surgical knives rather than fountain pens.[24] Indeed, "Advertisement for No Product" ("Réclame d'aucun produit"), the manuscript to which Aragon refers, was in fact written on an envelope that he had carefully unglued and folded flat, his handwriting covering the envelope's insides (Fig. 36). In this concrete way, Aragon turned his own writing into an act of surgical exploration, or perhaps of bodily desecration. As if con-

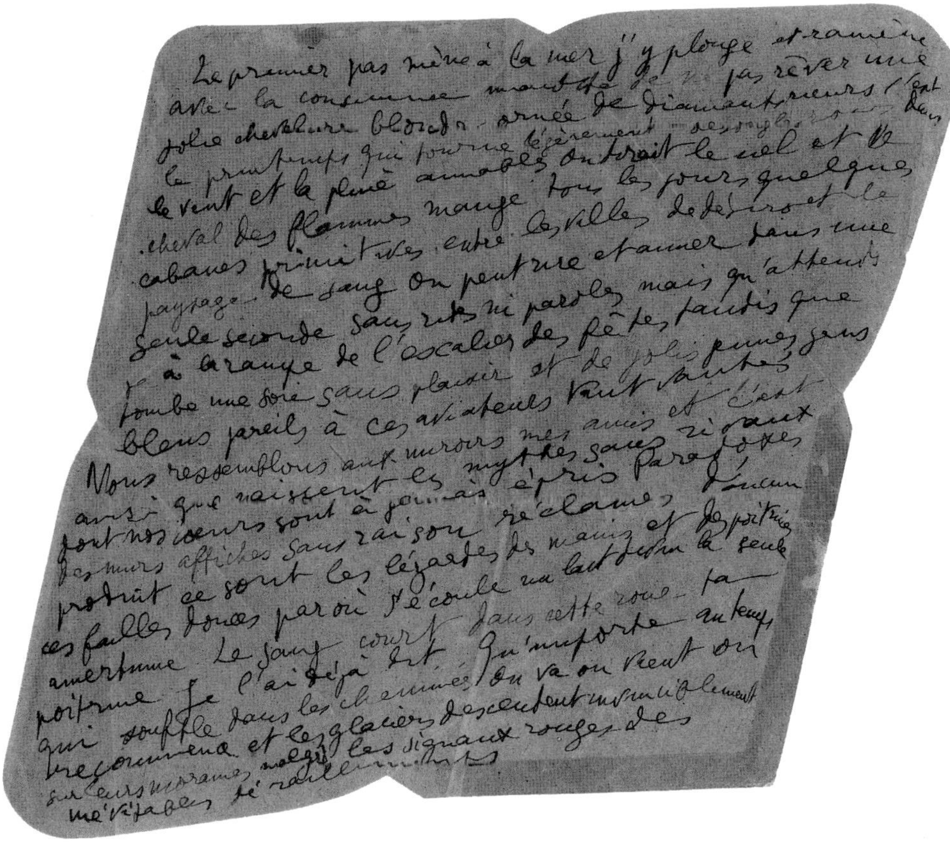

FIGURE 36 Louis Aragon, "Réclame d'aucun produit," 1920, written on an opened-up envelope. Bibliothèque Nationale de France, Department of Manuscripts.

juring up the rhetorical power of the moulages to vividly depict the "truth" of reconstruction, Aragon's poem materialized the act of writing as a culturally necessary form of surgery whose brutal imagery would puncture the smooth façade of the return to order: "Paradoxes of wall-posters without reason, advertisements for no product these are the lizards of hands and chests, these soft leaves over which runs a divine milk the only bitterness. Blood runs in this wheel, your chest."[25]

Aragon's poem is suffused with bodies opened and objectified, bodies that merge uncontrollably with their surroundings, blood running in this wheel, your chest, without differentiation between inside and out. Not only was this poem written on a page masquerading as a body—the open belly of the flattened-out gray envelope—but its language also violated the reader's expectations about what poetry could be. A chaotic melding of body and world, of milk and blood, this poem confuses the viewer's definition of literature in the wake of the war.

Of course, early surrealist literature often represented trauma in less overtly mortal terms. Breton's account of his first experience with psychiatry during the war, for example, discloses his drive to understand how the human mind works when trauma strikes. Breton had worked with a patient who had exhibited a high level of psychological repression and denial. The patient, Breton later recalled, claimed that the war was a sham, that the wounded were fakes, and that the dead had been taken from operating tables.[26] This idea that wounded soldiers were actors painted up for a gory theater performance very likely haunted Breton: his patient's story implicitly captured the rhetorical sleight of hand of the collections at Val-de-Grâce, which grouped the moulages to recast their horrors as emblems of physical and cultural repair. The human mind, like the surgeons at Val-de-Grâce, routinely repressed trauma by masking its horrors; only by doing so could the patient live a relatively normal life.

Like ghastly counterparts to the soldier's fantasy of a *trompe l'oeil* war, which protected him from assimilating the terrible physical and mental costs of the conflict, the moulages buried physical trauma beneath reconstructed flesh. Ironically, innovative plastic surgery was the one area in which any sort of "trickery" or dissimulation was permitted during the war because repression of the physical signs of war on soldiers' bodies was essential to promote regeneration. As historian Marc Roudebush points out in his work on male hysteria in France during the Great War, soldiers who faked psychological or physical injury could be prosecuted for their attempts to evade military service.[27]

These examples suggest that Aragon and Breton learned certain lessons about the mechanics of visual rhetoric from the French government's efforts to assuage the public's anxiety about the war's devastation. Even if the narratives of repair and renewal gave a positive spin to the war's violation of the male body, a number of surrealists recognized that the logic of that discourse contained several potentially corrosive elements: the physical presence of *mutilés de guerre* on city streets and the potential consequences to the nation if the unruly mind of the shell-shocked veteran could not be brought under control. Could the surrealists break through the cultural amnesia that was to be an antidote to traumatic memories of the war by refusing to let people forget what had happened? Could images that forced viewers to confront the realities of wartime carnage stave off easy statements of national rebirth and claims that the war, although unfortunate, would make France better, stronger, and more powerful than it had ever been?

Figuring Fragmentation

> But the human head which opens, flies and closes on its thoughts like a fan, the head falling on its hair as if on a lace pillow, the fragile and weightless head which holds itself in equilib-

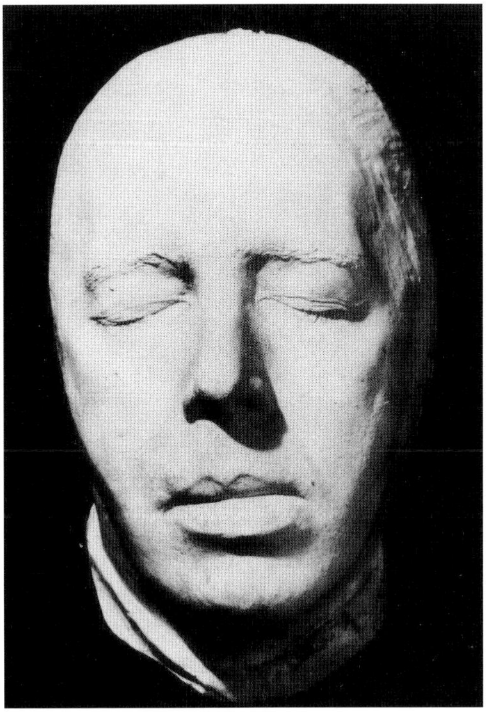

FIGURE 37 René Iché, plaster mask of André Breton, ca. 1930. © 2006 Artists Rights Society (ARS), New York/ADAGP, Paris.

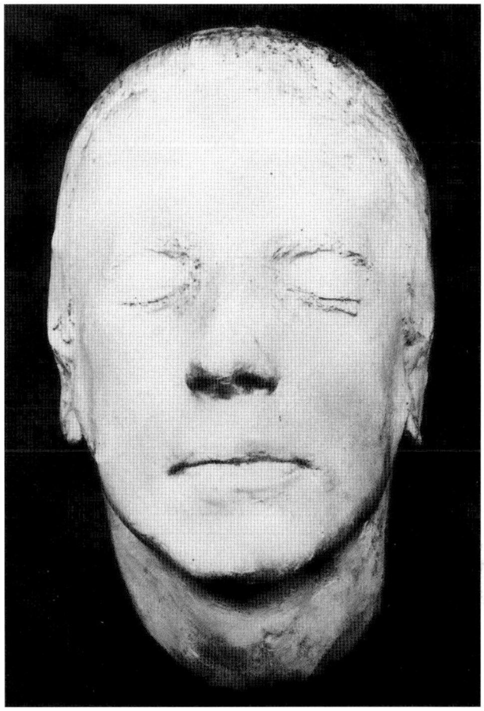

FIGURE 38 René Iché, plaster mask of Paul Eluard, ca. 1930. © 2006 Artists Rights Society (ARS), New York/ADAGP, Paris.

> rium between the true and the false, striated with blue like the dolls of New Mexico, the head from which one will mold a mask after my death, this head around which Max Ernst is like the river which never encounters a dam. The rationalism and the mysticism that disputes with the softness of Derain's hat are under the feet of Max Ernst. André Breton, "Surrealism and Painting," 1927

Once upon a time, some ten years after the end of the war, André Breton and Paul Eluard pretended that they were dead (Figs. 37 and 38). With closed eyes and slack lips, the plaster self-portraits they made with the help of sculptor René Iché mimic the look and feel of corpses.[28] These objects, which hung face-to-face in Breton's studio on the rue Fontaine for many years, make a powerful comparison with the moulages that were still on display at the Musée du Val-de-Grâce, even in 1930. With documentary precision, these plaster masks objectify and replicate the facial features of their models: stiff eyebrows, wrinkled eyelids, plump lips, and jowly chins. Reminiscent of the portrait sculptures and death masks that were popular in the eighteenth and nineteenth centuries as commemorative images of *grands hommes,* or "great men," Breton's and Eluard's moulages validate their position within that intellectual tradition while simultaneously framing them as victims of an untimely, youthful demise. Importantly, their masks repeat the visual effect of the moulages on view at Val-de-Grâce and make a visual comparison—if unconsciously recognized—between the *grand homme* and the *mutilé de guerre.* What are we to make of the men's decision to make death masks when they were still relatively young? Do these masks suggest death as a model for surrealist identity? Do they represent a drive to master the experience of death through bodily identification and repetition?

As psychology historian Ruth Leys proposes in her work on the nature of trauma and its cures, traumatic experience commands a particular response by those who endure it. After an individual goes through a traumatic event, one way of making sense of the experience is to repeat it: to embody the experience in the flesh is a way to work through the trauma.[29] Leys argues that psychic trauma "involve[s] a particular kind of memory system that in the absence of object-perceptions registers the trauma . . . 'bodily,' rather than through symbolic substitution and representation." Trauma is experienced *inside,* and it is therefore locked into one's flesh. "Traumatic memory," she concludes, is thus "*incarnated memory* . . . It can only be experienced in the mode of a repetition or acting out in the present, not in the mode of conscious recollection."[30]

Leys's account, based on her reading of papers on psychic trauma by psychoanalysts Abraham Kardiner and Sandor Ferenczi (Kardiner's on the war neuroses first published in 1932; Ferenczi's, in 1921), provides a way to think about why so many surrealist artists and writers made work that referenced or juxtaposed body parts. By repeating dismemberment—whether male or female (although women's bodies have more often been the focus of surrealist work)—the bodies we think of as quintessentially surrealist transform the human figure into a carnal sign of traumatic experience. If psychic trauma is physically embedded in people's bodies, as Leys suggests, might surrealist images of dismembered bodies displace traumatic experience onto the surrealist object, thereby enabling the beholder to master the trauma through visual experience? Did physically unmutilated men like Breton or Aragon explore the war's violence in their art by replaying the violations they had witnessed on so many *other* men's bodies? In some ways, their work seems to acknowledge the horror of what they saw by incorporating wartime violations of the body. At the same time, such imagery appears to contradict representations of the return to order because it continually emphasizes physical destruction. By focusing on dismemberment, surrealist artists and writers endowed the terrible experiences of the war with a physical and mental permanence.[31] After all, physical evidence of the war's brutality and violence was slowly disappearing from the bodies that inhabited French towns and cities in the 1920s.

Robert Desnos' text "Pénalités de l'Enfer ou Nouvelles Hébrides" exemplifies this tendency within surrealism to elevate images of partial or wounded bodies to cultural icons, in contrast to the prevailing taste for vigorous and robust images of postwar masculinity. His text situates ruined male bodies in a landscape of decay and fragmentation and seems to do so to conjure up the texture of wartime devastation. Desnos wrote "Pénalités de l'Enfer" at the beginning of 1922, just after his return from military service in North Africa.[32] Like Breton's vision of a "man cut in two," Desnos' writing shares an affinity with the structural organization of the collections at Val-de-Grâce. Throughout large portions of the text, Desnos describes men as matter, using imagery that illustrates their status as unfinished amalgams of disparate parts. Moreover, the words he uses to describe these bodies emphasize fragmentation, and the figures that people his book are nothing more than body parts whose presence in the text creates the sensation of seeing bodies cut, spliced, and tossed about. Reading their friend's work for the first time, Aragon and Breton surely found much to savor in Desnos' grisly prose:

> On the door of the room of Mr. and Mrs. Breton there was a terrifying inscription in chalk: "Number your slaughtered." I go back inside; there is the head of Benjamin Péret in the mirror. . . . The train passed rapidly. Péret jumped into this train . . . Not fast enough apparently. One of his arms, the left, remained in the space beneath the platform. Five hundred kilometers away Benjamin again made some signals so that I would send it to him. . . . The arm of Benjamin Péret I left it in this train station which marks the step, the arm of Benjamin Péret, alone in space, beneath the platform, indicates the exit, and beyond, the Grand Café du Progrès, and beyond . . . and beyond . . . [33]

Here we are, on the second page of Desnos' text, reading a frightening command to number the slaughtered. Then the figure of Benjamin Péret (one of the surrealist poets most closely associated with the group around Aragon and Breton) abruptly appears: first a head, then a wayward arm, he is in pieces, in the space beneath the platform, pointing to the exit and beyond. What are we to make of a dismembered arm that points the way out, especially when just a few pages later Péret's arm is ready to kill *n'importe qui*? "An arm passed by the opening. From the button on the sleeve I recognized the arm of Benjamin Péret that I had left in the train station. It directed itself towards me, grabbed my neck and would have strangled me if I had not pronounced the fateful word—Araucaria." A moment later, not satisfied with the narrator as his victim, Péret's arm is seen strangling corpses while producing loud cries as the corpses eventually escape down the street.[34] Throughout "Pénalités de l'Enfer," Desnos urges us to see his city as a place littered with fragments of human flesh and dead bodies: over there, a phallus stuck through with a needle; elsewhere, ears, mouths, and feet. Body parts fill the streets of Paris, and in Desnos' city (one reminiscent of the Comte de Lautréamont's), they have learned to speak:

"I would not know how to calculate the time," said the members that writhed on the sidewalk. I recognized the head of Bathtub and Greenery. They were cut in pieces and each part of their body spoke in chorus by categories:

> Mouths.—We bite the snowy summits at the flanks of heifers the color of foppish degenerates.
>
> Feet.—From flower of head to flower of skin here is the ideal of numerical shrimp. Abandon your teeth. Abandon your intestines. Abandon your eyeballs without music. And Niagara will burst out into African colonels devoured by the Burgraves.
>
> Intestines.—The wooden latch and the rending of steamers and music boxes have not resuscitated Christ. We have crawled long enough to find the boa constrictor but this one here is only a splendid burst of laughter in the hell of inoculated ears.[35]

Mouths, feet, and intestines speak in their own tongues; like diverse individuals, they appear on Desnos' page as different categories of performers in a morbid play. Here in Desnos' text the body part becomes a part of speech, with each piece functioning according to its anatomy and functionality. Paralleling the categorization process at Val-de-Grâce, Desnos' writing presents a compendium of potential activities for the disarticulated body.

His text also presages Breton's dream of a man cut in two. Spying an empty bottle, the protagonist grabs it, and the words "I am Guillaume Apollinaire" come pouring out of the bottle. And upon hearing Apollinaire's name—a poet revered by the surrealists—the narrator finds himself split in two:

> Immediately I felt paralyzed, blind and deaf on the left side. I soon perceived that it was nothing; my body had been separated in two from top to bottom. The other part stood before me. The section of body was eviscerated. I could judge my perspective by that of my half. Across the mirror I watched numbers interlace ceaselessly. Four bees flew around a poppy that I knew to be a lung. An electrical switch found itself almost at the center of all that. To my grand surprise my half spoke in these terms: "I, Guillaume Apollinaire, I borrow from you this fragment of your body you owe me."[36]

Sliced up the middle like a cut log, Desnos' subject is fractured, a man cut in two. Directly referencing Apollinaire's collagelike, fragmentary literary aesthetic in this passage—and perhaps indirectly referencing Lautréamont's petrified Maldoror or the bifurcated hermaphrodite discussed in Chapter 1—Desnos imagines male mutilation as a source of poetic transformation. His body is disfigured in the process of artistic creation. Using words like *evisceration,* and sliding one image of a poppy into one of a human lung, reveals his affinity for combining scientific and artistic imagery to surprise his readers. The slippage between one image and another, coupled with the bodily language of the text, suggest both the physical and the psychological dislocations catalyzed by traumatic experience—the same types of dislocations, surprises, and incongruities that Breton would celebrate in his manifesto two years later.

At the end of "Pénalités de l'Enfer," Desnos accentuates the link between bodily fragmentation and the idea of collective death—a link that might have conjured up memories about the war—by producing a map of a surrealist cemetery he called Cimitière de la Sémillante (Fig. 39). The image's center is labeled as a communal tomb *(fosse commune)*, and it contains the names of important surrealist precursors. Surrounding the central rectangular tomb are smaller, tomblike markers, each enumerated with a surrealist moniker. This cemetery is interesting not only because it focuses on the death of contemporary surrealist figures but because it seems to have been an organizational model for two surrealist group portraits that appeared in *La Révolution surréaliste:* one, a photo portrait of surrealist protagonists and precursors around a 1924 portrait of anarchist Germaine Berton; and a second, René Magritte's collage of surrealist mug shots around a painted female nude published in 1929 (Figs. 40 and 41).[37] Structural similarities between these later works and Desnos' *fosse commune* are readily apparent: In each case, a large central figure—in Desnos' piece, the communal grave—is framed by small portraits of surrealist individuals, each of whom is diligently identified by name.[38] In all three examples, the centralized rectangular figure is larger than the rest, suggesting collective identification: Desnos' collective tomb is filled with literary precursors to surrealism; in the image of Berton, the famous anarchist jostles with images of surrealists past and present, including Sigmund Freud; in Magritte's image, the object of the group's attention appears to be a demurely posed woman's body. Inscribed with the words "I do not see . . . [the woman] in the forest," the painting seems to be a collective dream of the individual men whose photographic portraits are pasted around the picture's edges.

The meaning of Magritte's image emerges from the juxtaposition of an objectified, nude female body and repeated images of wounded masculinity. For although the men could be asleep in these photo portraits, they also seem to feign death, as Breton and Eluard did with their plaster death masks. The inexpressive, documentary tone of these photo portraits—made at one of the first automated photo booths called the Photomaton—seem more related to the archival practices of late nineteenth- and early twentieth-century judiciary photography than to depictions of dreamy sleep.[39] With developments in 1908 that allowed use of the "mug shot" in the photography of corpses, these photo-booth images read like forensic portraits or updated, healed-over versions of the moulages of Val-de-Grâce. However, as in Breton and Eluard's death masks, instead of photographing the dead as if they were alive, as the police often did at the time (Fig. 42), these surrealist Photomaton portraits record the living as dead.[40] Apparently, others perceived them this way as well. Breton's surrealist nemesis Georges Bataille and his one-time colleagues Benjamin Péret and Raymond Queneau mined the corpselike imagery by using the same photograph of Breton to illustrate their 1930 polemic, *Un Cadavre* (A Corpse) (Fig. 43).

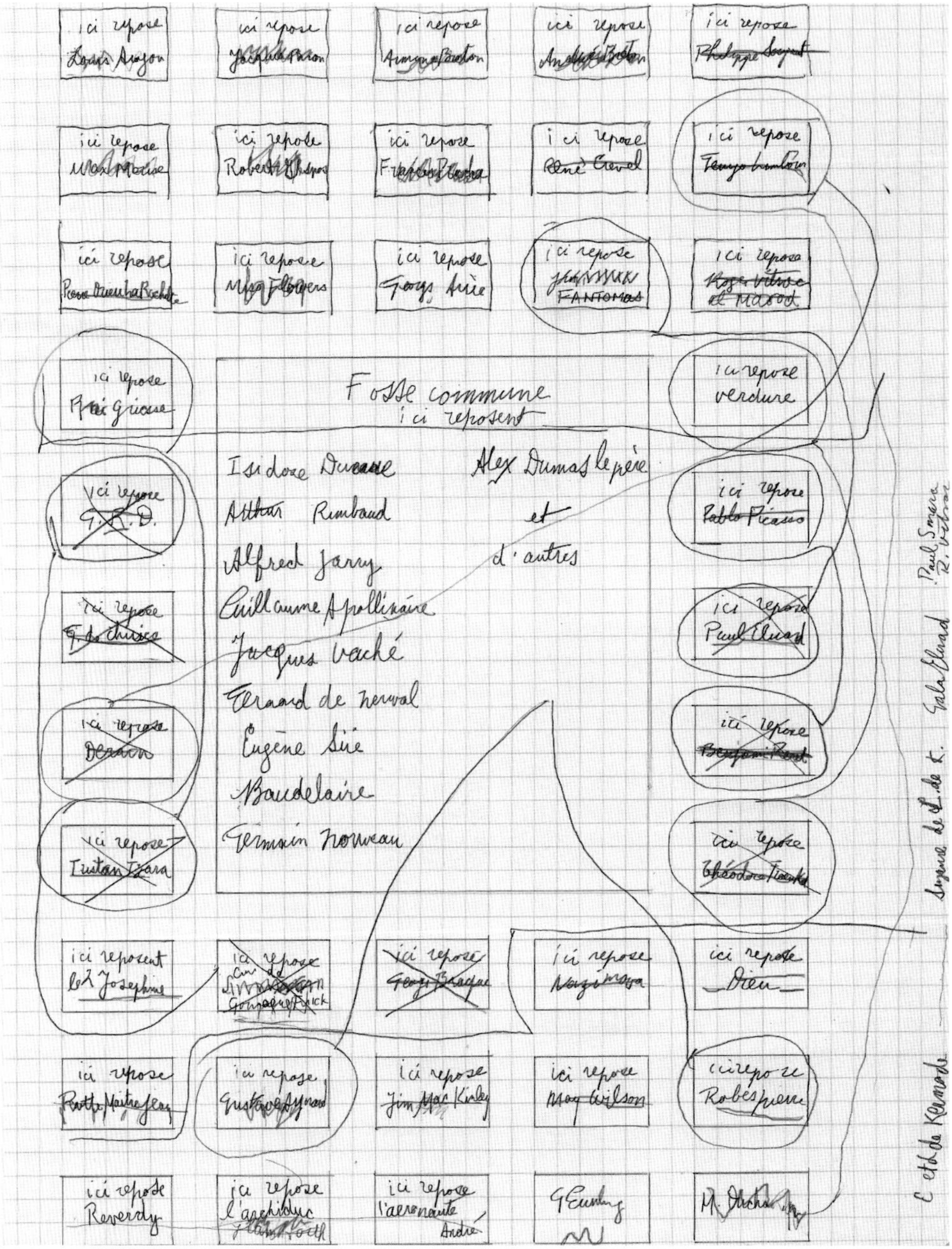

FIGURE 39 Robert Desnos, manuscript for "Cemetery of the Sémillante," ca. 1922. Bibliothèque Nationale de France, Department of Manuscripts.

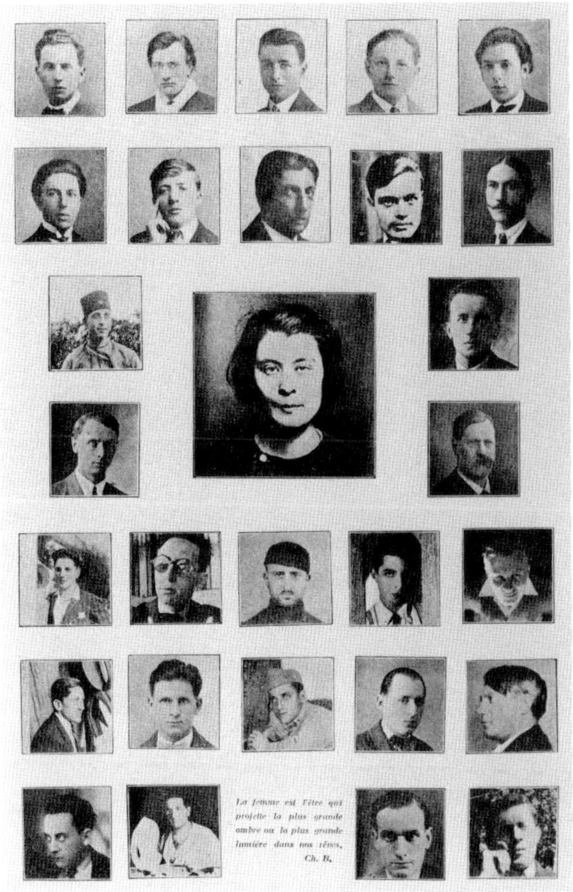

FIGURE 40
Photo collage of Germaine Berton, surrealists, and surrealist role models. In *La Révolution surréaliste* 1 (1 December 1924): 17.

Magritte's alphabetization of the portraits underscores the evidentiary impulse of the collage by mimicking the bureaucratic formula for listing the dead and wounded (echoing Desnos' words *numérotez vos abattis!*). Thus, the organization of the portraits seems to reference the archive as much as the collective dreams of men. The collage reiterates conventions of sexual difference, too, with the separation of male heads and female body playing up familiar ideas about the primacy of intellect and embodiment, respectively, across male and female subjects. Whether we read this male surrealist pantheon as dreaming or dead, femininity remains a crucial element within it. The visual opposition of the male frame and the female nude at its center suggests sexual differentiation while exaggerating the conflicts between realism (photography) and representation (painting), and between fragmentation (photo busts) and unity (painted nude). Most profoundly, this work has been regarded as an exemplary case

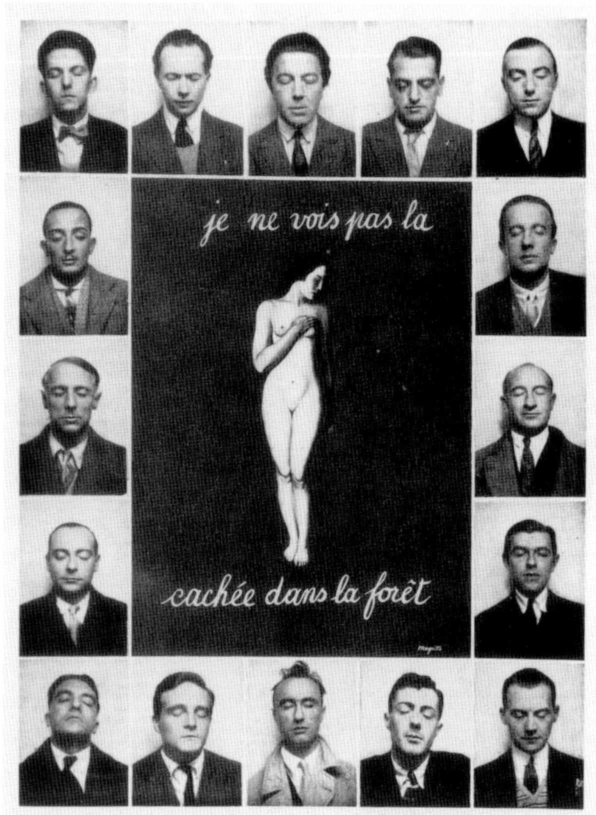

FIGURE 41
René Magritte, collage, 1929. In *La Revolution surréaliste* 12 (15 December 1929): 73.

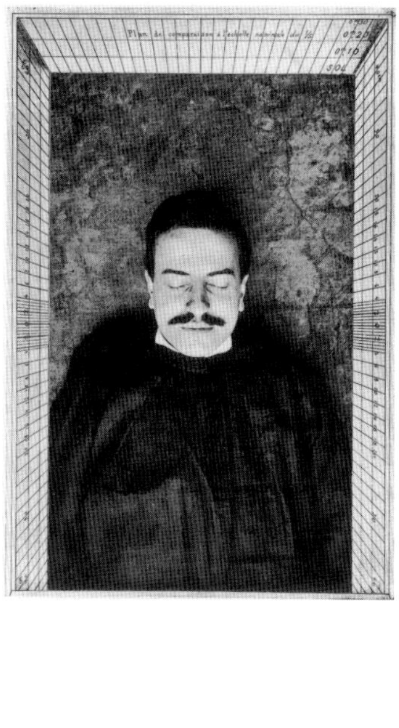

FIGURE 42
Louis Tomellini, photograph of a dead man (self-portrait) using the Bertillon method of judicial photography. In Dr. Louis Tomellini, *Metric Photography* (Lyon, 1908). Courtesy of the Bibliothèque Nationale de France.

UN CADAVRE

Il ne faut plus que mort cet homme fasse de la poussière.

André BRETON *(Un Cadavre, 1924.)*

PAPOLOGIE D'ANDRÉ BRETON

Le deuxième manifeste du Surréalisme n'est pas une révélation, mais c'est une réussite.

On ne fait pas mieux dans le genre hypocrite, faux-frère, pelotard, sacristain, et pour tout dire : flic et curé.

Car en somme : on vous dit que l'acte surréaliste le plux simple consiste, revolvers aux poings, à descendre dans la rue et à tirer au hasard, tant qu'on peut, dans la foule.

Mais l'inspecteur Breton serait sans doute déjà arrêté s'il n'avait pas tout de l'agent provocateur, tandis que chacun de ses petits amis se garde bien d'accomplir l'acte surréaliste le plus simple.

Cette impunité prouve également le mépris dans lequel un Etat, quel qu'il soit, tient justement les intellectuels. Principalement ceux qui, comme l'inspecteur Breton, mènent la petite vie sordide de l'intellectuel professionnel.

Les *révélations* touchant par exemple Naville ou Masson ont le caractère des chantages quotidiens exercés par les journaux vendus à la police. La méthode et le ton sont absolument les mêmes. Pour les autres appréciations sur d'anciens amis, chers parce que l'inspecteur Breton espérant qu'ignorant sa qualité ils le nommeraient président d'un Soviet local des Grands Hommes, elles ne dépassent pas les ignominies ordinaires des habitués de commissariat, ni les coups de pied en vache. A cette heure où sont maîtresses de la rue ces deux ordures : la littérature et la police, il ne faut s'étonner de rien. Aux deux extrêmes, comme Dieu et Diable, il y a Chiappe et Breton.

Que Dada ait abouti à çà, c'est une grande consolation pour l'humanité qui retourne à sa colique. — Mais dira-t-on, n'avez-vous pas aimé le surréalisme ? Mais oui : amours de jeunesse, amours ancillaires. D'ailleurs une récente enquête donne aux petits jeunes gens l'autorisation d'aimer même la femme d'un gendarme.

Ou la femme d'un curé. Car on pense bien que dans l'affaire le flic rejoint le curé : le frère Breton qui fait accommoder le prêtre à la sauce moutarde ne parle plus qu'en chaire. Il est plein de mandarin curaçao, sait ce qu'on peut tirer des femmes, mais il impose

G. RIBEMONT-DESSAIGNES.

(Voir la suite page 2)

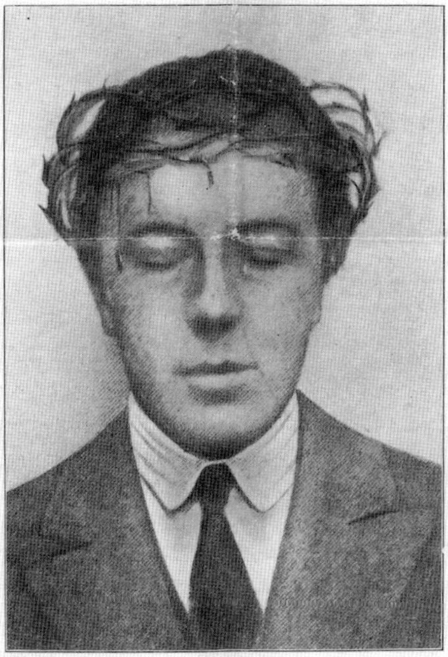

AUTO-PROPHÉTIE

Ce monde dans lequel je subis ce que je subis (n'y allez pas voir), ce monde moderne, enfin, diable ! que voulez-vous que j'y fasse ? La voix surréaliste se taira peut-être, je n'en suis plus à compter mes disparitions. Je n'entrerai plus, si peu que ce soit, dans le décompte merveilleux de mes années et de mes jours. Je serai comme Nijinsky, qu'on conduisit l'an dernier aux Ballets russes et qui ne comprit pas à quel spectacle il assistait.

ANDRÉ BRETON, *Manifeste du Surréalisme.*

MORT D'UN MONSIEUR

Hélas, je ne reverrai plus l'illustre Palotin du Monde Occidental, celui qui me faisait rire !

De son vivant, il écrivait, pour abréger le temps, disait-il, pour trouver des hommes et, lorsque par hasard il en trouvait, il avait atrocement peur et, leur faisant le coup de l'amitié bouleversante, il guettait le moment où il pourrait les salir.

Un jour il crut voir passer en rêve un Vaisseau-Fantôme et sentit les galons du capitaine Bordure lui pousser sur la tête, il se regarda sérieusement dans la glace et se trouva beau.

Ce fut la fin, il devint bègue du cœur et confondit tout, le désespoir et le mal de foie, la Bible et les chants de Maldoror, Dieu et Dieu, l'encre et le foutre, les barricades et le divan de Mme Sabatier, le marquis de Sade et Jean Lorrain, la Révolution Russe et la révolution surréaliste (1).

Pion lyrique il distribua des diplômes aux grands amoureux, des jours d'indulgences aux débutants en désespoir et se lamenta sur la grande pitié des poètes de France.

« Est-il vrai, écrivait-il, que les Patries veulent le plus tôt possible le sang de leurs grands hommes ? »

Excellent musicien il joua pendant un certain temps du luth de classe sous les fenêtres du Parti communiste, reçut des briques sur la tête, et repartit déçu, aigri, maitrechanter dans les cours d'amour.

Il ne pouvait pas jouer sans tricher, il trichait d'ailleurs très mal et cachait des boules de billard dans ses manches ; quand elles tombaient par terre avec un bruit désagréable devant ses fidèles très gênés il disait que c'était de l'humour.

C'était un grand honnête homme, il mettait parfois sa toque de juge par dessus son képi, et faisait de la Morale ou de la critique d'art, mais il cachait difficilement les cicatrices que lui avaient laissées le croc à phynances de la peinture moderne.

Un jour il criait contre le prêtres, le lendemain il se croyait évêque ou pape en Avignon, prenait un billet pour aller voir et revenait quelques jours après plus révolutionnaire que jamais et pleurait bientôt de grosses larmes de rage le 1er mai parce qu'il n'avait pas trouvé

Jacques PREVERT.

(Voir la suite page 2)

FIGURE 43 André Breton's mug shot, cover of *Un Cadavre,* 1930. Courtesy of the Research Library, The Getty Research Institute, Los Angeles.

of surrealist misogyny.[41] Yet the collage, although usually read in a way that emphasizes male dreamers and female objectification, also represents a material conflict that parallels the perceived irreconcilability of sexual difference. Magritte's collage juxtaposes painted canvas and Photomaton-brand gelatin silver print, as well as the confused yet gendered readings that attend those media (painting as "high culture," Photomaton as "mass culture"), as if to demonstrate the fictional quality of our assumptions. Though the choices of media support the apparently "essential" qualities of masculinity and femininity (male intellectual capacity equals the realist medium of photography; female sensuality equals the coloristic appeal of painting), the violent juxtaposition of these qualities, the contradictory way that they resonate as mass or elite forms, and the emphasis upon death undermine one's ability to read the collage as a conventional story about sexual difference. Look closely: if the surrealist men look dead, like the subjects of a forensic specialist's camera, their female counterpart is herself dissolving; her arm has begun to disappear in the inky shadows at right. Thus, the deathly reading of the men in this image potentially alters our sense of this woman; she becomes susceptible to bodily fragmentation and is not immune to bodily decay. As if compensating—like the nurse who turned away from the amputee Bravais—for the losses incurred by men who were injured in the war, Magritte's image displaces the recognition of male vulnerability onto the painted female in this collage, and it does so by comparing her near plenitude to their near-dead, possibly dreaming, heads.

Collage and Collective Memory

> Shells, gas clouds, and flotillas of tanks—shattering, corroding, death.
> Dysentery, influenza, typhus—scalding, choking, death.
> Trenches, hospitals, the common grave—there are no other possibilities.
>
> Erich Maria Remarque, *All Quiet on the Western Front,* 1929

The year 1929 was an important one for surrealism. It encompassed both the death and the rebirth of Breton's surrealist group, a transformation one could see through the purges and reorganization of competing surrealist groups in the pages of *La Révolution surréaliste* and other surrealist publications. It was also the year that Erich Maria Remarque's *All Quiet on the Western Front* was translated from the original German into both French and English.[42] The book underscored the continuing need for the war's survivors to make sense of their experiences in the conflict. It was filled with traumatic images—hospitals, trenches, communal graves—seemingly to help readers work through their shocking memories by identifying with the language of the text. By repeating the smells, sights, and sounds of the trenches, Remarque's book was a powerful catalyst for producing both collective memory and therapeutic cure. And, as such, it was the sort of work that the surrealists set out to achieve in their own ways.

A desire to organize the war's traumatic experiences by making art seems to have played a

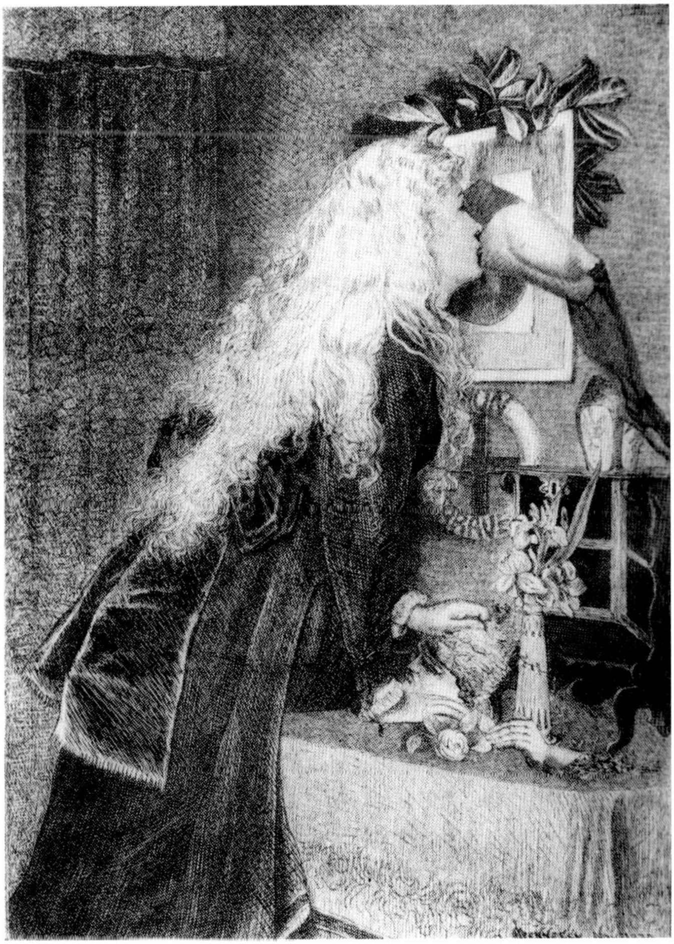

FIGURE 44
Max Ernst, *Altar of the Fatherland,* 1929.

role in Louis Aragon's decision to illustrate his important 1930 essay on collage, "Beyond Painting," with an image by Max Ernst called *Altar of the Fatherland* (Fig. 44). Ernst's image, one of over twenty examples of collage accompanying Aragon's 1930 text, seems to be a visual application of surrealism's aesthetics of dismemberment.[43] Whereas Aragon's text emphasizes dislocation in ways that resonate with Breton's "man cut in two," Desnos' body parts from "Pénalités de l'Enfer," or the single moulages at Val-de-Grâce, Ernst's seamless collage technique reflects an important aspect of the visual legacy of Val-de-Grâce: the aestheticization of male bodily trauma. This altar, made up of a few severed limbs, seems to have attracted attention because of its representation of a patriotic woman's fervent attention to the wounded male body. Instead of taking the tack that Magritte did in his collage, by showing the female body receiving the wounds of the dead men around her, this woman celebrates male sacrifice with a kiss but remains untouched by physical violence.

Completed in 1929 as part of the unfinished "Selected Pieces of the History of France," Ernst's collage altar underscores the importance of shielding the manipulation of pictorial rhetoric from view to create a semblance of historical unity.[44] Although the trauma of the cutting process is usually visible in collage practice, Ernst deliberately represses it here. Coupled with the use of engravings that seem to be cut from the same cloth, the relative invisibility of the act of cutting parallels the narrative suppression of trauma in the displays at Val-de-Grâce and in the rhetoric of interwar reconstruction. The apparent integration of the paper used for the collage—unlike Magritte's juxtaposition of media—helps ensure the viewer's complicity with the image's narrative agenda. Yet oddly, the cutting and pasting of collage technique has morphed into the content of the image: here, as in the war itself, personal and collective memory emerges from an altar constructed from severed limbs. The woman supporting herself on the altar celebrates the body part's role in French history and kisses the leg before her as if it were a religious icon. As her lips caress the flesh, she takes on the role of a dutiful, obedient subject. Although she acknowledges men's physical sacrifices, she nonetheless worships at an altar made from their bodies, highlighting a causal relationship between national allegiance, male sacrifice, and female desire. The opposition of the worshipping woman and the male leg partakes of conventional ideas about sexual difference during wartime: men would protect, even to death, the domestic ideal represented by the figure of woman. In this way, Ernst's altar mimics a widespread desire to reaffirm traditional social roles for men and women in the years immediately following World War I, thereby undermining its legitimacy; his seamless collage technique joins the reverent woman to the man's dangling leg with ease. But the collage also shows the ethical dilemma that arises when one stages national commemoration with images of trauma. Historical monuments are not usually made from the flesh of the soldiers killed or maimed in the wars they commemorate. *Altar of the Fatherland* is no ordinary monument because it recasts a traditional form of commemoration in the language of trauma. In this collage, the contrast between the apparently seamless surface and the narrative content dripping with violence helps expose the mechanics of interwar visual rhetoric: a viewer would need to aestheticize bodily trauma to go along with the logic of that rhetoric. Although we saw mutilation transmuted into a stage in cultural evolution at Val-de-Grâce, Ernst's collage reflects a subtle understanding of the risks of using the human body as social glue.

Altar of the Fatherland successfully pointed to the weakness and hypocrisy of official discourse about reconstruction, even though it never had wide circulation. Many surrealist works, however, failed to mobilize effective critiques of the state-promoted aesthetics of dismemberment, largely because they depended on the same rhetorical structures. Aragon seemed best to grasp the ominous ramifications of this aestheticization of trauma, dislocation, and dismemberment for the surrealist project. In "Introduction to 1930" in the final issue of *La Révolution surréaliste* (December 1929), Aragon mused that the modern—a conception that likely included surrealism's version of modernity—with its surprises, deracinations, transformations, and shocks, had failed to deliver the overarching critique it seemed to promise. He implied that just as the modern had been commodified, so had surrealism:

> The modern today is not in the hands of poets. It is in the hands of cops . . . just as painting is no longer in the hands of painters, but in the hands of those who, preserved by white batons and brownings, feed them. . . . It is the return of the censor to the unconscious. . . . The government may be reassured. We have followed its instructions. There is today, in France, a modern style, thanks to the exposition of 1925. It is for this reason that I can no longer go to a café: so many cafés have become modern. But the style, inspired from on high, does not stop at decoration. It invades little by little all the domains.[45]

The various forms of physical and cultural disturbance that marked the *mutilé de guerre*'s body at Val-de-Grâce, and which the surrealists had adopted as a model in the early 1920s, had been made over into the safely fashionable styles of streamlined efficiency known as art déco. Unlike the clunky, disturbing replacement of an amputated arm with a visibly disjunctive new body part that is also a tool, this machine-age, postwar "modern style" seemed to be the visual incarnation of the integration of human and machine. Just as the injured veteran's body was remade to make him a more productive member of postwar society, members of the Parisian art world busied themselves producing work aimed at "repressing the trauma of war" by celebrating the new machine age or infusing their work with nostalgia for a prewar existence.[46] Although at first seduced by the potential for advertising and other new visual and mechanical technologies to create a surrealist culture, surrealists like Aragon eventually realized that the works that had seemed the best weapons against the steamroller of postwar progress looked increasingly like vehicles for consumption instead of revolution. Rather than deploying fragmentation, dismemberment, and trauma to critique the idealized rhetoric of the return to order, surrealism's aestheticization of dismemberment seemed only to have increased the speed with which publicists and the government could exploit such images. As we shall see in the next chapter, by the late 1920s, visual shock, via symbolic repetition of the horrific mutilations of the war, had become a prerequisite for consumer desire.

Presciently, I think, Aragon realized the implications of this link between the aesthetics of dismemberment and the power of the state to control its subjects' experiences and desires. On the precipice of a new decade, Aragon saw that he and his surrealist friends might well have turned visual culture into a weapon for political and economic consolidation rather than a tool of social transformation. And, unfortunately for the victims of the emergent fascist movements that aimed to produce and control national cultures in the 1930s and 1940s, Aragon seems to have been on to something.

CHAPTER THREE

The Advertisement of Emasculation

ANDRÉ KERTÉSZ IN SURREALIST PARIS

André Kertész moved to Paris in the summer of 1925, at a time when the events of World War I had apparently begun to fade from people's minds as they went about their daily lives. By then France seemed well along in its postwar recovery, as evidenced by the celebratory displays at the Ministry of Commerce's Exposition Internationale des Arts Décoratifs et Industriels Modernes held from April to October of that year.[1] As we have already seen, images of a healthy and robust France—idealized mothers or virile laborers—were familiar fare during the early 1920s. As Romy Golan notes, such images of wholeness were an "antidote" to the trauma of the war; moreover, the increased production of art that centered on feminized, corporealized bodies during the 1920s presented a pictorial corollary to the nation's postwar rebirth.[2]

Throughout the late 1920s, Kertész—like the surrealists he knew through friendships with Man Ray and Brassaï—was fascinated less by images of physical and industrial rebirth than by conflicting evidence about the effects of the war on France's male populace. A cursory glance at his work from this period shows that he often trained his camera on the bodies of weak or damaged men—drunks, amputees, or the homeless—who were part of the urban landscape. Using sharp visual juxtaposition, Kertész exposed the tenuousness of the state's strategy to tie postwar reconstruction to male labor's production of flashy new consumer goods. His men were anything but the robust workers or dapper gentlemen visible in war-bond posters, product advertisements, and upscale shop windows. Although Kertész drew on the visual power and conceptual surprises of contemporary advertising, he did so in ways that often questioned whether the men he saw on the Paris streets were really more efficient, productive, and stronger than ever before. His photographs of weakened, mutilated, and disenfranchised men captured the ironic yet wrenching distance between people's fantasies about the well-being of postwar manhood and the reality of men's lives after the war. In powerful ways, these photographs are conceptually connected to the moulages at Val-de-Grâce, which emphasized rejuvenation of the soldier's body through graphic comparisons of physical mutilation and surgical treatment. Yet Kertész's images juxtapose the dreams concocted by the purveyors of commodity culture with the facts of urban existence in 1920s Paris.

A clear example of this preoccupation with bringing together competing ideas of postwar manhood is Kertész's 1928 photograph of a man seated at a Parisian café (Fig. 45). By contrasting the man slouching at a small table in the foreground with the splendidly erect man in the Ovomaltine poster behind him, the photograph highlights the split between healthy and afflicted varieties of manhood.[3] The number of plates on the café table—each small plate recording a drink consumed—and the man's flaccid posture indicate that he has been drinking for some time now, and he has probably not been drinking the nutritious, high-energy beverage prominently advertised by the straining metallic figure behind him. Although Ovomaltine was widely advertised at the time as a healthy, energy-boosting drink (an ideal hinted at by the half-legible text *"donne des for[ces],"* or "gives strength," beneath the Ovomaltine brand name), the café patron's listlessness undermines the poster's optimistic rhetoric. The disconnect between these two examples of masculinity—one vulnerable, one robust—shows Kertész's sensitivity to the contradictory messages about manhood that were visible on Paris streets in the 1920s. Whereas at Val-de-Grâce the French state promoted a coherent social body through images of the rehabilitation of injured men, Kertész's photographs depict men who have yet to be physically or emotionally rehabilitated. Using a crisply focused style and taking his pictures from a distance in a documentary-like fashion, Kertész indicates that masculinity remained under pressure in the mid- to late 1920s, the hopes for men's rehabilitation notwithstanding.

In many ways, Kertész's photographs record interwar France's cultural unconscious. They mirror the nation's fascination with—and disavowal of—male trauma by repeating and working through that trauma in pictorial form and calling attention to the reality that reconstruction aimed to erase. Although Kertész was not an official member of the surrealist group, his photographs often echo surrealist imagery, especially in their use of juxtaposition, visual shock, and visual comparison to communicate—techniques that were common in cutting-edge advertising and publicity at the time.[4] Rather than directly celebrating masculinity in the postwar years, Kertész's photographs push viewers to scrutinize contradictory evidence of the status of manhood that they might not normally notice, or would prefer to avoid. Many of his photographs parallel the media-saturated world of Louis Aragon's *Paysan de Paris* or Desnos' Bébé Cadum, in which advertising techniques disrupt conventional ideas about the social

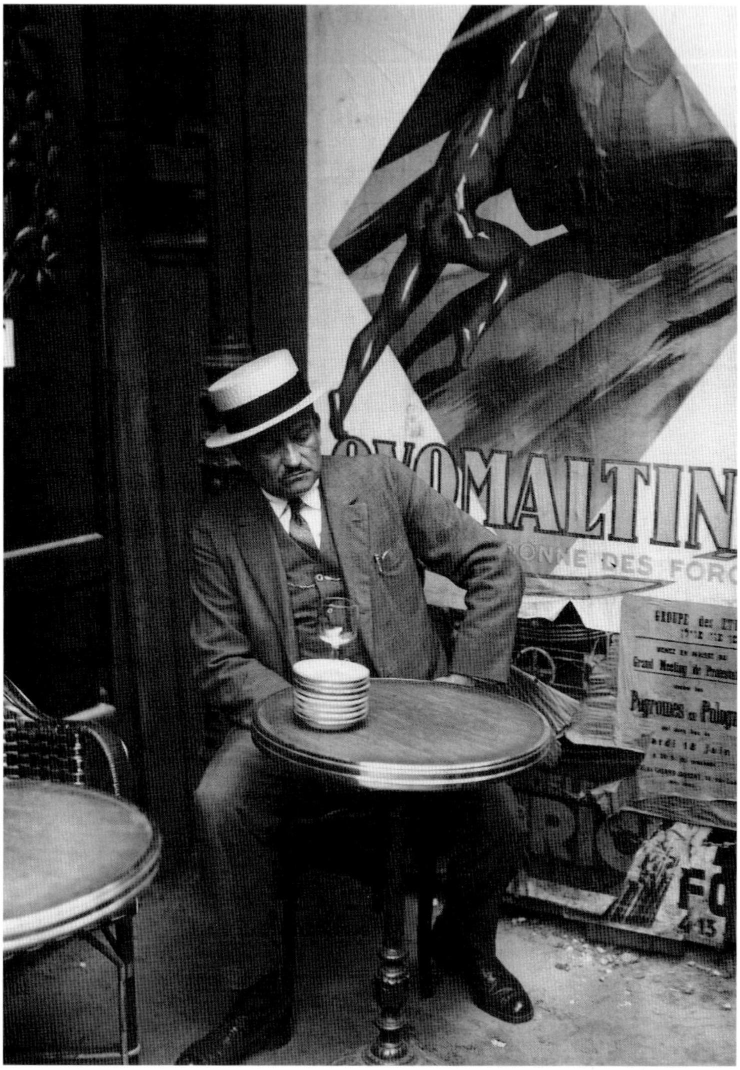

FIGURE 45
André Kertész, *Man at a Paris Café,* 1928. Photo André Kertész © Ministère de la Culture, France.

order. As we investigate Kertész's photographs of men from the late 1920s in the sections that follow, I propose that we think of his photographs as an ad campaign for a more complicated understanding of the war's impact on the social body of France and as a visual narrative exploring the links between commodity culture and postwar masculinity.

Intriguingly, the 1920s saw an explosion in advertising theory and the business of publicity in France, part of which focused on advertisements that sought to sell products to men. For the first time, the advertising industry began to target men using the strategies it had previously reserved for women.[5] But perhaps this shift made sense, for who else but the *mutilés de guerre* needed to buy new limbs as well as new tools to function productively in postwar industrial society? Despite the optimism about rebuilding men's bodies, and regardless of how many new products were available for men after the war—whether arms and legs or hats and shoes—Kertész's photographs pointed out that reconstruction was not assured. Because the emerging publicity industry saw the male war returnees as an important class of consumers, it favored increasingly idealized images of men. Much as the surrealists emphasized dismemberment and mutilation, Kertész advanced images of conflicted, anxiety-ridden masculinity that contradicted, or at least complicated, the reigning narratives about France's achievements in social and industrial reconstruction.

Kertész's Anxious Men

It is one thing to see pictures of the war's dead and wounded in an illustrated magazine, where soldiers' bodies lie twisted in communal graves many miles away from one's study or café table. It is quite another to walk by a man whose traumatized flesh forces one to see him as the casualty of a war machine. Walking along the Seine one day in 1926, André Kertész stopped to take a photograph that reflected this disturbing truth (Fig. 46). The scene that captured his attention was not a *bouquiniste*'s display of books but two men standing on a quai near Saint-Michel. The man on the left is a *mutilé de guerre,* his somewhat shabbily dressed figure framed by the crutches that must make up for his missing leg. The photograph compares his body with that of the larger, undamaged man by framing the two figures as reflections of one another.[6] By representing the *mutilé de guerre* as both an object of national sacrifice (one might presume his injuries are a result of the war) and the subject of reconstruction (one might read the two-legged man to his right as a symbol of possible rehabilitation), the photograph implies that recovery is incomplete. The framing of the shot demands that the two bodies be read as a pair, even though their clothing and their physical forms suggest differences of class and corporeal integrity. Their proximity to one another, combined with the physical disparities between them, demands that they be understood as competing possibilities for manhood, rather than as indicators of the potential of physical and social redemption. The photograph's juxtaposition of the men presents different views of the war's effects—as if enabling the viewer to see two sides of the same coin in a single glance. Kertész's comparison urges us to glance back and forth between the two men and thus seems to document at once the impossibility of forgetting the war's mutilation of such men and the promise of their restoration. We might see the man without a leg as an embodiment of postwar French society's phantom limb, a limb that has been lost or left behind but that remains a nagging presence in its ghostly absence.[7]

The back-and-forth visual movement created by the photograph's framing subtly mimics a

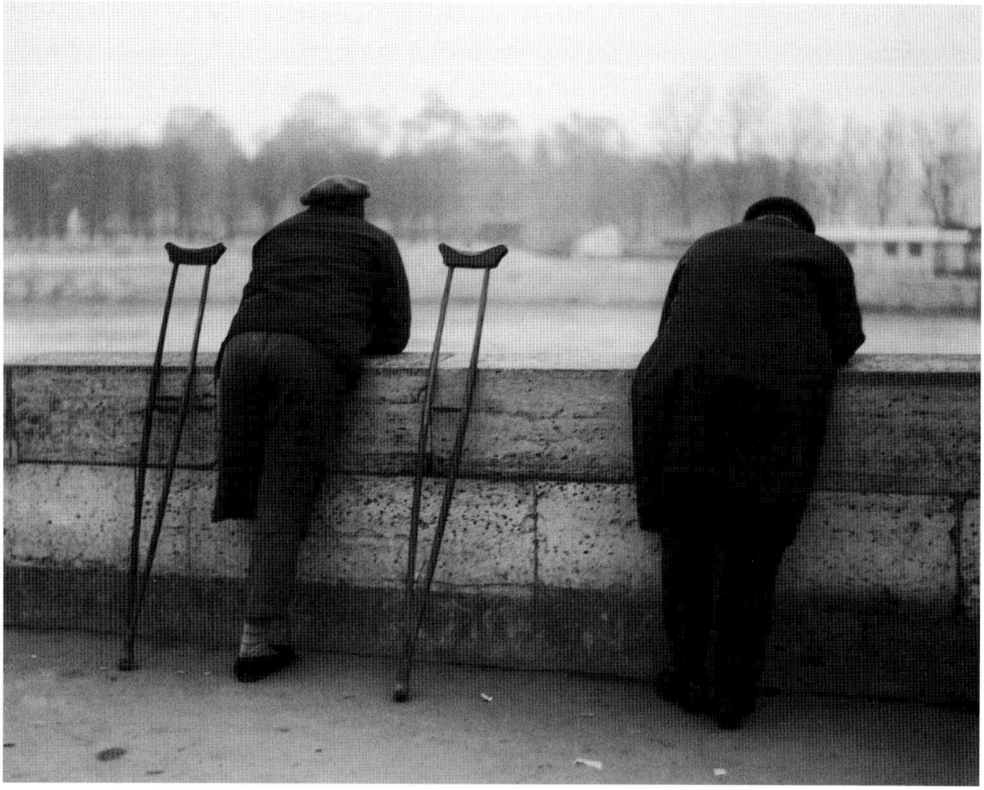

FIGURE 46 André Kertész, *On the Quai Saint-Michel,* 1926. Photo André Kertész © Ministère de la Culture, France.

dialectical experience favored by the surrealists. By making visible the war's brutality and violence toward men in this way—in conjunction with an image of a complete male body—the photograph underscores why political and business interests were eager to repress evidence of the war's savagery to safeguard the promise of a healthy society. In a more subtle way, it also alludes to the commodification of the male body at Val-de-Grâce, where the museum displays focused on making men better than they were before through cutting-edge scientific technology. The photograph doesn't subsume the injured man with the cured one; rather, it presents the two men as competing possibilities.

The comparison between an amputee and a two-legged man subtly inserts the logic of modernity, whose ties to the industrialization of the postwar male body is viscerally insured by the physical differences of their bodies. One could assume that modern progress will secure the injured man's future through technological innovation. But in this instance, the wounded man remains in physical and, potentially, economic limbo. Trauma, the image proposes, will not be erased by reconstruction in this instance; instead, the mutilated male body counters the rhetoric of seamless transformation through its fragmentary, shocking visibility.

Kertész's image has an affinity with Walter Benjamin's idea of the power of the "outmoded" object to awaken the beholder to his or her historical oppression. In Benjamin's view, such an object—for example, an article of clothing that looked up-to-date when you bought it but ten years later seems like the sloughed-off skin of a different, earlier you—prompts an awakening because of the way it brings past and present together in violent contradiction.[8] Reconstruction in Kertész's hands is a collectively held myth that works only if one forgets or ignores the past. In its comparative structure, Kertész's photograph rejects this kind of historical amnesia and insists instead upon visualizing the past, present, and future as mutually dependent elements rather than as sequential links in a temporal chain. Thus, the amputee's body concretizes the past by visibly carrying the war's brutality into the present, while the promise of a productive future appears in his counterpart's wholeness; but between the two men lies evidence that past and present remain unsettled, with the past not completely erased nor the future secured. The photograph asks the viewer to imagine this space between the men's bodies. For progress to become concrete, in other words, the *mutilé de guerre* would have to disappear, or at least become unimportant. The parity promoted in the photograph makes the viewer uncertain about this tragic story's end.

Kertész's pictorial logic also found echoes in the work of the prominent photography critic Pierre Mac Orlan. In his 1928 essay "Photography: The Social Fantastic," Mac Orlan theorized photographs as objects with the potential to visualize things that one might not otherwise see or recognize. Photography could represent those "fantastic forms of life that require at least an instant of immobility in order to be perceived."[9] According to Mac Orlan, photography, by freezing temporal succession, exposes the space of ideological construction: the moment between before and after or between old and new, a moment the surrealists mined again and again as a structuring absence within the narrative of the return to order. In Mac Orlan's account of photography, the camera freezes the invisible elements that tie one moment to the next. Invisibility becomes an object, worthy of attention because it forces the beholder to see ideological construction concretely: a process, in the case of postwar France, in which the burial of trauma is a prerequisite for successful rebirth. In light of Mac Orlan's observations, the expressive power of Kertész's men along the river Seine depends on the successful immobilization of the amputee's wounded body at a moment in the narrative when its rehabilitation is promised but not yet achieved.

The dialectical account of trauma and its therapeutic cure in the image of the two men at the Seine is echoed in a photograph Kertész made in 1927 of a battered prosthetic leg lying on an old iron bed. Rather than implying the difficulty of regenerating masculinity, this photograph objectifies male mutilation by isolating male lack in the form of a sculptural object (Fig.

47). Under Kertész's intimate gaze, this artificial body part seems magically to turn itself into an image of phallic unity. The chipped prosthetic leg sits unceremoniously atop a mounded blanket, its bulk demanding attention because of the way it appears to fill the bed. With its flattened top at rest on a wrinkled pillow and its black shoe nearly touching the bed's frame at bottom, the leg appears as a stand-in for the person who would usually sleep there. Representing the absent body, the prosthetic device emphasizes the body's incompleteness. Oddly, this mechanical substitution reads as both a body part—the section of calf and foot below an amputee's knee—and as a unified whole. The mechanical nature of the leg gives it its unity, and the way that it hints at bodily fragmentation, even as it promises to complete the body that will use it, provides a focus for Kertész.

A subtle difference exists between this photograph's emphasis on a partial body and the comparison of the two men along the Seine. This leg also mimics the elongated form of a phallus, signifying both a lost limb and the body's loss of authority. Instead of filling in the bodily gaps created by amputation, the image of the battered leg prompts the viewer to imagine its absent owner: Is the leg's owner hobbling around the edges of the bed on a stump? Is he hopping? Or must he crawl? This image represents the injured male body as both artificially complete and pitiably lacking, as both part and whole. Finally, the fact that the limb is numbered like a specimen or a product on an assembly line — the number 13 stenciled above it on the wall suggests as much — helps to produce a sense of this prosthetic device as one of many. That sensation is augmented by the visible excision of the rest of the world by the photographic frame. This leg, the viewer imagines, is just one of thousands like it that are used to supplement, and make productive again, the bodies of mutilated veterans.

Because both of Kertész's images invite multiple readings of the brutalized or weakened male body, they reveal a contradiction within the rhetoric of reconstruction: phallic plenitude depends on several ways of repressing male dismemberment. The contrast between an amputee and a man with two legs signals the possibility, if not the achievement, of reconstruction. The two men appear to represent the passage from mutilation to regeneration, with dismemberment sidling up alongside a complete, and unmarred, male body. Implicit in this depiction of the logic of reconstruction—and, of course, Western viewers, who typically read from left to right, tend to read the photograph as moving from part to whole and from absence to presence—is an unwillingness to allow the beholder to grab hold of either position. In the portrait of a prosthetic leg, masculinity overcomes partiality by disavowing the existence of bodily lack. Thus, the framing of the prosthetic limb changes the object from a sign of male lack into a symbol of phallic male power. These two photographs thus depict differences *within* masculinity. Usually repressed by physical or cultural means, these differences become visible in Kertész's work; his photographs are concrete, realist objects against which one can compare narratives of progress, recovery, and healthy manhood.

Rhetoric about reconstruction emphasized the need to renew traditional roles to help

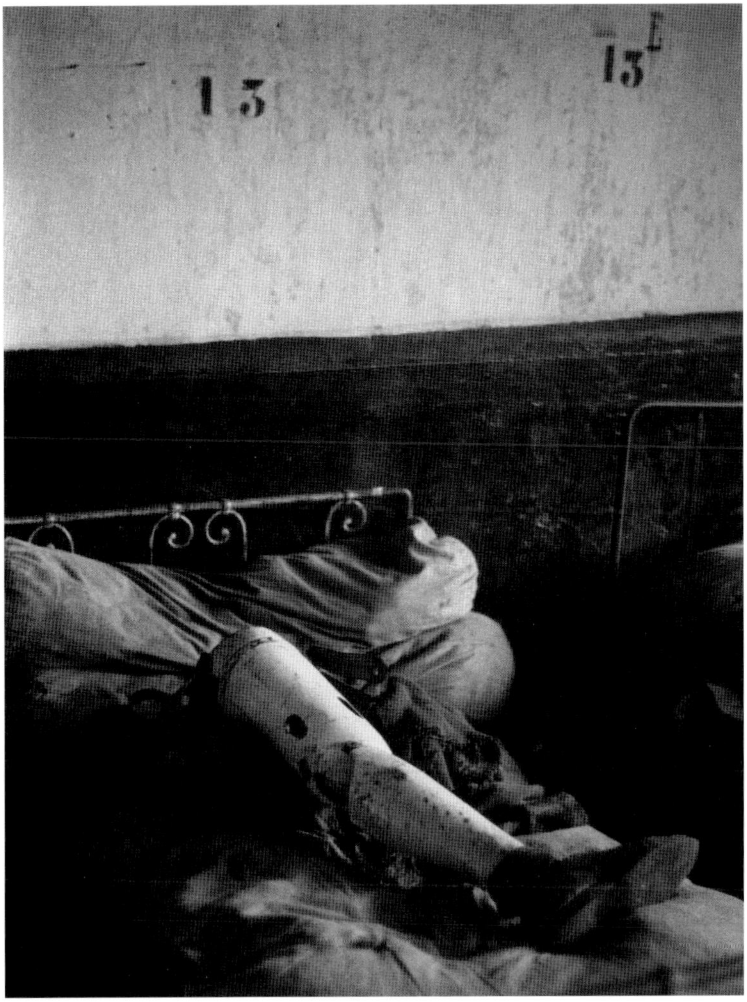

FIGURE 47
André Kertész, *Leg (Hôtel de Reveil)*, 1927. Photo André Kertész © Ministère de la Culture, France.

France avoid further physical or moral decay after the war. Indeed, stable gender positions seemed as crucial to postwar reconstruction as did work on the economic and physical infrastructures of the nation. But the war dramatically altered people's perceptions of their proper social roles. Indeed, the 1920s were a watershed in French history because they ushered in increasingly fluid, at times confused, ideas about sex and gender identities.

Kertész's 1928 image of a flower vendor on the Champs-Élysées (Fig. 48) not only expresses the palpable presence of male mutilation and vulnerability on the Paris streets but also underscores the link between anxiety about male emasculation and fears about women's changing roles in postwar French society. The photograph depicts an incipient commercial exchange between a man and a woman. Yet the image of a legless man confronting a well-heeled modern woman effectively inverts conventional narratives of sexual difference. Briefcase in hand, this businesslike, self-assured woman strides headlong into the *métro*. The vendor's neediness is poignant next to the woman's brusque self-sufficiency; his proffered posy stands for a conventional set of gender roles that she has no interest in buying. While his torso mimics the gestures of heterosexual courtship, his missing legs announce his physical inadequacy, recalling the censored wartime photographs of Bravais and his nurse in Chapter 2. The striding young woman's lack of interest appears to present a threat to both his manhood and his ability to make a living. The photograph situates the man's body somewhere between the traditional polarities of sexual difference, setting a third element—the damaged masculinity he represents—against two conventional representations of gender: the unimpaired male figure who strolls into the photograph's upper-left corner and the young woman with her briefcase. The healthy, active male counterpart to the vendor's squat legless body literalizes the deformation of idealized masculinity. Yet even this second image of manhood inside the photographic frame revolves around the contrast between the mutilated, grasping flower vendor and the coolly dismissive modern woman. Male viewers whose ideas about manhood included a properly submissive role for women would have seen this modern incarnation of femininity as a problem, for the woman undermines the possibility of returning to the social order of the prewar years.

The tense yet poignant content of this photograph shows that Kertész saw the streets of Paris as battlegrounds in which people fought over the nature of the social order, including the way sexual identities should or should not conform to traditional concepts of individual and collective identity. Precisely because of her widely-commented-upon physical appearance—slim, trim, and bobbed—the modern woman, not unlike the amputee, embodied the society in flux. At a time when many men lost cultural and economic authority along with their legs or their arms, the streamlined, self-confident *garçonne* demonstrated that she, too, had changed. In this new world, modern women were winning social and sexual freedom at the cost of traditional male-female relations, especially because their new identities suggested the transformation of masculinity as well.

By 1934 Kertész's interest in the political valence of the body on the streets of Paris not only centered on sexual difference but also highlighted the importance of an idealized, mass-produced image of manhood to public life. Masculinity had become an increasingly familiar commodity in the years after World War I. In *On the Paris Boulevards* (Fig. 49), Kertész interrogates the relations between the sexes as they were being redefined by consumer culture—an idea that was implicit in his image of the flower vendor's exchange with an uninterested female customer. The photograph of a Paris street plastered with advertisements for the popular apéritif Dubonnet captures the texture of the postwar culture, in which men, too, had become the

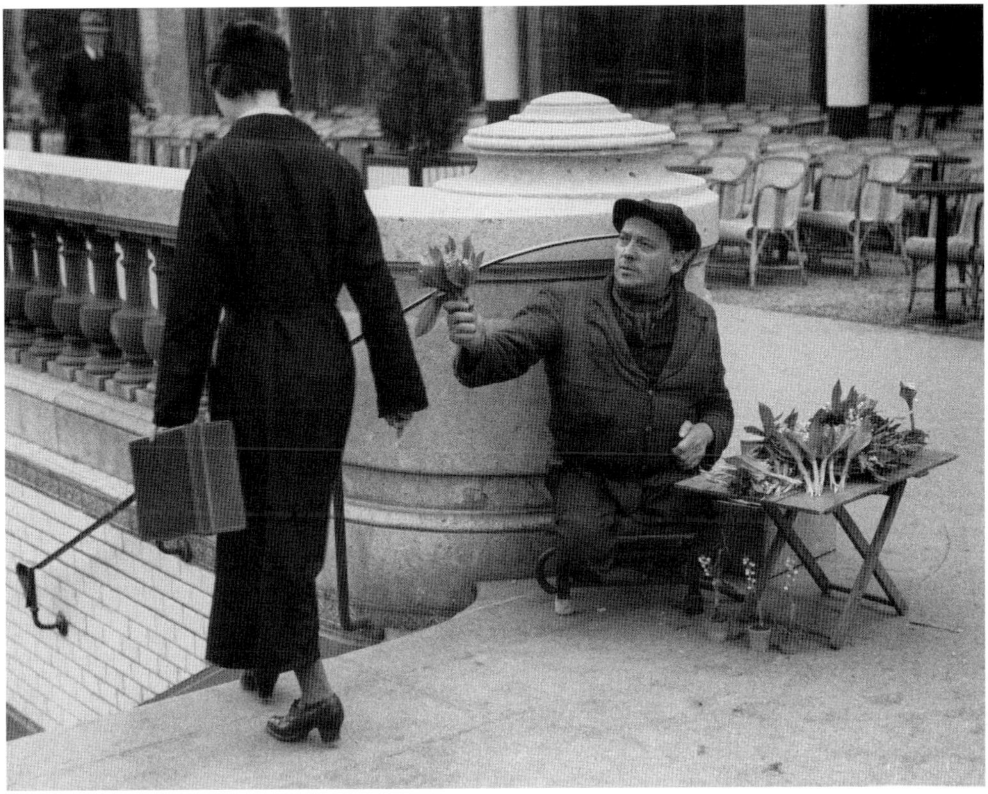

FIGURE 48 André Kertész, *Muguet seller on the Champs-Élysées*, 1928. Photo André Kertész © Ministère de la Culture, France.

objects of the consumer's gaze. In this case, an image of men drinking, set in contrast to a top-hat–wearing masculinized *bourgeoise,* seems to replicate itself across the city wall. The repetition of modern-style male figures indicates the firm grip that male customers had on consumer culture by the early 1930s; men as well as women were, by this point, integral partners in the development of the postwar French economy. Yet, on the whole, this photograph seems most interested in showing the types of manhood with which male viewers might identify at the time. The repeated forms of drinking men in the Dubonnet posters conflate industrially produced men with the real thing, suggesting that masculinity is multiple—that is, that many kinds of masculinity exist in the world and that men are welcome to choose their identities as they would select shoes, soap, or booze.

If men were increasingly able to choose their masculine identities as they did other products, wasn't the existing, traditional definition of manhood at risk of disappearing? This idea

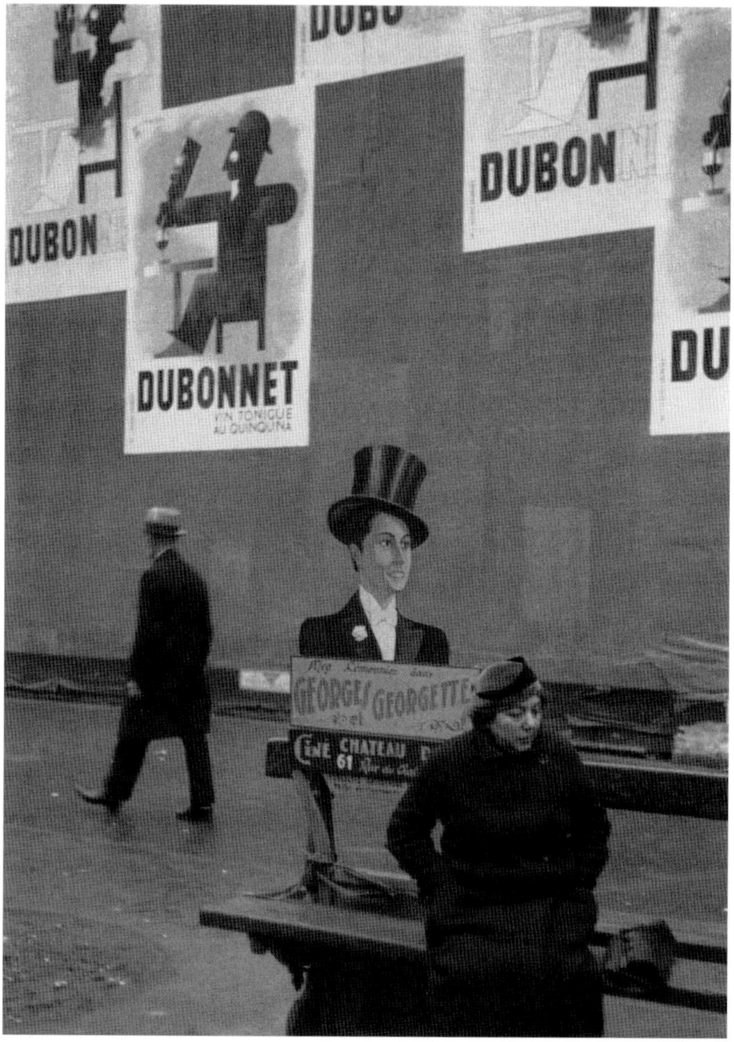

FIGURE 49
André Kertész, *On the Paris Boulevards (Dubo, Dubon, Dubonnet)*, 1934. Photo André Kertész © Ministère de la Culture, France.

was not new in the early 1930s: widely reproduced images like the 1926 advertising poster for a theatrical performance "L'Homme sans Tête" (Man without a head; Fig. 50) clearly indicate that French culture recognized the need for men to juggle identities. In ways much more subtle than those in the theater advertisement, Kertész's 1934 photograph breaks new ground by proffering several images of masculinity for the viewer to contemplate simultaneously (even as it obscures the face of the man striding away at upper left). Yet its recourse to the familiar bifurcation of masculine and feminine is also clear: the picture on the bench hinders the

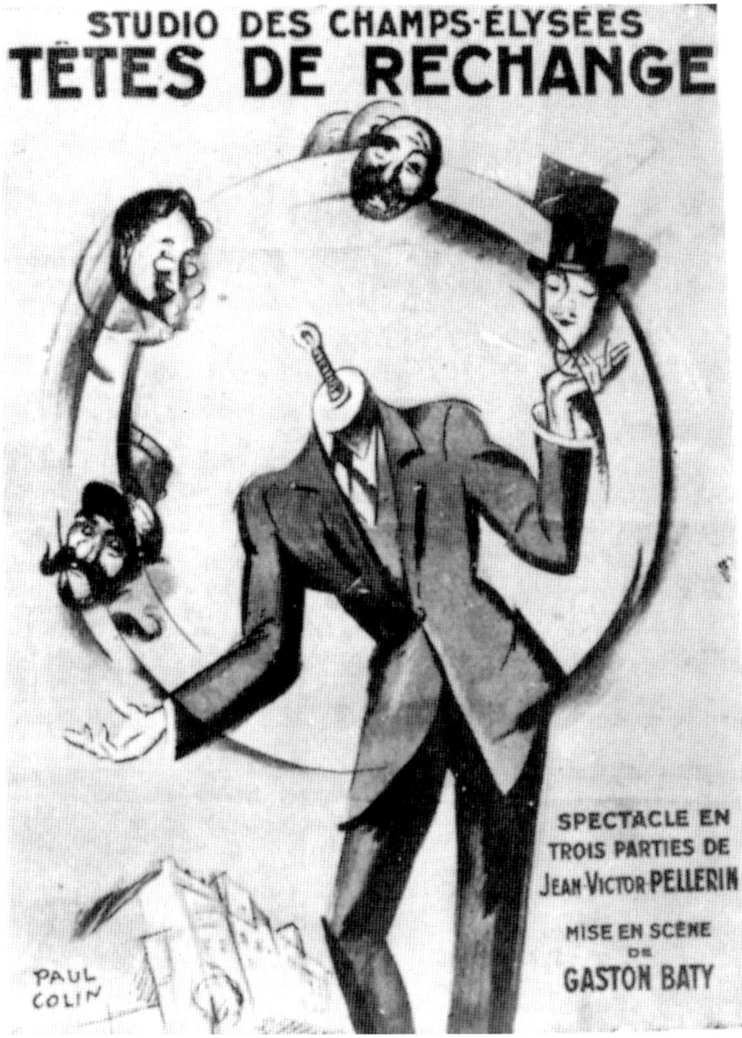

FIGURE 50
Poster for theater production (man juggling heads). In *L'Art Vivant* (1 June 1926), 429.

woman seated there from interacting with the varied images of men behind her. The photograph offers a further twist: even as the advertisement on the bench separates male from female, it joins them by juxtaposing the masculine name "Georges" and the feminine name "Georgette." Gender identities pile up, shift, and transform within this photograph as the viewer's eye moves around the surface, choosing from a menu of visual and textual indicators that stress fragmentary yet still-legible gender positions. Why assume, Kertész's photo seems to ask, that only one type of man is possible if several types of women evidently exist? Like other consumer products, masculinity had diverse meanings by the early 1930s that now rivaled the myriad possibilities traditionally presumed for femininity. The mutilated male was only one of the new forms of masculinity. As Kertész's image of the flower vendor at the *métro* entrance reveals, reintegration of the mutilated male body into a hypermasculinized postwar French culture remained incomplete as the 1920s came to a close. A sense of economic, physical, and psychic desperation permeates these photographs, suggesting that the return to order had failed.

In 1929 the commercialization of male trauma became a more explicit focus of Kertész's work, particularly in a series of photographs of the famously one-legged African-American dancer Clayton "Peg-Leg" Bates (Fig. 51). Bates performed in Parisian jazz clubs in the late 1920s, and his popularity was buoyed not only by the allegedly "exotic" fact that he was black but also by the way his act spectacularly emphasized his body's mutilation. Shot from above Bates's legs and torso, Kertész's photograph focuses our gaze on the join between the performer's thigh and his wooden limb. The image's use of a differential focus makes the viewer keenly aware of the way in which the leather strap holds Bates's stump and limb together, accentuating the space between flesh and wood. With this tight framing, the photograph forces one to contemplate masculine dismemberment at close range. Instead of making the prosthetic limb the object of the viewer's gaze, as does Kertész's 1927 photograph of a limb on a bed, this photograph treats the prosthesis as a supplement so that it can foreground the dancer's special talent. Whereas the earlier photographs of prosthetic limbs either repressed male trauma or suggested its cure, this image spectacularizes an incomplete male body to generate publicity. "Peg-Leg" Bates's widespread popular appeal, and Kertész's commission to photograph his body, shows that in only a few years after the war's end, the traumatized male body had gone from tragic symbol to commercial sensation. The commercialization of dismemberment in this dancer who drew crowds because of his differences from his Parisian audience (not only was he an amputee, but he was black) suggest that by 1929 showing the weaknesses of postwar manhood had become more acceptable than it had been in the early 1920s. Yet this photograph also suggests that Kertész, like Bates's audiences, continued to be intrigued by the imagery of male bodily trauma, although now the picture magazines that Kertész worked for were also selling damaged male bodies to their readers. The German illustrated magazine *Münchner Illustrierte Presse* published several photographs from Kertész's shoot with Bates in 1929. Although this photograph of Bates's leg did not appear in the issue, it did become part of the collection of the well-known surrealist gallery owner Julien Levy as early as 1932.[10]

Although photographs like Kertész's are not usually associated with the surrealist movement, their focus on male dismemberment and their structural oscillation between one reading and another—between spectacular entertainment and traumatic recognition—parallel surrealism's dialectical process of seeing. Thus, considering Kertész's Parisian men within

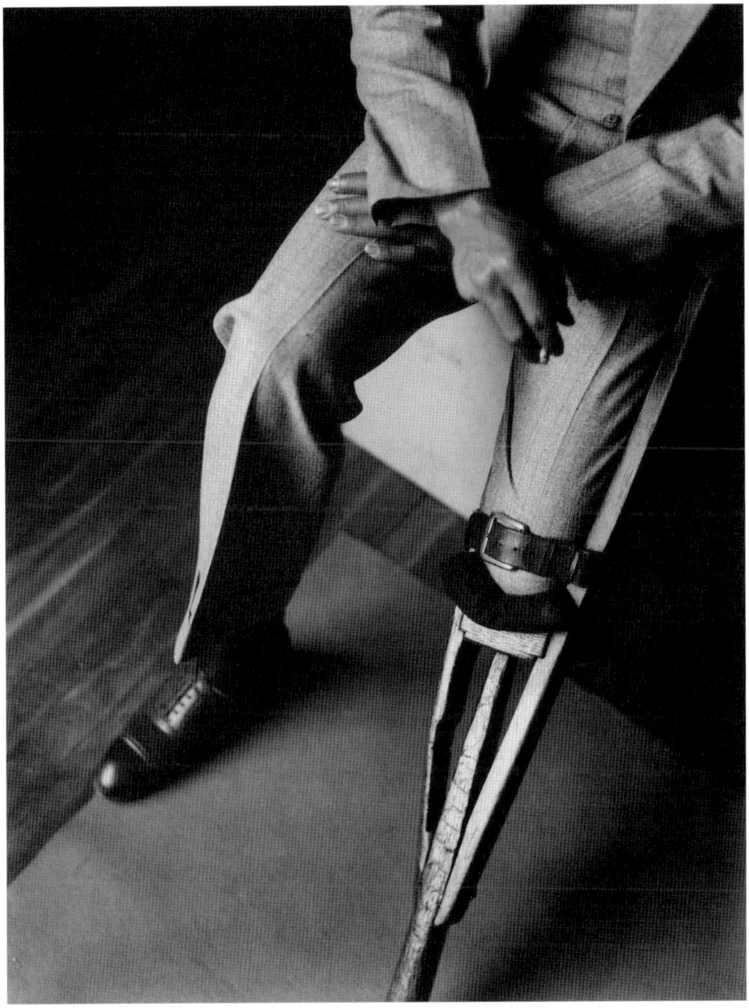

FIGURE 51
André Kertész, *Clayton "Peg-Leg" Bates,* 1929. Photo André Kertész © Ministère de la Culture, France.

surrealism's historical and aesthetic context offers interesting insights. His photographs depict city streets as disturbing outdoor museums filled with objects whose fragmentary natures can catalyze surrealist visual experience. These photographs of men, which he made over a period of years, reflect a surrealist approach in their presentation of the disturbingly physical contradictions within masculinity being worked out in the public realm. In these photographs—the two men along the Seine, the prosthetic leg at rest on a flophouse bed, or "Peg-Leg" Bates's spectacularized prosthesis—Kertész shows that by the late 1920s images of male dismemberment had become not just signs of trauma but also figures of fascination and desire. An image like the one of Bates's leg was not just a snappy ad to remind viewers of the dancer's skill in the face of physical adversity; it might also have prompted viewers to remember the terror of the war lurking behind the exotic pleasures of postwar nightlife. Kertész seems to have realized, however, that he could incorporate his experimental representations of the damaged male body into a more readily salable female form: that of the distorted female body, whose strangeness, following the precedent of surrealist literary and photographic practices of the late 1920s, made it a particularly seductive figure of surrealist desire.

Fantasies of Distortion: Emasculation, Anxiety, and the Marketing of the Female Nude

The Kertész work most often linked with surrealism is his series of photographic female nudes, *Distortions*. The series was commissioned in early 1933 by A.-P. Barancy, editor of the saucy magazine *Le Sourire*, and was accompanied by a poetic text proclaiming the photographs to be a "window open onto the beyond"; six months later several of the "distortions" appeared in the influential illustrated graphic-arts journal *Arts et Métiers Graphiques*.[11] Many commentators disagree with Barancy's description, however, arguing that these female nudes are more like surrealist pinups. Shot at close range with a strange mix of attention to the details of skin and a blurring of the distorting mirror, they read as bodies that exist to be looked at, a fact that encouraged their circulation in *Le Sourire*, a magazine that made money by titillating its audience. Kertész's use of fun-house mirrors to produce these odd female bodies further emphasizes the series' voyeuristic qualities, embedding the process of visual objectification into the making of the photographs: the mirror looked at these women's bodies and reproduced them as deformed.

This objectified sensibility is perhaps not too much of a surprise, for *Le Sourire*'s stock-in-trade was the sale of soft-core erotica. The magazine aimed to excite its viewers with racy articles, images, and advertisements; listings of pornographic films, erotic photographs and bondage apparel, for example, are plentiful in the magazine's classified-advertisement section. *Arts et Métiers Graphiques,* in contrast, aimed to educate its audience of professional designers, photographers, and publicists about design issues, including developments in commercial photography. As we consider *Distortions* as a body of work, we should thus keep in mind the editorial interests of the two magazines; yet we should also consider the genesis and history of these images and their subsequent reception. The series first appeared in 1933 in somewhat truncated form in these two publications. However, when the photographs were published on a much larger scale for the first time in 1976, curators and critics did not describe them as part of a commercial commission. Rather, they presented the work as evidence of Kertész's status as a serious, avant-garde artist. Critic Hilton Kramer claimed that the appearance of these images in 1976 marked the rediscovery of a "hidden chapter" of Kertész's working life and encouraged his readers to see these photographic nudes as "belonging to the same period that produced Dalí's dreamscapes and Picasso's *Girl Before a Mirror,*" a period of provocative surrealist image making.[12]

For Kramer, the distorted nudes "celebrated" their female subjects. But feminist critics of surrealism have countered Kramer's view with persuasive arguments about the images' misogyny, a familiar criticism of surrealism because of its apparent objectification and violation of the female body. In many surrealist representations of women, for example, the model's relationship to the viewer seems to be a "one-way venture," as Mary Ann Caws says, "far from the erotics of exchange, open only to a willing relation of dominator and dominated."[13] However, some works by male surrealists are deeply ambivalent about how to represent their female subjects. One can, depending on the construction of a particular surrealist image, come away with both a positive and a negative image of femininity, Caws suggests.[14] In an important essay on Kertész's female distortions, Carol Armstrong extends the logic of this argument about surrealism's ambivalent approach to the female body by arguing that the distortions simultaneously encourage an objectifying, deforming male gaze and register the models' self-reflexive, self-aware gazes upon their own bodies.[15]

The notion that the distortions reflect an awareness of the models' subjectivity even as they are objects of Kertész's gaze has important links to the history of the photographs' production, although that history has until now been buried in the archive. Scholars have generally recognized that *Distortions* has an antecedent in Kertész's photograph of a male swimmer underwater (1917), in which the swimmer's body is distorted by the shimmering surface of water, and they have assumed that Kertész used fun-house mirrors to distort his subjects only when he photographed female bodies in 1933. My research shows, however, that Kertész first used the distorting mirror, in 1929, to transform the look of *male* bodies. Until now, this key precedent in the use of the male body has been absent from the literature about Kertész's work.[16] Using a mirror nearly identical to the one he would later use for the 1933 *Le Sourire* commission, Kertész photographed himself and his friend Carlo Rim at Luna Park, an amusement park on the outskirts of Paris. The discovery of the glass negatives for these photos depicting distorted men is significant because it changes the series' history and has the potential to change our understanding of Kertész's later work.

Because the distorted males have not featured in discussions of Kertész's 1933 series of female nudes, readings of his later work have tended to point to its inherent violence as proof of its misogyny. Often, scholars cite the female distortions as examples of a possessive "male gaze," because of the directness with which the photographs fragment, fetishize, and objectify the female body (Fig. 52). Although the strangely tortured bodies in this series clearly reflect a phallocentric, possessive gaze, I am persuaded by Carol Armstrong's argument that the photographs' emphatic presentation of the process of picture taking both exaggerates and negates

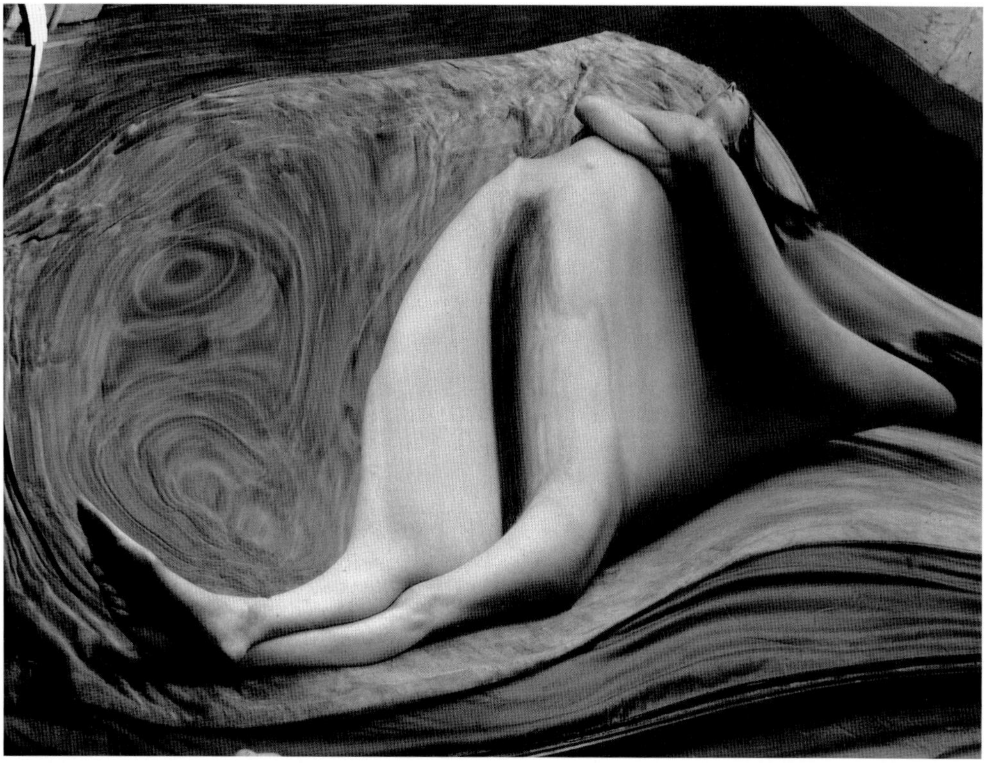

FIGURE 52 André Kertész, *Distortion #148,* 1933. Photo André Kertész © Ministère de la Culture, France.

this male gaze.[17] Armstrong's argument for the photographs' ambivalent perspectives on the female body, which she calls "possessive" and "reflexive" points of view, is supported by the discovery of the images of distorted men. That group of negatives documents a chronological and aesthetic shift in Kertész's use of the distorting mirror's effects. Kertész's distortions of females almost seem to provide photographic disavowal of his earlier deformations of the male body, displacing anxiety about the deformed male body onto the bodies of women.

In many ways, the two distortions series together extend Kertész's earlier approach to the male body as a locus of cultural conflict, social anxiety, and fantasies of emasculation, yet they are very different in look and feel from his documentary-like images of men on the streets of Paris. Both groups of distortions move away from the portraitlike, crisply detailed documents of damaged manhood toward images that make bodies look as if they are inherently deformed (the female nudes) rather than victimized by external degradation (such as alcohol, poverty, and homelessness) or wartime violence (amputation). By removing the streets and cafés that provided context for his earlier images of men, his mirror-based distortion work (although, to be sure, the images of distorted females suffered the most intense contextual cutting) effectively turned the bodies into commodities. Taken together, the two groups of distortions push viewers to recognize that the commodification of trauma crossed the gender divide. Men's and women's bodies had become sources of a voyeuristic, manipulative kind of visual pleasure.

Because the distortions of women were commissioned and published by the mass-circulation commercial magazine *Le Sourire,* we cannot be surprised that one editor saw them as windows onto a world of fantasy and desire. After all, female passivity and possession were a common recipe that marketers used to capture their audiences' attention. In 1933 the editors of *Le Sourire* saw good reason to publish photographs of female bodies that relied on a fetishizing aesthetic, with certain body parts appearing in focus and others blurred or stretched to the point of unrecognizability. If we consider that this strategy was first carried out on men's bodies—especially interesting in that the men in the photographs are Kertész and his friend Rim—what relation might we discover between those early male versions and their later female offspring?

The most striking thing about the negatives of distorted men is that so many of them foreground the men's gazes at their deformed bodies. In a text that accompanied three distorted portraits of himself in an August 1930 issue of *VU,* Rim described his desire to see his body in the process of transformation (Fig. 53): "I want to see the fattest man in the world, the biggest man in the world, the smallest man in the world. They went on vacation, a sailor told me. . . . Too bad, I will offer myself anyway this spectacle at the gallery of distorting mirrors where I will be, for an instant, the Barnum of my own metamorphoses."[18]

Like a catalog of the body types one could see on a visit to the amusement park, Rim's text exaggerates the power of the distorting mirror over his body, even as he relishes the spectacle of his own deformation. He self-consciously imagines himself ringmaster of his own transformation. Yet because the mirrors produced self-images that were less than flattering, this sense of self-mastery was eroded by his obvious lack of control over his image; he was also victim of the mirror's brutal, specular vision. Yet Rim evidently enjoyed seeing himself mutated enough to repeat the experience—granted, as a voyeur this time, and his image is difficult to see in the darkened background of this print—for he attended at least one of Kertész's shoots for the female images in 1933 (Fig. 54).[19]

Several of the distortion negatives in which both Rim and Kertész appear underscore the men's mutual pleasure in the physical changes wrought by the mirror: they appear to greet the changes lightheartedly in contrast to the quiet pessimism of the photographs of male amputees earlier in this chapter. In one such photograph (Fig. 55), Kertész's stumpy, tripod-wielding figure stands in front of Rim's elongated body in a way that heightens the viewer's awareness of a complex circuit of gazes at work in the photograph. At the same time, Rim watches himself watching Kertész take the picture. Kertész's look, which obviously mimics

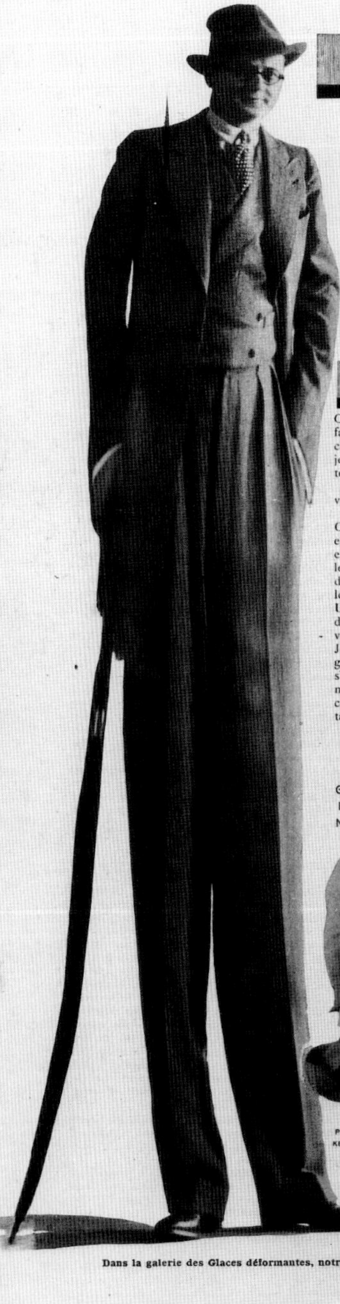

LUNA PARK

OU

LA CLEF DES SONGES

PAR CARLO RIM

PHOTOS KERTÉSZ & UNIVERSAL

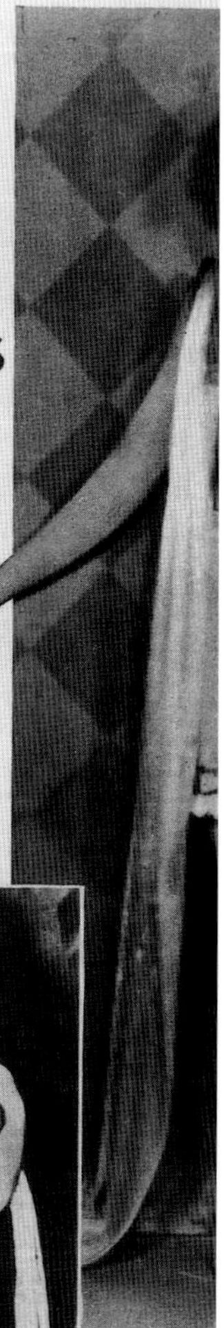

Les drapeaux tricolores ont regagné le débarras d'où ils ne sortent qu'une fois l'an, au 14 Juillet. L'heure des adieux est venue. Leurs compagnons des longs soirs d'hiver, les filets à crevettes, vont s'enfuir à leur tour, mais pour plus longtemps. C'est l'été. Gloutonnes, les valises, vidant tiroirs et armoires, veulent se faire aussi grosses que les malles. Tout à l'heure ce sera le drame des clefs et des billets égarés. La catastrophe finale du train bondé (« — Et je t'avais bien dit de retenir nos places, mais Monsieur n'en fait qu'à sa tête ! »)

Les mouchoirs s'agitent dans le tumulte aigu des départs. Paris se vide à coups de sifflet.

Luna-Park est, pour ceux qui restent, une consolation et un symbole. Ce petit royaume absurde est à l'image du monde raisonnable puisqu'il est aussi fou que lui. Luna-Park, synthèse et caricature de l'Univers, est à la fois aérodrome, gare, océan, montagne, port, autodrome — et les voyages qu'on y fait sont les plus beaux du monde, car ils sont sans durée. Dès le seuil, on est englouti dans la foule hurlante. Cela sent le cambouis, la gomme à mâcher, le magnésium, la sueur, le nougat. Une espèce de frénésie mécanique s'empare de tous et l'on a soudain l'impression que ce sont les "attractions" qui vont s'amuser de nous, jusqu'à satiété. On songe au Jugement dernier, aux abattoirs de Chicago, à la guerre future. L'homme, souriant et docile, s'abandonne à la machine comme on se livre au masseur. Durant deux heures, il sera pétri, bousculé, écartelé. Il aura le droit de monter sur les tables, de marcher sur l'eau ou sur les mains, de

LE GÉANT ET LE NAIN

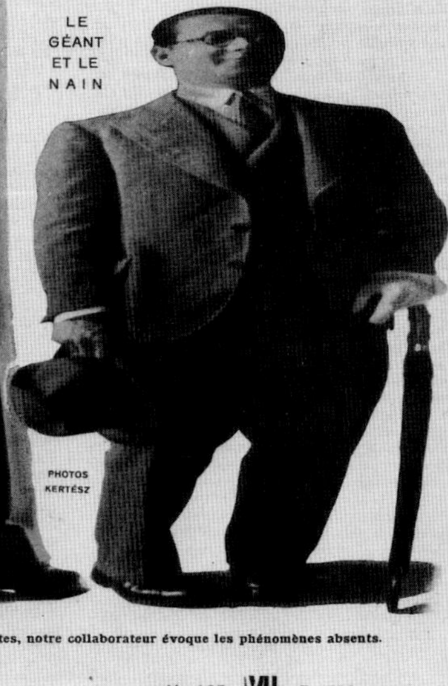

PHOTOS KERTÉSZ

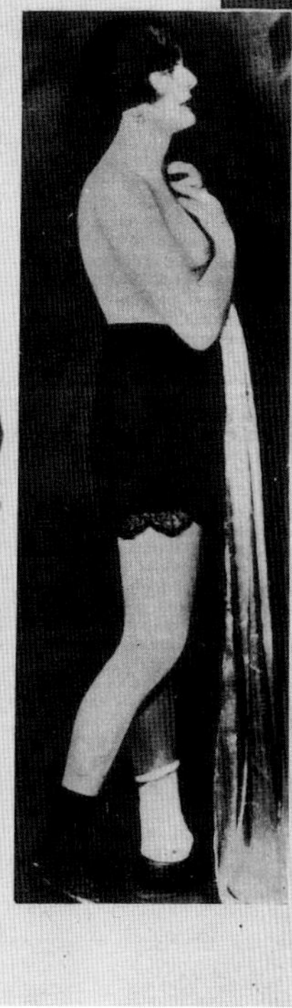

Zinida
est âg
dire E
"mons

← ELLE

Dans la galerie des Glaces déformantes, notre collaborateur évoque les phénomènes absents.

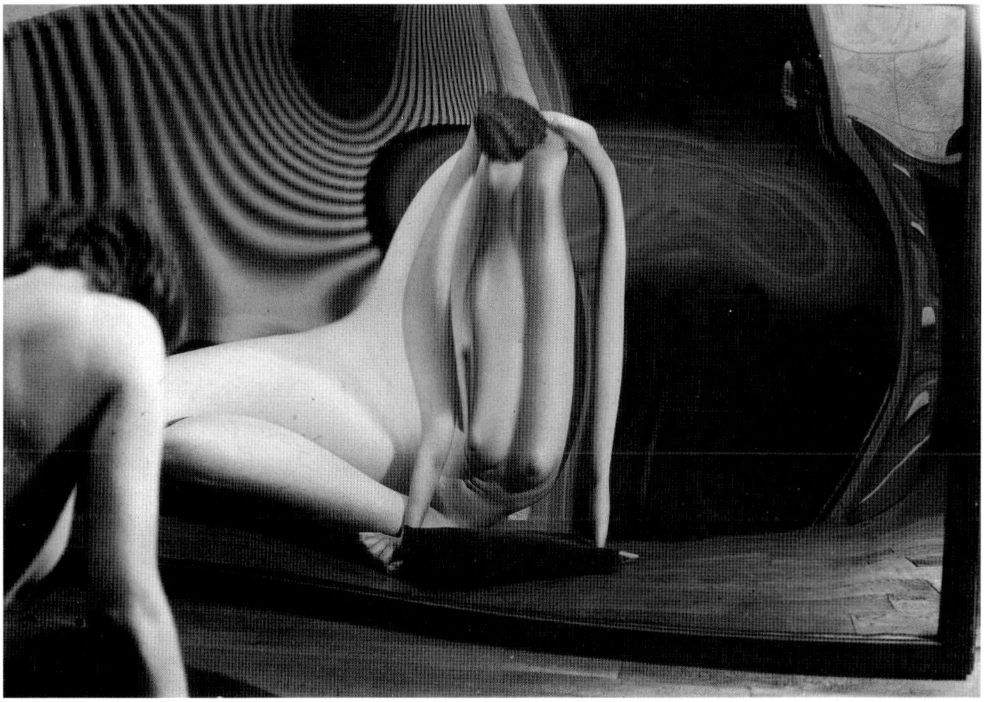

FIGURE 54 André Kertész, *Distortion #39*, uncropped negative, (Carlo Rim and Kertész visible in background to right of model), 1933. Photo André Kertész © Ministère de la Culture, France.

(and is augmented by) the camera's powers of objectification, seems at first to accentuate his mastery of his subjects. Yet Kertész's body, regardless of his apparent control over the camera, is distorted anyway: one foot looks like a scrawny, shrunken stump, and the other appears bloated, with its swollen contours suggesting infection or congenital disease. This experiment reveals that Kertész, too, is victim of the mirror's powerful gaze.

The photographer's presence at the edges of his female model's body in *Distortion #91* from the 1933 series (Fig. 56) suggests a strong connection between the two groups of distortions, documenting the tight relationship they share in the picture-taking process. The presence of Kertész's distorted body in this image reveals that the distorted images of men are in fact the source material for and the generators of the female ones upon which he now trains his camera. Kertész's apparent power over the female bodies he photographs depends, in fact,

FIGURE 53 André Kertész, distorted images of Carlo Rim, 1930. In Carlo Rim, "Luna Park ou la clef des songes," *VU* 125 (August 1930): 786.

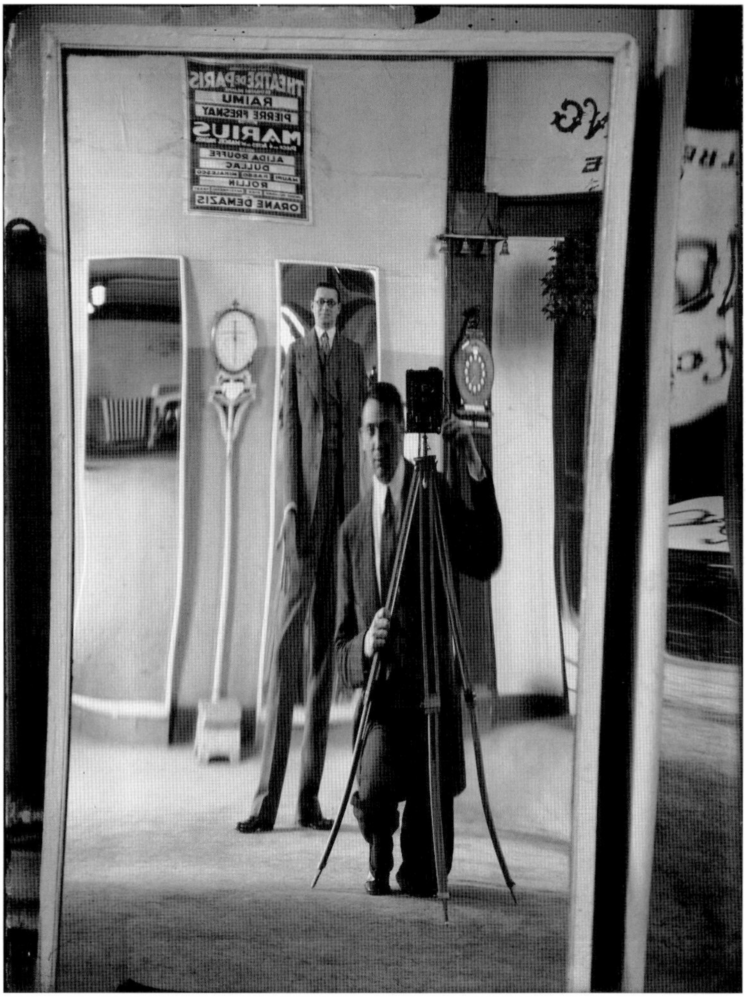

FIGURE 55
André Kertész, distorted image of André Kertész and Carlo Rim at Luna Park, 1929. Photo André Kertész © Ministère de la Culture, France.

upon the ability of the picture-taking process to alter everything it touches; the camera actively deforms the bodies it sees, whether they are male or female. Thus, *Distortion #91* records physical distortion as a by-product of photographic seeing: notice how the inverted representations of Kertész are joined by the tripod's bent leg. Camera and tripod appear at once to extend Kertész's visual control of the world and to deform him. The photograph shows Kertész's body quite literally as a framing device for his image of the woman: he shrinks behind the chair and tripod into the dark ground of the image. At the same time, the nude female figure at the center of the frame expands across the photograph's surface like the star of the show (her body's

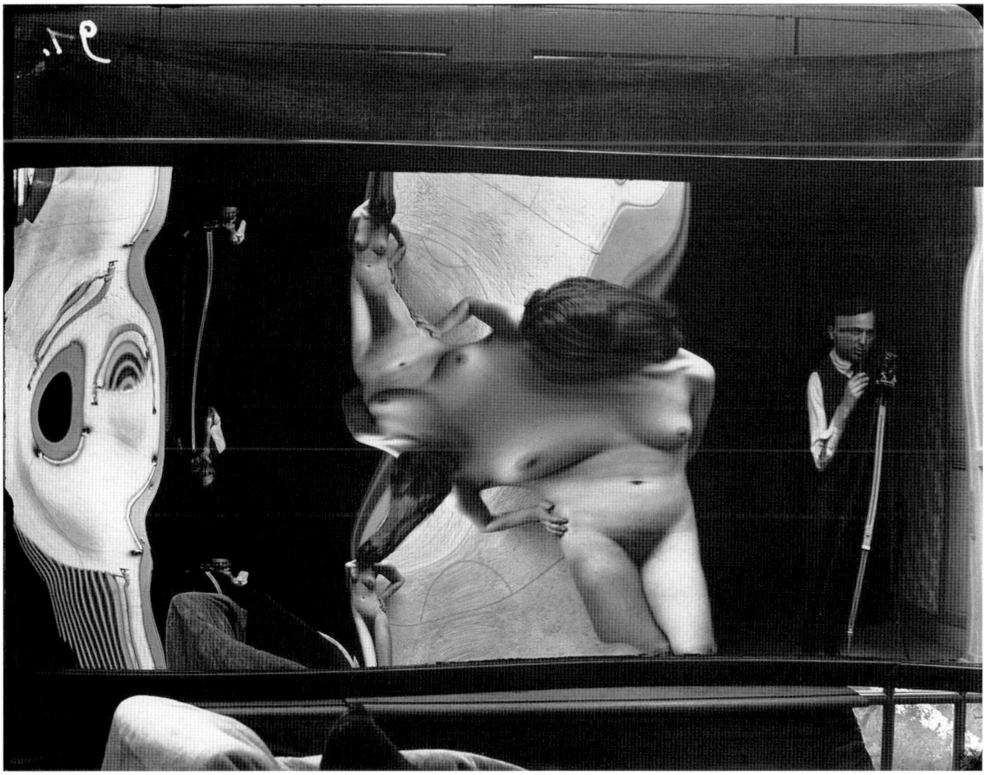

FIGURE 56 André Kertész, *Distortion #91,* uncropped negative, 1933. Photo André Kertész © Ministère de la Culture, France.

expanded shape is also oddly starlike). This reading, of course, does not rescue Kertész from the charge that in this image, he extends the tradition of male artists' mastery of their female models exemplified in works like Ingres' *Grande Odalisque* (1814) or Matisse's *Blue Nude: Souvenir de Biskra* (1907). Crucially, however, in *Distortion #91,* the distorting mirror mutates bodies of both men and women; both Kertész and his model are twisted, stretched, and deformed. Even so, this apparent democracy of distortion falls short of upending art history's conventional economy of sexual power: Kertész wears clothes, and his model does not.

Because we can see the photographic apparatus so vividly in this example, we are reminded that the primary source of deformation is photography, not any innate qualities in the female's (allegedly anatomically lacking) body. Bodily deformation thus appears as an effect of photographic seeing rather than as a statement by the figure in front of the camera. For this reason, *Distortion #91* is a useful demonstration of Kertész's pictorial method. He and his model are deformed together, albeit differently (according to conventional markers of sex and social status). The image preserves traces of Kertész's use of the fun-house mirror as a distorting tool (first men, then women) while maintaining a focus on the female body.

Intriguingly, when this negative was first published in the 1976 book, the photograph was cropped to exclude Kertész's body, effectively erasing the traces of the work's origins in the male bodily distortions that preceded them (Fig. 57). The effect of this editorial work—which took place while Kertész was alive, but which he did in concert with his editors—was not only to accentuate the physical deformity as inherent to the female body but also to hide the fact of male vulnerability (and any resulting anxiety). This choice not only stifled any sense of male emasculation but impeded a more complex understanding of the project's roots in experiments with male distortion.

Indeed, the removal of most traces of the male body's connection to the distortions of the female body (as in *#91*) had a profound impact on people's understanding of the distorted images of females (both then and now). When several of the photographs were published in *Arts et Métiers Graphiques* in September 1933—cropped so that the viewer could not see either the mirror or the photographer's body—the accompanying text ignored the camera's role in the distortion. "The nature of this magic mirror," wrote Bertrand Guégan, "is to vary the systems of distortion according to the way the object changes itself." ["Le propre de ce miroir magique est de varier les systèmes de déformation selon que l'objet *se déplace."*] [20] Guégan's use of the reflexive verb form *("se déplace")* emphasizes the way in which the photographically distorted body-object seems to transform itself under the camera's watchful yet objective (non-distorting) eye. This approach amounts to photographic surveillance, with a subtle twist: according to Guégan, these women participate in their own objectification in ways that suggest they have always been deformed and displayed.[21]

The idea of the female body's allegedly inherent deformation was surely familiar to those aware of Freud's account of the Oedipus complex and the young male child's horror at his mother's lack of a penis. We must remember that Kertész's male distortions reflect wounded male bodies as well as a process in which they appear to take on the physical lack normally associated with femininity. In Freud's story, the little boy averts his gaze from the source of his anxiety to focus on a fetish object.[22] If we consider the history of Kertész's two distortion series as the photographic transference of bodily deformation from men to women, the logic of his choice seems to parallel that in the Freudian narrative (although I can find no evidence that Kertész read Freud at the time). Instead of continuing to make photographs that depicted male lack (as in the earlier male distortions), Kertész began to make photographs that averted the viewer's gaze from that lack toward a fetish: the fragmented, distorted female body. Very likely, the constraints of a market system in which images of deformed men may not have sold very well also encouraged Kertész to leave behind his early experiments to make market-friendly images of women.

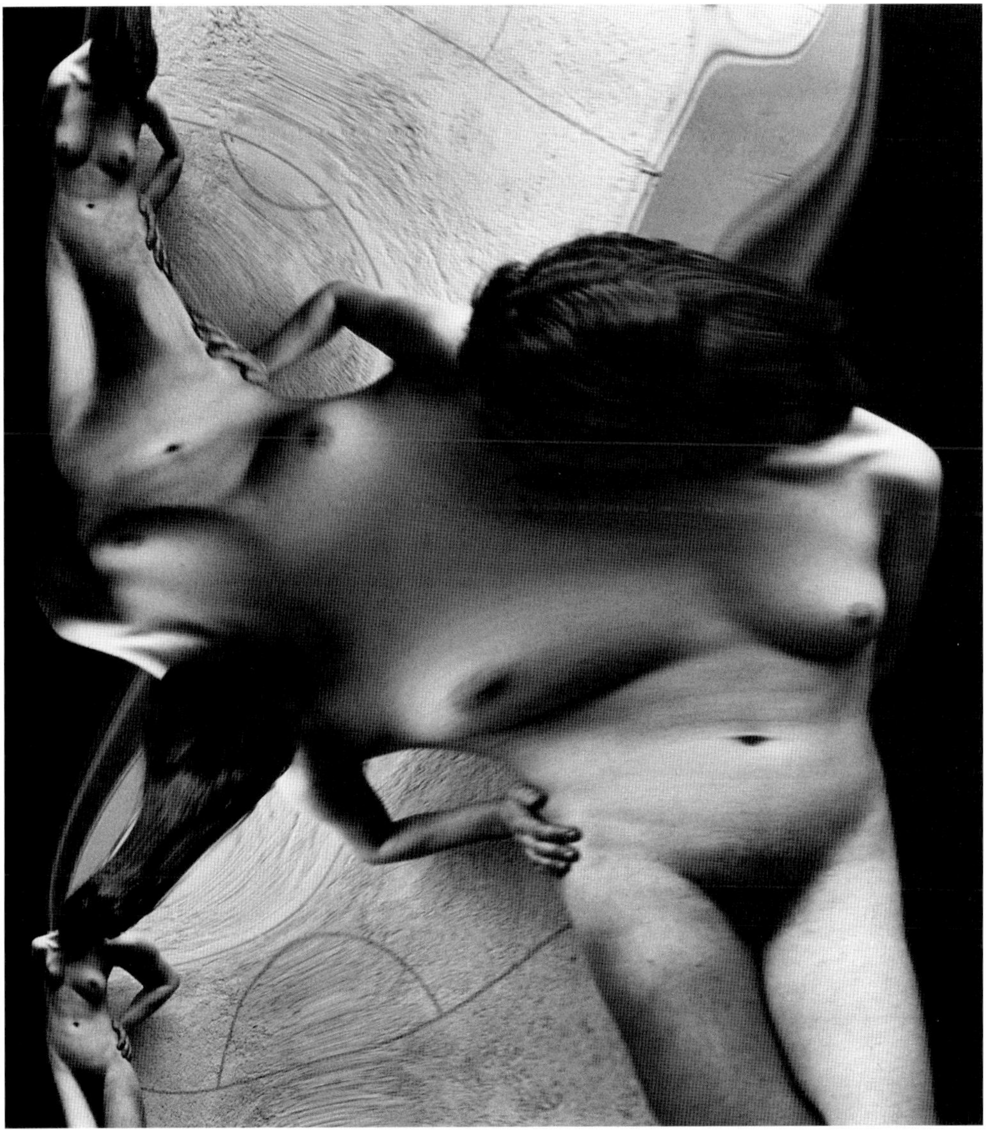

FIGURE 57 André Kertész, *Distortion #91*, 1933. Photo André Kertész © Ministère de la Culture, France.

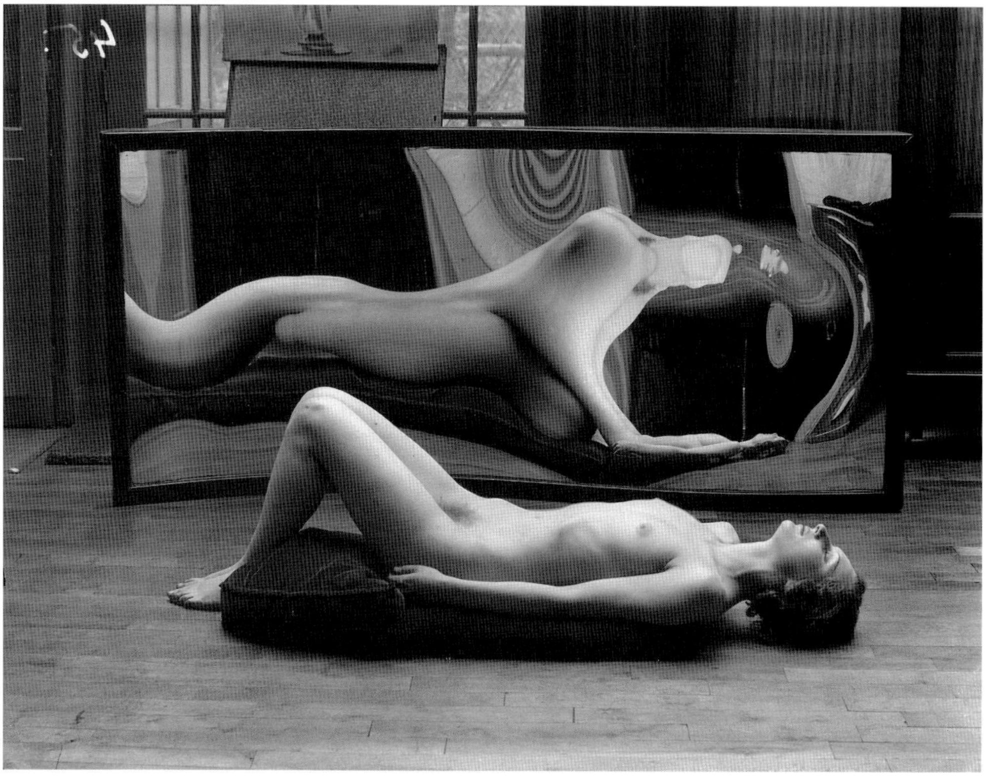

FIGURE 58 André Kertész, *Distortion #45*, uncropped negative, 1933. Photo André Kertész © Ministère de la Culture, France.

Several unpublished glass negatives from the series of female distortions capture the process of turning women's bodies into fragmented objects of delectation—a process that announces itself as a fiction—even though their published form maintained the illusion that the female body is intrinsically deformed. KRT 289V (Fig. 58), for example, vividly documents the distance between the nude model lying on a cushion and the distorted figure produced by the mirror. Stepping back and away from his subject, Kertész shows us the mirror in its entirety, as well as the elongated female body positioned opposite it—effectively laying bare the fact that the distorted bodies are the products of an elaborate studio setup. Compare this staged image to a related image, *Distortion #41* (Fig. 59)—apparently of the same model, from a slightly different angle—in which the space between model and mirror has evaporated, compelling us to conclude that the deformations are emanating from the body itself. The photograph's tight framing of the body thus cuts out the mirror's role and makes the model look essentially distorted.

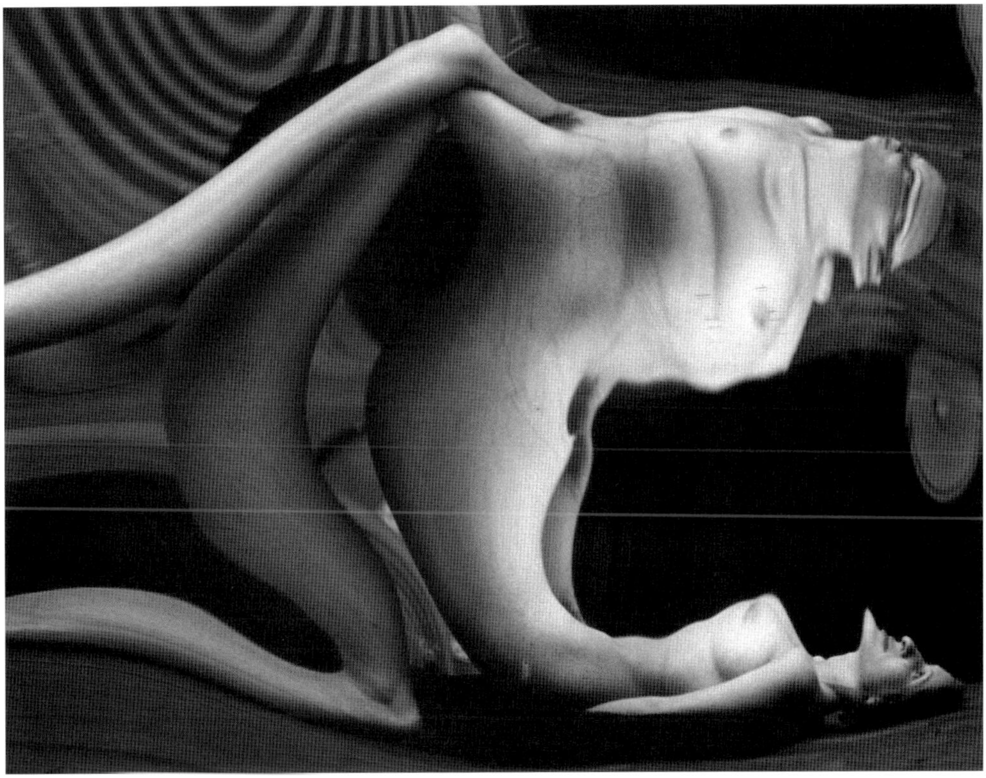

FIGURE 59 André Kertész, *Distortion #41*, 1933. Photo André Kertész © Ministère de la Culture, France.

Comparing the original glass negatives with cropped, published versions of a number of the *Distortions* reveals that editors regularly cut out the mirror's role in making the women look deformed. Instead of exposing the voyeuristic mechanics of the photographer's studio practice, the published photographs repress the body's relationship to the wider visual, aesthetic, and commercial contexts within which Kertész worked. An objectifying gaze folds itself into the female body, and the image's tight framing squeezes self-analysis and potential autoeroticism out of the picture. Lost in this process of pictorial compression is the complexity of Kertész's enterprise, in which both photographer and model might derive pleasure—he, from seeing, and even photographing his own transformations; she, from seeing herself from surprising and unexpected points of view. Moreover, as the space around the bodies constricts to the minimum necessary for their recognition as bodies, Kertész's distortions visually detach the female nudes from their history as descendants of objectified, distorted men. The published versions, in other words, focus one's attention so tightly on those slithery, mobile

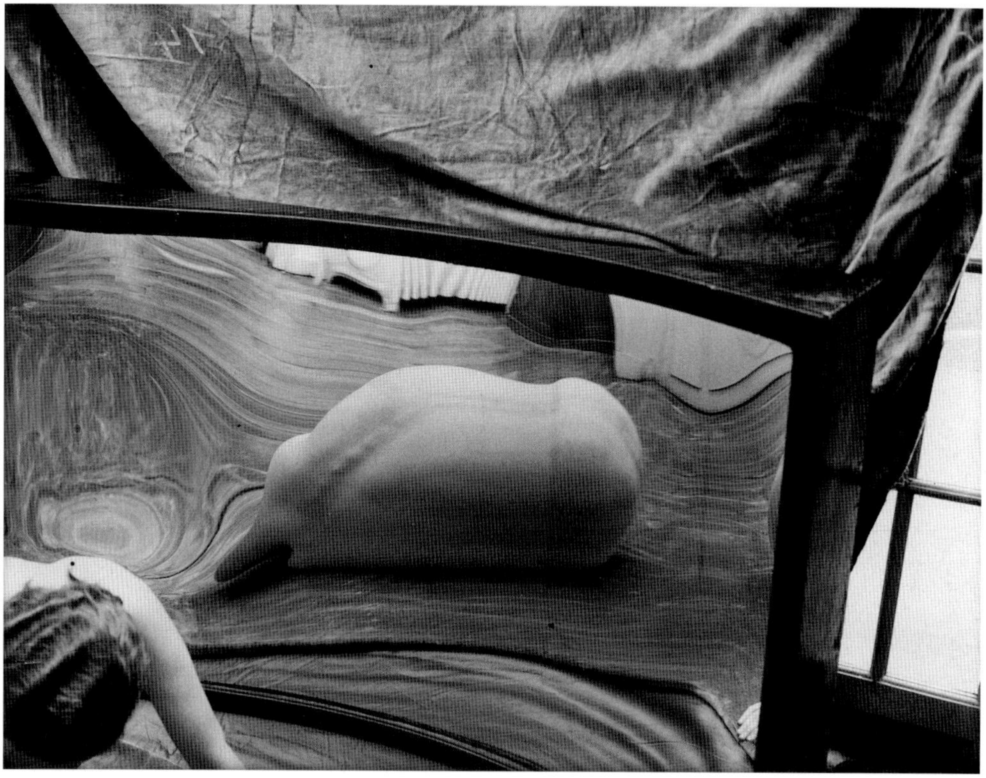

FIGURE 60 André Kertész, *Distortion #143*, uncropped negative, 1933. Photo André Kertész © Ministère de la Culture, France.

women's bodies that accessing their "prehistory" is nearly impossible. This prehistory would show us that anxiety about male deformation was displaced—for commercial, aesthetic, or personal reasons, we cannot tell—onto the bodies of women.

A similar erasure of the image's process of production occurs in a distortion that manipulates the pictorial frame to turn the mirrored female body into a phallus. If we compare KRT 877V (Fig. 60) and *Distortion #143* (Fig. 61), we notice that the model's unadulterated head and shoulder remain visible in the far left of the published image. Yet the uncropped original negative shows us that the mirror and the photographer are the culprits, because the woman's lumpen flesh sits as if contained by the mirror, while her body and the cues about her position within the studio (the cloth draped above and over the window to block out the light from the street outside) in the original negative suggest that she inhabits the studio alongside the pho-

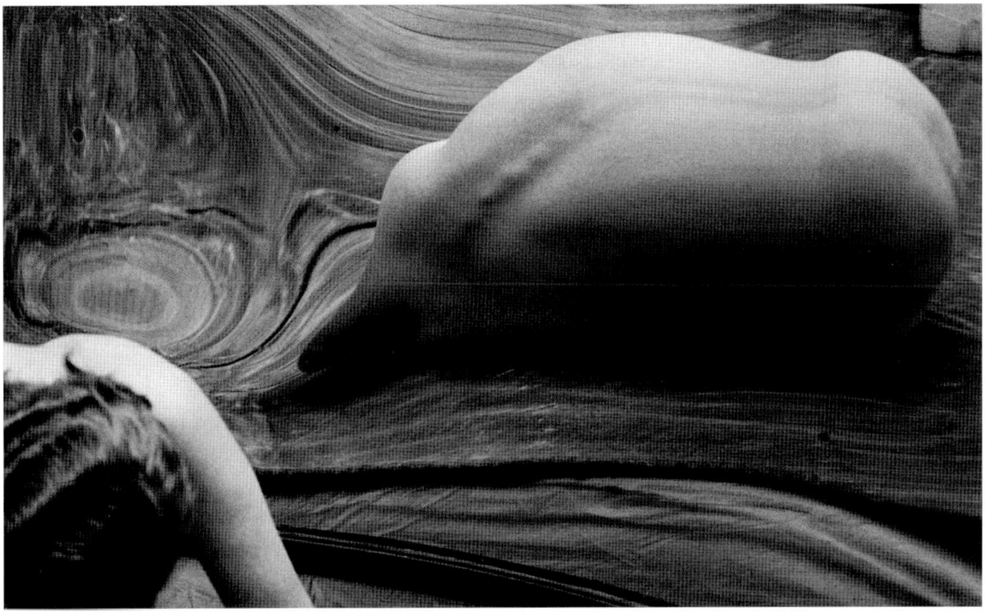

FIGURE 61 André Kertész, *Distortion #143*, 1933. Photo André Kertész © Ministère de la Culture, France.

tographer rather than that she has become the pinheaded, penile form that nearly fills the frame of the published version.

When we analyze the female distortions in concert with their earlier male counterparts, we learn not only that Kertész liked photographing male deformation but that he saw male and female bodies as equally pliant photographic objects. Moreover, reclaiming this "prehistory" of Kertész's 1933 *Distortions* reveals that the facts of male anxiety and deformation were defining aspects of the later female nudes and allows us to consider the idea that the transference of that anxiety from the male to the female body parallels the displacement of male fears about emasculation onto the hardened, unflinching figure of the modern French woman. This hidden history of *Distortions* shows us a series of linked procedures: first, the process of male deformation; second, a recognizable similarity between the deformed male body and its apparently "lacking" female descendant; and third, the publication of images in which the anxiety-producing deformations that were once the domain of the ruined postwar man became essential to Kertész's fantasies about the postwar woman.

An exceptional example of this slippage between male mutilation/lack and the displacement of male anxiety via the distortion of women's bodies is a photograph of Carlo Rim, KRT 2852V, from the 1929 series, that exaggerates and wounds his masculinity (Fig. 62). The repeating stack of torsos accentuates Rim's manhood, taking the shape of a great phallic object. Yet this phallus gapes open: the vertical torso is punctuated by a series of folds (produced by his jacket's lapels) that look suspiciously like the shape of a vagina. By conflating metaphors for masculinity and femininity, the photograph depicts the integral connection between the male body's phallicism and the female sex. Male embodiment (the column) appears to be built from visual evidence of the female body's deformation: the repeating, flared openings that puncture Rim's torso. These openings mimic the imagined cut of castration, effectively turning Rim's phallically organized figure into a symbol of male lack and assailing the male body's usual position of privilege with the threat of physical violation.

The surrealists, as we are by now well aware, were not strangers to male victimization and emasculation. Whether at Val-de-Grâce or in Robert Desnos' meditations on the fragmentary male body in "Pénalités de l'Enfer," fear of emasculation was widespread, and the surrealists took advantage of this fear in their deployment of images of male dismemberment. In a poignant passage from "Pénalités de l'Enfer," Desnos recounts a dreamlike sequence of male anxiety about castration. Thinking that he has raised a gun to get his customers under control, a bartender realizes that he is holding nothing more deadly than his own castrated member: "The barman raised his revolver. 'Raise your hands,' he cried. All the customers obeyed. Only I began to laugh: 'This revolver is nothing but a severed penis; this man is a eunuch.' The barman did not move. I touched it. He put the thing in his pocket and left."[23]

Carlo Rim's expanding yet carved-out torso echoes the anxiety about the status of male power that Desnos' image captures. Standing with short, squat legs and with his umbrella planted firmly on the ground, Rim's figure grows into a phallic form via the mirror's reflection, but it has also become a phallus racked by anxiety about the threat of castration by the female sex. It is both phallus and vagina, a space in which the process of emasculation has begun, yet it retains the traces of its phallic roots in the columnar shape of Rim's repeating figure.

We can see the power of this visual conflation of signs of sexual difference in Rim's repeating torso by comparing the photograph with two similar images of the female body in *Distortion #121* [KRT 856V2] (Fig. 63) and its original glass negative KRT 856VNR0 (Fig. 64). In *Distortion #121,* a cropped, columnlike female torso mimics the 1929 image of Rim as phallus, although this time the image is woman as breast: both figures, in other words, are reduced to their corporeal "essentials" by Kertész's production. Yet in the 1933 version, the body is female, naked, and distorted so as to appear like a headless stack of breasts and arms: the published

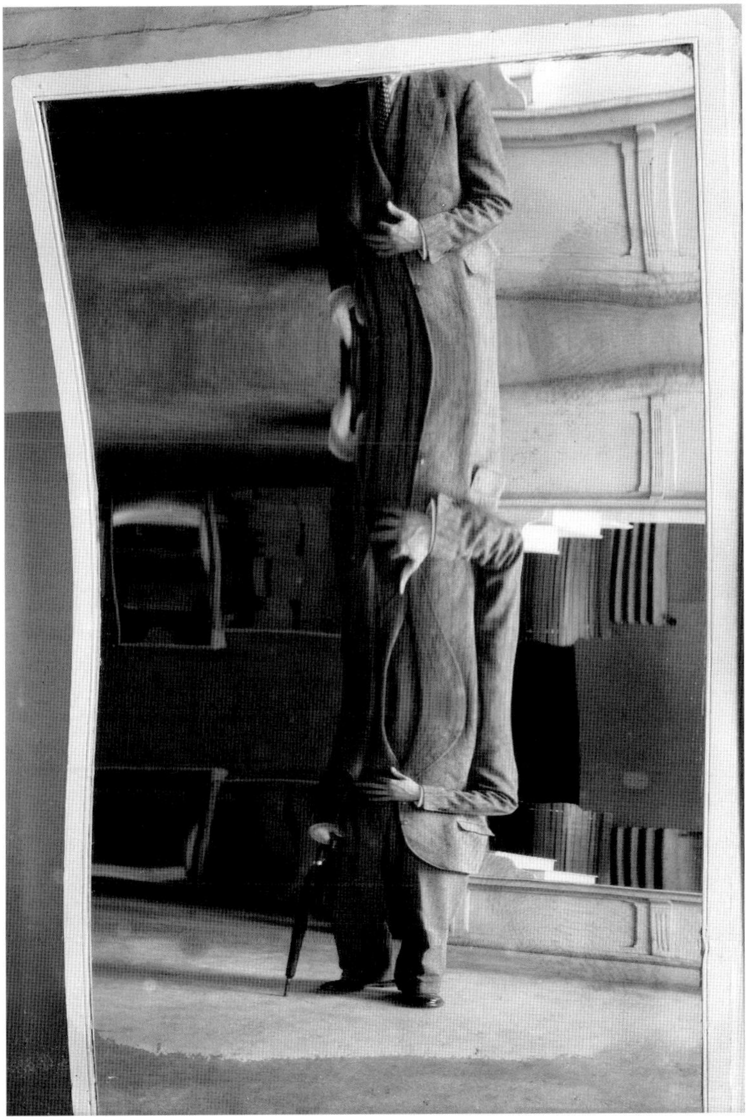

FIGURE 62
André Kertész, Carlo Rim, distortion, 1929. Photo André Kertész © Ministère de la Culture, France.

image has clearly been cropped to accentuate her headlessness (in contrast to the full frame of the glass negative in which heads are visible). Unlike the conflation of phallic and vaginal forms in the previous image of Rim's erect torso, the nude female body in this image reveals no confusion of male and female. Instead, the image pares the female body down to her essential, sex-linked characteristic: the breast.[24]

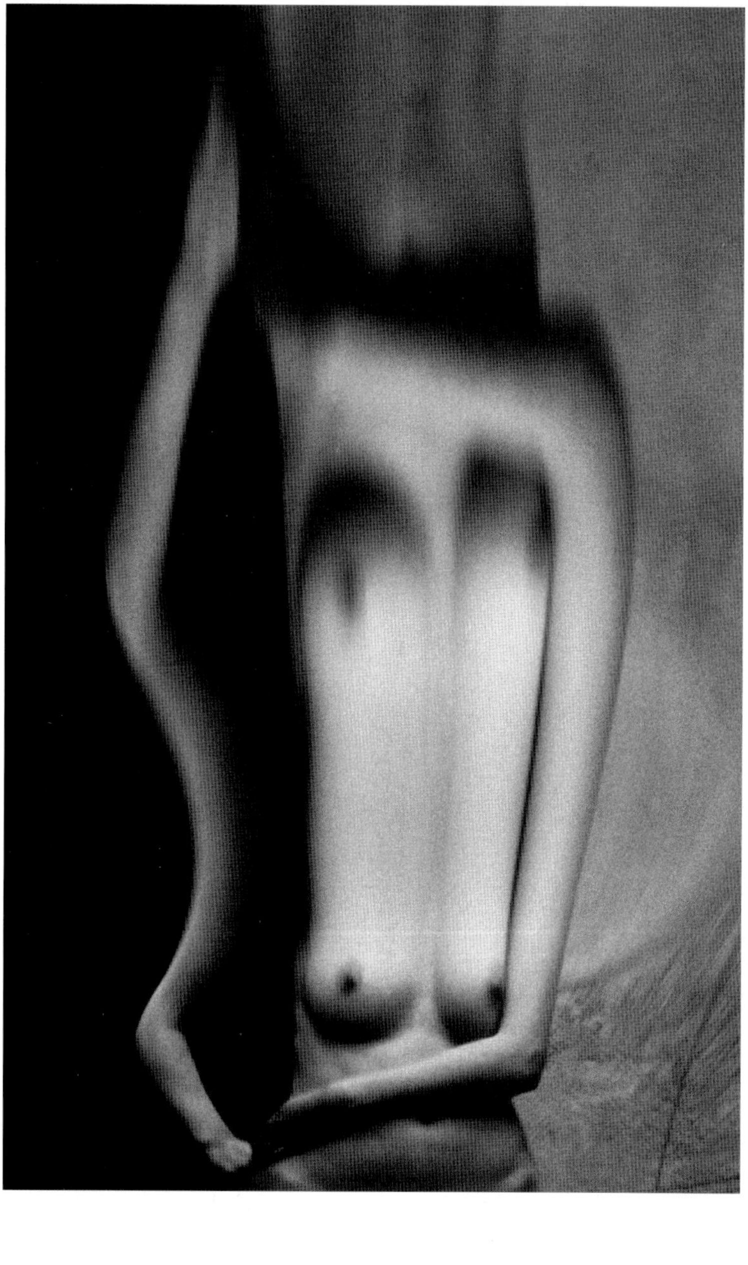

FIGURE 63
André Kertész,
Distortion #121, 1933.
Photo André Kertész
© Ministère de la
Culture, France.

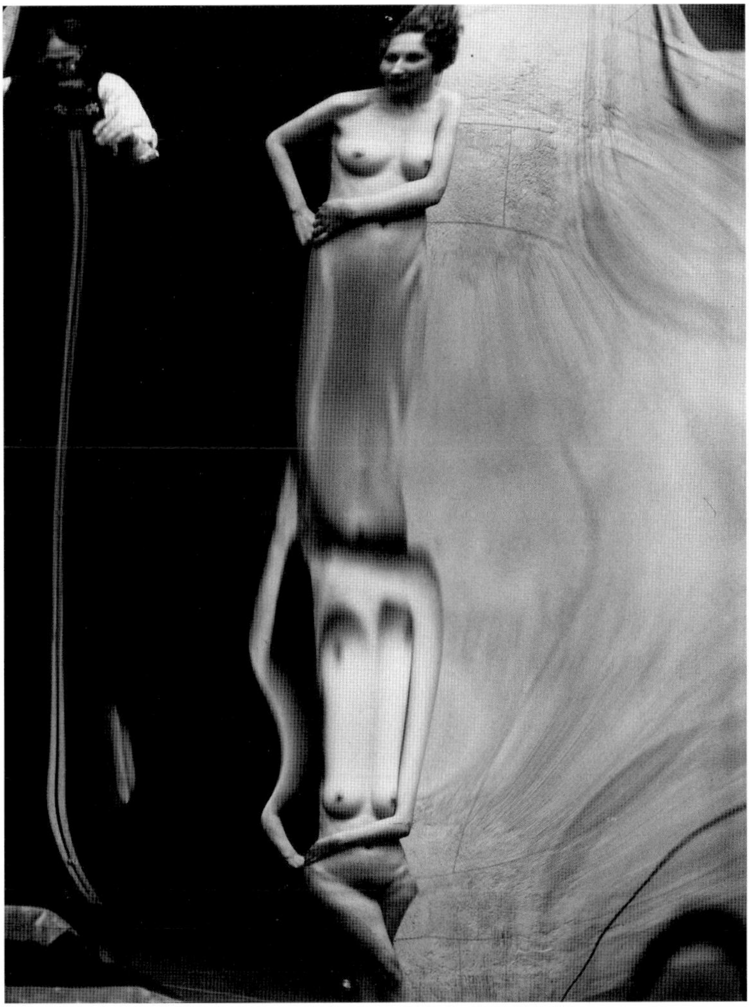

FIGURE 64
André Kertész, *Distortion #121,* uncropped negative, 1933. Photo André Kertész © Ministère de la Culture, France.

The controlling, constraining gaze that permeates the studio nudes of 1933 is a brittle shell of the more fluid (if equally contrived) surprises that Kertész and Rim found when they first looked at themselves in the mirrors at Luna Park. The later nudes codified the initial sense of play and wonder—the experience of grasping the self as another, "deformed . . . yet true," as Rim said—into a studio enterprise whose main goal was to sell pictures that would pique the desires of the readers of a soft-core illustrated magazine.[25] Because Kertész was being paid to make pictures that fit the editorial profile of *Le Sourire,* his 1933 distortions necessarily played to a predominantly male crowd that expected to be aroused rather than disturbed. Now that we can finally see the female distortions alongside their distorted male counterparts from 1929, we can begin to understand why the female distortions affect their viewers so powerfully. Maybe they do their work so well not just because they are grotesquely seductive but also because this seduction is born of, and taps into, men's unconscious fears of mutilation and loss.[26]

⊙ ⊙ ⊙

Because of the documentary impulses of Kertész's photographs—the *mutilés* and other anxious men and the two groups of distortions—we might consider this work to be an effort to produce a *mission héliographique surréaliste*—a quasi-documentary record of the anxieties about and transformations of gender that dominated surrealism's own projects in the interwar years.[27] Although this chapter is necessarily a limited narrative about Kertész's exploration of his male subjects, Kertész's photographs show that Paris was permeated by anxiety about gender identity and the commodification of the individual. If "Peg-Leg" Bates's popularity with his audiences stemmed from his ability to turn the sign of male trauma into entertainment, Kertész's photographs of Bates, Parisian men, and distortions critiqued this transformation. His photographs depicted the *process* by which gender anxiety and male trauma were made over into palatably safe consumer products, new forms of entertainment.

In this way, Kertész recalls another photographer who produced a body of work that both imaged the changing nature of Paris and its inhabitants and took aim at the ways in which industrialization and the rise of industrialized consumer culture were mobilizing that change: Eugène Atget.[28] Kertész, with his vivid juxtapositions of simulated and flesh-and-blood bodies and tightly framed distortions, is an updated postwar version of the surrealists' self-proclaimed photographic precursor, Atget; indeed, the distortions seem to mobilize a structure of seeing that is similar to that in Atget's photographs of storefronts and shop windows. Both photographers represented Paris as a city of commerce, but a city whose streets and shop windows reflected both the promise and the terror of the burgeoning commodity culture. Yet Kertész's images are surrealist documentary photographs in that they fuse empirical observation and subjective experience; his photographs of men document the reality of the Paris street while encouraging the viewer to see the images as if within a dream.[29] Although I argue that we should view Kertész's distortions of female bodies as descendants of his distortions of male bodies, I also imagine them to be relatives of documents like Atget's 1908 photograph *Au Tambour* (Fig. 65). If one were to cut this photograph down to show just the door of the depicted establishment, the image would begin to look something like one of Kertész's distortions: visual indistinctness would overtake the crispness of Atget's descriptive force, and the reflective glass surface of the restaurant's front door would blur and mutate the photographer's own figure and camera. The connection between Atget and Kertész is perhaps most evident in this photograph because of the way that the glass in the door no longer works as a transparent

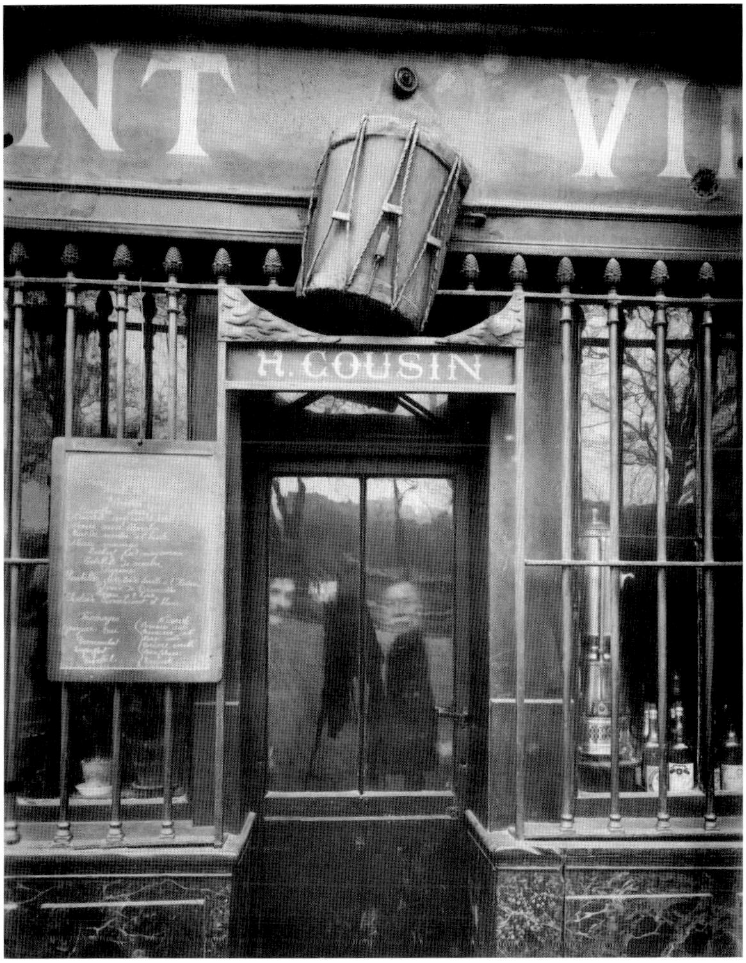

FIGURE 65
Eugène Atget, *Au Tambour, 63, quai de la Tournelle, Paris,* 1908. Courtesy of the George Eastman House, Rochester, New York.

membrane separating inside from out. The window merges with the bodies it depicts, and the camera is sandwiched between them, implicated as the catalyst for the collapse of spatial and corporeal difference.

In Atget's work, however, this type of distortion appears infrequently. More often, his photographs depict the shop window as a metaphor for consumer society, showing how the arrangement of the window's displays aims to attract the passing crowd's attention. In contrast, Kertész's distortions document the process that turns gendered subjects, men and women alike, into commodities. His photographs of Paris men—the amputee, the drunk, the flower vendor, the exotic yet damaged male performer—offer evidence of the incompleteness of the postwar project to produce "new and improved" men for commerce, industry, and social stability. Indeed, these photographs gain power from their emphasis on the contradictions in contemporary advertising's effort to classify various types of men as "brands" of masculinity. The distortions of male and female bodies continue this exploration of gender anxiety and consumer culture by first acknowledging male dismemberment and deformation and then transforming the resulting anxiety into a recipe for commercial success by grafting it onto the bodies of naked women. Kertész distorts his female nudes so that their bodies no longer appear to be deformed by the mirror but are naturally and inherently deformed by the cropping of the negatives for publication.

By confusing the boundaries between the sexes and effectively merging the concepts of male dismemberment and female castration—as in his image of Carlo Rim's vaginally inscribed torso—Kertész imagined a surrealist rebuttal to the rhetoric of a seamlessly reconstructed masculinity. And he did so in a visual language of shock, fragmentation, and distortion born of contemporary advertising and publicity techniques. The visual surprise of these images was a means of capturing the attention of a blasé or complacent audience. In this way, Kertész caricatured not only the selling of new varieties of postwar masculinity, but he also implicitly linked postwar manhood to the allegedly weak and wounded nature of essential femininity. Kertész's anxious or castrated men were anathema to the postwar society, which was bent on rehabilitating manhood with rationalized industrial methods. Whereas the legless flower vendor's rejection by the businesslike young *garçonne* might solicit either sympathy or anxiety, the *Distortions* turned away from men's anxieties about the weak and mutilated state of postwar manhood by imagining that women were the ones who were passive and deformed. We should thus consider Kertész's photographs of men—dismembered, distorted, and otherwise equated with the wounded status presumed of the female sex—to be concrete traces of a hidden male anxiety in his representations of women. The distorted female figures whose tortured, bulging forms disturb us are not just catalysts for male fantasies of erotic power; they are symbols of an ongoing drive to repress male fear of emasculation and impotence.

CHAPTER FOUR

Man Ray, Lee Miller, and the Photography of Surrealist Sexuality

Creeping anxiety about a decline in French cultural morality in the years after World War I often took the shape of a woman: a "loose" or sexually liberated woman, a *garçonne,* a woman who did not want to have a child. She had male counterparts: libertines, perverts, addicts, homosexuals. The war seemed to have violated not only the nation's physical and economic infrastructure but its moral, ethical, and social structures as well. For some, as we have seen, the boundaries between the sexes seemed to be dissolving and French society's sexually differentiated model of human interaction appeared to be eroding from within. France seemed to be, as Pierre Drieu la Rochelle said in 1927, a "civilization without sexes."[1] The nation was "sapped" of energy; it had been "rendered . . . metaphorically feminine, porous, and permeable"; it was a disturbingly feminized place in the wake of the war's violence.[2] Ironically, while such writers described the nation in feminizing terms, they also noted that women were becoming more like men. And men—whether the neurotic, shell-shocked veteran; the pervert for whom the war had transformed his taste for violence into a sexual obsession; or the decadent, effeminate homosexual—were also a topic of anxious conversation. In contrast to hope for the rebirth of a new, healthy nation, the apparent increase in deviant sexual and ethical behavior among both men and women symbolized the republic's decline. Nervousness about the effects of the war on individual conduct and morality not only made deviance and perversion popular topics for the scientific and medical communities at the time. The surrealists, seizing upon this anxiety for their own ends, celebrated its emergence by making images and texts that promoted ambiguous or deviant sexualities. By amplifying the cultural confusion about the fluidity and ambiguity of sex-gender roles in their work, the surrealists made visible the psychologically unmoored, desire-driven society that they hoped would derail the return to social order.

Man Ray and Lee Miller's photographs called into question strictly defined categories of gender, thereby undermining the concept of so-called normal sexuality upon which traditional family ties depended. During the time they worked together, from 1929 into the early 1930s, they created photographs that appeared to revel in eroticism, sexual ambiguity, and perversion. They made some work together; other work, they made apart; at times, one or both made images that spoke to the other's images. Visceral, engaging, and at times conceptually confusing, their photographs consistently tried to stretch viewers' imaginations. Certain images explored the traditional art-historical relationship between male artist and female model. Other photographs disclosed the existence of gender ambiguity and inversion. Still others chronicled and promoted unconventional desires, fantasies, and sex acts that one associates with the privacy of one's bedroom or the underground economy of pornography. Analyzed as a whole, their work appears to be an extended dialogue about aspects of sexuality and sexual identity that appealed to both of them, although sometimes for different reasons. By moving to Paris, Lee Miller, an aspiring photographer and New York fashion model, was able to explore some of the social customs that she and other young women of her day appeared to reject with their cropped hair and independent ways.

An image of Miller's neck (Fig. 66) informs us of the richness and complexity of her collaboration with Man Ray. This photograph seems at first to show the female body in its familiar role as object of the male photographer's gaze. Yet Miller's extended role as model, editor, and printer of the first version of this photograph—a photograph generally attributed to Man Ray—prompts us to study her collaboration with Man Ray more closely.[3]

Their work often promotes the sensation of instability through pictorial oscillations that require viewers to find their own meanings in the photographs. For example, some photographs offer multiple viewing positions to encourage viewers to conflate conventional and unconventional ideas about sexuality. Though Miller was an independent-minded woman and Ray a key member of the surrealist group, their work did not always buck convention. Yet their marshaling of images of the unexpected, ambivalent, abnormal, or perverse defined them as surrealist photographers. And the range of venues in which their work appeared at the time enabled them to explore many aspects of sexuality and eroticism. Although some of their images appeared in surrealist journals or exhibitions, others circulated in limited editions or remained confined to their studios as small work prints or negatives and were never printed. That some images entered the public realm while others remained private highlights the exploratory quality of their work and their own uncertainties about their work's ability to find an accepting audience. The first work to be published tended to view the body with a dominat-

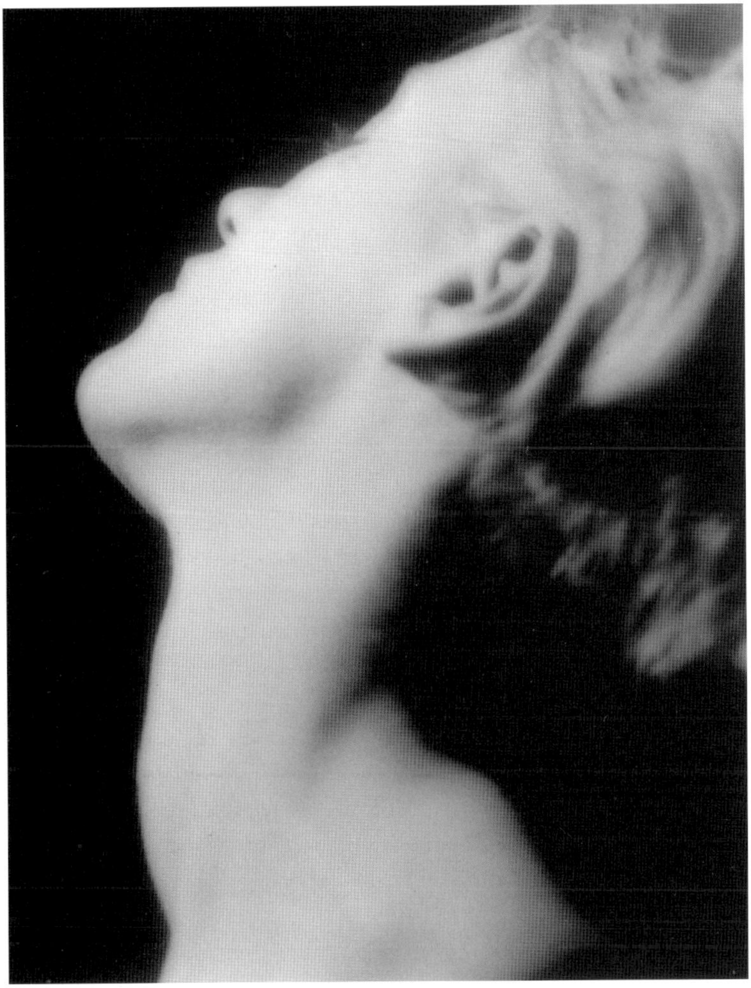

FIGURE 66
Man Ray, *Neck (portrait of Lee Miller)*, 1929. Courtesy of the Lee Miller Archives, East Sussex, England. © 2006 Man Ray Trust/Artists Rights Society (ARS), New York/ADAGP, Paris.

ing or possessive male gaze. Other work, some of which still partook of this gaze, explored alternative sexualities and sexual practices in edgy ways that likely precluded regular appearances in the public realm. In this chapter, I hope to erase the opposition that the art-historical literature typically sets up between two "types" of work by Miller and Ray, because their working methods suggest that they did not see their work as inhabiting either the professional "public" realm or the personal "private" one. By breaching such conceptual boundaries, we can consider that their photographs actually propose several compelling outcomes: the erosion of boundaries between public and private life, accepted and rejected artistic content, male and female identity, and erotic and perverse desire. To see such connections between these diverse bodies of work is to recognize that the photographs also neutralize our ability to render an image either "appropriate" or "inappropriate" to surrealism; we have to adopt multiple viewing positions that in turn encourage multiple definitions of surrealism. Because Ray and Miller were inconsistent in the way they imaged sexual difference and sexual practice, they seem to have been more interested in exploring options for an erotically challenging personal life than in codifying surrealist sexuality. And though some critics and historians continue to divide these artists' work into categories (for ease of analysis, one imagines), causing this inconsistency to fade from view, we can agree on the impact of their diverse and interlinked bodies of work: Their photographs recorded alternative concepts of sex, gender, and desire that made some viewers uncomfortable and that the promoters of a morally certain return to order were at pains to ignore.

Picturing Lee Miller

The biographical writing on Lee Miller and Man Ray shows that their collaboration has been central to their reputations and that their reputations depend on conventional ideas about the way gender shapes an artist's life and work. Although some of their most widely published photographs seem to reject rigid categories of sexual difference and artistic identity (Figs. 73 and 74), the bulk of the published monographs about the pair rely on the type of sexualized perspective that is common in the literature about male and female artists.[4] The first published interview with Lee Miller, "My Man Ray" (1975) in *Art in America,* exemplifies this approach. The interview is illustrated with a large Man Ray profile portrait of Miller that exaggerates the photographer's control of his model by depicting her body as a product of his hand (Fig. 67).[5] The thick black line that traces the contours of her head and neck is the result of the solarization technique that Man Ray commonly used in his surrealist work. Thus, both the title of the interview and the image chosen to represent Miller's voice reinforce her work's intimate connection to Man Ray's reputation. The explicit references to Man Ray throughout the interview rehearse a fact familiar to anyone who has conducted research on women artists: that women's art gains prominence through its association with men's and that male artists' reputations usually depend on perceptions of their sexual power over women and their ability to create important work.

The most widely accepted (and often-repeated) story about Man Ray and Lee Miller's collaboration is one about their first meeting in 1929. As Miller's biographers tell the story, she traveled to Paris hoping to meet the well-known surrealist photographer Man Ray. She then sought him out in one of his favorite cafés and informed the nonplussed Man Ray that she was his new photographic assistant. He resisted her efforts to work with him, but she refused to take no for an answer. Soon after, she moved in with him, at which point, the story goes, their tur-

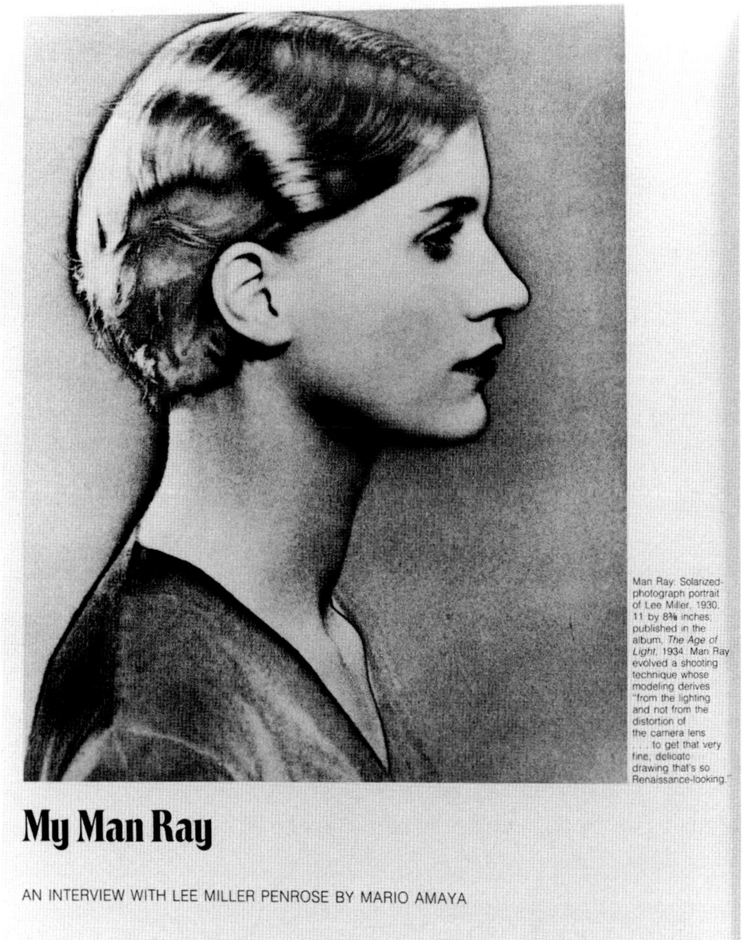
Man Ray: Solarized-photograph portrait of Lee Miller, 1930, 11 by 8⅜ inches; published in the album, *The Age of Light*, 1934. Man Ray evolved a shooting technique whose modeling derives "from the lighting and not from the distortion of the camera lens . . . to get that very fine, delicate drawing that's so Renaissance-looking."

My Man Ray

AN INTERVIEW WITH LEE MILLER PENROSE BY MARIO AMAYA

FIGURE 67
Man Ray, solarized profile portrait of Lee Miller, 1930. In Mario Amaya's interview with Lee Miller, "My Man Ray," *Art in America* 63 (May–June 1975): 54. © 2006 Man Ray Trust/Artists Rights Society (ARS), New York/ADAGP, Paris.

bulent collaboration began. Although Miller later took an apartment so that she could make her own work, starred in a Jean Cocteau film (*Blood of A Poet*, 1930), and eventually moved back to New York in 1932 to start her own photography studio, art historians have consistently defined her surrealist credentials by her proximity to Man Ray: her connection to him afforded her access to the male-dominated surrealist circle.[6]

Ray and Miller apparently invented the technique of solarization together—a technique that rapidly came to represent a specifically surrealist look in the early 1930s—and this collaboration has bound them together in the published record. In describing this discovery, most writers use highly coded, gender-specific language. Miller, ever the beautiful younger woman, plays the passive role to Man Ray's active one. Her role as the "unconscious" female contrasts with Man Ray's rationalist control of the new process. In the 1975 interview, Miller remembered the event in this way:

> Something crawled across my foot in the darkroom and I let out a yell and turned on the light. I never did find out what it was, a mouse or what. Then I quickly realized that the film was totally exposed: there in the development tanks, ready to be taken out, were a dozen practically fully-developed negatives of a nude against a black background. Man Ray grabbed them, put them in the hypo and looked at them later. He didn't even bother to bawl me out, since I was so sunk. When he looked at them, the unexposed parts of the negative, which had been the black background, had been exposed by this sharp light that had been turned on and they had developed, and came right up to the edge of the white, nude body. But the background and the image couldn't heal together, so there was a line left which he called a "solarization."[7]

Although Miller was knowledgeable about the technical aspects of photography, she deemphasized this aspect of her practice, even when asked about it years later. She instead cast her own behavior as that of a "typical woman" whose fear of mice unleashed the technique for which Man Ray would become famous.

Nonetheless, Miller's account also subtly records her role in the discovery. Although she underscores Man Ray's active role, her description records the experience of seeing the solarized image as a first witness. "When he looked at them," she reports, "the unexposed parts of the negative, which had been the black background, had been exposed by this sharp light that had been turned on and they had developed, and came right up to the edge of the white, nude body." Although she clearly uses the pronoun *he,* her words remind us of her presence as a collaborator who recognized the stunning visual effect of the velvet-black thickening at the edge of the nude, an effect with which she, too, experimented.

Later in the interview, Miller turns the conversation back to the origins of solarization to highlight Man Ray's role as a pioneer. "About the solarizations, it was all very well my making that one accidental discovery," she interjected (nearly interrupting the interviewer to make her point). "But then Man had to set about how to control it and make it come out exactly the way he wanted to each time."[8] Miller presents Man Ray as the master of the new technique, a calculation that necessarily limited her ability to attain creative authority. Antony Penrose argues that this deference to Man Ray's abilities proves the depth of Miller's interest in fostering an environment of collective productivity. Yet one could also argue that Miller's words evidence her desire to gain professional visibility by highlighting her relationship with Man Ray and to show (albeit in a conventional and gender-coded way) that she was an integral part of the process. Miller grasped the traditional role held out to her and used it to clearly define herself as Man Ray's artistic muse so that she, too, could become a player within the surrealist group.[9]

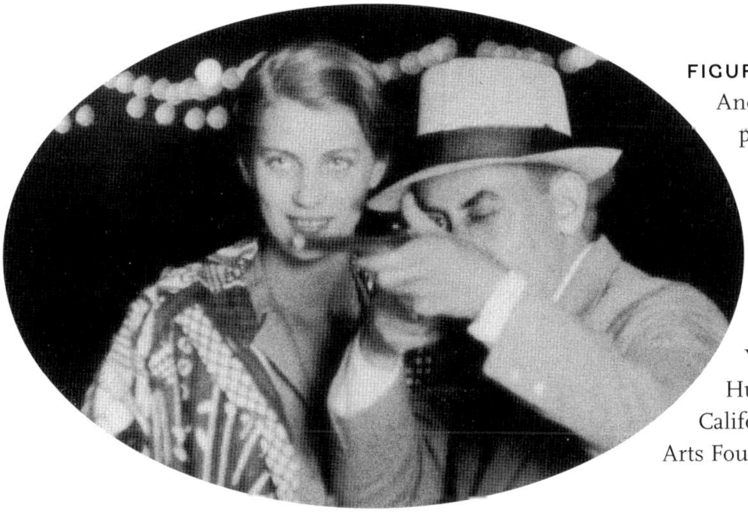

FIGURE 68
Anonymous, photograph postcard of Lee Miller and Man Ray at a Paris fair. Published on an interior title page in Jane Livingston, *Lee Miller: Photographer* (New York: Thames & Hudson; Los Angeles: California/International Arts Foundation, 1989).

Sadly, she erased her presence in their shared studio in concrete ways as the years passed, notably by destroying a large part of her work from the years in Paris.[10] Because of that destruction, historians have linked the few works that remain from her years in Paris even more closely to Man Ray's position as the surrealist house photographer.

Man Ray again receives credit for shaping Miller's artistic identity on the title page of the catalog for the first retrospective exhibition of Miller's work in 1989, a show that introduced her practice and ratified its importance to twentieth-century art by coupling the two photographers (Fig. 68).[11] A photograph of the two at an amusement park at the beginning of the catalog mimics the structure of Miller's biography, presenting Lee Miller as Man Ray's social companion. Similar pairings have appeared in Man Ray's work. However, in one example depicting Ray, Miller, Max Ernst, and his partner, Marie-Berthe Aurenche, the link between female muse and male artist is inverted and replicated across two surrealist couples (Fig. 69). The image upends the conventional hierarchies of heterosexual surrealist coupling: the two women in the group, Miller and Aurenche, take control of the creative process by grabbing hold of their male partners. This image refreshingly depicts surrealist women as more than models or muses; here they act for themselves, exploring the boundaries of surrealist identity by manipulating the movement's usual sexual protocols, and they do so with their boyfriends' visible approval. Yet as the growing scholarship on surrealist art and literature reminds us, women within the surrealist movement were viewed primarily as catalysts for male discovery or as the objects of male fantasy rather than as artists in their own right. Although a number of women had begun participating in surrealist activities by the late 1920s and early 1930s, many of them, like

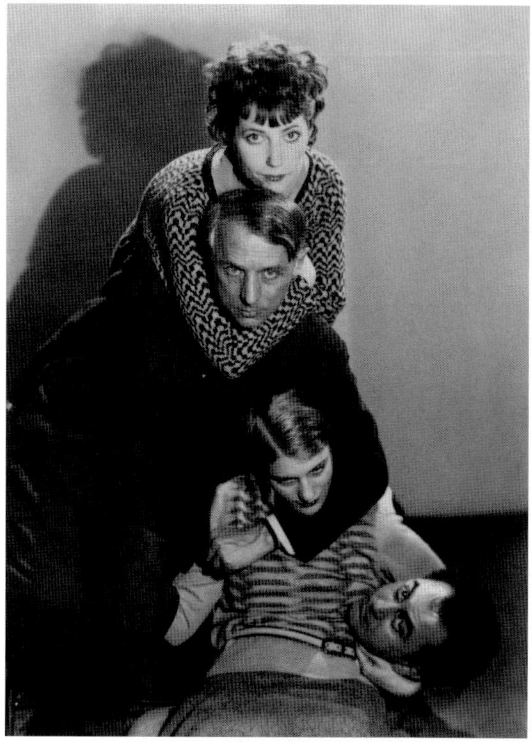

FIGURE 69
Man Ray, *Marie-Berthe Aurenche, Max Ernst, Lee Miller, Man Ray*, 1932. Courtesy of Telimage, Paris. © 2006 Man Ray Trust/ Artists Rights Society (ARS), New York/ ADAGP, Paris.

Miller, gained access to the group initially through "typical" domestic attachments—as lovers or wives of the male surrealists—not by virtue of their work alone.

Miller apparently understood the need to make such a tradeoff—assuming the role of muse rather than taking charge as an artist—to achieve the status of a surrealist photographer. She undertook a complex negotiation of her position with respect to Man Ray that included artistic innovation as well as critique and compromise. That she did so within a collaborative relationship that strained under the weight of its inconsistent mixture of antiestablishment ideals, feminist impulses, and misogynistic behavior is crucial to an understanding of her work. It is also key to making sense of Man Ray's work. The tensions about gender, sexuality, and artistic identity in their collaboration pushed them both to produce some of their most compelling surrealist photographs. The element that is hard for us to remember today is their images' refusal to recognize any difference between public and private lives in representing sex.

Conversing with Surrealism

Lee Miller saw the contradictions in surrealism's approach to gender politics and sexual identity from a position at the edges of the male surrealist group. And as Susan Suleiman has pointed out, the surrealists in general (among other male avant-gardes) cultivated a similar stance in relation to the mainstream cultural milieu.[12] And much as the surrealists critiqued the dominant culture, Miller often carried on a dialogue with Man Ray's images of women in her work. Using her own visual language, she reformulated his images of female (dis)embodiment. Although she relied upon Man Ray's status for her place in the surrealist milieu, she also challenged his role as a typically controlling male artist by depicting femininities that successfully evaded the more familiar forms of objectification and fetishization for which he is best known. In one instance, in 1929, she subverted the logic of a particularly misogynistic image that Man Ray had made of her by appropriating the image for her own purposes. After retrieving a negative he had thrown away—the image he'd shot of her neck tipped back at a disorienting, twisting angle (see Fig. 66)—she printed it on her own and usurped his authorship.[13]

After this transgression of his artistic authority, Man Ray's opinion of Miller's surrealist identity changed rapidly. He reportedly erupted with rage when Miller claimed that the image had become hers once she selected and printed it, and he kicked her out of the studio. Upon her return, she found the print pinned to the wall, the image of her distended throat slashed by his pen and dripping with the blood-red ink of a fountain pen.[14] He quickly, and publicly, recast their relationship along gendered lines: he published the photograph as his own in a special issue of the design magazine *Arts et Métiers Graphiques.* In addition, the photograph appeared just after a fashion portrait he had taken of her.[15] Because readers did not know the image's complex parentage at the time of its publication, Man Ray's effort to reclaim the photograph publicly is revealing. It was his way of putting Miller in her place as his model rather than acknowledging her as his photographic rival.

Although Man Ray apparently wanted to reclaim control over Miller's photographic incursions into his practice, she continued to appropriate aspects of his work for her own artistic ends. She wanted to gain surrealist status, and one way she did so was to insert herself in the long-running and visible photographic dialogue that Man Ray had been conducting for years with his friend Marcel Duchamp. The relationship between Man Ray and Duchamp was important for both men, particularly in their well-known collaboration on the creation of Duchamp's female alter ego, Rrose Sélavy (Fig. 70). Man Ray photographed Rrose regularly during the 1920s, and as late as 1934, he included a text of hers, "Men Before the Mirror," in his first published monograph. Although Rrose was actually Duchamp in drag, the text she wrote for Man Ray's book of photographs exposed an image of surrealist masculinity that was embodied, sensate, and grounded in the physical world—just like a "typical" woman:

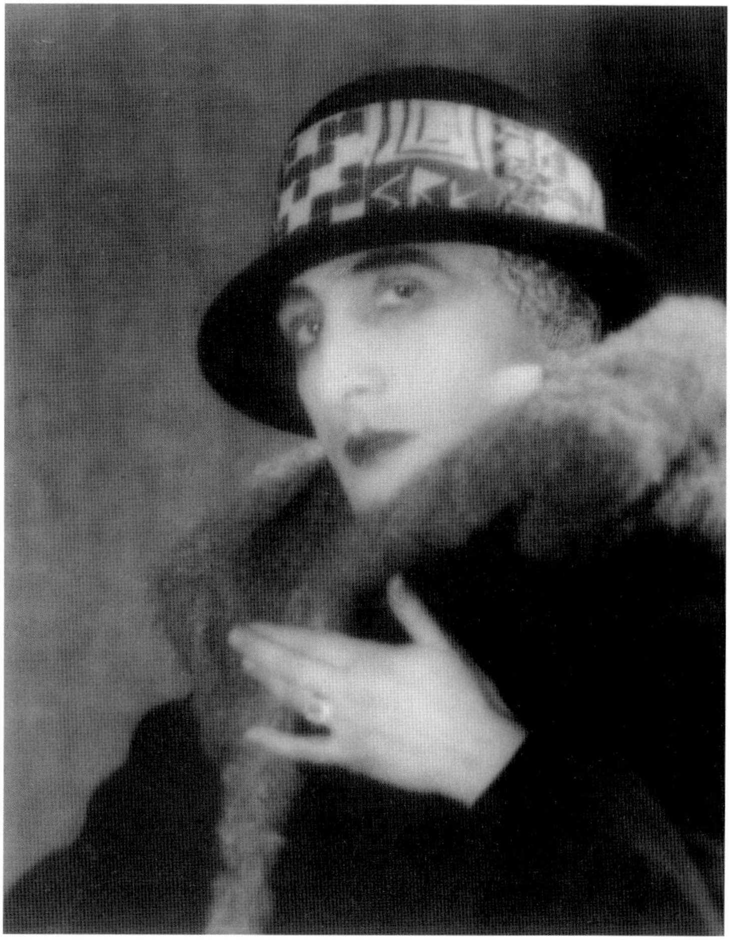

FIGURE 70
Man Ray, *Rrose Sélavy (Marcel Duchamp)*, 1923. The J. Paul Getty Museum, Los Angeles. © 2006 Man Ray Trust/ Artists Rights Society (ARS), New York/ ADAGP, Paris.

Slim hands with long fingers or short, that grasp forth. The nape of a neck that rises steeply to lose itself in the forest's edge of the hair, the tender curve of the skin behind an ear, the mysterious mussel of the navel, the flat pebbles of the knee-caps, the joints of their ankles, which a hand envelops to hold them back from a leap—and beyond the farther and still unknown region of the body, much older than it, much more worn, open to all happenings: this face, always this face which they know so well. For they have a body only at night and most only in the arms of a woman. But with them goes always, ever present their face. The mirror looks at them. They collect themselves. Carefully, as if tying a cravat, they compose their features. Insolent, serious and conscious of their looks they turn around to face the world.[16]

Rrose's words construct an image of manhood that is dramatically physical: sensual, pleasurable, and embodied. Through visually allusive language that asks the reader to imagine touching the male body in various places, Rrose's male body becomes a series of concrete, earthbound forms. For her, men's bodies are bound to the tactile, objectified realm usually reserved for women: their navels are mussels to eat; the napes of their necks, like cool forest glades. The prominence of male sensuality in this passage undermines traditional ideas about masculinity's presumed connection to rationality and the life of the mind. And like women, Rrose's men are objects of the gaze (in this case the female gaze); they have begun to recognize that their masculine identities are perhaps nothing more than elaborate public masks.

If Rrose's description of men before the mirror reflects a stereotypically feminine emphasis on the body, one of Man Ray's photographs of Duchamp with shaving cream on his face underscores the key role of gender in their man-to-man collaboration (Fig. 71). Man Ray exaggerates Duchamp's manhood by ironically photographing his face covered with peaks of shaving cream. As if offering a counterproposal to the feminization of Duchamp's body in his guise as Rrose, these images seem to reclaim traditional masculinity (through the superficial signal of shaving) while also drawing attention to machismo as hyperbole through the vast amounts of shaving cream enshrouding Duchamp and through his devilish appearance.

In 1929, to insert herself directly into the Man Ray–Duchamp collaboration, Lee Miller recreated the two men's earlier shaving-cream collaboration by depicting Man Ray shaving (Fig. 72). The effect of this appropriation is twofold. First, Miller equates her work to Man Ray's by mimicking the content of his earlier images of the cream-covered Duchamp. Second, Miller assumes Man Ray's position as photographic producer and casts him as her photographic model (a role she had already begun to play exquisitely in their work together). This inversion of their working relationship is key to Miller's effort to create her own surrealist identity, for it situates her as a photographer in her own right who is keenly aware of her position within the surrealist avant-garde.

Miller's image of Man Ray shaving does more than situate her in the inner sanctum of Man Ray's artistic community. It also raises questions about Man Ray's masculinity by objectifying his face. Her decision to photograph him during an intimate morning activity indicates the tenor of Miller's approach to her partner. Not only do we see the famous photographer engaged in domestic activity, but the print (through dodging and burning, most likely) erases the hard edges and lacks the firm contours of a conventionally crisp, descriptive portrait. Moreover, the profile format—possibly reflecting Miller's interest in reformulating his solarized portrait of her (see Fig. 67)—suggests that she sought to create an iconic image of Man Ray's masculinity. Instead of mimicking the firm contours in Man Ray's solarized portrait of Miller, Miller's image depends on the shaving cream (as well as some dodging in the lower half of the image) to give the impression that Man Ray's face has dissolved into the image's surface. As if taking up Rrose's account of manhood as embodiment *avant la lettre,* Miller's

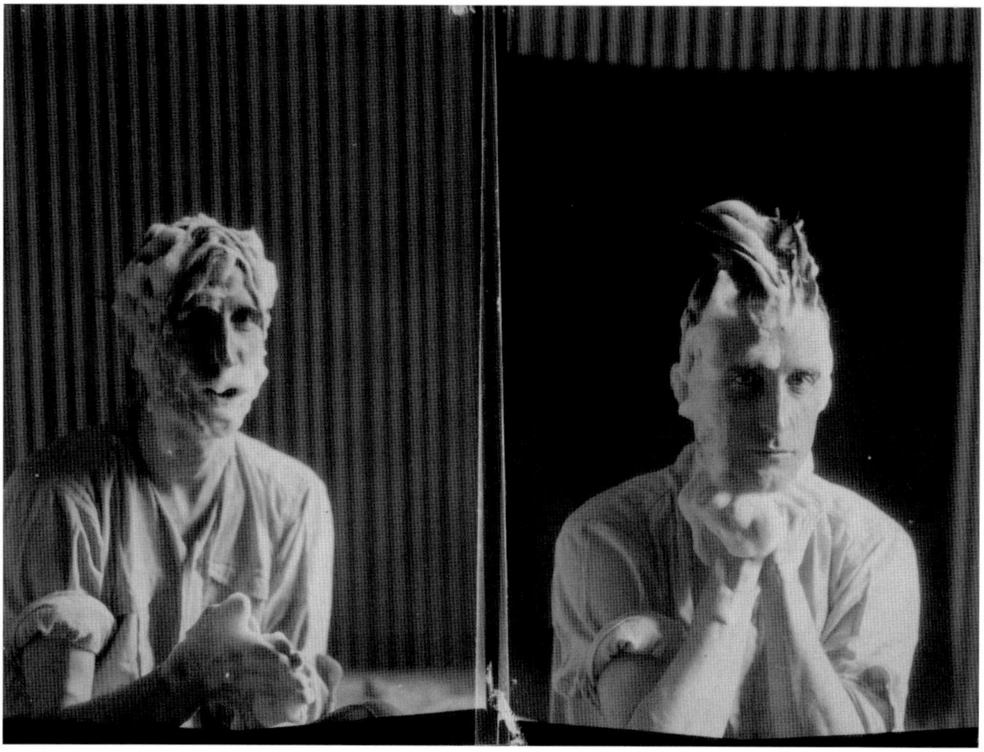

FIGURE 71 Man Ray, *Marcel Duchamp, Obligation for the Monte Carlo Roulette,* 1924. Musée National d'Art Moderne, Centre Georges Pompidou, Paris. CNAC/MNAM/Dist. Réunion des Musées Nationaux/Art Resource, New York. © 2006 Man Ray Trust/Artists Rights Society (ARS), New York/ADAGP, Paris.

image not only dissolves Man Ray's throat and shoulders into the paper's surface but also denotes his face as a surface to be marked. The shape and fluidity of the patch of shaving cream just under his ear simulates the activity of a painter's brush, encouraging us to view Man Ray both as a projection of a stereotypically masculine form of activity (painting) and as a man whose body is matter. As Miller depicts him, Man Ray is someone who cares about, and for, his body. Thus, his artistic identity becomes less than conventional in Miller's hands. Her image questions the portrait's capacity to tell the truth about its subject. While relying upon the traditional profile format, she turns her intimate gaze to the physicality of the artist's morning ritual, emphasizing the artifice of the male artist's public persona. She suggests that this ritual is tied more often to the symbols of technical or intellectual mastery than to personal hygiene.

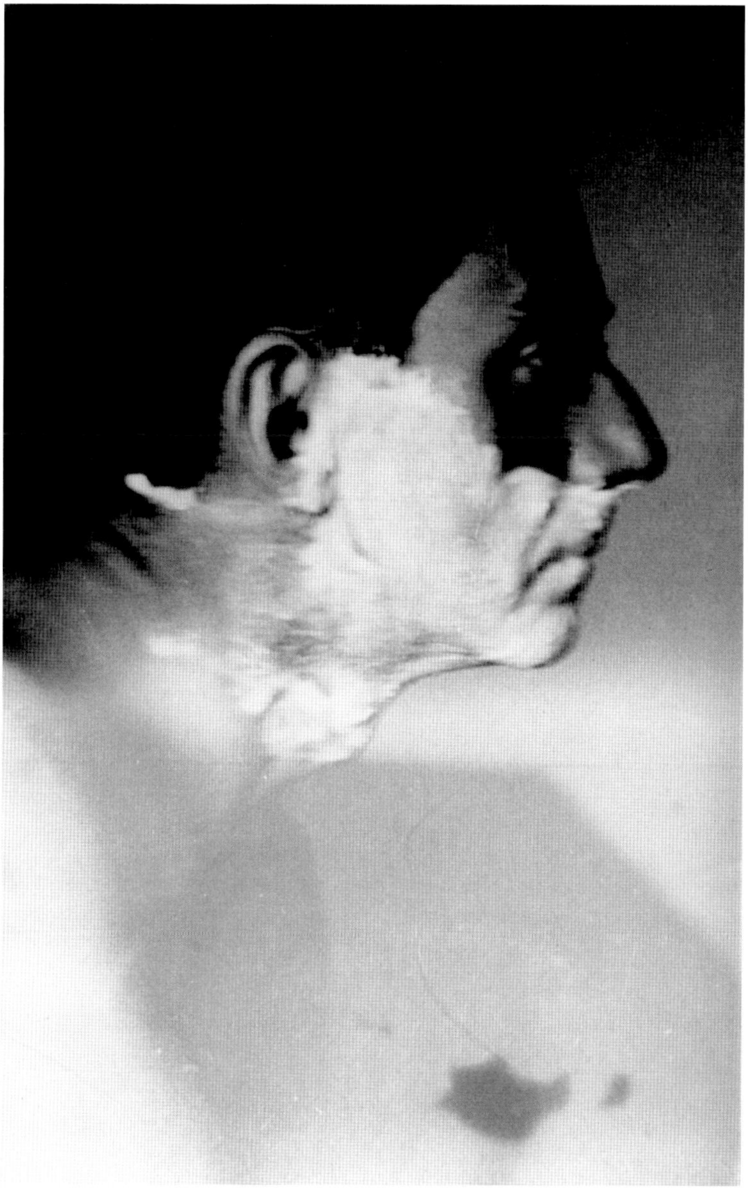

FIGURE 72
Lee Miller, *Man Ray Shaving,* 1929. Courtesy of the Lee Miller Archives, East Sussex, England.

Miller's reference to Man Ray's images of the soapy Duchamp transforms his work into her own, if only by catalyzing a process of pictorial appropriation in the minds of viewers familiar with Man Ray's work. Speaking in a voice like Man Ray's, she inserts herself into his previous conversation with Duchamp, articulating subject and object positions simultaneously. She essentially acquiesces to his public persona to link herself to Man Ray's position at the center of the surrealist group, yet her appropriation also yields a potential for critique.[17] Taking up Man Ray's role as the photographer of surrealism, Miller makes photographs that look just enough like his to warrant comparison. Miller's photograph of her partner shaving thus traverses a terrain that both honors his achievement and highlights the common, superficial ways in which male artists like him assert their public identities by announcing their machismo. Miller's appropriation of Man Ray's image of Duchamp, and her reframing of that image to create a stepping-stone to her own surrealist identity exposed the gendered assumptions in the male artist–female model relationship that the Ray-Duchamp collaboration so often mocked—especially when Duchamp became Rrose. Miller tested her surrealist credentials by knowingly using some of Man Ray's pictorial habits for her own purposes. By implanting herself in his avant-garde past in this way, she pictured him as he had so often pictured her: as a signature of his own sex. Thus, she refused the boundaries between male and female artistic identities by treating these identities as roles rather than essential elements of personhood. In this way, Miller's appropriation of Man Ray's surrealist portraiture enabled her to consider questioning the conventional gender hierarchies of the avant-garde by reframing male artistic identity with the camera's unflinching eye. Perhaps Miller could give Man Ray the experience of being looked at as a woman, if only for an instant.

Reimagining the Surrealist Body

Portraiture was not the only photographic genre Miller used to converse with Man Ray. The female nude—the signal form of female embodiment as other for which he was widely known—offered her an even greater opportunity to revise the pictorial language of surrealist photography he had perfected. Of course, Man Ray wasn't alone among the surrealists in his fascination with women. As feminist scholars like Gauthier, Chadwick, Caws, and Suleiman have pointed out, in surrealist art and literature, the female body is the quintessential object through which a male artist can act out his fantasies and desires of possession. Quite a few male surrealists imagined that women have better, more natural access to the unconscious than men do. We have seen how André Kertész incorporated the signs of female lack into his images of Carlo Rim and how Breton and Aragon celebrated female hysteria as a "supreme form of surrealist expression."[18]

Miller's approach to the female nude, however, evaded the familiar scenarios of female objectification for which her partner was known. We can compare his photograph, *La Prière,* for example (Fig. 73), to her *Untitled (nude, bending forward)* (Fig. 74). The relationship of the body to the photograph's framing edge is critical in both images. *La Prière* shows us a pair of demurely shielded buttocks, whose off-center position heightens the sense of participating in a voyeuristic experience. This body's decapitation and its seemingly self-imposed repetition of forms—the pattern of twos that begins with the buttocks and ends with the feet—seem to solicit an objectifying gaze that emphasizes the orderly analysis of the body as a collection of parts.[19]

One might also experience an urge to identify with this scene of bodily compression, feeling the sensation of knees touching abdomen, buttocks resting on the balls of the feet, and left hand pressing against right. The texture of flesh also enhances such identification because the skin's pores mimic the grain of the photographic surface. This flesh is palpable, particularly in the way that its texture pricks the picture's gelatin-silver membrane. The body's folding over onto itself thus reads as an erotic moment of prayer, perhaps, or even an instance of self-absorbed contemplation.

However, we cannot help but sense another mode of looking that makes us want to cover up the body's orifices to ward off the fetishist's glance. The photograph's dramatic, raking light source and skewed angle of approach to the figure within the frame produces a bodily inventory. This nude becomes a series of objects piled on top of each other; the viewer is hard pressed to see these parts, neatly arranged in rows, as elements of an integral whole. The clarity of the folded-over body at the center of the photograph contrasts with the amorphous shapes that begin to appear in the upper corners of the print, effectively dramatizing the easy readability of the central form.

Miller possibly conceived *Untitled (nude, bending forward)* as a response to Man Ray's codification of the female body. She frames and lights her figure so that potential energy and motion are stored within the amorphous structure of the body. Unlike Man Ray's tidy packaging of the female body, Miller's image appears to be much less certain about its subject's spatial location. Whereas Man Ray classifies body parts with a horizontal arrangement—feet, hands, buttocks, each staged on a well-lit surface so that one can quickly see them and establish visual control—Miller's nude is awash in confusion. Her grainy figure undulates across the surface of the photograph, appearing as an amorphous, shifting presence whose identification is uncertain and just out of reach. The location of the body in Miller's photograph, whose gender is unclear, compels the viewer's attention. The figure's spatial location is resolutely indeterminate, thereby driving us to look more closely. Yet instead of finding resolution in looking, we find new questions. Where is the figure standing? Are the rounded features at the top buttocks? Or are they shoulders, with the figure's neck bent over and its arms producing dark creases at the sides of the curve that might be a waist? What *kind* of body are we looking at? If we imagine the figure bending toward us, buttocks at top, its head could flash up momentarily and demand a confrontation with our gaze. Or, if the body is turned away from our look, it

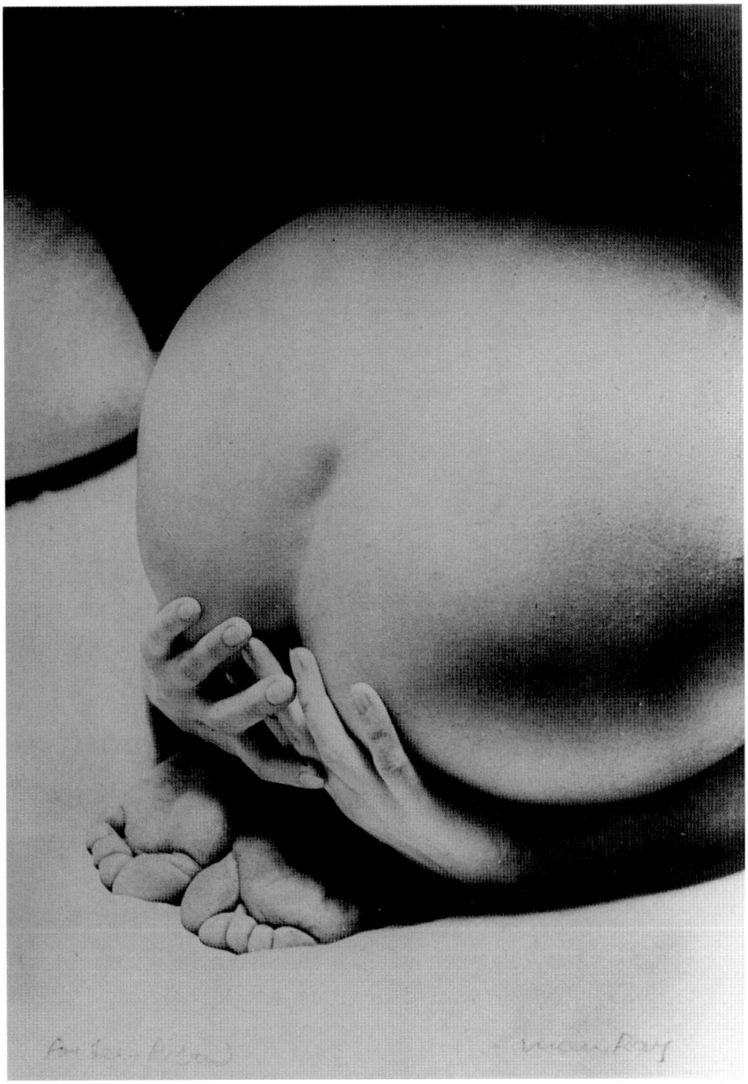

FIGURE 73
Man Ray, *La Prière (The Prayer)*, 1930. Courtesy of the Lee Miller Archives, East Sussex, England. © 2006 Man Ray Trust/Artists Rights Society (ARS), New York/ADAGP, Paris.

might both court and reject our scrutiny. In both these scenarios, Miller's nude is less available for a fetishistic or voyeuristic gaze than is Man Ray's. Her figure demands that the beholder find his or her own way of seeing the body, as if from multiple points of view. In this multiplication of possible perspectives, Miller's nude suggests more of an integral whole, even if head, hands, and legs remain outside the photographic frame. Her work uses the physical (and

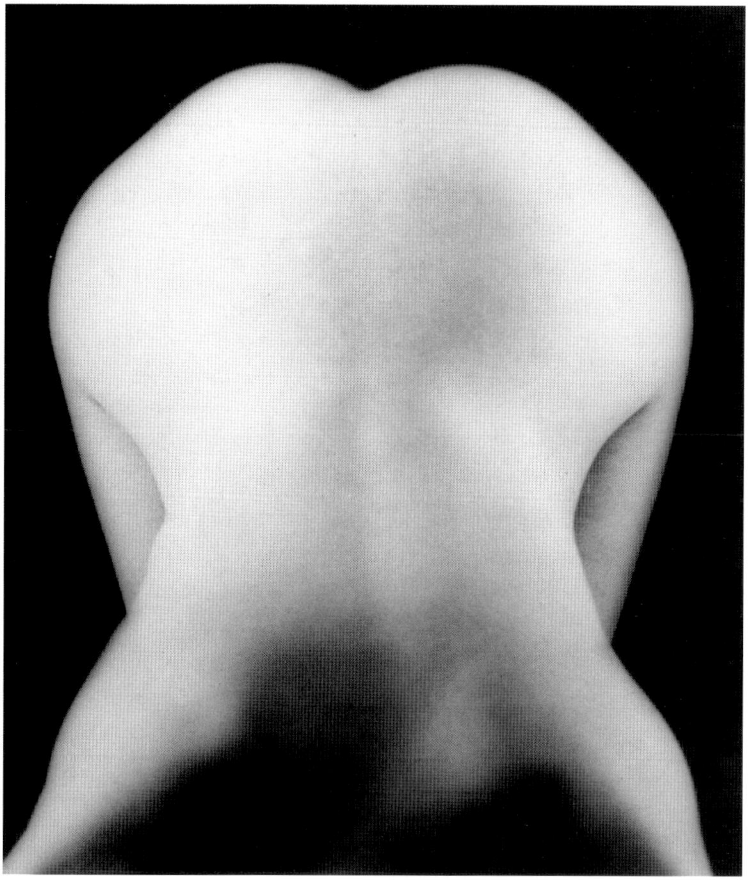

FIGURE 74
Lee Miller, *Untitled (nude, bending forward)*, ca. 1930. Julien Levy Collection, gift of Jean Levy and the estate of Julien Levy, 1988.157.54. Reproduction, The Art Institute of Chicago.

allegedly psychological) instability of the concept of femininity to critique Man Ray's interest in freezing and fragmenting the female body to emphasize its status as an object of masculine (surrealist) desire.

By conversing artistically with the man at the center of surrealist photography, Miller created a place for herself within surrealism. Images such as *Untitled (nude, bending forward)* admit respect for the work of Man Ray and other surrealist photographers. Yet they often turn away from the penetrating, aggressive positions staked out by Man Ray in photographs like *La Prière* or *Homage to Sade* (Fig. 86) and by the fashion photographers for whom Miller posed in the 1920s and early 1930s. Through her interrogation and internalization of the visual dialectics of surrealism, Miller's own surrealism emerges, and her surrealism both speaks of its sources and resists the tenor of their embodiments.

Feminist critics have argued quite rightly, as we have seen, that surrealism's appropriation of tropes of femininity—the figure of woman as embodied, desiring, hysterical, unruly—was but another refinement of techniques of male domination. Man Ray's storied career supports this argument. He was a successful photographer in surrealism and fashion because of the skill with which he deployed the female body as a fetish—whether through cropping, creative lighting, or other means of fragmentation. Other of his photographs, however, remain for the most part outside the canon of his work. Frequently unpublished, released in limited editions, or circulated only among friends, these less-familiar photographs conjure a range of fantasies and anxieties about masculine embodiment that speak to surrealism's sexual agenda, which sought to associate the masculine with the feminine and reveal perverse (by conventional standards) practices to counter the moralistic proclamations of social conservatives.

Upon close inspection of these photographs, we can begin to see that this portion of Man Ray's work registers some uncertainty, perhaps even fear, about the power that an embodied, sexualized femininity—in particular the feminine power of Lee Miller—might have over him.[20] These less widely reproduced images show a chink in Man Ray's misogynist armor. In them, a kind of passivity bubbles to the surface of a fractured masculinity. Although rare, Man Ray's momentary recognition of an ambiguous relationship between masculinity and femininity seems to have resulted from his recognition that the boundary separating men from women, which he and other male artists of his generation had taken for granted, was beginning to weaken.

The Anxiety of Self-Representation

Many surrealists believed that women were more hysterical, embodied, and tied to the drives of the unconscious than men—despite medical reports of male hysteria during the war. By aligning themselves with typically feminine traits and conditions—the hysterical woman and her uncontrolled desires; the female's deep link to nature, the body, and its leakages and ruptures—the surrealists imagined that they would counter the authoritarian, rationalist model of social organization in which the paternalistic authority of the state reigned supreme. Accordingly, they celebrated women primarily for their presumably "natural" lack of reason, their inherent carnality, their affinities with the body and sexuality, and their psychological, intellectual, and physical passivity.[21]

André Breton's literary character Nadja, a mad but beautiful Parisian woman who starred in his novel of the same name, and Dr. Charcot's celebrated hysterical patient Augustine are exemplary cases of the types of women that interested surrealist men. These women's apparent inability to control their physical appetites and psychological conflicts made them attractive. Breton claimed that Nadja was a symbol of human emancipation because she had generated a "private conspiracy" against "logic . . . the most hateful of prisons."[22] Defining hysteria

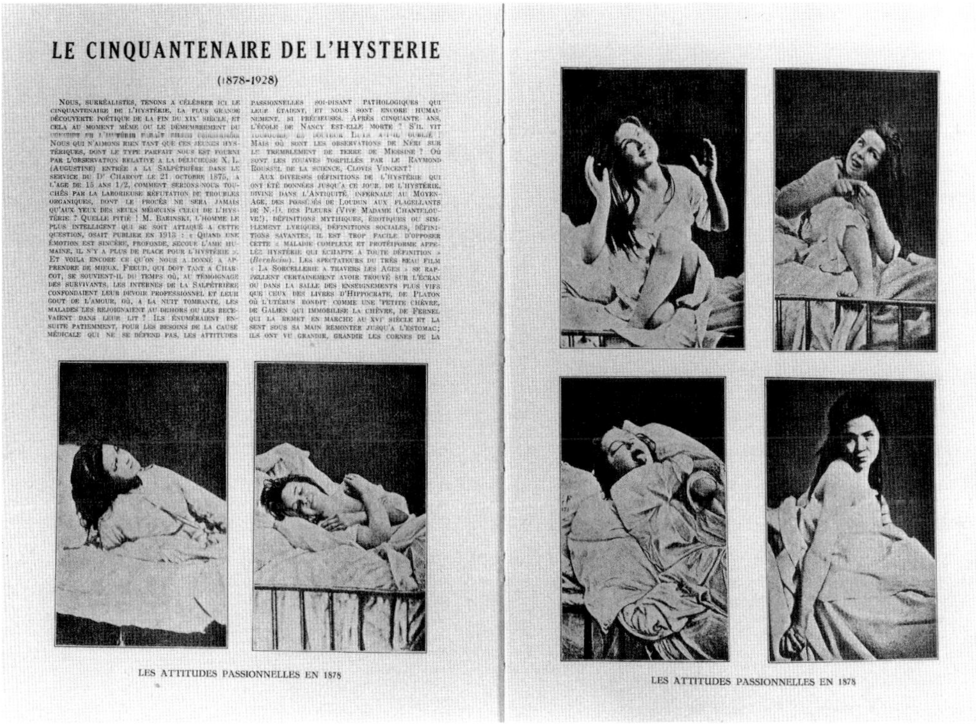

LE CINQUANTENAIRE DE L'HYSTERIE

(1878-1928)

Nous, surréalistes, tenons à célébrer ici le cinquantenaire de l'hystérie, la plus grande découverte poétique de la fin du XIXe siècle, et cela au moment même où le démembrement du [illegible] Nous qui n'aimons rien tant que ces jeunes hystériques, dont le type parfait nous est fourni par l'observation relative à la délicieuse X. L. (Augustine) entrée à la Salpêtrière dans le service du Dr Charcot le 21 octobre 1875, à l'âge de 15 ans 1/2, comment serions-nous touchés par la laborieuse réfutation de troubles organiques, dont le procès ne sera jamais qu'aux yeux des seuls médecins celui de l'hystérie ? Quelle pitié ! M. Babinski, l'homme le plus intelligent qui se soit attaqué à cette question, osait publier en 1913 : « Quand une émotion est sincère, profonde, secoue l'âme humaine, il n'y a plus de place pour l'hystérie ». Et voilà encore ce qu'on nous a donné à apprendre de mieux. Freud, qui doit tant à Charcot, se souvient-il du temps où, au témoignage des survivants, les internes de la Salpêtrière confondaient leur devoir professionnel et leur goût de l'amour, où, à la nuit tombante, les malades les rejoignaient au dehors ou les recevaient dans leur lit ? Ils énuméraient ensuite patiemment, pour les besoins de la cause médicale qui ne se défend pas, les attitudes passionnelles soi-disant pathologiques qui leur étaient, et nous sont encore humainement, si précieuses. Après cinquante ans, l'École de Nancy est-elle morte ? S'il vit toujours, le docteur Luys a-t-il oublié ? Mais où sont les observations de Néri sur le tremblement de terre de Messine ? Où sont les zouaves torpillés par le Raymond Roussel de la science, Clovis Vincent ?

Aux diverses définitions de l'hystérie qui ont été données jusqu'à ce jour, de l'hystérie, divine dans l'Antiquité, infernale au Moyen-Age, des possédés de Loudun aux flagellants de N.-D. des Pleurs (Vive Madame Chantelouve !), définitions mythiques, érotiques ou simplement lyriques, définitions sociales, définitions savantes, il est trop facile d'opposer cette « maladie complexe et protéiforme appelée hystérie qui échappe à toute définition » (*Bernheim*). Les spectateurs du très beau film « La Sorcellerie à travers les Ages » se rappellent certainement avoir trouvé sur l'écran ou dans la salle des enseignements plus vifs que ceux des livres d'Hippocrate, de Platon où l'utérus bondit comme une petite chèvre, de Galien qui immobilise la chèvre, de Fernel qui la remet en marche au XVIe siècle et la sent sous sa main remonter jusqu'à l'estomac ; ils ont vu grandir, grandir les cornes de la

LES ATTITUDES PASSIONNELLES EN 1878

LES ATTITUDES PASSIONNELLES EN 1878

FIGURE 75 Photographs of Augustine from "Le Cinquantenaire de l'hystérie," 1928. In *La Révolution surréaliste* 11 (15 March 1928): 20–21.

in 1928 as "a mental state . . . characterized by the subversion of relations between the subject and the moral world," Breton and Aragon argued that hysteria be understood not as a "pathological phenomenon" but as "a supreme means of expression."[23] For them, the female hysteric embodied moral subversion. The female hysteric's body and her unconscious desires were inseparable, so her convulsive states of being must be the recordings, literally, of her unconscious at work. The surrealists' decision to publish these two images of Charcot's patient Augustine in an issue of *La Révolution surréaliste* enabled them to define hysteria as a crucial model for unleashing the power of the unconscious (Fig. 75). If one followed Augustine's example, one might be able to liberate the mind and body from the brittle strictures of a repressed, conventionalized society. Importantly, Nadja's first public appearance in *La Révolution surréaliste* was in the same issue.[24] Thus, both Augustine and Nadja became exquisite models for surrealism, in ways that Lee Miller echoed in her oscillating, amorphous images of bodily instability—such as that in *Untitled (nude, bending forward)*. For surrealist men, then, appropriating the affect and mentality of such women appeared to be a way to fashion new identities for themselves that contrasted with the authoritarian model of male bourgeois citizenship within which many of them had been raised.

Although Man Ray's work generally appeared to envision domination of the female body, he also recorded a rather ambiguous image of masculinity in two similar versions of *Self-Portrait with Bathrobe* from about 1930 (Fig. 76).[25] The limited, essentially private status of this image—it was not published at the time—offered Man Ray the space to enact and document the potential for a nontraditional male sexuality. Breton, in fact, argued as early as 1929 that surrealists might have to withdraw their work from the public realm to enable its imagined transgressive nature to survive the increasingly repressive cultural climate of the time. "The approval of the public," he reminded his friends and colleagues in 1929, "is to be avoided like the plague."[26] As we saw with Kertész's initial forays into using the fun-house distorting mirror on the male body—his images also were not published at the time—work that remained within private or limited circulation often enabled members of the surrealist group to explore issues and ideas of a sensitive, inflammatory nature without fear of public scorn. Although such choices also likely stemmed from the desire to maintain the fiction of male power and dominance, their mere existence (even if they are not well known) is crucial historical information that helps us see that exploring alternative masculinities was a potentially frightening enterprise for these men.

Even within the surrealist collective, Man Ray's exploration of passive masculinity in *Self-Portrait with Bathrobe* would likely have met with some resistance. For although the surrealists celebrated femininity's apparently direct link to the unconscious, they did not necessarily want a male surrealist to envision himself in the position of a woman, either physically (as the object of the male gaze) or psychologically (as a passive, uncertain, or vulnerable individual). Sigmund Freud argued in his *Three Essays on the Theory of Sexuality* (published in French for the first time in 1923) that all human subjects are essentially, and from the first moment of conception, bisexual.[27] "A certain degree of anatomical hermaphroditism occurs normally," according to Freud. And in his view, "In every normal male or female individual, traces are found of the apparatus of the opposite sex. . . . [A]n originally bisexual physical disposition has, in the course of evolution, become modified into a unisexual one, leaving behind only a few traces of the sex that has become atrophied."[28]

And although Freud surmised that a bisexual disposition plays a role in inversion (homosexuality), he was uncertain about the effect of a bisexual disposition on an individual's choice of object. As he said, even in cases of inversion, the sexual instinct and the sexual object appear

FIGURE 76 Man Ray, *Self-Portrait with Bathrobe,* ca. 1930. Courtesy of Telimage, Paris. © 2006 Man Ray Trust/Artist Rights Society (ARS), New York/ADAGP, Paris.

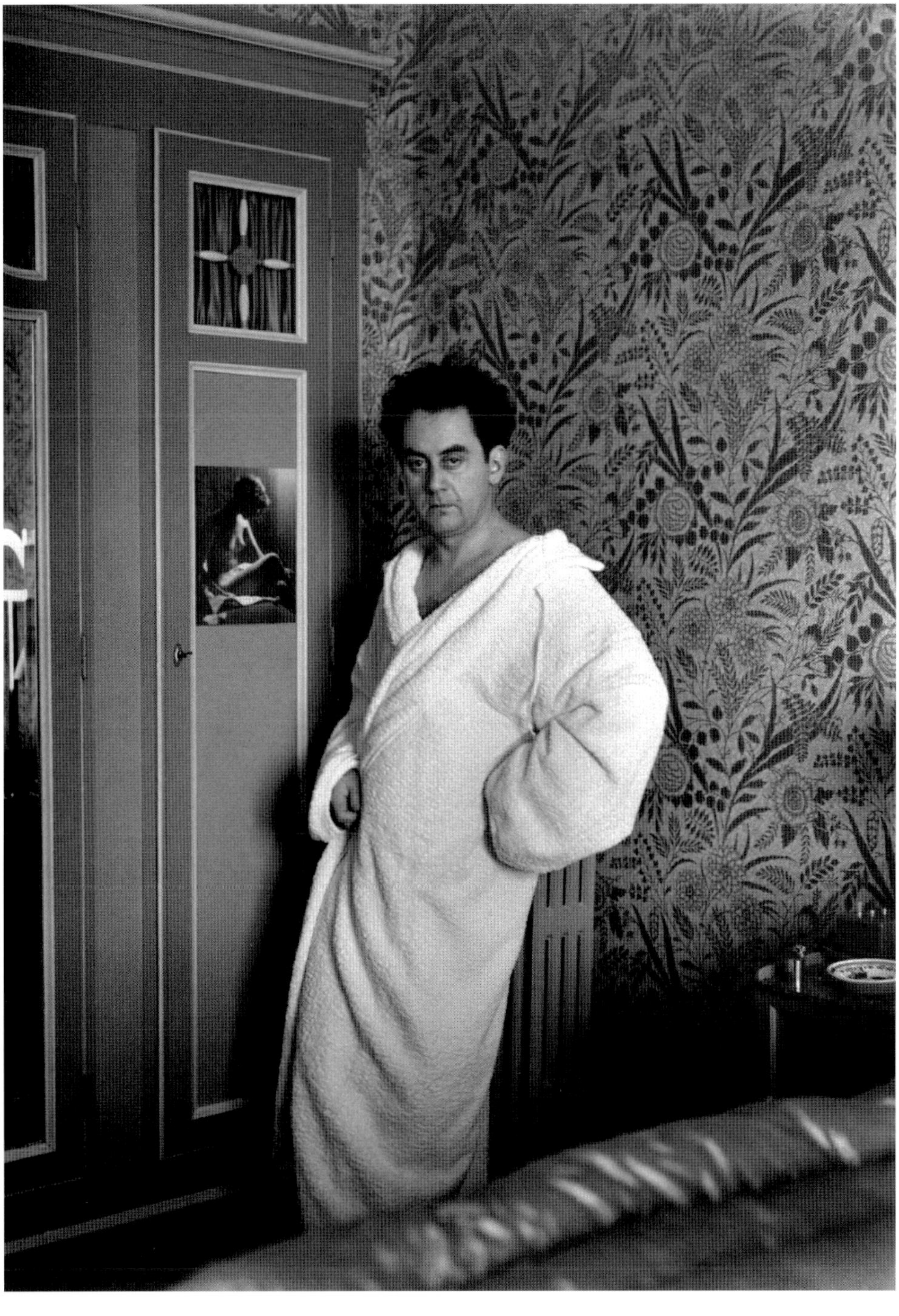

to be "merely soldered together," suggesting that human subjects may possess multiple combinations of object choice and instinct.[29] I propose that we explore the deflated affect of Man Ray's *Self-Portrait with Bathrobe* in concert with Freud's identification of a fundamentally bisexual disposition in all human beings, because Freud's theory sheds useful light on this odd photograph. Although Man Ray does not seem in real danger of becoming a truly passive character in this image, his interest in trying out "passivity"—his pose echoes those of the fashion models he regularly photographed, as we shall soon see—reflects ambivalence about the rigid contours of sexuality. Maybe his sexuality, at least the one he is thinking about in this photograph, is more fractured and diverse than the ideally masculine or feminine positions that Freud staked out in his discussions of human sexual development.[30] Confusion about whether this image conveys a passive or active subject appears to be the photograph's focus.

In this image, Man Ray depicts himself dressed in a white robe, peering out at the viewer from a room that appears to be a bedroom. His body is visually juxtaposed with that of Lee Miller, whose photograph is tacked to the wall behind him. The intimate setting (in addition to its self-referentiality) prods us to read the image as a sort of confession: Man Ray stands before us, as if interrupted in his morning routine. The photograph's apparently spontaneous intimacy is key to its truth-value, for this tone suggests the photographer's lack of calculation. Apparently caught off guard, Man Ray presents a self-image that reads more as self-exposure than as carefully crafted fiction.

The selection of pose and the insertion of an image of Miller (Fig. 77) exaggerate Man Ray's separation from Miller even as they insist upon his desire for her (or at least for the type of femininity she represents). An in-frame visual comparison of the two provides a dramatic contrast between the paunchy, aging figure of Man Ray and the warmly sensual, idealized image of Lee Miller's nude body. The comparison does more than appropriate Miller as Man Ray's model and lover of choice. It also registers Man Ray's anxiety about his personal and professional relationships with Miller. Man Ray is unlike Miller here, both in his bodily presence and in his desirability. Whereas Miller is unclothed, self-absorbed, and perhaps even narcissistically engaged in the pleasure of self-appraisal, Man Ray looks out reticently at the viewer, seemingly aware of his own unwillingness to reveal himself in the way that he imagines Miller willing to do.

By pairing himself with his current lover in his self-portrait, Man Ray alludes to a previous moment in his life and work, represented by the more self-assured and cocky 1927 photographic portrait of himself and Kiki de Montparnasse (Fig. 78). This image of Man and Kiki is rife with stereotypes of male-female interaction, particularly in Man's impersonation of a cheeky sailor who has come ashore to partake of Kiki's provocatively posed body. If Man played customer to Kiki's madam in the earlier photograph, how might we read the relationship between him and Miller in *Self-Portrait with Bathrobe*? In its intimate setting, this later image echoes the erotic narrative in the image with Kiki. Yet in his self-portrait, Man Ray has appro-

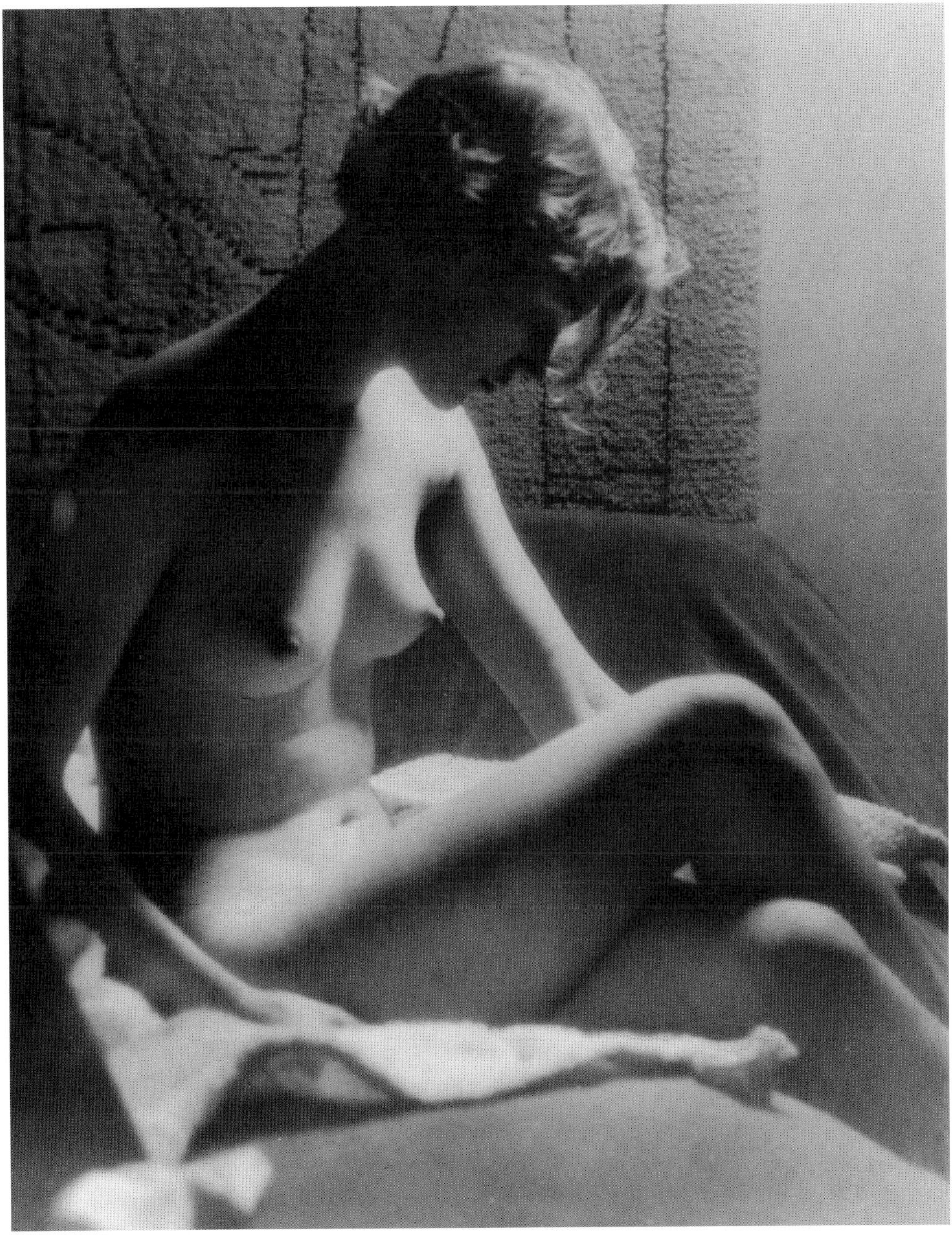

FIGURE 77 Man Ray, *Lee Miller, Paris,* 1929. Courtesy of the Lee Miller Archives, East Sussex, England. © 2006 Man Ray Trust/Artist Rights Society (ARS), New York/ADAGP, Paris.

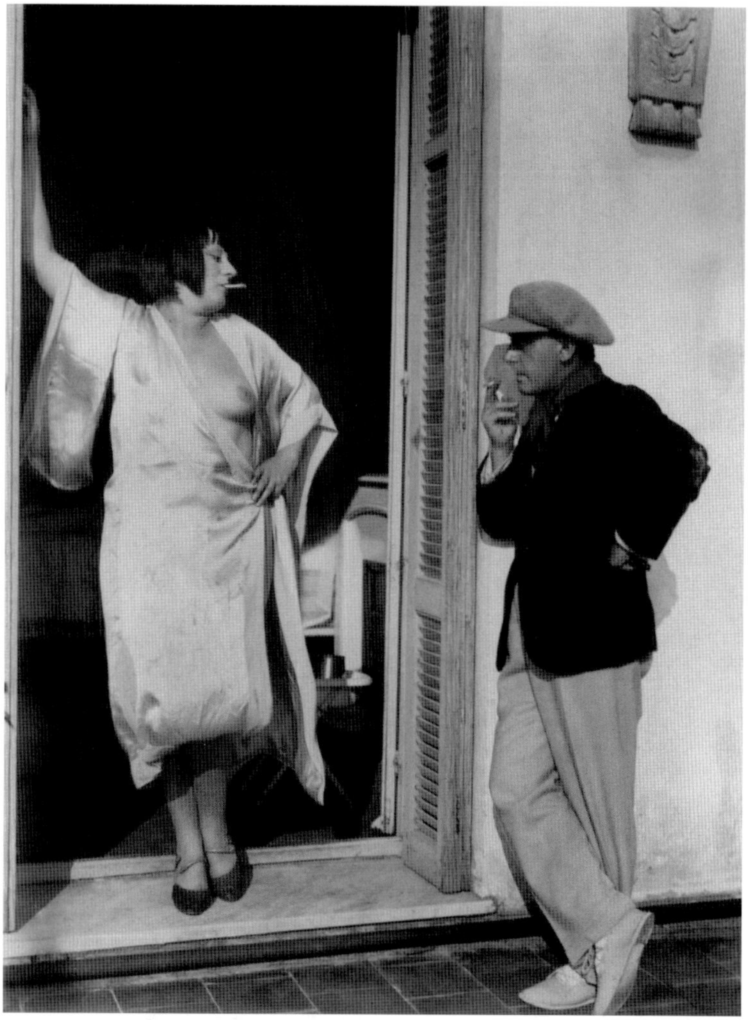

FIGURE 78
Man Ray, *La Prostitution (Prostitution)*, 1927. Courtesy of Telimage, Paris. © 2006 Man Ray Trust/ Artist Rights Society (ARS), New York/ ADAGP, Paris.

priated Kiki's pose from the 1927 picture. He uses elements of his usual photographic iconography in depicting his own body, although the bathrobe portrait also manages to retain traces of a more conventional male-female opposition than is common in surrealist work.

This integration of poses proposes a merger of the conventional positions, or roles, of masculinity (active) and femininity (passive). First, the white terry robe that Man Ray wears looks suspiciously like the one upon which Miller sits in the photograph on the wall behind him. Second, Man Ray's pose and attire mirror the staginess of his own fashion photography (Fig.

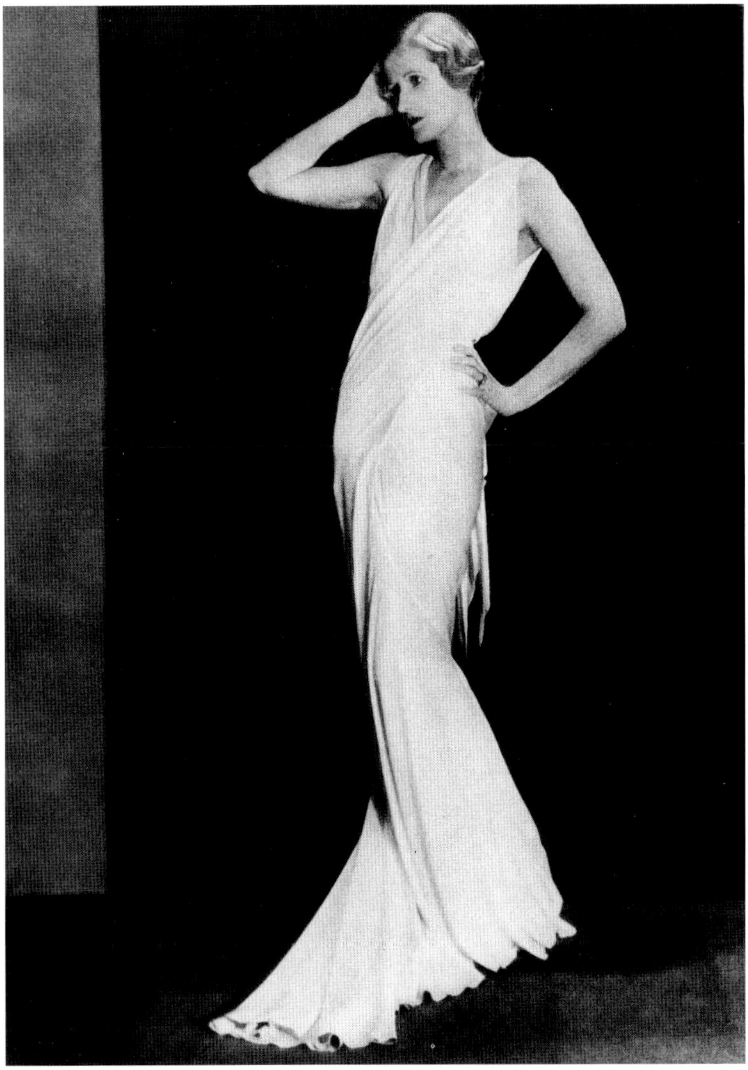

FIGURE 79
Man Ray, fashion image. In *Photographs by Man Ray 1920 Paris 1934* (1934). © 2006 Man Ray Trust/Artist Rights Society (ARS), New York/ADAGP, Paris.

79). He moves his right arm forward to hold the robe closed, while his other arm rests confidently across his hips in a familiarly glamorous gesture. This mimicry of his models' poses, coupled with the direct link to Miller's recently removed robe, underscores Man Ray's comparison of his own body's position in the photograph with those of the women he usually photographed (like Miller). He puts himself into his model's shoes by performing her poses. Yet, even as he does so, Man Ray reasserts his masculinity by staging that pose in a photograph that remains tightly connected to the traditional relationship between male artist and female model: Miller, after all, remains pinned to the wall in a nude photograph, and seen against her image in that way, Ray's robe wearing can be interpreted as a self-portrait after sex; he needs only to pick up a cigarette to seal the bargain. Although Ray refrains from showing us his body, his simulation of the three female models discussed above suggests his desire to imagine himself as the object of the camera's (male) gaze. He longs to be seen, potentially by a woman, yet that woman is in the picture as the disinterested, self-absorbed Lee Miller.

In his 1914 essay "On Narcissism," Sigmund Freud describes the form of narcissism he most often met in women, and with it, a form of male anxiety that we can see in Man Ray's bathrobe image. Freud's account describes the female subject's intensification of her original narcissism as an effect of her being looked at by men. With the onset of puberty, the sexually developed woman "experiences an intensification of her original narcissism" that is "unfavorable to the development of a true object-choice." "Women," he continues,

> especially if they grow up with good looks, develop a certain self-contentment which compensates them for the social restrictions that are imposed upon them in their choice of object. Strictly speaking, it is only themselves that such women love. . . . Such women have the greatest fascination for men, not only for aesthetic reasons, since as a rule they are the most beautiful, but also because of a combination of interesting psychological factors. For it seems very evident that another person's narcissism has a great attraction for those who have renounced part of their own narcissism and are in search of object-love.[31]

Freud argues that narcissism attracts men seeking object love because of their own inaccessibility or self-sufficiency; thus, the narcissist exists in a state like the self-absorption of children, criminals, and women. Yet the narcissist's charm is doubled-edged, causing dissatisfaction in the (presumably male, heterosexual) lover, for it creates "doubts" about the woman's love, apparently because of her "enigmatic nature."[32]

As if echoing Man Ray's anxiety about Miller's self-sufficiency—which he laid bare in letters to her exposing his jealousy of her efforts to go her own way—the photograph of Miller pinned to the wall shows her as uninterested in the world around her.[33] She appears to be fully absorbed in experiencing her own body, seemingly denying Man Ray and the beholder (for they are one and the same) access to her persona. Although this moment of narcissistic self-regard potentially excludes the viewer, Miller's position in front of the camera also creates a voyeuristic experience for the beholder. Thus, even as this picture within a picture suggests that Man Ray is anxious about Miller's self-absorption, the robe's appearance in both images makes palpable his wish to be the object of desire—Miller's perhaps. But then another twist emerges, and one realizes that the photograph also reiterates the familiar opposition of clothed male and nude female that abounds in art history (Manet's *Déjeuner sur l'Herbe* comes to mind). Man Ray wants to control Miller's body and command her attention in the small nude portrait, even as she evades such intimacy with her inward-looking pose. And although the decision to present himself in a robe like hers prompts a comparison between their bodies as objects of the camera's gaze, Man Ray's clothed body takes the form of a great phallus, thus aligning itself visually with another more masculine model: the great sculpture of Balzac by Auguste Rodin.[34] In investigating the internal relationships between these two images, we can read Man Ray's fantasy of masculine power in several ways. Man Ray claims male potency through his upright pose and the display of his conquest of Miller; yet Miller, even when pinned up like a specimen, remains inaccessible because she is embroiled in her own moment of self-reflection. Thus, the circuit of gazes within this self-portrait may reflect both his fantasy of gaining control over Miller and the worry that this thought may be wishful thinking.

One final detail of the self-portrait accentuates Man Ray's unease in the face of Miller's eroticized self-absorption. The instinct to cover himself with a robe, yet expose her body, belies his worry about self-exposure. As Miller herself said about men in 1932, "Men are much more self-conscious than women. . . . Women are used to being looked at."[35] By covering his body, Ray sets up a contrast with Miller's apparent comfort with her nudity.[36] Thus, although Man Ray promoted himself as a stereotypically controlling male artist again and again throughout his career as a photographer, his underlying anxiety about his ability to maintain such a position in the face of visual scrutiny seems to suffuse this photograph.

Perhaps being more like Miller—comfortable in her body, unruffled by the experience of objectification, and maybe even gleaning pleasure and power from it—offered Man Ray a way to reimagine his masculinity. The photograph proposes a revised image of manhood with subversive potential, encouraging a view of masculinity that partakes of both active and passive "currents." In many ways, the complex structure of Man Ray's identification with Miller (to the point of appropriation) suggests this duality of impulse. Man Ray wants to imagine himself more like Miller, to be and to have what she has (his love, his admiring gaze). Yet if he is to substitute his body for hers in this and other images, he must also replace her as if she were his rival. A displacement of anxieties about his body and his photography occurs here. Wanting what Miller has—confidence in her body's desirability, perhaps, or her ability to one-up her older mentor (as she did by taking credit for his negative of her outstretched neck)—Man Ray imagines possessing Miller as an object and eliminating her as a rival by stepping into her shoes. The oscillation between passive and active positions in *Self-Portrait with Bathrobe* thus reflects anxiety about his masculine erotic potential to attract a woman like Miller and his fear that his attraction to her could lead to a type of photographic emasculation. After all, she had already proved herself capable not only of appropriating his work but of recasting his previous collaboration with Duchamp as a precursor to their own.

Man Ray's ambivalent sexuality in this image grows out of his personal and professional relationships with Miller, but it also likely stemmed from ongoing cultural anxiety about the emasculation of French culture after the war. During the 1920s, ideas about the existence of a so-called third sex and debates about the rise of an emphatically "homosexual aesthetic" became increasingly popular.[37] If we read Man Ray's ambiguously masculine self-portrait in the context of such debates about sexual indeterminacy, we can see that the image might have seemed to embody a nontraditional image of manhood in which the masculine mind has succumbed to a fantasy (even if only a momentary one) about becoming more like the other, the female.[38] Imagining himself as other in his self-portrait thus makes visible Man Ray's fraught masculinity. Because this portrait mimics certain aspects of feminine passivity, it enables us to see how a man might recognize the fictional quality of the ideal image of integral masculinity that drove the return to order. But we do not yet see the manipulation of that recognition to promote an actively deviant form of masculinity. In Man Ray's photography, the balance between an anxious masculinity and a deviant one seems to tilt consistently toward perversity; and of course images of perversity were more comfortably salable parts of his surrealist work than were examples such as this rare photograph of his masculine unease.

Perversity and Postwar Masculinity

Even before the war, pornography was viewed as a root cause of France's decadence and emasculation. After the war, however, writers, critics, and politicians explicitly contrasted pornography and male perversion with idealized images of robust postwar masculinity for social or political gain. Men who had been through the war and had not become homosexuals or "perverts" were viewed as symbols of national reconstruction, whereas men who acted in "deviant" ways were increasingly subjects of analysis and pathologization in the medical literature.

As historian Carolyn Dean has suggested, postwar debates about French cultural decline often centered on the need to protect the masculine social body from symbolic forms of "sexual violence" or from the "shame, desecration, and subjugation" that many French men and women had experienced as a result of the war. Cultural commentators of the period saw (and feared) a connection between the compromised social body, masculinity, and degeneration. And they saw this connection in the apparently increasing number of men who were adulterers, social deviants, or homosexuals.[39] Indeed, the need for a concept of "deviant" masculinity was evident everywhere, for it helped define respectable masculinity in negative terms.[40]

Pushing against the use of "good" and "bad" versions of manhood to secure social order, the surrealists invested a good deal of time and effort in their own campaign for surrealist forms of sexuality, which actively courted perversion, deviance, and pornographic effects. By 1924—the year of Breton's first manifesto of surrealism—surrealist artists and writers, as well as other members of the French intellectual community, had become quite familiar with Sigmund Freud's argument that sexuality holds a primary position in the development of the human psyche. That year, in fact, was called the "Saison Freud," or "Season of Freud" because of the popularity of Freud's work in intellectual and artistic circles.[41]

The embrace of Freudian theory in Paris was not to everyone's liking, however. Some commentators critiqued the increasingly open discussion of sexuality, sexual perversion, psychological neuroses, and the unconscious drives that shape subjectivity as a sign of social decay. Others, however, believed that the exposure of perversion and decadence might ward off a hidden menace: the psychosexual instability of masculinity. The surrealists, for their part, delighted in representing perversion instead of fending it off. For them, perversion in its many forms was a symbol of a liberated unconscious; its presence seemed to signal the freedom to express one's deepest sexual desires without fear of social, moral, or ethical strictures. By advancing nontraditional images of sexuality—including the disturbed masculinity of Gaston Modot's perverse character in Buñuel and Dalí's *L'Âge d'Or,* Man Ray's passive-aggressive *Self-Portrait with Bathrobe,* and Kertész's mutilated and distorted men—the surrealists promoted antiestablishment concepts of social and sexual decorum.

We need to view this effort to create alternative masculinities against the backdrop of interwar French attitudes about male sexuality, in particular, male homosexuality. By the mid-1920s, for example, a number of critics in the French literary community acknowledged that a new genre of *"la littérature homosexuelle"* had emerged in the years after the war. Thus, at the same time that the French legislature was pursuing pronatalist social policies, the literary community was debating the potential connections between creativity, homosexuality, and the "modern woman." As if to quantify this apparent trend toward homosexuality in artistic production, the conservative literary journal *Les Marges* circulated a survey on *la littérature homosexuelle* to a diverse group of critics and then published the results in March 1926.[42] Several respondents were concerned about homosexual themes in contemporary art and literature. Not only did a genre of homosexual literature exist, but it seemed to be turning into a marketable commodity.[43] Commentators tried to surmise the causes of this new aesthetic and decided that (1) the war had forced men to spend too much time together, causing them to seek comfort and solace in one another's company; (2) the postwar emphasis on sport (the Paris Olympics had just taken place in 1924) increased male-to-male physical contact; and (3) women, particularly *les garçonnes,* were looking and acting more like men, so a heterosexist logic demanded that men would "naturally" find other men sexually desirable. The masculinization of the female body *à la garçonne*—the *garçonnes'* adoption of so-called homosexual aesthetics by cutting their hair, slimming down their bodies, forgoing motherhood, and pursuing athletics—was thus blamed for the rise of a homosexual subculture.[44] Because *women* now looked more like men, men were beginning to desire themselves, and each other, narcissistically.

Angelo Hesnard was an important popularizer and advocate of Freud in France. His *Psychologie homosexuelle* (1929) aimed to describe and categorize the homosexual psyche using a Freudian conception of the male homosexual's primary narcissism, which included a deep attachment to and identification with the mother and an autoerotic attraction to people of one's own sex.[45] This idea was nothing new in its Freudian view of female sexuality as integrally narcissistic. However, Hesnard's work broke new ground in finding male identification with the female—coupled with a strong dose of male narcissism—to be an essential precursor of nontraditional (homosexual) male sexuality. Hesnard, following Freud (although not to the letter, by any means), imagined male narcissism and male homosexuality to be symptoms of a "perverse" masculinity.

In a particularly virulent response to the *Les Marges* questionnaire, the conservative critic Camille Mauclair demonstrated how closely some members of the French literary community now linked homosexuality (a term that commentators of the time often used interchangeably with the terms *pederasty* or *inversion*), perversion, and surrealism as dangerous cultural anomalies: "You see the indignation raised recently by the infected manifesto where the surrealists spat on France. All the press had sworn no longer to print their names. And still I see them speaking politely again of Soupault, Crevel, and the other signatories of this garbage. We very well forgot the Boches [slang for Germans]; we will forget the pederasts as we will the surrealists."[46]

Mauclair's attack relied upon a crucial assumption. In his mind, surrealism and homosexuality were related cultural phenomena that had the potential to disrupt, or "infect," the social and cultural order of France. Like German soldiers, homosexual men *and* the surrealists threatened French virility. Unlike the alien "Boches," however, surrealists and male homosexuals threatened the nation from *within,* like a disease.

In light of such discussions within the French literary and artistic community during the 1920s, one can begin to understand why Man Ray's photographic self-portrait emphasizing ambivalence about his masculinity—and particularly, the ambiguous emphasis on both an active and a passive masculinity—could have signaled danger to critics fearing masculinity's decay. Man Ray's reticence to publish this image may well indicate his own sense of the image's problematic relationship to an idealized image of manhood. Other photographs by Man Ray depicting more palatable forms of perversion—particularly those representing sadomasochistic (S-M) pleasure derived from apparently willing female bodies—did appear in the surrealist journals. That these images were published, and others depicting uncertain masculinity were not, is important. Like the cropped female distortions that Kertész published in 1933 (whereas his male distortions barely saw the light of day), these images reinscribed familiar oppositions between the active and desiring male gaze and the passive, compliant female body even while emphasizing nontraditional sexual desire and practice. Although this pattern persisted in surrealist work in the 1920s and 1930s, at several points the surrealist group managed to achieve a degree of complexity in its analysis of human sexuality and unconscious desire. One such instance occurred during the freewheeling discussions about sexuality that the surrealists eventually published in the late 1920s as *Recherches sur la Sexualité.*

Sex and the Clinical Gaze

With the growing reliance on psychoanalytic concepts to interpret postwar culture came increased interest in many sectors of French society in cataloging, analyzing, and commenting upon sexuality's role in the formation of individual and collective identities. In March 1928 the surrealist group publicly announced its commitment to investigating sex as a cultural phenomenon when it published the transcripts of two research sessions on sexuality ("Recherches sur la sexualité," hereafter shortened to *Recherches* in light of the articles' later publication in book form) run by the surrealist Centrale, the research arm of the surrealist collective.[47]

The surrealists' interest in making public matters that were normally private, such as one's sexual history and sexual preferences, prompted their publication of the *Recherches.* The research turned a quasi-clinical gaze to the subject of sex and sexuality with the aim of being as nonjudgmental as possible. No topic was off-limits. Fetishism, onanism, and homosexuality; the desirability of a *ménage à trois,* simultaneous orgasm, and masturbation; preferences for different parts of a lover's body as well as sexual positions; and the practice of bestiality all had a place in the group's published conversations. Unlike the more private or intimate context of *Self-Portrait with Bathrobe,* the *Recherches'* public appearance put forward sexual practices and sexualities as appropriate content for their surrealist "revolution." And in many cases, the *Recherches* opened up new terrain. At times, the transcripts seem to record personal confessions, presenting the sort of sexual narratives upon which Freud based his psychoanalytic method. Yet unlike Freud's work, which focused primarily on female patients (although, of course, he occasionally analyzed male patients, such as Little Hans and the Wolf-Man), the preponderance of male participants in the survey skewed the focus toward male sexuality.[48]

As if playing the role of scientists, participants usually approached their task with matter-of-factness: How desirable is mutual orgasm with a woman? Must one link male orgasm and ejaculation? How desirable is anal sex? What do people think about homosexuality? The explicit description of sexual practices and desires seemed to offer an entrée to sexual liberation through discourse.[49] The surrealists hoped that the *Recherches'* descriptions of sexual practice and desire would open readers' eyes to their own experiences and liberate them. Discussing fantasies or lived experience in print not only might create a connection with readers but might also suggest new possibilities, desires, and techniques to them. Still, though the participants discussed a wide range of issues, the majority of the statements by the predominantly male participants dismissed women's experiences. And for all their efforts to promote new ideas about sexuality and sexual practice, the participants stuck to rather traditional ideas about sex and sexual difference in many of their questions and answers.

Some anxiety about the stability of male sexuality also permeated the discussions, revealing that members of the group were uneasy about exploring their own sexual assumptions and sexual habits. For example, during the second session—the only one in which Man Ray participated—Aragon complained that Breton had proposed an unsupportable system of differentiation that categorized men as either normal or pathological in their sexualities. Breton raised the specter of male sexual dysfunction by saying that a man's orgasm would always be accompanied by ejaculation unless the individual were a "pathological case." In response, Aragon quickly objected to the moralizing implications of Breton's analysis: "I want to signal that for the first time in the course of this debate the word 'pathological' has come into play. This seems to imply on the part of certain among us an idea of the normal man. I rise against this idea."[50]

Aragon, unlike Breton, assumed the existence of a plurality of masculinities that were neither normal nor abnormal. He was unable to support Breton's idea of a "normal" man, and in so doing, raised a critical point about the methodology of the *Recherches*. The group's investigation of male sexuality was not monolithic. Aragon, for one, refrained from passing judgment throughout the *Recherches*, apparently trying to be as clinical and analytic as possible to encourage frank, wide-ranging discussion.

A brief look at Man Ray's comments in the session in which he participated may help us understand the multifaceted character of his public and private utterances on the topic of sex. His statements reveal a more complex sexual self-portrait than one might expect from a man whose photographic and personal control over women is a familiar part of his artistic biography. Although his words reveal no shame, for example, in being watched while having sex, he also names fellatio as his favorite sexual activity (largely because, as he says, it happens to him so rarely).[51] In contrast to other participants' statements, Man Ray's recorded remarks about male homosexuality are relatively judgment free. "I don't see any great physical distinction between the love of a man for a woman and homosexuality," he remarks at one point during the conversation. He qualifies his statement by explaining that "emotional relations between men" are "worse" than those between men and women.[52] In the end, however, Man Ray's statements center on presenting his own sexual history as one of conquest. Blithely remembering an incident in his boyhood, he discloses that he knowingly inflicted pain on an even younger female partner.[53] Although this statement was the first time that Man Ray publicly aligned himself with a sadistic approach to sexual practice, it would not be the last.

A bit of digging into Man Ray's published work shows that he produced some starkly clinical, quasi-pornographic photographs of sexual intercourse in a collaborative book with the poets Louis Aragon and Benjamin Péret. Entitled *1929*, the book was a short but lavish production of erotic poems by Aragon and Péret interleaved with four explicit photographs by Man Ray. The photographs do not illustrate the poems per se, yet their graphic, in-your-face quality is closely attuned to the raw language of the poets' work (Figs. 80, 81, and 82). Published in an initial run of 214 copies, *1929* used gritty and graphic sexual imagery that recalls the *Recherches'* clinical approach to the depiction and analysis of sex.[54] Man Ray's photographs—each keyed to

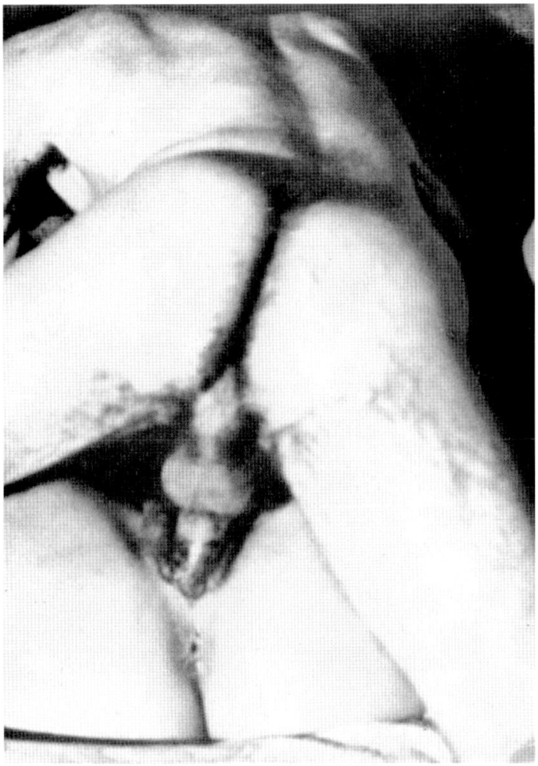

FIGURE 80
Man Ray, *Printemps (Spring)*, ca. 1929. In Benjamin Péret and Louis Aragon, *1929* (Paris, 1929). © 2006 Man Ray Trust/Artist Rights Society (ARS), New York/ADAGP, Paris.

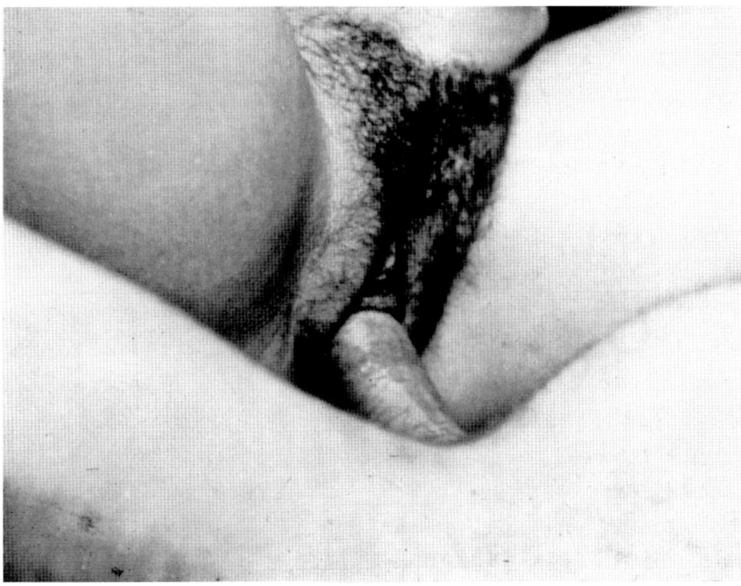

FIGURE 81
Man Ray, *Été (Summer)*, ca. 1929. In Benjamin Péret and Louis Aragon, *1929* (Paris, 1929). © 2006 Man Ray Trust/Artist Rights Society (ARS), New York/ADAGP, Paris.

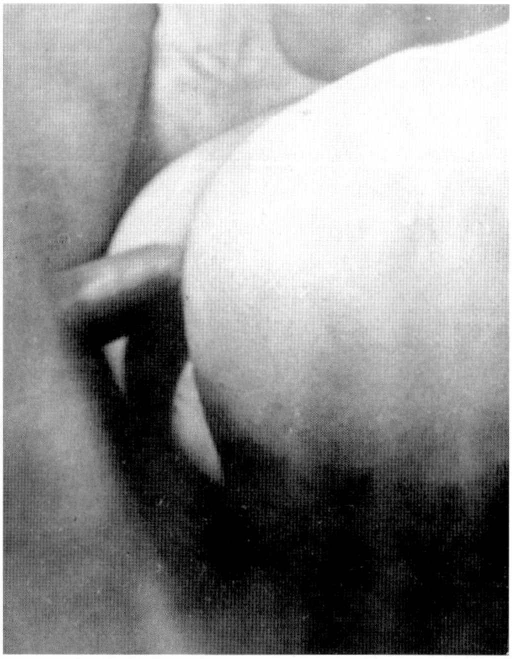

FIGURE 82
Man Ray, *Hiver (Winter)*, ca. 1929. In Benjamin Péret and Louis Aragon, *1929* (Paris, 1929). © 2006 Man Ray Trust/Artist Rights Society (ARS), New York/ADAGP, Paris.

a season of the year and functioning as a "chapter" break in the text—are tightly framed close-ups of sexual activity. They include male-female vaginal penetration, female fellatio of the male, a slightly less direct allusion to anal penetration of the female by the male, and an ambiguously gendered coupling in which a penis appears ready to merge with a pair of buttocks. The images are shot at close range—in one case from the perspective of a male participant (see Fig. 81), in another from the point of view of a third party (see Fig.80)—and their tight framing and grainy texture suggest the analytic investigations of a sexologist whose main interest is the particulars of the sexual act rather than the pictorial appeal of the image as art. Man Ray's unflinching gaze at these fragmentary yet direct sexual couplings suggests a will to depict sexual intercourse as both a bodily process (through tightly framed views of body parts in different situations) and an important, singular event (through the visually dramatic selection of specific moments in the unfolding process of sexual intercourse).

The book's direct, no-nonsense approach to imaging intimate sexual acts likely dictated its limited print run, its foreign publication, and the Bibliothèque Nationale's decision to catalog it in the *enfer* (literally, "hell") section of the library reserved for seditious and pornographic texts.[55] Although the *Recherches* were aimed at a broader public audience than *1929* was, both texts validate explicit sexual description as a surrealist strategy for instigating a dialogue about the power of sexuality in human culture. The *Recherches* and *1929* each promote sexuality as a topic of public discourse (even if the public for each work was somewhat limited). Man Ray's clinical investigations into sex and its practical variants were not limited to his work on *1929*, however. He consistently framed his artistic identity—particularly with respect to his relationship with Lee Miller—as a deviant one well into the early 1930s. But, as we will see in the following sections of this chapter, these images did not only support the image of a controlling male artist, they also documented Ray and Miller's participation in overtly sadomasochistic forms of sexual play and activity. Whether this choice was part of an elaborate staging of their relationship as "perverse" to secure their surrealist credentials, I do not know. I do know, however, that their collaboration included a body of work that encouraged viewers to see their relationship as one that clearly deviated from accepted sexual norms.

Sade, Sexuality, and the Photography of Perversion

The surrealists who wrote most about sexuality in the mid- to late 1920s and early 1930s based much of their thinking on Freud's revelations about the normalcy of an allegedly "deviant" sexuality at the core of human sexual life. For this reason, Freud's work may be key to understanding surrealist sexuality. In *Three Essays on Sexuality,* Freud says that the subject's inherently bisexual makeup allows "normal" sexuality to embrace a wide range of alternative or unconventional possibilities, including the appropriately nondeviant, heterosexual object choice. Thus, he saw the "normal" sexual instinct as a matter of endless variation, with the possibility of multiple object choices by the sexualized human subject.[56]

In 1933, some ten years after the appearance of Freud's text on sexuality, Maurice Heine, editor and scholar of Sade's work and also Man Ray's friend and neighbor, published a text with important echoes of Freud's ideas about sexual aberration. Heine's essay, "Psycho-Biological Classification of Sexual Paresthesias," extends the logic of Freud's account of human bisexuality to the subject of Sadeian forms of sexual perversion. Heine makes this linkage explicit in a diagram in his article (Fig. 83). The explanatory diagram gives visual form to the notion that an integral relationship exists between normal sexuality and sexual perversions: the two sides of sexuality appear as plants deriving from the same psychophysical root.

Heine's text analyzes the so-called perversions of the sexual instinct—sadism, sadomasochism, fetishism, pedophilia, necrophilia, bestiality, and so on—using a schema that aims to study them without passing judgment upon their validity or morality. Moreover, as he remarks at the end of his brief essay, the advantage of studying these perversions without prejudice is that the "intermediary cases" teach one the most about true human sexual and biological instincts. Noting that such cases were already present in Sade's work as early as 1785—and thus Sade's modeling of such cases is an integral part of Heine's analyses of sexual perversions—Heine suggests that his schema shows the fundamental unity of the perversions,

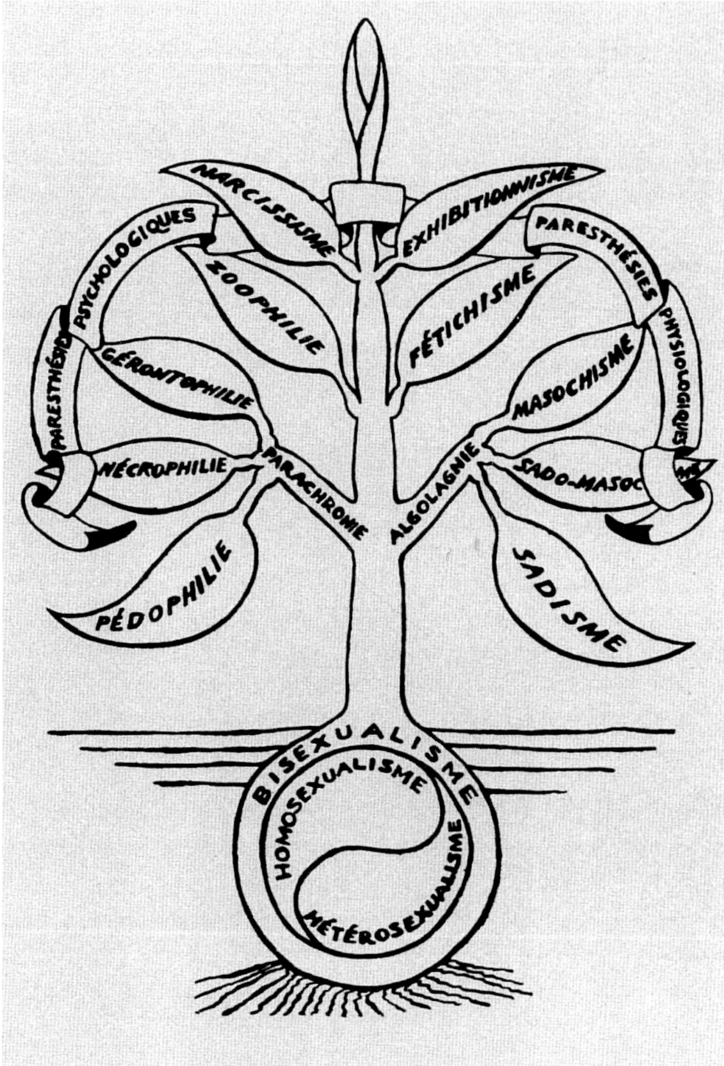

FIGURE 83
Maurice Heine, drawing from "Note sur un classement Psycho-Biologique des Paresthésies sexuelles." In *Minotaure* 3–4 (1933): 36.

which, regardless of their particular manifestations, are "nonetheless reducible to a common source."[57] Heine's case for the commonality of perversion—or at least the possibility that it could emerge in every human subject—benefited surrealism in the 1930s by pressing forward an understanding of perversion as the unconscious or other of "normal" human sexuality. The discovery and active deployment of the sexual unconscious might help transform these "perverse" desires into weapons against the moribund state of the postwar social and sexual order.

For Man Ray and Lee Miller, and for a number of other surrealists at the time, the Marquis de Sade was as much of a psychosexual touchstone as was Freud. Analyses of sexual perversion were central to both Freud's and Sade's writing, and the surrealists who wrote most about sexuality in the late 1920s and early 1930s drew equally from these two authors' work.[58] Indeed, by the early 1930s, particularly in the journal *Le Surréalisme au Service de la Révolution (SASDLR)*, Sade seems to have eclipsed Freud as a favorite surrealist topic.[59]

Man Ray consistently sought a self-image that associated him with Sade-like perversion and deviance—sexual or otherwise.[60] Not only did Man Ray value his friendship with the Sade scholar and editor Maurice Heine during the 1930s, but subsequent interviews with him reveal a lifelong appreciation for Sade's writing.[61] His interest in attacking sexual conventions is clear in an essay published toward the beginning of an issue of *Minotaure* in which Heine's sexual etiology also appeared. The essay indicates the role he might have envisioned for his more private photographic work in the early 1930s and shows him to be a risk taker willing to endure persecution for his surrealist beliefs.

> Each one of us, due to his timidity, cannot go beyond a certain limit without being outraged. He who . . . has succeeded, for himself, in pushing further than this limit, necessarily awakens a sentiment of antagonism in those who, in order to accept the conventions admissible for everyone, show no initiative. And this antagonism generally takes the form of an insignificant mockery, a criticism, or even a persecution. In every case this apparent outrage is preferable to the monstrous habits excused by etiquette and aestheticism.[62]

The etiquette and aestheticism of the return to order appear to be Man Ray's targets here. And he publicly announces that he will endure ridicule and persecution to pursue cultural provocation with his photography. He is willing to sacrifice comfort and acceptance to push beyond the boundaries of conventional society. Although he clearly pushed at these boundaries in photographs that partake of a Sadeian aesthetic, we can also read the photographs as Man Ray's efforts to depict himself as a Sadeian fellow traveler at a time when he was one of the most popular fashion photographers of the day.

A significant portion of the photographs that Man Ray and Lee Miller produced during their collaboration present their relationship as a specifically Sadeian, sexual one. Even if these images do not aim to depict the two as sexual pioneers, they effectively propose throwing conventional sexual activity out the window of the surrealist bedroom. Although many of Man Ray's photographs evoke conventional scenarios of masculine power and feminine passivity—*La Prière*, for example (see Fig. 73), and the various images he made of Miller's cropped and available torso (Fig. 84)—others that he made during the early 1930s traverse the less common paths of same-sex desire (Fig. 85) and Sadeian taste (Figs. 86 and 87). Miller not only modeled for the image of two women kissing in Figure 85 but was likely a catalyst of Man

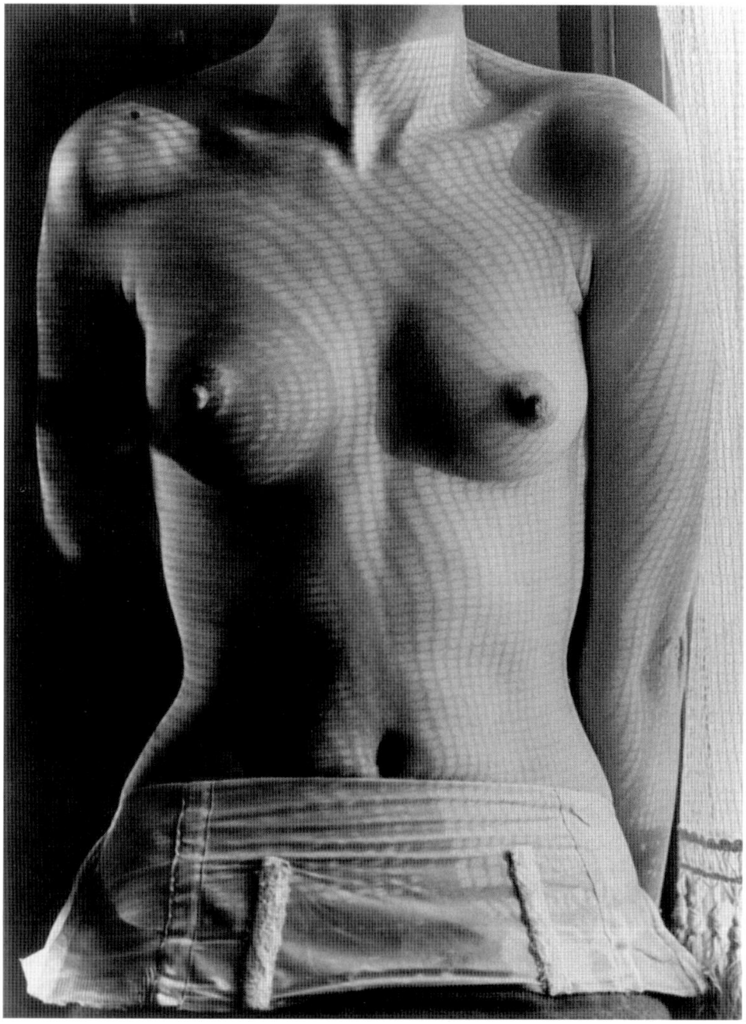

FIGURE 84
Man Ray, *Shadow Patterns on Torso (Lee Miller)*, 1930. Courtesy of the Lee Miller Archives, East Sussex, England. © 2006 Man Ray Trust/Artist Rights Society (ARS), New York/ADAGP, Paris.

Ray's interest in the subject: its unconventional imaging of lesbian eroticism could have fulfilled a common, voyeuristic male fantasy. In contrast, Man Ray's image of a pair of buttocks with a hand-drawn, inverted cross atop not only equates an inverted cross with the male sexual organs but also celebrates anal eroticism. Although the image of two women kissing was never published, *Monument to D. A. F. Sade* (see Fig. 87) was one of a number of works that Man Ray published at the time that directly expressed appreciation for the Marquis de Sade. Miller also experimented with this type of imagery, in one case (Fig. 88) reworking Man Ray's *Homage to*

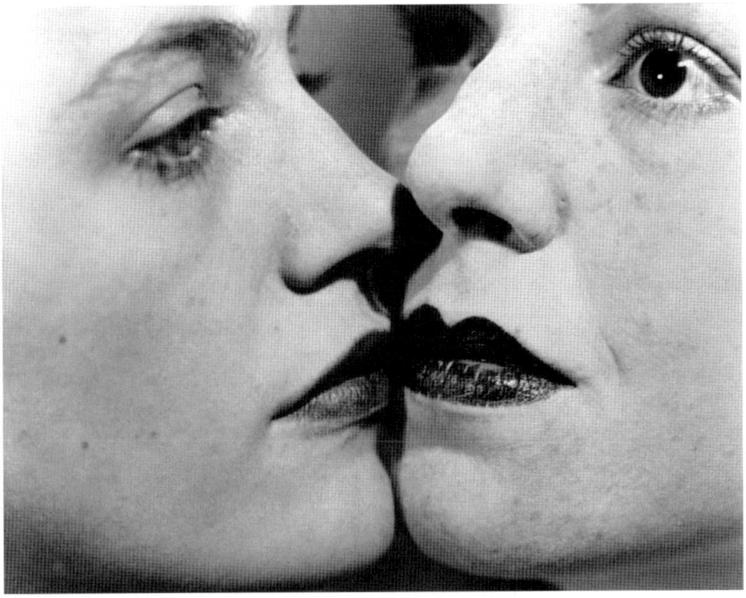

FIGURE 85
Man Ray, *Le Baiser (The Kiss)*, 1932. Courtesy of Telimage, Paris. © 2006 Man Ray Trust/Artist Rights Society (ARS), New York/ADAGP, Paris.

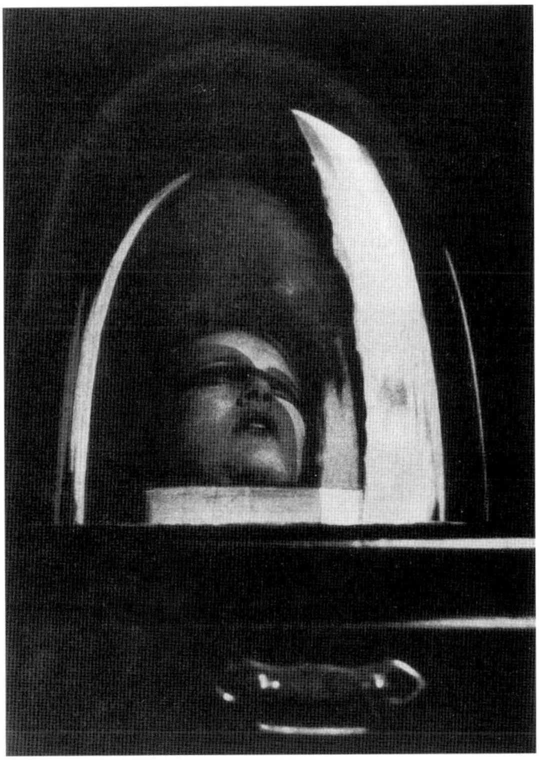

FIGURE 86
Man Ray, *Homage to D. A. F Sade*, 1930. In *Le Surréalisme au Service de la Révolution* 2 (1930). © 2006 Man Ray Trust/Artist Rights Society (ARS), New York/ADAGP, Paris.

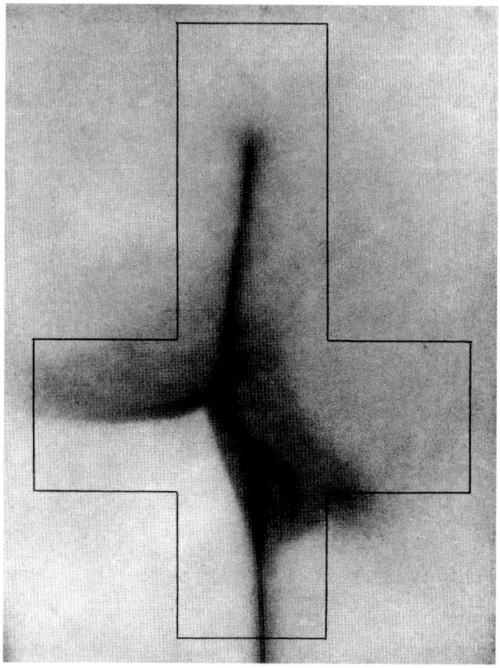

FIGURE 87
Man Ray, *Monument to D. A. F. Sade,* 1933. In *Le Surréalisme au Service de la Révolution* 5 (1933). © 2006 Man Ray Trust/Artist Rights Society (ARS), New York/ADAGP, Paris.

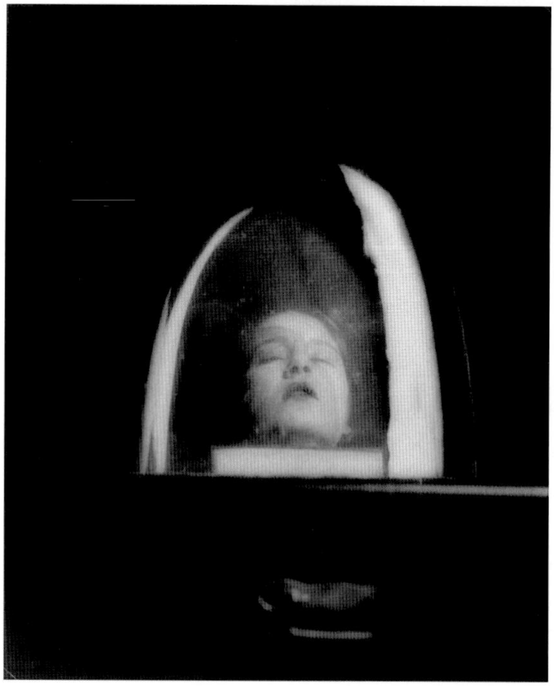

FIGURE 88
Lee Miller, *Head (Tanja Ramm) in Bell Jar,* 1930. Courtesy of the Lee Miller Archives, East Sussex, England.

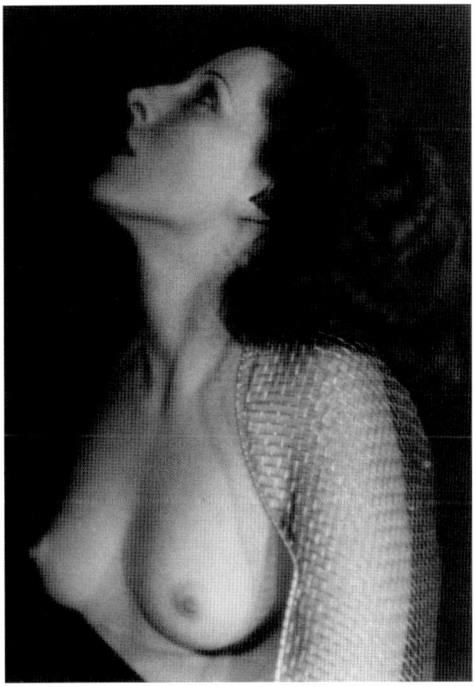

FIGURE 89 Lee Miller, *Woman with Saber Guard*, ca. 1930. Courtesy of the Lee Miller Archives, East Sussex, England.

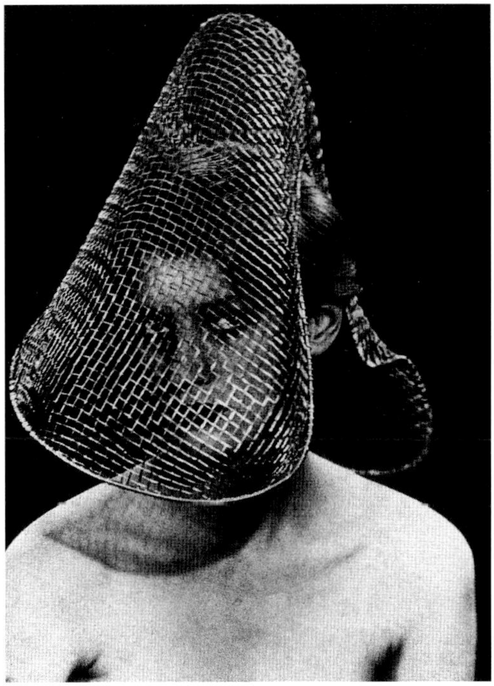

FIGURE 90 Man Ray, *Lee Miller Wearing a Saber Guard*, 1930. In *Le Surréalisme au Service de la Révolution* 1 (1930). © 2006 Man Ray Trust/Artist Rights Society (ARS), New York/ADAGP, Paris.

Sade (see Fig. 86), and in another (Fig. 89) depicting her own female model wearing the same metal saber guard that she had modeled for Man Ray (Fig. 90).[63]

As if to reinforce control over his increasingly prominent photographic partner, while also claiming an affinity with Sadeian tastes, Man Ray offered his image of Miller wearing a metal-mesh saber guard (see Fig. 90) to *Le Surréalisme au Service de la Révolution*, which published it in July 1930.[64] Lee's gaze out at the viewer acknowledges, somewhat resignedly, her participation as a model for Man Ray's work. Strikingly, this image of Miller appears with a caption alluding to the Marquis de Sade's scandalous practices. Captioned "these young girls being the last to have distinguished themselves in a scandal of the haunted house," the image was one of a small group that Man Ray made of Miller manipulating the mesh guard—at times wearing it on her shoulder, holding it in her lap, or, as published in *SASDLR*, wearing it over her face like a mask. In this published selection, Man Ray's image of Miller proposes that she is a captive in the ominous house described in the image's caption—which was from a text by André Breton that appeared in an earlier section of the issue.[65]

The image of Miller in *SASDLR* advertises her status as a caged subject of Man Ray's camera. His name's visibility beneath her photograph tightens the link between her role as a model and his sexual reputation, and thus the mask seems all the more to entrap her even as it provides a kind of facial protection. Man Ray's gaze at Miller's naked torso implies a violent approach to her body in that the mesh saber guard is a protective device. In this way, the image reinforces traditional gender roles by equating bodily control of Miller with Man Ray's actions. Because many of the journal's readers would have recognized Miller as Man Ray's current lover, the photograph also invites the reader to imagine the couple's investment in exploring alternative forms of sexual gratification, including sadistic and masochistic pleasures.

Marketing Sadomasochism

In making their personal lives public, Ray and Miller sometimes alluded to apparently perverse sexual interactions. They did so not just to publicize their sex lives but also to represent their identities as explicitly subversive. Man Ray's photographs during the early 1930s, in fact, moved from documenting sexual perversion to selling perversion as a surrealist product. Many of the sexually experimental photographs have remained largely outside the canon of Man Ray's familiar images. The existence of work prints and celluloid negatives revealing this strain in Man Ray's work, however, tells us that photographing sexual perversion was one way for Man Ray to reinforce his and Miller's surrealist credentials.

In a mostly unpublished series of six small vintage prints by Man Ray from about 1930—only one of the series, to my knowledge, has been published, and then not until 1985—the forms of sexual perversion in Sadeian literature become matters of contemporary fashion and avant-garde taste in Man Ray's hands (Figs. 91 through 94). Lee Miller appears with the American author William Seabrook, a man well known for his eccentric sexual tastes and sadomasochistic preferences.[66] Although Seabrook apparently commissioned these images from Man Ray, Miller's participation is important. Her presence not only figures Seabrook's fantasy of his own relation to Miller, but Man Ray, by photographing his lover at play with Seabrook, also shows his own investment in unconventional forms of sexual gratification and the value of the unconventional images for marketing his (and Miller's) surrealist identities.

Miller wears a wide metal collar that Man Ray apparently designed for William Seabrook's wife.[67] Four of the photographs depict Miller and Seabrook together, and two are images of Miller alone. In Figure 91, Miller, photographed without Seabrook yet wearing the metal collar, appears to be a model for the newest in S-M accessories. The halolike effect of the backlighting that surrounds her head and shoulders combines with the crispness of the image to create a photograph akin to a typical Man Ray fashion shot—although here the product is one that

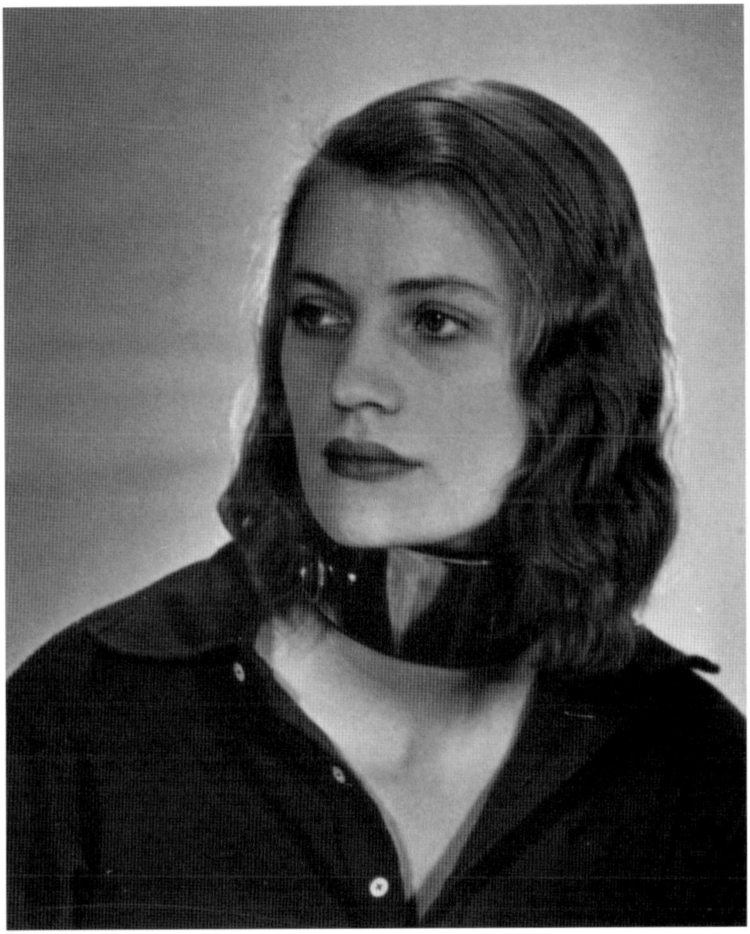

FIGURE 91
Man Ray, *Lee Miller,* ca. 1929–30. Musée National d'Art Moderne, Paris. CNAC/MNAM /Dist. Réunion des Musées Nationaux, Paris/ Art Resource, NY. © 2006 Man Ray Trust/Artist Rights Society (ARS), New York/ADAGP, Paris.

suits the well-heeled feminine masochist. In a familiar way, Miller turns her head to the side to look off frame, just as she has in many of Man Ray's fashion photographs.

The four photographs in which Seabrook and Miller market unconventional sexual practices are not simply ciphers of Seabrook's imagination; they are also Man Ray's creations. In Figure 92, Seabrook enacts fetishistic pleasure as he looks, touches, and seems ready to inhale the scent of Miller's hair. In Figure 93, the wide metal collar takes center stage, both as an object and as the catalyst of a particular physical event. Miller's head, prominently articulated by Man Ray's use of focused light as well as Seabrook's firm grasp of the metal collar, is pulled back and to the side, as if to more easily expose the collar's design elements, as well as to enact

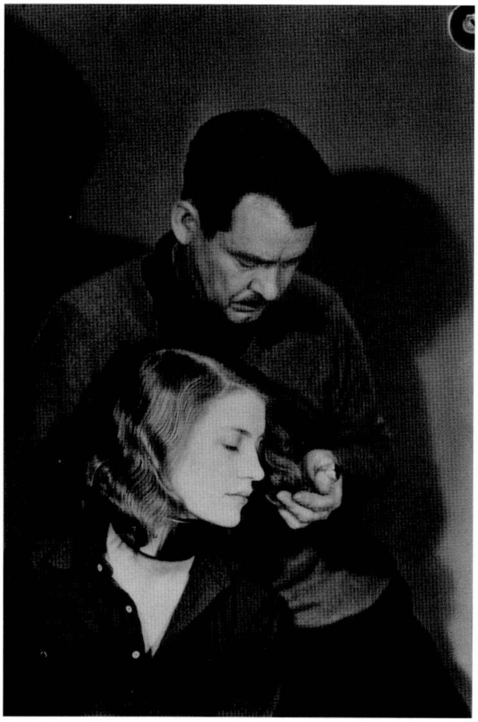

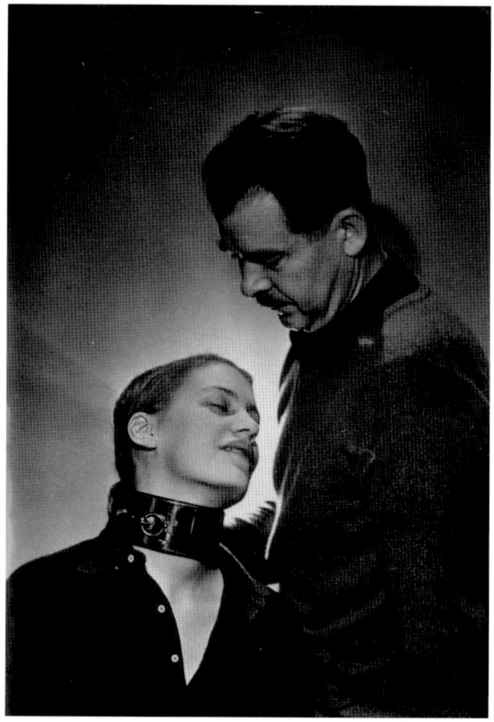

one way to use the collar in practice. Figure 94 further emphasizes the actions inspired by the metal collar, showing Seabrook's hand more prominently as the source of Miller's bodily position, with his fist holding tightly to the collar's protruding rings.

Because of the subtle, stagy lighting and the conspicuous position of the collar in these photographs, Man Ray's images seem to be advertisements for both the collar and sadomasochistic sexuality. Rather than advertising a hat, a dress, or even a corset, Man Ray depicts Miller as the beautiful wearer of his newly designed collar as well as the object of Seabrook's (and potentially his own) sadomasochistic desire. The collar's prominent encircling of Miller's neck, its visibly refined detailing, and her submission to Seabrook's physical pressure emphasize Miller's allegiance to (if not her personal appreciation of) the fashionability of sadomasochistic sexuality in surrealism. By placing sadomasochistic products at the center of these fashion portraits, Seabrook, Ray, and Miller essentially articulate the contours of a surrealist ad campaign for a transformed set of sexual expectations. Or, better yet, the images document Ray and Miller's willingness to experiment with their sexual identities in representation, if not in practice or in the eye of the public.

In addition to creating the fashion-oriented portraits of Miller and Seabrook, however, Man

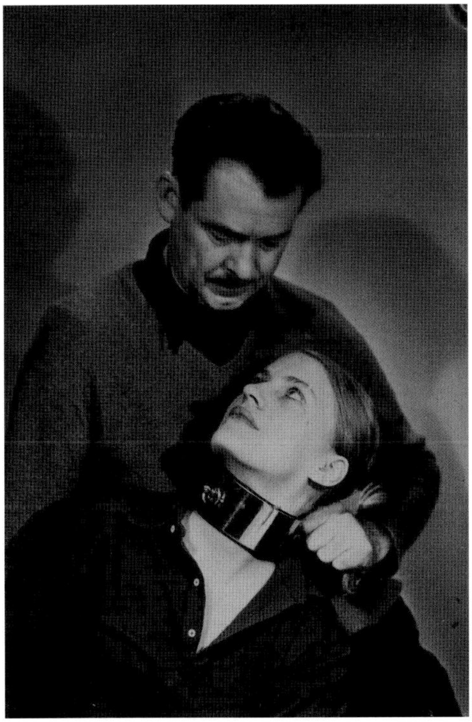

FIGURES 92, 93, 94
Man Ray, *Lee Miller and William Seabrook,* ca. 1929–30. Musée National d'Art Moderne, Paris. CNAC/MNAM/Dist. Réunion des Musées Nationaux, Paris/Art Resource, NY. © 2006 Man Ray Trust/Artist Rights Society (ARS), New York/ADAGP, Paris.

Ray explored sadomasochistic sexual activity in a documentary style. The resulting work, a group of celluloid negatives that the Musée National d'Art Moderne in Paris acquired in 1994, was apparently also a Seabrook commission. The photographs seem bent upon documenting the types of activities that Seabrook and his varied partners favored, and their style hews more closely to a style I would call anthropological: that is, they reveal a compelling interest in the positions, the subjects, the accoutrements, and the banal details of each event (whips, cuffs, gloves, and a suitcase to hold this paraphernalia; a telephone, light switches, vibrant wallpaper, and modernist-inspired furniture; the residue of cocktails or a small meal). Reinforcing this ethnographic feel is the apparent artlessness of the photographs. Composition, lighting, and the boldly graphic style we usually expect from Man Ray here give way to interest in the activities going on in front of the camera.

In one of the photographs (Fig. 95), a nude woman hangs from the ceiling with hands bound behind her back, her toes barely touching the ground. Her body is tense, yet it droops to the floor like a doll's. The fashion aesthetic of the S-M portraits of Miller and Seabrook has evaporated. Instead, Man Ray has captured a moment in an unfolding drama: the rope binding the woman's wrists cuts across the right corner of the image, alluding to an off-frame partici-

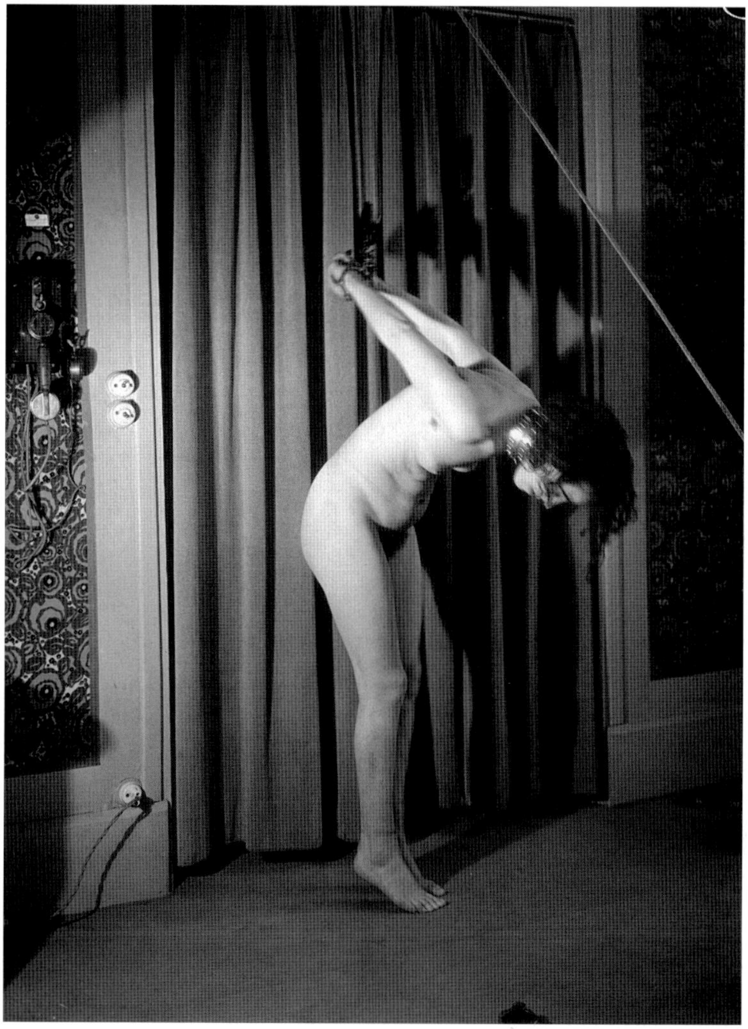

FIGURE 95
Man Ray, *The Fantasies of Mr. Seabrook: Woman Suspended,* ca. 1930. Musée National d'Art Moderne, Paris. CNAC/MNAM/Dist. Réunion des Musées Nationaux, Paris/Art Resource, New York. © 2006 Man Ray Trust/Artist Rights Society (ARS), New York/ADAGP, Paris.

pant. This detail encourages the viewer to imagine the process of creating a bondage event; and the blur of the body's movement solidifies this effect by suggesting that the event is taking place before our eyes. The inclusion of the telephone and light fixtures at left, however, suggests a "do-it-yourself" effect: a domestic environment is a fine location for such S-M play. Other negatives from this series more explicitly document the unfolding of an S-M narrative: In one (Fig. 96), a leather-clad dominatrix stuffs paper into the mouth of a nude woman who has been securely bound by leather belts and lies in a fetal position on the floor. In another

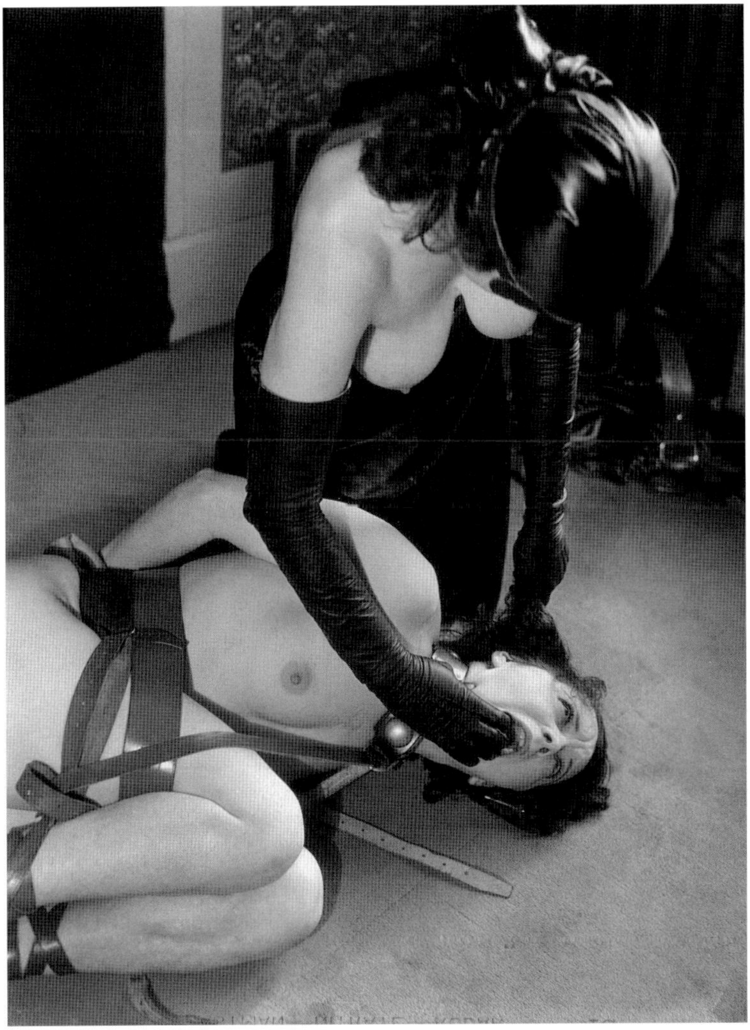

FIGURE 96
Man Ray, *The Fantasies of Mr. Seabrook,* ca. 1930. Musée National d'Art Moderne, Paris. CNAC/MNAM/Dist. Réunion des Musées Nationaux, Paris/Art Resource, New York. © 2006 Man Ray Trust/Artist Rights Society (ARS), New York/ADAGP, Paris.

(Fig. 97), the same dominatrix and a helper collaborate in their domination of the woman. A large pair of pliers wielded by the dominatrix grip the bound woman's right breast; the dominatrix's assistant applies a large screwdriver to her prey's genitals. Notably, the couch behind the figures and the floor in the left corner of the image are arrayed with tools of the masochist's trade: a pair of handcuffs, ropes, different sizes of leather straps. The glassware, alcohol bottles, and stray electrical cords that converge around the table at right, and the radiator next to the couch, stress a different interpretation. These apparently extraneous (yet dutifully pho-

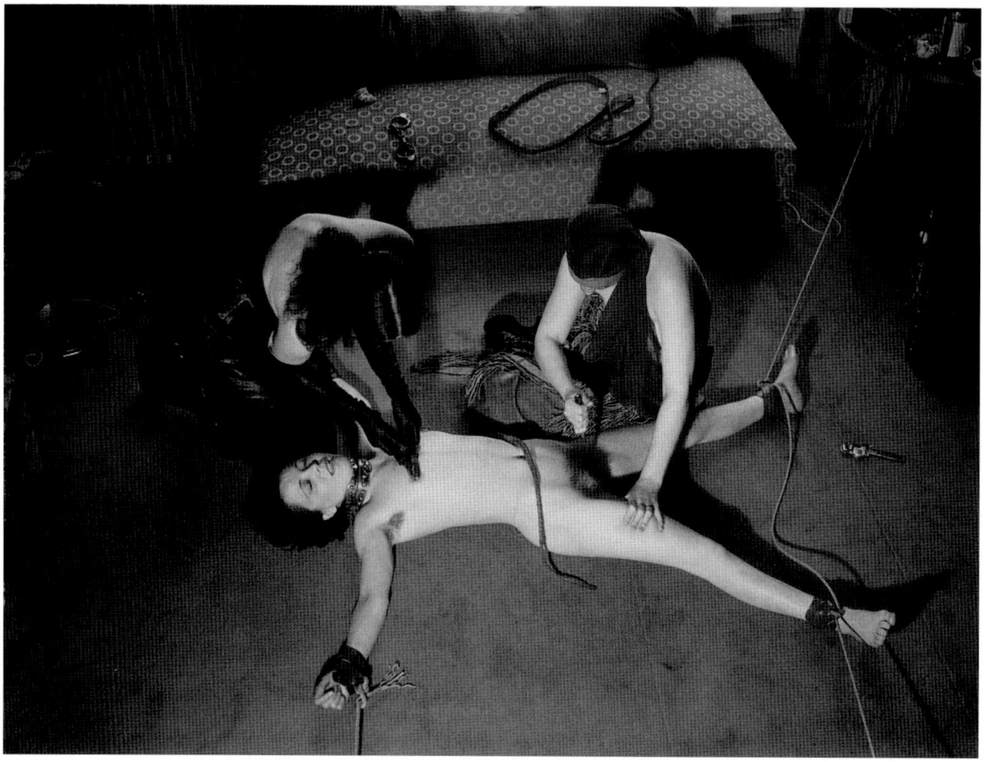

FIGURE 97 Man Ray, *The Fantasies of Mr. Seabrook*, ca. 1930. Musée National d'Art Moderne, Paris. CNAC/MNAM/Dist. Réunion des Musées Nationaux, Paris/Art Resource, New York. © 2006 Man Ray Trust/Artist Rights Society (ARS), New York/ADAGP, Paris.

tographed) details encourage the viewer to see this image as a spontaneous record of an event rather than as a carefully staged story or "shoot." Yet this quasi-documentary quality is called into question by the studied placement of the objects on the couch and the lonely wrench on the carpet to the right of the bound woman's legs.

Whereas the vintage photographs of Miller and Seabrook advertised a beautifully iconic image of S-M play through the glamorously stilled, isolated studio images of the two participants, the less seductive, grittier light and texture of these "anthropological" images suggest that these photographs are records of a real event—either because we can see signs of ongoing inhabitation of the space (phones, glasses half full, pillows bearing impressions of use) or because we read movement in the splayed body (as in the photograph of the woman whose slightly blurred, suspended body suggests movement in response to her binding)—rather than a fabricated advertisement. Nonetheless, we would be wrong to assume that the neat

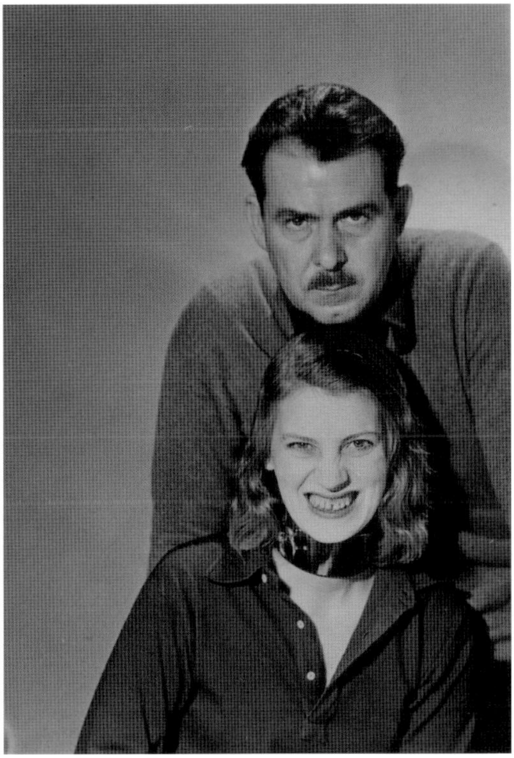

FIGURE 98
Man Ray, *Lee Miller and William Seabrook,* ca. 1930. Musée National d'Art Moderne, Paris. CNAC/MNAM/Dist. Réunion des Musées Nationaux, Paris/ Art Resource, NY. © 2006 Man Ray Trust/Artist Rights Society (ARS), New York/ADAGP, Paris.

organization of the image of a spread-eagled woman, for example, has nothing to do with Man Ray's careful approach to fashion composition. These bodies of previously inaccessible, sexually experimental documents by Man Ray are historically significant because they underscore how fantasies (if not realities) of sexual transgression permeated Man Ray's production of a perversely surrealist self-image. They emerge like the repressed material of the bourgeois male psyche, threatening to disturb their viewers' assumptions about sex in the early 1930s and further, to validate aberrant forms of desire.

But Miller's relationship to this part of Man Ray's work—as well as her willingness to participate in his demonstrations of a new product line for the sadomasochistic set—exposes the complexity of her place in the surrealist milieu, which derived from her position within Man Ray's sphere of influence. Ray could move easily from public to private and back again with his photography, even as he made sexually explicit and transgressive images. Whether she had the option to go "public" in the way that he did, we can only speculate. One surprising image from the S-M portrait shoot with Seabrook, however, suggests that Miller found a way to document her refusal to submit completely to the role of a willingly passive female partner (Fig. 98). In this final image from the shoot, Miller nearly growls back at the camera, at Man Ray, as if to contest the position in which she finds herself. Here, through her forceful, knowingly confrontational stance, Miller both courts and rejects her status as the object of masculine desire.

The public articulation of heretofore-private activities and desires, coupled with the Ray-Miller penchant for manipulating conventional or stereotypical representations of gender, made their practice exquisitely surrealist in the years around 1930. By expressly demanding that their viewers confront alternative sexualities, desires, and practices, they effectively took the apparently private spaces of the bedroom and the unconscious and pushed them into the light for viewing, analysis, and perhaps even admiration. In this way, they created their own collaborative version of photographic surrealism. They fashioned surrealist identities on the backs of sexual ambiguity, deviance, and perversion, and they did so by asking their viewers to confront their own assumptions about permissible ways of talking about and having sex. Although people at the time (and to a certain degree, people today as well) generally regarded sexuality, sexual activity, and erotic desire as the stuff of *la vie privée* (private life), if the surrealists had their way, these issues would become central to conversations about postwar life.

CHAPTER FIVE

The Lessons of Barbette

SURREALISM, FASCISM, AND THE POLITICS OF SEXUAL METAMORPHOSIS

Barbette is the sphinx of transformists. He compels each spectator to ask himself the riddle:—Girl or boy? Girl or boy? To which Barbette-sphinx will reply—And you?

ANONYMOUS, "Barbette et le Barbettisme"

In 1926 Man Ray made a series of photographs of the transvestite music-hall performer Barbette at the urging of Jean Cocteau. Barbette was a legend already, as much of a cultural icon to Parisian audiences as Michael Jackson was to fans of the late twentieth century.[1] Barbette was the stage name, and alternate persona, of a young male acrobat from Texas named Van der Clyde. He transformed himself into Barbette by donning feminine attire and performing an acrobatic routine as a woman. The popularity of Barbette's act hinged on the successful creation of an illusion of femininity that she renounced at the end. When the curtain dropped and her number appeared to be over, the performer returned to the stage, removed her wig, and proved that she was actually a man.

Barbette's performance confused the well-defined gender roles that lay at the heart of France's "return to order" by blurring the lines between masculinity and femininity. Her convincing portrayals pressed her audiences to acknowledge that the body could not always be trusted to tell the truth about gender. Even her name—Barbette—disturbed the usual boundaries between male and female: it is a feminized version of the French word *barbe*, or beard; thus, the root of her name reflected a common index of virile masculinity.[2] Her well-orchestrated performance of gender ambiguity attracted diverse audiences, from aficionados of popular entertainment to surrealist artists and writers, in the 1920s and early 1930s. Her number was popular not only because of its commercialization of sexualized performance but also because it publicly rendered gender identity as a visual and cultural experience that audiences could read and interpret in different ways. This chapter explores the similarities and differences in two key readings of *le numéro Barbette* that emerged from surrealism in the early 1920s, in the work of Man Ray and of Pierre Drieu la Rochelle. Although both these men identified with surrealism at the time they first engaged with Barbette's performance, they extracted different elements from her presentation of gender instability and used these elements for their own aesthetic purposes. In their eyes, her sexual indeterminacy was a metaphor for postwar French society's difficulty dealing with the promise of, and anxiety about, a world without distinct sexes.

Barbette made her first appearance in a surrealist context in 1929—three years after Man Ray photographed her—in an issue of the surrealist-friendly Belgian journal *Variétés* (Fig. 99).[3] The journal photographs, which appear to be stock publicity photographs, compare her female and male identities using the same type of "before-and-after" rhetoric we have seen both at Val-de-Grâce and in Kertész's pairing of two men at the edge of the Seine. In this case, however, the photo spread depicts the same physical body in both a masculine and a feminine persona. The juxtaposition of the two identities across the same body (and across the same page) seems aimed to expose the conventionality of sexual difference; it also seems ready to declare that conventionality a fiction, encouraging us to read the two figures as the two sides of a coin. On the left, hovering in an indeterminate yet theatrical space, Barbette averts her gaze slightly from the viewer and enacts the demureness of an objectified female subject. Her sinuous pose accentuates the delicate conformation of buttocks, legs, and elegantly pointed toes usually attributed to women, and her deflected gaze encourages the viewer's voyeuristic pleasure in looking without being looked at. Van der Clyde, in contrast, stares directly out at the viewer from a street corner, his facial expression and rooted stance reflecting an aggressively masculinized subject position. Whereas Barbette inhabits a dark, amorphously interior space of fantasy, Van der Clyde is out on the street, so we see a familiar sexual equation: the passive, private female versus the active, public male. But because the same body represents both states of being, the layout encourages the viewer to see sexual difference as a matter of pose, gesture, and context rather than an inherent quality of the flesh. Although the images depend on stereotypical ideas about masculinity and femininity, and about the public and private spheres, the convincing portrayal of both qualities at once demands that viewers consider that the body may be an unreliable marker of sexual identity. The editors of *Variétés* apparently found Barbette compelling because she bucked conventional ideas about human beings and attested publicly to the arbitrariness of the relationship between sexual organs and gender identity.

We can see, then, that *le numéro Barbette* was more than an anomaly on the music-hall circuit; Barbette's commercial success shows us that the surrealists' interest in disrupting traditional notions of sex and sexuality were part of French popular culture and that audiences were already primed to consume the gender instability that the surrealists wanted to sell. Just as

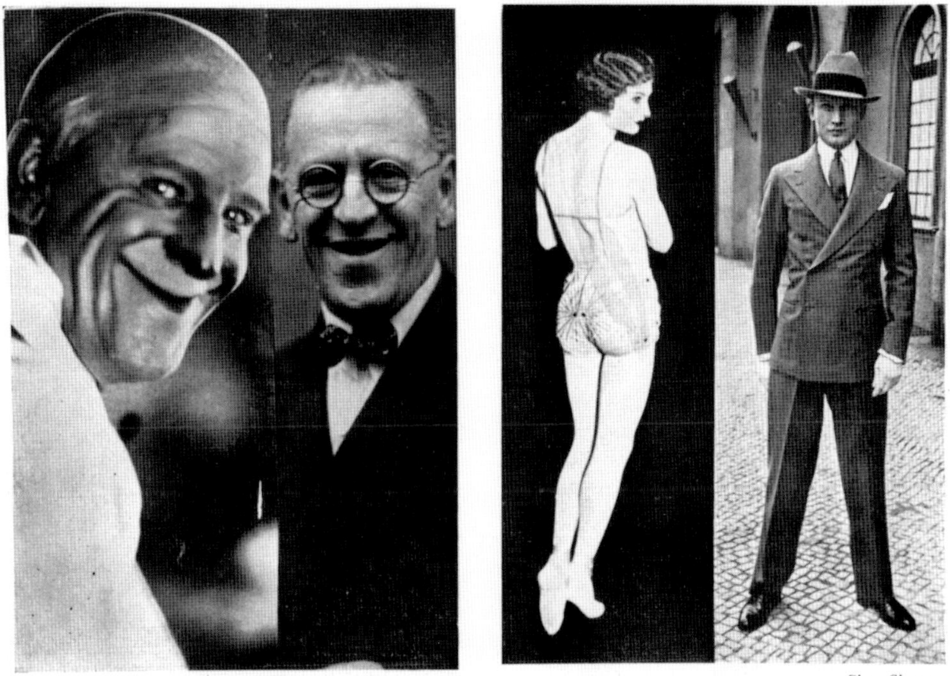

FIGURE 99 *(At right)* Barbette–Van der Clyde, 1929. In *Variétés* 7 (November 1929).

Kertész's photographs seemed to market new forms of masculinity that were already in view on the streets of Paris, Man Ray's images of Barbette emphasized the disintegrating boundaries between the sexes in postwar society. However, Man Ray's Barbette photographs pushed viewers to imagine how social change might occur rather than simply to accept such change as a spectacular form of eroticized entertainment.

Le numéro Barbette

Members of Barbette's audience were seduced by her performance because it seemed the work of an authentically female physique. And Barbette was not one to dissuade them, as she repeatedly emphasized this bodily authenticity when she spoke about her act. In a 1929 *VU* magazine interview, for example, she emphasized her body's important role in creating a convincing illusion of femininity. Admitting that she refrained from eating during the day to maintain her svelte figure, she also noted that her diet forced her to give up the gifts of food some fans gave her: she sadly returned one admirer's gift of a luxurious bit of *foie gras* because she worried that the delicacy would fatten her up.[4] She had to maintain her body's delicate balance—between the high level of muscular fitness required for her performance and the expectation of a slender female form— to successfully project a feminine identity.

Pierre Bost dedicated a section of his 1931 history of the circus and the music hall to a discussion of the physical nature of Barbette's femininity. Echoing Barbette's belief that muscular conditioning was essential to her preparation, Bost highlights her bodily presence and physical strength in his description of her performance:

> The acrobat . . . leaves half his chest to be discovered, and . . . retain[s] only a pair of drawers around his loins; this nudity is the first mark of the sincerity of the game. The contraction of the muscles, the movements of air, are present to our eyes like unimpeachable witnesses to success; a nude athlete cannot fake his weight, and it can be strongly moving to see, in certain strength exercises that are difficult to perform, in the athlete's stretched and strained body, an abdomen panting and jumping like a furious animal.[5]

Bost focused on the character of Barbette's flesh, the veracity of her "slender pink body" and, as a sign of the difficulty of the acrobatic performance, her heaving belly.[6] Barbette's raw power could have given away her secret if she had not been a master of gender dissimulation; her act worked only if Van der Clyde's body passed as a woman's.

To satisfy the audience's hunger for proof of her femininity and to quell any suspicions about her "true" identity, Barbette began her act with an explicit revelation of her figure. After walking down a staircase onto the stage (Fig. 100), she removed parts of her costume so that the audience could clearly see her body. Sometimes she heightened the sensuality of the moment by performing this portion of the act while reclining on a divan (Fig. 101). Her languid pose and the deliberateness with which she undressed, dramatizing her act's similarity to a strip tease, seemed to confirm her identity: "On stage, against the curtains of black velvet, a young woman with a gilded silver wig, helmeted with plumes and diamond tufts, trailing costly lamés and metallic lace, . . . disrobes on a couch. Some precious rugs lead up to the couch. . . . The woman stands nude, breasts and genitals jeweled with stones . . . and she leaps onto the high wire."[7]

After disrobing to the point of near nudity, Barbette would leap onto the high wire, drawing praise for a costume that emphasized her womanliness. Suggestively shaped fabric and jewels were sewn onto the sheer material that covered her breasts and pubis to accentuate her femaleness. Van der Clyde's orchestration of femininity was thus a two-part process: first he put on a woman's costume, and then he removed most of the costume to show that Barbette's body was female. Barbette passed as a woman not only because of her use of elaborate clothing, makeup, and jewels but also because her physique and her attitude were recognizably feminine.[8] Only

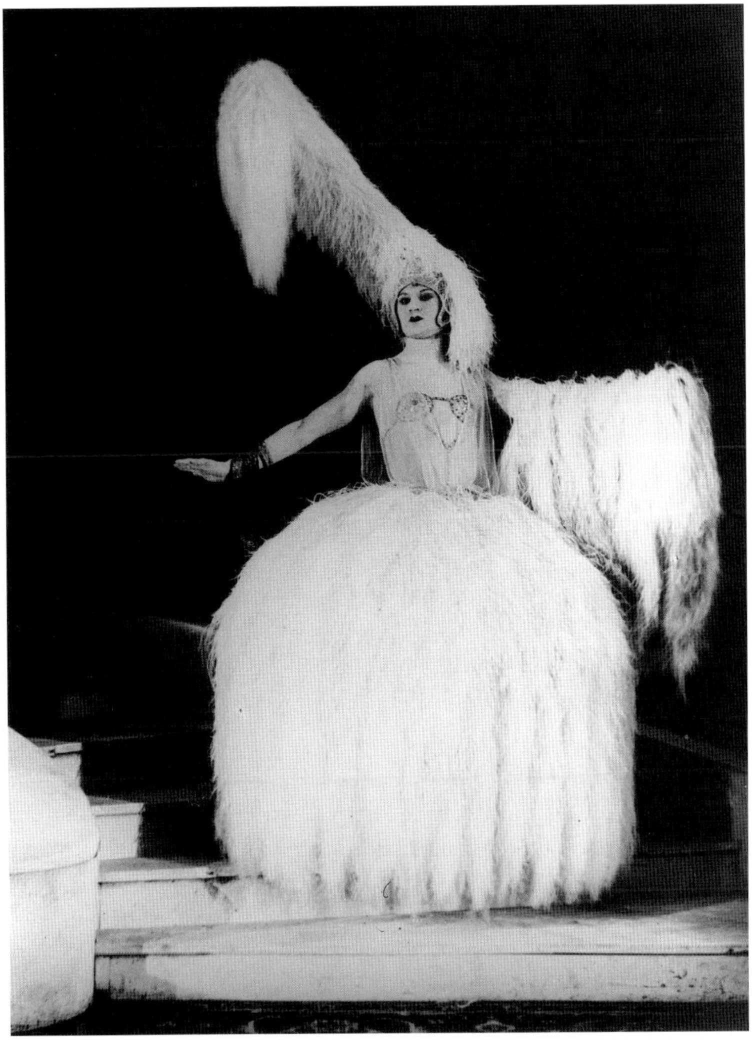

FIGURE 100
Man Ray, *Barbette*, 1926. © 2006 Man Ray Trust/Artist Rights Society (ARS), New York/ADAGP, Paris.

by obscuring her male anatomy and carefully measuring the proper degree of physical exercise could Van der Clyde become Barbette. As one critic remarked, "He never practices, contrary to his acrobat comrades. Because he believes that he would lose his line of feminine sveltesse, absolutely necessary to the character of magical illusion that he has created."[9] To persuade audiences to believe in Barbette's femininity, Van der Clyde carefully sculpted his body to make it appear as womanly as possible. Yet by refraining from extended physical conditioning,

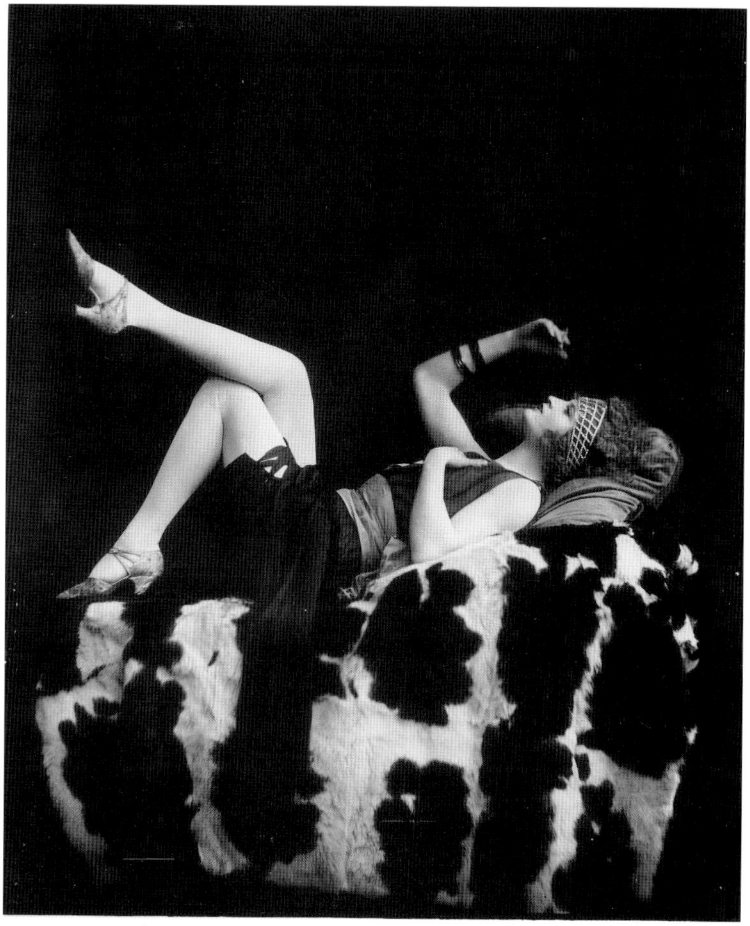

FIGURE 101
Barbette on a Divan, undated. Courtesy of the Bibliothèque Nationale de France, Paris (Opéra).

he ran the risk of failure: although his minimal training made him look more feminine, it could also lead to injury.

A second element that critics noted in *le numéro Barbette* was the process of mental transformation from man to woman that occurred during the hours of preparation before each performance. Like an artist, Barbette applied makeup and manipulated her body to recast her identity in a feminine mold. Thus, her act also depended on an aesthetic impulse—the ability to apply gender with an artist's materials:

> Barbette arrives at the music-hall at least three hours early. . . . His makeup is a work of art and patience. . . . In order to achieve the physical, and also psychological, metamorphosis of Barbette, the makeup begins with a first sketch of the face, then it is the bust

> the artist renders, then he sheaths his legs in a maillot and returns to his table, in front of the mirror, in order to perfect this astonishing and expressive face of which he makes a sort of master portrait. Barbette proceeds with . . . precision . . . in order to impregnate himself spiritually as well.[10]

Both physical and psychological metamorphoses depended on the artistic reorientation of the body's surface, coupled with a more time-consuming process of "spiritual impregnation" to enable Barbette to become feminine from within. She didn't rely solely on external elements like makeup and costume to become feminine; she also struck observers as psychologically feminine. This nexus of physical and psychological transformation from man to woman and back again was central to Man Ray's exploration of Barbette. The series of photographs he made of her in 1926 appears to be a conceptual precursor of Man Ray's ambiguously gendered images of men, from his own *Self-Portrait with Bathrobe* to the section "Men Before the Mirror" in the first survey of his photography in 1934.[11]

Man Ray's Barbette

Unlike the somewhat static photographs of Barbette in the *Variétés* spread, Man Ray's images of *le numéro Barbette* offer vivid photographic descriptions of her performance's subversive potential by focusing on the *process* of her transformation. The best known of his Barbette images (Fig. 102) echoes the surrealist interest in gender instability, not only by showing a body whose sex seems to be changing before our eyes but also by pictorially describing male emasculation as a prerequisite for Barbette's femininity. In this image, Barbette is attaching her stockings to a girdle that Van der Clyde used to cover and flatten his genitals. The thick, white girdle fabric denies us a clear view of Barbette's sexual anatomy, even as her pose centers our attention upon it: in the midst of a stocking adjustment, she has propped one leg up onto a chair in a pose that exposes her corseted crotch. Man Ray's use of a raking, focused light directs our attention to this region of Barbette's body, too, starkly illuminating the contours of her thigh and genital region. Yet the binding of the genitals displaces our attention to other parts of her body as we look in vain to see her sexual anatomy. Our gaze alights first, perhaps, upon the blond pin-curled hair and theatrical makeup, both of which contrast with the flat, muscular torso. The contrast between her feminized head and masculine chest creates confusion. Does the suppression of masculinity—visible in the binding of the male sex organs—make her feminine? Or does the ambiguity of her body's gendered codes challenge the viewer's sense of what makes a body more female or more male?

In a 1926 commentary on Barbette's performance in *Nouvelle Revue française,* Jean Cocteau saw traumatic content in Man Ray's photograph and described Barbette as a "bandage-maker's Apollo."[12] Man Ray's image intriguingly depicts Barbette's manhood at the moment of conversion suggested by Cocteau: a spectacular moment of self-inflicted, if symbolic, castration. The girdle does not just suppress the bulk of Van der Clyde's organs but implicitly functions like a bandage worn to cover injury to the male body. Because Barbette can emerge only after Van der Clyde conceals his organs in this way, she not only registers anxiety about emasculation, but her physique inverts the usual cues an audience would use to figure out her sexual identity. Man Ray presents Barbette's femininity as dependent on suppressing Van der Clyde's manhood rather than on producing a visibly female sexual organ like a breast.

The people who paid to see Barbette perform were not party to the studied process of transformation that Man Ray captured with his camera. Thus, audiences reportedly were terrifically surprised when Barbette's wig came off at the end of the show to reveal Van der Clyde's shaven head and young man's bodily gestures. Audience members apparently responded in different ways to Barbette's elaborate performance. Cocteau noted that Barbette's mutable act was so successful because it engaged so many viewers simultaneously: "He pleases those who see in him the woman, those who understand in him the man, and others for whom the soul is inflamed by the supernatural sex of this beauty."[13] Cocteau was not alone in seeing the fluid, convincing display of gender ambiguity as the key to Barbette's popularity. Contemporary music-hall critic and historian Maurice Verne reported that male members of Barbette's audiences often felt deceived by the performance. According to Verne, male spectators wanted the "voluptuous illusion" of Barbette's femininity to continue without interruption. Female spectators, in contrast, were reportedly relieved to discover that Barbette was actually a man: Van der Clyde's dramatic revelation reduced their anxiety about this beautiful female "rival."[14]

Although Verne's is only one interpretation of Barbette's act—whose male-centered and heterosexist impulses we should acknowledge—a strong likelihood exists that the pleasure of being seduced by Barbette's sexual metamorphosis was probably more unsettling than Verne's account allows. One can imagine both male and female spectators delighting in the delicious surprise of this amorphous, uncertain image of the gendered body, particularly because the experience of having one's assumptions overthrown by the thrill of misrecognition would have added a layer of surprise to the already-seductive performance. *Le numéro Barbette* promised a more titillating spectacle, and much more to talk about after the show, than did music-hall performances by the popular chanteuse Mistinguett or even the "exotic" American dancer Josephine Baker. Through Barbette's performance, audiences could experience the pleasure of discovering new sexual terrain through a mutably sexed body that aroused their curiosity and confused their expectations. Given all the publicity surrounding *le numéro Barbette,* audiences probably knew what to expect when they purchased their tickets to the performance. However, even critics refrained from breaking her seductive spell, choosing to perpetuate the myth of

FIGURE 102 Man Ray, *Barbette,* 1926. In *Photographs by Man Ray 1920 Paris 1934* (1934). © 2006 Man Ray Trust/Artist Rights Society (ARS), New York/ADAGP, Paris.

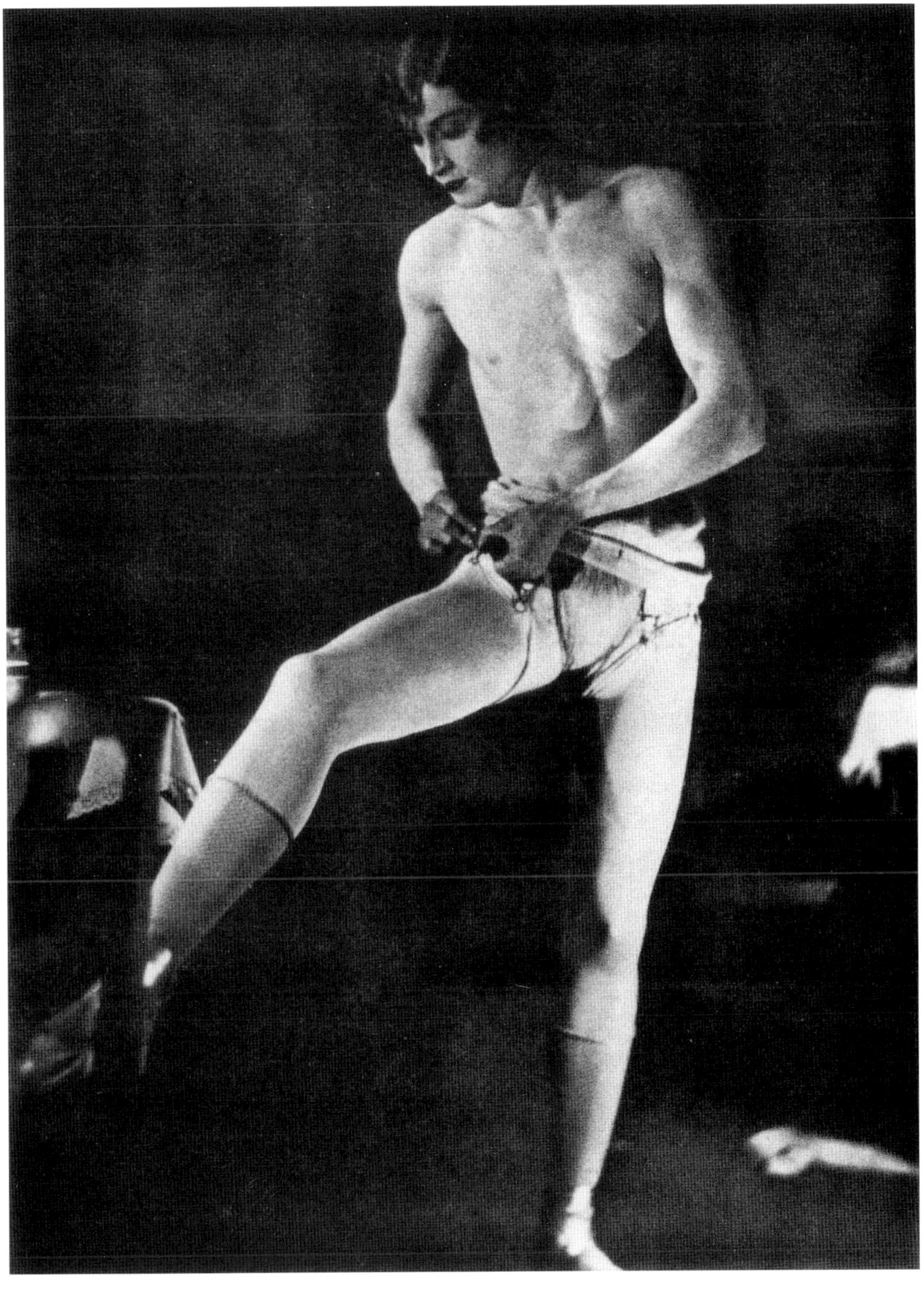

her femininity in their reviews until the very last sentence in which they described her spectacular finale.

Viewed against a postwar backdrop of male trauma and emasculation, Barbette's oscillation between femininity and masculinity, and her act's rejection of a rigid categorization of gender identity, were likely magnets for Man Ray and his surrealist friends. As we saw in Kertész's photographs of male amputees and male distortions, documenting male compromise and ambiguity was a key strategy for critiquing the success of postwar reconstruction and the rhetoric that supported it. *Le numéro Barbette* invited spectators not only to consider gender ambiguity a fact of contemporary life but also to imagine possibilities for eroding the hierarchies of the traditional sex-gender system. The lasting popularity of Barbette's act (she performed well into the mid-1930s) suggests that she successfully packaged postwar anxiety about gender stability as a salable commodity.[15] The fact that Paris audiences flocked to see her for nearly ten years suggests that they enjoyed seeing gender instability enacted before their eyes. Because her act confined the risks of social upheaval to the music-hall stage, spectators could explore their feelings about the breakdown of boundaries between the sexes without facing real or lasting societal change. The image of a liberated, powerful, modern woman, capable of usurping some of manhood's terrain, was already a source of cultural anxiety in the mid-1920s. Even the word *la garçonne*—a feminized version of the French word for boy, *le garçon,* coined by novelist Victor Margueritte in 1922—suggested that this new woman had willfully appropriated a masculine attitude in her identity and her public life. Barbette was a *garçonne*-like figure. When a member of her audience walked back into the streets of Paris after seeing her performance, Barbette's conflated sexual identity would recede into the mysteries of the theatrical experience. Her performance might stir up anxieties that her audiences could work through, but the real effects of her transformations would rarely dare to follow a theatergoer home.

For the surrealists, too, Barbette challenged traditional ideas about the transparency of connections between the physical body and the cultural one. She pried gender away from sex and treated her body as an elaborate screen onto which the beholder could project his or her own assumptions, fantasies, and desires. In other words, *le numéro Barbette* presaged the demise of a unified concept of sexual difference. More than a spectacular form of popular entertainment, *le numéro Barbette* embodied a complicated debate about the nature and function of gender in French culture and revealed the body as a tool for shaping social and political discourse. As for Man Ray, Barbette helped him stake out a position as an unconventional surrealist portrait photographer.

In Man Ray's first published monograph, *Photographs by Man Ray 1920 Paris 1934,* the picture of Barbette in the act of suppressing her male genitals (see Fig. 102) appeared at the end of a section of the book that claimed to depict "men before the mirror."[16] This section was prefaced by a text of the same name (attributed to Rrose Sélavy) and included portraits of many of the men who were card-carrying members of the Parisian avant-garde. Tristan Tzara, Paul

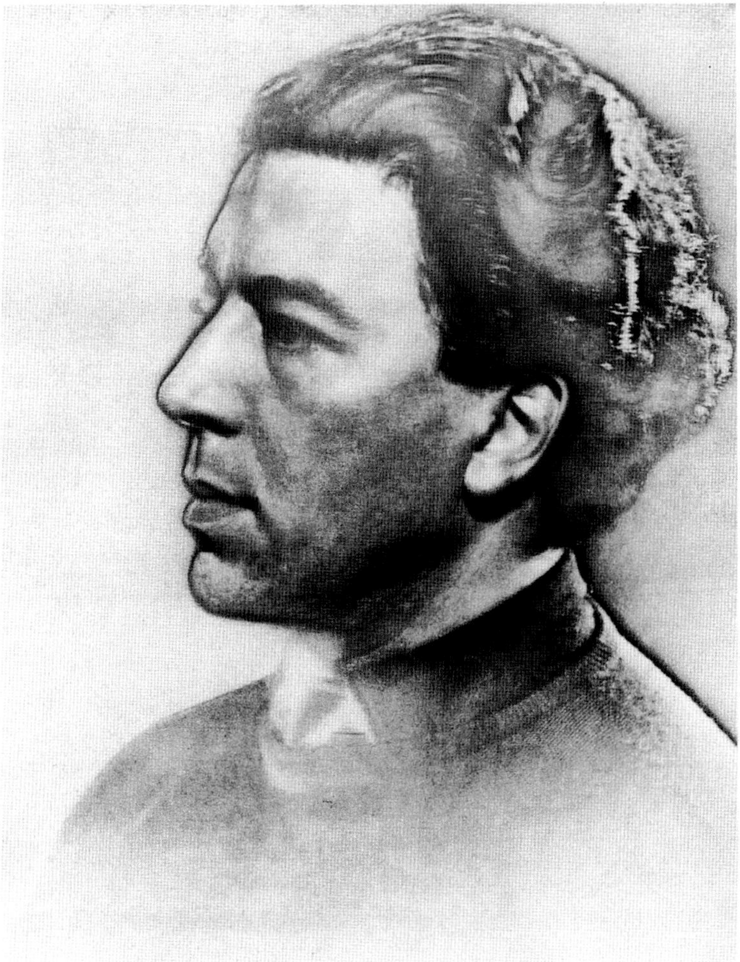

FIGURE 103
Man Ray, *André Breton,* 1934. In *Photographs by Man Ray 1920 Paris 1934* (1934). © 2006 Man Ray Trust/Artist Rights Society (ARS), New York/ADAGP, Paris.

Eluard, Pablo Picasso, Man Ray, Marcel Duchamp, and André Breton all made appearances in this group. Interestingly, the bulk of the portraits were quite conventional in format, using frontal or profile poses and a bust-length format. Several of these images, such as the one of André Breton, promoted a surrealist aesthetic by using the technique of solarization that Man Ray and Lee Miller had discovered in 1929 (Fig. 103). Significantly, however, only one image deviated from the portrait format: the photograph of Barbette. Unlabeled and shown in full-length format, the Barbette image suggests that the performer's notoriety preceded her, because she was the only figure who went unnamed.[17] By showing her entire body, the photograph reiterates her importance, even as her figure remains an enigma. Her unconventional appearance and her unexpected position at the end of a long line of great avant-garde male portraits seemed calculated to guarantee a surrealist *frisson* for the viewer.

The presumption that the audience would know Barbette's story and would link it to Man Ray's catalog of avant-garde masculinities was crucial to Man Ray's placement of her portrait. By including the portrait, the section "Men Before the Mirror" demanded that viewers question the stability of the identities of the men within the avant-garde. Another set of portraits that conflated the fixed boundaries of gender appeared at the end of the section "Visages of Women" that preceded the male avant-garde portraits. There, Man Ray threw down a gender-bending gauntlet by situating a masculine-looking portrait of Gertrude Stein directly before a German-language version of Rrose Sélavy's text "Men Before the Mirror." By setting up contradictory image comparisons—Stein's portrait across from the text about men and the image of Barbette's becoming a woman at the end of the male portraits—the book aimed to destabilize readers' assumptions about the nature of femininity and masculinity.[18]

The half-dressed Barbette's appearance at the end of Man Ray's portraits of men suggests that her femininity was *both* illusion and reality, for she shows how porous the boundaries might be between masculinity and femininity, particularly within the circle of artists and writers associated with surrealism. By inserting her into a compendium of *grands hommes* in this way, Man Ray suggested that viewers see the series as a critique of traditional masculinity. The monograph may also have been a counterproposal to the increasing unrest within French society at the time it was published. In the wake of the February 1934 fascist riots in Paris, Barbette's ambiguously gendered public persona may have signaled a dangerous turn of events for those on the French right for whom porous social and sexual boundaries signaled cultural decay. In 1934, after all, with Hitler's recent rise to power in Germany and the increasing visibility of fascist parties in France, Barbette's indeterminacy was proof of the growing popularity of the surrealists' agenda of sexual and social confusion. Not everyone who decried the surrealist agenda saw Barbette as a threat, however. For the fascist writer Pierre Drieu la Rochelle—who had been close to Louis Aragon and the surrealists during the early 1920s—Barbette modeled a new way of understanding the power of gender ambiguity in postwar French culture. Unlike his surrealist friends, however, Drieu offered an interpretation of Barbette's unstable gender that promised an exceptionally integrated social body—at a time when society seemed to be fracturing.

Another Barbette

In 1924, the year that he reviewed Barbette's music-hall act for the *Nouvelle Revue française,* the prominent Parisian writer and critic Pierre Drieu la Rochelle was not only a close friend of Louis Aragon's but a surrealist fellow traveler. He had participated in several dada events, including the trial of Maurice Barrès (1921) and the production of the 1924 pamphlet *Un Cadavre*

(A Corpse), which attacked the work and the public commemoration of the recently interred French literary giant, Anatole France, whom they viewed as an outmoded figure. He also seems to have been prominent enough in the group to warrant an appearance in Robert Desnos' surrealist cemetery in "Pénalités de l'Enfer" (see Fig. 39 in Chapter 2). Although Drieu broke publicly with the surrealists beginning in 1925, before then he appeared to be sympathetic to many of the group's literary and cultural goals. Thus, that he found *le numéro Barbette* worthy of critical attention is perhaps not surprising.

Before turning his attention to Barbette, Drieu had been writing for several years after the war about the negative consequences of the conflict's degradation of the once-robust French man. In a 1922 essay, he worried about an increasing "decadence of the creative spirit" as well as an increase in male submissiveness after the war, and he dreamed of an intellectual, moral, and physical reintegration that could alleviate the threat to European culture posed by postwar dislocations and mechanization.[19] His writing in the immediate postwar years consistently explored ways to re-create a strong society from the ashes of the war. For Drieu, postwar man had been emasculated by the machinelike intensity of modern technology. With both workers and soldiers relegated to increasingly passive roles in society, this new man dreamed not of enhancing his virile energies through active, creative work but of satisfying his physical and emotional desires in passive acts of consumption: drinking, eating, and nonprocreative eroticism. In his 1925 novel (dedicated to Aragon), *L'Homme couvert de femmes,* for example, Drieu's male protagonist, Gilles, anxiously oscillates between an obsession with sexual gratification and impotence. For Drieu, men who surrendered to bodily pleasure instead of acting forcefully guaranteed their own extinction.[20] Instead of fostering sterility, onanism, inversion, alcoholism, and drug use, he longed to reinvigorate the "infantilized" postwar man through "intellectual, moral and corporeal reintegration."[21]

In contrast to Drieu's anxiety about male decadence, his response to *le numéro Barbette* was enthusiasm about the act's corporeal integration of social and sexual opposites—male and female. After watching Barbette's act in 1924, Drieu reported that her powerful, streamlined body was crucial to her success. "What a difference between this great, nervous amazon and the swollen females that one sees elsewhere, with muscles wrapped in fat," he wrote, marveling at her figure's ideal athleticism. "She is muscled," he remarked, "ready for anything."[22] Barbette's trim physicality pleased Drieu. He described her powerfully androgynous, "effaced" hips as the physical traces of a crucial form of male-female integration that he would one day lionize as the source of reinvigorated creative power. Yet his admiration of her ideal body type had a catch. He notes in his review that Barbette's abrupt removal of her golden wig crushed the viewer's fantasy of a muscular, active femininity. The "truth" of her body thus soured his appreciation of her assertive, vigorous performance, causing him to begin to see Barbette as an effeminate man. "Suddenly she turns herself with a brusque gesture, new, unexpected," writes Drieu. "She removes a wig; she now has close-shaven hair. Hesitation: Because of the makeup and because one can expect everything, triple-level delusions. In the next instant, the beautiful American has become a man."[23] The slip from a muscular, robust female to a man who looks a little too much like a woman was for Drieu at this time a problematic, if provocative, proposition.

Drieu la Rochelle's relationship to the surrealist group has not generated much ink in the history of the movement, particularly in discussions of surrealist aesthetics. But in his and the surrealists' attention to *le numéro Barbette,* we see a moment of common interest before Drieu converted to a fascist aesthetic in 1934. (Scholars typically cite his publication of *Socialisme fasciste* as the event that cemented the change in his political agenda.)[24] Barbette's ambiguous interpretation of gender roles put forth sexuality as a means of contesting the return to order, which is why her act was so attractive to Drieu and his surrealist friends. At the time of Drieu's review—two years before Man Ray's photo session and five years before *Variétés* published its version of Barbette–Van der Clyde—he seemed relatively in step with surrealist ideas about the potential for gender ambiguity to catalyze personal and social transformation. By 1925, however, when Drieu penned a controversial attack on surrealism for the increasingly overt political content of its activities, he began to diverge from the path that he had so often walked alongside his surrealist friends. And by 1927, Drieu had severed nearly all his ties to the group because of the surrealists' commitment to communism.[25]

Drieu's argument—which he first put forward in *Socialisme fasciste*—was extranationalist: he believed in a myth of a new postwar Europe that would grow out of a more fluid, ambiguous notion of community. If Europeans and their governments could transcend national, cultural, and linguistic boundaries, a new European community could emerge.[26] Both at the level of political theorization and in keeping with his perception of increasingly weak and undifferentiated concepts of class and gender, Drieu longed to repair the "civilization without sexes." He proposed shoring up the best elements of the social and the individual bodies first and then fusing them into a totality that would move beyond traditional national or sexual categorization. If, as George Mosse reminds us, "fascist style demanded a strictness of form which did not allow for ambiguities or vague definitions," we can see why Drieu's formulation lies outside the usual recipes for understanding fascism.[27] By acknowledging social and political differences at the outset and then transforming these differences into a new image of the individual and the state that would transcend traditional concepts of nation and gender, his model seems to parallel his earlier appreciation for Barbette's hybrid androgyny. A fusion of masculine and feminine elements within Van der Clyde's body created the illusion of Barbette's lithe, androgynous performance. Echoing Van der Clyde's suppression of difference to create a new individual, Barbette, Drieu's conception of fascism was that it created a new political figure to act as an "intermediary between the old right and the old left." Neither promoting "a politics of equilibrium . . . nor of balance," Drieu saw fascism as "a politics of fusion."[28] Barbette seems to parallel Drieu's political model of fusing elements to create an extranationalist Europe because she illustrated the fusion of female (beauty, grace, creative force) and male (active, muscular, physical power) in her performance. Her femininity was active, her muscles no longer enshrouded by the ballast of postwar physical decadence and dissolution.

Drieu's early appreciation of the erasure of sexual difference in Barbette and his subsequent desire for an extranational political culture in *Socialisme fasciste* suggest that he continued to engage with surrealist ideas about the dissolution of the bourgeois social order. He learned to read the body's sexual ambiguity through a surrealist lens. To compare his and the surrealists' images of Barbette is to realize that they shared an appreciation for her vivid yet anxiety-producing conflation of genders. Yet Drieu's assumptions about the use-value of her androgyny led him to a very different conclusion from that of the surrealists. Although Drieu's aesthetic and political trajectory diverged dramatically from that of the surrealists in the 1930s, Barbette's imaging of gender ambiguity taught him something important about the body's fundamentally malleable state: that one might be able to reinvent the individual by transcending difference and fusing the best qualities of both sexes. He later incorporated this lesson into his unconventional approach to the development of a unified fascist body politic.[29]

Aspects of Drieu's interpretation of Barbette seem to have infiltrated his characterization of the key figure of Dora in his 1939 fascist novel *Gilles*. In this novel—a parable of Drieu's trajectory from surrealist fellow traveler to supporter of violent fascist revolt—Drieu's idealization of "intellectual, moral and corporeal integration" presents a particularly chilling fantasy of personal and collective homogeneity.[30] Whereas Drieu's 1924 review of Barbette cited such homogeneity as a disturbing potential outcome of Barbette's physical and psychological ambiguity, in *Gilles* he promotes the androgynous, youthful American woman Dora as an antidote to the wrecked postwar man. He essentially recasts Barbette's ambivalently gendered surrealist body as a unified (fascist) whole.

The novel introduces Dora as one of several lovers of the book's male protagonist Gilles. In ways that uncannily repeat key elements of Drieu's approving description of Barbette's body fifteen years earlier, Dora overwhelms Gilles with her power and her physicality:

> Dora was not beautiful if one looked at her face. Nothing admirable in these small dark eyes, this stubby, unformed nose. But her body manifested the beauty of a race and, in contrast with the unsuccessful face, the triumph of the body was all the more moving. . . . Long legs, long hips; long hips on long legs. A powerful chest, dancing on a supple waist. Higher, in the clouds, straight and large shoulders. . . . Higher still, beyond the clouds, the solar profusion of blond hair.[31]

In his description of Dora, Drieu founds a new fascist order on the idea of an integrated body whose androgynous beauty, supple movement, muscular power, and (even) blond hair echo the image of Barbette. Taking her "large body in his hands," Gilles "held tight to an idea of life that had been dear to him . . . a certain idea of force and nobility."[32] To Gilles, Dora is a powerful woman endowed with the "ample ribs of an athletesse on which were softly superimposed these mother's breasts"; she "evoked the best of man"; she was a "Doric beauty" whose "pure and homogeneous substance" was like "marble" to his touch.[33] Dora's name quite literally implies the solidity of a classical heritage (the Doric order and, oddly, Freud's most prominent hysterical patient of the same name) and her flesh is like marble to Gilles's touch. She reflected Drieu's interest not only in the masculinization of the female body but also in the integration of race, force, and nobility within a fascist aesthetic.

In contrast to Drieu's description of Dora—athletic, blond, physically perfect, beautiful in her representation of a race—his characterization of Gilles some pages later reflects visceral fear about male emasculation. He reveals these feelings of terror, however, only in the moment when Gilles embarks upon an erotic encounter with the female body, in this case, that of a prostitute.

> He wanted to undress before her. . . . She was surprised to discover his body. This body was disconcerting: it was bipartite like an anatomy diagram. On one side it was the body of a bright and almost athletic man, with a large rooted neck, a straight and full shoulder, an ample chest, a narrow hip, a well-fit knee; on the other side, it was a lightning-stricken carcass, tormented, warped, dessicated, puny. This was the side of war, of slaughter, of torture, of death.[34]

The splitting of the masculine subject in this image of Gilles's bipartite body operates in direct contrast to the integration of femininity and masculinity in Dora. Drieu's tormented carcass of a man is cowed by the specter of the female body. His impotence is an outgrowth of his unstable, bifurcated self. Thus, if Dora echoes the conflation of the sexes Drieu once saw in *le numéro Barbette,* her idealized femininity conflicts directly with the unincorporated, disaggregated halves of damaged masculinity: On one side, Drieu describes a man who is fit and has his full strength; on the other side is half a man whose desiccated decrepitude exposes the ravages of a violating war. Male emasculation, in this fascist novel, occurs in the body and does so at the moment of sexual revelation, when the injured man confronts a healthier, robust—if decadent in her role as a prostitute—female counterpart. Whereas the prostitute to whom Gilles exposes his body remains clothed, the sight of Gilles's disturbingly schizophrenic physique confounds her assumptions about masculinity: she is unable to reconcile the sight of "virile solidity" with that of a tortured carcass. And as the novel closes, Drieu makes clear that Gilles must take up arms against the decadent society that has produced this psychophysical "splitting" and emasculation to produce a new postwar fascist man. Thus, male emasculation, in Drieu's scenario, stems from Gilles's memories of the idealized Doric beauty of his former female lover. In contrast to Gilles, whose body is dis-integrated, split in two, partly virile and partly weak, Dora is an ideally unified figure of feminine power and productivity—one who might well serve as a model for the emerging fascist man. The lesson that Drieu learned from *le numéro Barbette,* I suggest, is that a truly revolutionary culture would succeed only if it could rally the body politic around a new physical logic that fused male and female into an integral, robust whole. Perfection would be achieved when masculine force and female creativity triumphed over a stylized, desiccated, "decadent" persona. (Critics and politicians on the left and the right accused men and women alike of being decadent through "inversion" of the usual structures of sexual identity: men were feminized, and women relinquished their female "natures" in favor of greater independence.) If the body of Drieu's new fascist woman would be more like a man's, fusion with this new woman would be the only way to heal the currently impaired masculinity.

Scholars often note that the model of the fascist male body rejects hybridity and confusion in favor of an armored, virile ideal. As Hal Foster (and Klaus Theweleit before him) has argued, "fascist armoring . . . is pledged against all comminglings urged by sexuality." Thus, some people may be surprised to find that Drieu's fascist bodily ideal evades such arguments about the need to shore up the male body's defenses against the "feminine forces of sexuality and death."[35] Rather, his account of the ideal fascist body—individual as well as collective—imagines that the feminine and masculine could be powerful only if expertly fused into a unified whole. Unlike the German fascist aesthetics that armored the male body, and by extension a new German nation, against the terror of hybridity, fluidity, and passivity, Drieu's idealized fascist form relied on recognizing each gender's strengths.[36] This model would select these strengths and then fuse them into a new postwar subject that evaded polarization. Instead of envisioning a fragmented body, Drieu preferred to imagine a body politic that reintegrated the fractious, ambiguous elements of the war-ravaged social body into a fascist unity.

Acknowledging continuing polarization of the "intellectual" class and the "manual" or working class in some of the great cities, Drieu saw that a traditionally binary (Marxian) model of class conflict was no longer relevant because individuals were increasingly able to hold multiple social and political positions.[37] "We see not a replacement of one class by another," wrote Drieu, "but the fusion of ancient elements in a new formation that corresponds to new needs."[38]

In Drieu's realization of the necessity to merge or conflate the sexes, we can glimpse the impact of the surrealist bodily aesthetic on his development of a fascist political agenda. His was a two-part solution: first, to illuminate the best aspects of manhood and womanhood, and then—echoing his extranationalist theory of political regeneration—to incorporate the most powerful, productive elements of masculinity and femininity into a reorganized, unified body. Drieu's ideal body did not resecure the boundaries between the sexes; rather, it fused the essential characteristics of the modern woman and the idealized action of the wartime man into a newborn fascist individual. And this fusion would occur because of the need to protect the tormented man whose body had been cut in two by the war and cultural decadence, polarized as a noble and a degraded self. Whereas Barbette encouraged the surrealists to envision gender categories as fictive, she suggested to Drieu a protofascist body—and by extension, a body politic—in which the virile power of a man would fuse directly with the beauty and creative energy of a woman.[39]

Discussions of the relations between modernism, the avant-gardes, and fascism are relatively few in current accounts of interwar culture. In discussing surrealist art, Therese Lichtenstein has productively interpreted Hans Bellmer's dolls in terms of their dialogue with the idealized fascist bodies favored by Nazi artistic culture.[40] However, interpretations of French fascism have mostly centered on the constitution of fascist political ideology or, more recently, the production of fascist literature. Only a few scholars of interwar art history have challenged us to consider the dialectical nature of cultural production at that time by exploring the specific conditions under which modernist and avant-garde practices intersected with fascist ones.[41] In other words, the possible links between surrealism and fascism (however tenuous or negatively received) have been slow to attract attention.[42] Although Drieu's intimacy with Aragon and the surrealists in the early 1920s is well known among literary scholars, his aesthetic and political trajectory inside and outside the group has remained largely invisible to historians of surrealist art and literature. How, then, did someone like Drieu move from a position of some intimacy with surrealism to his role as one of the most prominent fascist intellectuals in France during the 1930s? The more I struggle with this question, the more I believe that Drieu must have learned from surrealism's aesthetics of dismemberment and destabilization—particularly in relation to the problematic nature of postwar gender and sexuality—and later mutated the idea into his vision of fascist unification.

Although the surrealists and Drieu shared an interest in gender ambiguity—formed in the crucible of surrealist Paris—their divergent paths in the late 1920s and 1930s reveal how differently one could use gender instability as a form of aesthetic or cultural critique. (Even so, we need to acknowledge that both Drieu and the surrealists believed that traditional views of gender had been destroyed by the early 1920s.) Whereas the surrealists embraced the destabilized and fragmentary imagery of Barbette's performance, Drieu grew increasingly anxious about the disarticulation of tradition she represented as the years passed. He soon became publicly antagonistic to the surrealists' demonstration of the body—which, for them, always seemed to be a metaphor for a larger social body—as perpetually dismembered. Man Ray's photograph of Barbette in the process of becoming a woman not only emphasized this fact of perpetual change but showed gender ambiguity in a state of suspended animation. Rather than securing a place for the re-created, integral body, then, his photograph of Barbette with her genitals bound and her pin curls flowing emphasized the impossibility of re-creating a unified social body.

Drieu and the surrealists also shared the belief that bourgeois culture was vulnerable if one attacked the strict categories of gender at the center of bourgeois domestic and public life. And Drieu—like his surrealist friends—recognized the power of Barbette's depiction of psychological and social instability to reshape audiences' experience of their world. Drieu took this lesson from surrealism but transformed its message to serve a different purpose. His approach to cultural representation—reorganization and fusion of a disaggregation of elements to create a new object—carried vestiges of the surrealist method. But Drieu moved away from the surrealist investment in dismemberment by accentuating reconstruction of the human subject through unification of disparate elements. Whereas the surrealists celebrated Freud, Sade, and Marx for their deconstructive achievements, Drieu rejected the anarchic potential of these men's ideas in favor of an imagined unity that would create not only a new, postwar man but also a modern, efficient, homogeneous European society. In a political parallel of his fantasy about Barbette's (and Dora's) fusion of the masculine and feminine, Drieu assumed that deconstruction of the nation-state system would lay the groundwork for a new postwar Europe.[43]

Barbette's gender ambiguity encouraged two distinct views of the aesthetic and political potential of the body. The ambiguity of her performance not only suggested a critique of conventional ideas about sexual difference, but, in the case of Drieu, offered a model of aesthetic and political change in which the fusion of apparently opposing views would generate a whole: the active, creative beauty of the ideal fascist subject or an extranational fascist Europe. Whatever way the interpretive pendulum swung at the time, *le numéro Barbette* helps us see that, for a brief moment at least, the ambiguously gendered body encouraged competing ideas about how to put gender ambiguity in the service of revolutionary politics. Just as *le numéro Barbette* manipulated the presumed boundaries between the sexes, it encouraged dramatically different interpretations of the implications of sexual ambiguity for postwar culture. Thus, Barbette shows us a moment—difficult to acknowledge and rarely mentioned—when surrealism's aestheticization of gender instability and Drieu's brand of fascism were closer than one might want to think.

CONCLUSION

A Postscript on Masculinity and Reconstruction

Why were women's bodies so often the site of surrealist experimentation? What did the mostly male members of the surrealist collective hope to achieve with such work? Did a connection exist between these images and the maiming and killing of so many men during the war? To answer these questions, I unearthed little-known archival material and revisited canonical surrealist texts and images like Lautréamont's *Chants de Maldoror* and Kertész's *Distortions*. In this book, I approach surrealism and its history analytically, looking at how the surrealists conceived of and produced works that reflect contradictory ideas of postwar manhood.

The case studies I include here reveal that the mostly male members of the surrealist group around Breton did indeed celebrate and appropriate the feminine in order to negate establishment culture. But they also turned their gaze to men, although much of the work in which they did so has remained at the periphery of surrealism's history. The images I discovered of damaged, ambivalently gendered, unstable, and even deviant masculinities are absent from mainstream art-historical accounts of surrealism. To develop an account of surrealist masculinity required looking at what the surrealists did not do and say in their work as well as what they did. Reading around the edges of surrealist production, I show that some of the work produced by the best-known surrealist artists did not always share the stylistic and theoretical preoccupations of the surrealist canon.

The Kertész we know as the maker of sensational, distorted images of women had another side to his practice: his uncertain photographs of deformed men actually preceded the images of violated women for which he is best known. The apparent misogyny of his distorted females masked an anxiety about male identity to which the earlier distortions of males gave voice. The female distortions were first published in 1933 and again in the 1970s, whereas the images of distorted men that preceded them remained on shelves in the Kertész archive until now. Because the male images were withheld from circulation, they never found a place in the history of Kertész's photography.

This divorce of Kertész's distorted males from accounts of his practice epitomizes the difficulties that face those who are interested in surrealism. Many depictions of women are reproduced in the expanding literature on the surrealist movement, but those of men rarely appear in such publications. This situation has roots in the surrealists' own inaction; they refrained from promoting and circulating these depictions. Because surrealist images of women are more widely available for study and analysis than are those of men, the collecting and publishing practices of museums, galleries, and scholars reinforce this situation. The stylistic orientation of art history itself, moreover, rarely presents opportunities to discuss such work: if the content or visual effects of a work diverge from those that scholars commonly recognize as surrealist, the work may never receive sustained scholarly analysis. The temptation to analyze surrealism in terms of competing "orthodox" and "dissident" approaches may contribute to this tendency to minimize the possible connections between surrealist representations of femininity and images of masculinity. Then, too, during the 1920s and 1930s (and, one could argue, even today) artists had greater success making and selling images of women in compromised, vulnerable, or sexualized positions than they did making similar images of men.

The surrealists were wedded to the masculinist culture of their time even as they raised their voices for a revolution of both mind and action. It seems clear now that their work did little to achieve the sexual or political liberation that their manifestos, programs, and actions so often proclaimed. Yet some of the images I've presented here—of dismemberment, mutilation, sexual ambiguity, gender anxiety, and displaced fears of male loss—show that several of the men associated with surrealism recognized that the concept of masculinity was neither stable nor monolithic after the war. The ideal of a timeless, heroized masculinity had lost its power in the face of the war's devastating impact on the lives of so many men. Male anxiety, as well as desire, seemed worth exploring—not just because the surrealists were interested in exploring the unconscious but also because to explore male anxiety and gender confusion was to challenge the hierarchy of a capitalist society and its idealized image of bourgeois masculine power. Whether the surrealists' challenge to this paradigm succeeded, however, is another question.

⊙ ⊙ ⊙

> The growth of perversions is not a moralizing theme that obsessed the . . . Victorians. It is the real product of the encroachment of a type of power on bodies and their pleasures. . . .

> The implantation of perversions is an instrument-effect: it is through the isolation, intensification, and consolidation of peripheral sexualities that the relations of power to sex and pleasure branched out and multiplied, measured the body, and penetrated modes of conduct. Michel Foucault, *The History of Sexuality*

> The truth is that the new type of man demanded by the rationalization of production and work cannot be developed until the sexual instinct has been suitably regulated and until it too has been rationalized. Antonio Gramsci, "Some Aspects of the Sexual Question"

The surrealists tried to construct a liberated future by creating works that effected alternative ways of behaving in postwar France. In an increasingly regulated and commodified society, driven more and more by practices of industrialization in work and leisure, the surrealists came to believe that the sexual drives through which the unconscious expressed itself were crucial to their revolutionary agenda. As France recovered economically from the war, men and women toiled in factories that adopted Taylorist models of assembly-line labor. Although labor became more efficient as a result, individuals grew increasingly cut off from the objects they produced. Individual workers could not master the overall production process, instead experiencing their labor as a fragment of a larger, ungraspable whole. The advertising techniques that emerged after the war bore an uncanny similarity to this piecemeal form of labor: the trend in advertising imagery was to dramatically fragment bodies and commodities to draw attention to products and to whet consumers' appetites for buying the real (complete) thing. Although factory techniques alienated workers from the products of their labor, workers could still buy goods that (as advertisers hoped) satisfied their desire for a feeling of completeness. The surrealists learned from advertising, medicine, and economic technologies how efficacious the fragment could be, but they used that knowledge to pursue a counterculture outcome. By deploying advertising images in novel ways—as in the sequence in *L'Âge d'Or* in which such images encourage antisocial acts because they prick viewers' unconscious—the surrealists aimed to advertise something other than a commodity or social stability. They hoped their "ads," images that elicited surrealist desires, would help market their brand of cultural revolution. The problem—from my perspective as a feminist scholar—was that their brand of revolution depended heavily on displacing anxiety about male emasculation onto the female body.

The growing body of popular and academic writing on surrealist work makes it clear that this surrealist agenda for social transformation failed. The myriad surrealist works that dramatize femininity as "other," deviant, deformed, or violated are legendary for consistently promoting a power differential between men and women and for drawing on gender stereotypes. One can easily find images of women's bodies that mimic the seductively deforming effects of Man Ray's fashion photography. But where, if ever, does one find similar images of men? Viewed at a distance, surrealist images of the 1920s and 1930s seem to have laid the groundwork for an increasingly sexualized rhetoric in the mass media while opening up new terrain for social and sexual regulation.

In the end, the idea that these experiments with the unconscious might instill the desire to behave differently was wishful thinking. The technologies that surrealists borrowed from medicine, advertising, and pornography—which they thought they could turn to different purposes—did not catalyze individual or collective revolt against sexual or social convention. Instead, the work they created by appropriating such technologies seemed to do nothing more than showcase a surrealist "style." Their best-laid plans resulted not in social transformation but in institutional consolidation. They were defeated by a powerful, industrialized culture whose capacity to shape personal and public experience they underestimated.

In December 1929 Louis Aragon wrote an essay that hinted at the likely failure of the surrealist revolution. He pointed out that the surrealists' appropriation of the advertising techniques of fragmentation and repetition had been rapidly incorporated into the "modern" style on display at the 1925 International Exposition of Modern Industrial and Decorative Arts. The fragment—that cipher of dismemberment; sign of unmet, unconscious desires; and catalyst for alternative states of reality—became the central feature in a mass-market version of "avant-gardism." In so doing, it lost its critical edge and, with it, any power to incite the cultural revolution the surrealists so much desired.

Instead of creating new ways to see and understand one's relation to the world, the surrealists' strategies to disrupt social conventions in the end strengthened the forces of social and political conservatism in the 1930s. Aragon, no longer believing that surrealist work could revolutionize contemporary culture, acknowledged late in 1929 the imminent "return of censorship to the unconscious *(la revanche de la censure sur l'inconscient)*."[1]

Aragon's words offer a fitting conclusion to my account of surrealism and masculinity. They dramatize the promise, and the terror, of the work he and his friends had started after the war—the images of unbridled social and sexual energy that would promote individual liberation and undermine the bourgeois state by recognizing and celebrating the power of unconscious desire. For a time, at least, the surrealists believed that the unconscious could be mobilized to attack the social oppression that the war, and the ensuing call for a national "return to order," had brought into being.

Written some five years after Breton's "Surrealist Manifesto" announced the advent of the surrealist collective, Aragon's words presage T. J. Clark's "bad dream of modernism," a nightmare in which avant-garde explorations of new forms of consciousness simply make it easier for cultural institutions to colonize the spaces the avant-garde had cleared for the road to a liberated future.[2] The surrealist project produced no social or cultural utopia; instead, the surrealists' feminized, marginal, or deviant images prepared the way for postwar social regulation. In many respects, surrealism did less to unleash the unconscious and its unruly desires than to suggest how the techniques of mass marketing could appropriate them. Canonical accounts of surrealism have not examined its few depictions of masculinity—perhaps because these images have seemed to reflect the underside of the movement's claims to feminization, fantasy, and eroticism as the key weapons in their attack on bourgeois culture in the 1920s. The limited visibility of these works, both when they were made and today, suggests that masculinity—particularly images of male dismemberment, deformity, and weakness—can never be as marketable as femininity. Thus, instead of resisting social conservation by producing alternative sexualities and social roles, surrealism actually delivered the unconscious to the technocrats by reconstructing the gendered human subject. As we know, such social regulation was to become a powerful weapon in the hands of fascist ideologues.

NOTES

Unless otherwise noted, all translations throughout this book are my own.

Introduction. The Paradox of Surrealist Masculinity

1 Jean-Jacques Becker and Serge Berstein, *Victoire et frustrations, 1914–1929* (Paris: Seuil, 1990), 165–66.

2 These figures come from A. Sauvy, *Histoire économique de la France entre les deux guerres*, vol. 1 (Paris: Fayard, 1965), 442.

3 In 1811 the French population included 1,035 women for every 1,000 men. In 1921 that proportion was 1,103 women for every 1,000 men. But perhaps most significantly, the proportion of women to men rose dramatically according to age: 1,200 women for every 1,000 men ages twenty to twenty-four; 1,323 women to 1,000 men ages twenty-five to twenty-nine, and 1,253 women to 1,000 men ages thirty to thirty-four. See Becker and Berstein, *Victoire et frustrations*, 156. In one rather public example of anxiety about the impact on traditional family relations of the loss of so many young men, the magazine *J'ai Vu* published an *enquête* asking its readers to respond with ideas about what would become of the 1.5 million young women of marriageable age now that so many young men had been killed or maimed. See the two-part survey, "Enquête: que vont devenir les 1.500.000 jeunes filles à marier?" *J'ai Vu*,15 January 1920 and 1 March 1920.

4 Etienne Balibar, "The Nation Form: History and Ideology," in *Race, Nation, Class: Ambiguous*

Identities, ed. Etienne Balibar and Immanuel Wallerstein (London : Verso, 1991), 101. Balibar draws upon the work of Antonio Gramsci and Louis Althusser in this piece, and these three scholars have been instrumental in the development of my thinking about the connection between a critique of national identity and the surrealists' consistent reevaluations of individual gender identities. Antonio Gramsci remarks that the state creates a certain type of civilization and citizen and that it ought to be considered an "educator" of the populace, teaching its citizens to rationalize and create a particular national society. See "State and Civil Society," in *Selections from the Prison Notebooks of Antonio Gramsci*, eds. and trans. Quintin Hoare and Geoffrey Nowell Smith (New York: International Publishers, 1971), 242–43, 246–47. Louis Althusser's notion of the Ideological State Apparatuses (ISAs) is also key here, particularly his suggestion that the individual's gender and familial identities and identifications support the hegemony of the ruling class; in his formulation, of course, the family ISA and the educational ISA are key components (along with the church, another of the surrealists' bêtes-noires) that reproduce the ideological bases of capitalist production. See Althusser's "Ideology and Ideological State Apparatuses (Notes towards an Investigation)," in *Lenin and Philosophy*, trans. Ben Brewster (New York: Monthly Review Press, 1971), 140–57.

5 Kenneth Silver, *Esprit de Corps: The Art of the Parisian Avant-Garde and the First World War, 1914–1925* (Princeton, NJ: Princeton University Press, 1989), especially chs. 7 and 8; Romy Golan, *Modernity and Nostalgia: Art and Politics in France between the Wars* (New Haven, CT: Yale University Press, 1995).

6 Carolyn Dean's work on interwar French culture and anxiety about decadence and gender identity has been central to the development of my thinking. See her *The Frail Social Body: Pornography, Homosexuality and Other Fantasies in Interwar France* (Berkeley: University of California Press, 2000), and her chapter "History, Pornography and the Social Body," in *Surrealism: Desire Unbound*, ed. Jennifer Mundy (New Haven, CT: Yale University Press, 2001).

7 André Breton, *Conversations: The Autobiography of Surrealism*, trans. Mark Polizzotti (New York: Paragon House, 1993), 71–72.

8 André Breton, "Manifesto of Surrealism (1924)," and "Second Manifesto of Surrealism (1929)," both in *Manifestoes of Surrealism*, trans. Richard Seaver and Helen Weaver (Ann Arbor: University of Michigan Press, 1972), 3–47 and 119–187, respectively.

9 A growing body of literature dealing with women and surrealist art has appeared over the past thirty years. Some of the most important texts include Xavière Gauthier, *Surréalisme et sexualité* (Paris: Gallimard, 1971); "La Femme surréaliste," special issue, *Obliques* 14–15 (1977); Whitney Chadwick, *Women Artists and the Surrealist Movement* (Boston: Little, Brown, 1985); Mary Ann Caws, "Ladies Shot and Painted: Female Embodiment in Surrealist Art," in *The Female Body in Western Culture: Contemporary Perspectives*, ed. Susan Rubin Suleiman (Cambridge, MA: Harvard University Press, 1986); Susan Gubar, "Representing Pornography: Feminism, Criticism, and Depictions of Female Violation," *Critical Inquiry* 13 (1987): 712–41; Susan Rubin Suleiman, *Subversive Intent: Gender, Politics, and the Avant-Garde* (Cambridge, MA: Harvard University Press, 1990); Mary Ann Caws, Rudolf Kuenzli, and Gwen Raaberg, eds., *Surrealism and Women* (Cambridge, MA: MIT Press, 1990). Among the studies that articulate the connections between femininity and masculinity in dada and surrealist repre-

sentation are Hal Foster, *Compulsive Beauty* (Cambridge, MA: MIT Press, 1993); Amelia Jones, *Irrational Modernism: A Neurasthenic History of New York Dada* (Cambridge, MA: MIT Press, 2004); Therese Lichtenstein, *Behind Closed Doors: The Art of Hans Bellmer* (Berkeley: University of California Press, 2001); Sue Taylor, *Hans Bellmer: The Anatomy of Anxiety* (Cambridge, MA: MIT Press, 2000); and Robin Adèle Greeley, *Surrealism and the Spanish Civil War* (New Haven, CT: Yale University Press, 2006).

10 Indeed, Breton seems to have thrived on Nadja's apparent inability to control herself or to submit to the necessary structures of civic life. At the end of his text, he marvels: "I never supposed she could lose or might have already lost that minimal common sense which permits my friends and myself, for instance to *stand up* when a flag goes past, confining ourselves to not saluting it; so we do not side with whatever we feel sympathetic to on every occasion, nor permit ourselves the unparalleled joy of committing some splendid sacrilege, etc." *Nadja*, trans. Richard Howard (New York: Grove Press, 1960), 143.

11 Erika Billeter, ed., *La Femme et le surréalisme* (Lausanne: Musée Cantonal des Beaux-Arts, 1987).

12 Rosalind Krauss, "Corpus Delicti," in *L'Amour Fou: Photography and Surrealism* (New York: Abbeville, 1985), 95.

13 Ibid.

14 Rudolf Kuenzli, "Surrealism's Misogyny," in *Surrealism and Women*, ed. Mary Ann Caws, Rudolf Kuenzli, and Gwen Raaberg (Cambridge, MA: MIT Press, 1990), 17–25.

15 Hal Foster, "L'Amour Faux," *Art in America*, January 1986, 121. Indeed, Foster states that this conflation is an impossible one: "That this conjunction is impossible, that it hardly suffices as a resolution, is suggested by the fact that Bellmer felt compelled to pose his dolls in sadistic tableaux—in scenes that suggest the aftermath of rape, murder, child abuse." Rosalind Krauss's reading of Bellmer's "Doll" series as imaging construction as dismemberment is from her "Corpus Delicti," 86.

16 Hal Foster, "Armor Fou," *October* 56 (Spring 1991): 65.

17 Central to this reevaulation of historical analysis has been Michel Foucault's influential *The History of Sexuality*, vol. 1, *An Introduction*, trans. Robert Hurley (New York: Vintage, 1990).

18 Daniel Sherman notes that most popular representations of the postwar period were reticent to depict death. See Daniel J. Sherman, *The Construction of Memory in Interwar France* (Chicago: University of Chicago Press, 1999), 59.

19 Kaja Silverman, *Male Subjectivity at the Margins* (New York: Routledge, 1992), 55, 16.

20 Ibid., 42.

21 Ibid., 16.

Chapter 1. Anxiety and Perversion in Postwar Paris

1 See Amelia Jones, *Irrational Modernism: A Neurasthenic History of New York Dada* (Cambridge, MA: MIT Press, 2004), 35–56.

2 André Breton and Louis Aragon, "Le Cinquantenaire de l'hystérie," *La Révolution surréaliste* 11 (15 March 1928): 20–22.

3 Breton studied under Babinski, who was himself a student of Charcot's. Records at the Archives of the Service de Santé at Val-de-Grâce are littered with references to Babinski's, Charcot's, and Janet's work, although Babinski and Janet, by 1915, were much more important actors on the stage of wartime hysteria.

4 André Breton, "Manifesto of Surrealism (1924)," in *Manifestoes of Surrealism,* trans. Richard Seaver and Helen Lane (Ann Arbor, MI: University of Michigan Press), 1972, 26.

5 Ibid., 27–28.

6 A chronology of Breton's military medical service during the war, his work under Babinski, and his work with traumatized patients at Val-de-Grâce appears in *André Breton: La Beauté convulsive* (Paris: Musée National d'Art Moderne, 1991), 86–95.

7 Breton and Aragon, "Le Cinquantenaire de l'hystérie," 22.

8 Breton, "Manifesto of Surrealism (1924)," 37. The passage on the meeting of umbrella and sewing machine on a dissecting table appears in Chant Sixième, *Les Chants de Maldoror,* in Comte de Lautréamont [Isidore Ducasse], *Oeuvres complètes* (Paris: Gallimard, 1973), 233–34. Indications of the passage's key aesthetic role for surrealism appear in André Breton, *Conversations: The Autobiography of Surrealism,* trans. Mark Polizzotti (New York: Paragon, 1993), 32; "Le Cas Lautréamont," special issue, *Le Disque Vert,* 1925; Louis Aragon, "Lautréamont et nous," part I, *Les lettres françaises* (1–7 June 1967): 9; and "The Most Important Meeting of Your Life," *Minotaure* 3–4 (1933): 101, an *enquête* that included an illustration by Man Ray of the dissecting table, umbrella, and sewing machine.

9 Lautréamont, *Les Chants de Maldoror,* 81.

10 Philippe Soupault, *Lautréamont* (Paris: Seghers, 1946), 9.

11 Ibid., 15.

12 Philippe Soupault, "Le Cas Lautréamont," special issue, *Le Disque Vert* (1925): 13.

13 Lautréamont, *Les Chants de Maldoror,* 233–34.

14 Ibid., 265–66.

15 Ibid., 167–68. Soupault reproduces this extract from the Chant Deuxième in *Lautréamont,* 69–70.

16 Lautréamont, *Les Chants de Maldoror,* 207, 246.

17 On the themes of sadism and masochism in the work of Lautréamont and the Marquis de Sade, see Maurice Blanchot, *Lautréamont et Sade* (Paris: Éditions de Minuit, 1949), and Kazuya Tsukiyama, "Le Masochisme de Lautréamont," in *Lautréamont: Retour au texte,* ed. Henri Scepi and Jean-Luc Steinmetz (Poitiers: La Licorne, 2001), 99–109.

18 Extract of Lautréamont's *Chants de Maldoror* (Chant Deuxième), as reproduced in Soupault, *Lautréamont,* 69–70.

19 This first exquisite corpse appeared in *La Révolution surréaliste* 9–10 (1 October 1927): 8. Breton's description of the exquisite corpse appeared two years later in a footnote to André Breton, "Second manifeste du surréalisme," *La Révolution surréaliste* 12 (15 December 1929): 15.

20 *La Révolution surréaliste* 9–10 (1 October 1927): 8. Five *cadavres exquis* were published in this issue of the journal, with this masculine example first in the sequence.

21 "Eaux-Fortes (premiers états) de Salvador Dalí pour illustrer 'Les Chants de Maldoror,'" *Minotaure* 3–4 (December 1933): 37.

22 Sidra Stich, *Anxious Visions* (Berkeley: University Art Museum, 1990), 49.

23 André Breton, "Second Manifeste du Surréalisme," *La Révolution surréaliste* 12 (15 December 1929): 2.

24 Assistant Director Claude Heymann recalled years later that the film "could assume its true value only if it was structured precisely within the framework of a 'bourgeois' film." Paul Hammond, *L'Âge d'Or* (London: British Film Institute, 1997), 40. *L'Âge d'Or* needed bourgeois film as a foil for its message just as the surrealists depended on the social-political right to illuminate the film's critical potential.

25 Buñuel recollected some forty years after the film's production that "the ideas of the Surrealist Group are perfectly visible [in the film]." Paul Hammond, "Lost and Found: Buñuel, *L'Âge d'Or* and Surrealism," in *Luis Buñuel: New Readings*, ed. Peter William Evans and Isabel Santaolalla (London: British Film Institute, 2004), 16.

26 Hammond makes this point about the film's antifascism in "Lost and Found," 18–19.

27 Salvador Dalí, epigraph to the program for *L'Âge d'Or*, 1930, 1. [Reprint edition, supplement to the special issue "*L'Âge d'Or*. Correspondance Luis Buñuel–Charles de Noailles. Lettres et Documents (1929–1976)," in *Les Cahiers du Musée National d'Art Moderne* (Hors-Série / Archives), 1993.]

28 Salvador Dalí, "L'Âne pourri" (1930), in *Dalí*, trans. Dawn Ades and Michael R. Taylor (New York: Rizzoli, 2004), 551. This text first appeared in two works in 1930: *La Femme Visible* (Paris: Éditions surrealistes, 1930); and *Le Surréalisme au Service de la Révolution* 1 (July 1930), 9–12. Stills from *L'Âge d'Or* and paintings by Dalí appeared in the latter.

29 "D'un Scandale. Lettre ouverte á M. Paul Ginisty, président de la Censure," *Le Figaro* (7 December 1930), published in "*L'Âge d'Or*. Correspondance Luis Buñuel–Charles de Noailles," 174.

30 A pamphlet entitled "L'Affaire de '*L'Âge d'Or*'" was edited and circulated in January 1931. For a reprint, see José Pierre, ed. *Tracts surréalistes et declarations collectives, 1922–1939*, vol. 1 (Paris: Terrain Vague, 1980). It included a chronology of events, a questionnaire about the affair, excerpts from the program and from the Paris press, as well as several film stills and photographs of the damage incurred during the riot.

31 For more on the chronology of the film's public presentation and seizure, see "*L'Âge d'Or*. Correspondance Luis Buñuel–Charles de Noailles," 171–78, and Hammond, *L'Âge d'Or*, 58–69.

32 "L'Affaire de *L'Âge d'Or*," 192. This document explicitly raises questions about the links between police interdiction of the film and official encouragement of "fascist methods" in France. Paul Hammond notes that the film was a surrealist publicity coup in 1930 and that the publication of "L'Affaire de *L'Âge d'Or*" provides crucial insight into the surrealist group's understanding of the film's role, particularly into the group's alliance with the Communist Party and its sense of the film as a direct attempt to engage fascism in France.

33 For Dalí, this activity would be stronger and more horrible than the cut-eye sequence in Buñuel's *Andalusian Dog* (1929).

34 Salvador Dalí, letter to Luis Buñuel, undated, in "*L'Âge d'Or*. Correspondance Luis Buñuel–Charles de Noailles," 50.

35 On the reverse of the letter, Dalí described his initial plan to have Lys's upturned lips dissolve

into the "actual lips of a shaved vagina." See "*L'Âge d'Or.* Correspondance Luis Buñuel–Charles de Noaille,"50–53, for the letter (in French) and a facsimile of it with its drawing.

36 Salvador Dalí, letter to Luis Buñuel, undated, from the Archives of the Filmoteca Española, Madrid, letter no. 26 in "*L'Âge d'Or.* Correspondance Luis Buñuel–Charles de Noailles," 54.

37 Salvador Dalí, "Poetry of the Mass-Produced Utility," in *The Collected Writings of Salvador Dalí,* ed. Haim Finkelstein (Cambridge: Cambridge University Press, 1998), 58.

38 This idea that one image would suggest another—a structure paralleling my description of the advertisement and photograph that Modot sees in *L'Âge d'Or*—is connected to Dalí's concept of the paranoiac mechanism, which he outlines in "The Rotting Donkey" (1930), in Ades and Taylor, *Dalí,* 550–51.

39 In a letter to his patron, Charles de Noailles, Buñuel notes that Vigneau agreed to design and produce the posters for free (Vigneau's work was recognized in the film's onscreen credits). See Buñuel to Noailles, 8 February 1930 (Paris), in "*L'Âge d'Or.* Correspondance Luis Buñuel–Charles de Noailles," 46–48.

40 This association between the hand's movements and those of female masturbation was acknowledged at the time of the film's initial screening: a censor's report dated 10 December 1930 claimed that "the film represents a young woman (Lya Lys), dressed, stretched out on a sofa, a leg hanging loose, her hand raised to the level of her pubic region, gently turning her middle finger as if giving herself obscene contact." See "*L'Âge d'Or.* Correspondance Luis Buñuel–Charles de Noailles," 97.

41 The program for *L'Âge d'Or*'s screening at Studio 28 includes a text, signed by Aragon, Breton, Dalí, Péret, and others, that articulates how individual acts could be transformed by, or associated with, collective acts of revolt. See in particular the section "Aspect Social—Elements Subversives," 17–19.

42 See Robin Walz, *Pulp Surrealism: Insolent Popular Culture in Early Twentieth-Century Paris* (Berkeley: University of California Press, 2000); Kirk Varnedoe and Adam Gopnik, *High and Low: Modern Art and Popular Culture* (New York: Museum of Modern Art, 1990); Christian Bouqueret, *La Nouvelle Vision Photographique en France, 1920–1940* (Paris: Marval, 1998); and Marie-Emanuelle Chessel, *La Publicité. Naissance d'une profession, 1900–1940* (Paris: CNRS Éditions, 1998).

43 Louis Aragon, "Introduction à 1930," *La Révolution surréaliste* 12 (15 December 1929): 60.

44 Robert Desnos, *La Liberté ou L'Amour* (Paris: Gallimard, 1962), 34.

45 Walter Benjamin, Section G ["Expositions, publicité, Grandville"], in *Paris, Capitale du XIXe Siècle,* trans. Jean Lacoste (Paris: Editions du Cerf, 1993), 190.

46 Ibid., 192–93.

47 Walter S. Maas, "Subconscient et Publicité," *Arts et Métiers Graphiques* 1 (15 September 1927), 56–57.

48 For Louis Aragon's review of the exposition, see "Au bout du quai, les Arts Décoratifs!" *La Révolution surréaliste* 5 (15 October 1925): 26–27. The Siégel mannequin was part of a series of photos Man Ray completed as a commission for Siégel, one of which then appeared on the cover of *La Révolution surréaliste* (15 July 1925).

Chapter 2. The Aesthetics of Dismemberment

1 References to their meeting at Val-de-Grâce abound. Some of the most prominent sources include Louis Aragon, "Lautréamont et nous," part 1, *Les Lettres françaises* (1–7 June 1967), 5; *Aragon parle avec Dominique Arban* (Paris: Seghers, 1968), 28 ff.; Henri Béhar, *André Breton* (Paris: Calmann-Lévy, 1990), 53–58; André Breton, *Conversations: The Autobiography of Surrealism,* trans. Mark Polizzotti (New York: Paragon, 1993), 24–25; Marguerite Bonnet, *André Breton. Naissance de l'aventure surréaliste* (Paris: José Corti, 1975), 119; Hal Foster, *Compulsive Beauty* (Cambridge, MA: MIT Press, 1993), 1; *André Breton: La Beauté convulsive* (Paris: Musée National d'Art Moderne, Centre Georges Pompidou, 1991), 91; and Michel Sanouillet, *Dada à Paris* (Paris: J.-J. Pauvert, 1965), 85–86. Aragon noted the importance of the experience at Val-de-Grâce in other contexts as well, including the cryptic line "Le Val-de-Grâce: André Breton" from his "Project for a History of Contemporary Literature," in *The Dada Painters and Poets,* ed. Robert Motherwell (Cambridge, MA: Harvard University Press, 1981), 230 [originally published in *Littérature,* Paris, 1922]. Breton finally received his auxiliary medical certificate on 1 July 1919. For a detailed account of Breton's time at Val-de-Grâce, see *Breton: La Beauté convulsive.*

2 Such activity, although not equivalent to a soldier's experience during the war, suggests how Aragon and Breton might have repeated the soldier's experiences in the trenches, listening to the wounded cry out between gun battles. As Antoine Prost has shown, soldiers often had to listen, sometimes all night long, to the screams and cries of the wounded on both sides. As one soldier said, "It was terrible to hear the wounded of both sides crying out screaming and on quiet nights you could hear it a long way off and no way to relieve them unless they were close—our job was to watch and listen. After moments of quiet the groaning began again far off and came closer, explosions machine-gun fire that often finished off the wounded all the noise covered the cries of the dying." M. Camille Moyniez, 67th Infantry, 1st Battalion, 3rd Company, quoted in Antoine Prost, *In the Wake of War. 'Les anciens combattants' and French Society,* trans. Helen McPhail (Oxford: Berg, 1992), 5.

3 On the process of making the moulages, as well as their photographic and sculptural accuracy, see Sophie Delaporte, *Les Gueules Cassées. Les blessés de la face de la Grande Guerre* (Paris: Éditions Noêsis, 1996).

4 Marc Roudebush, writing about the infamous case of Vincent Deschamps, a soldier who was tried in August 1916 for assaulting a superior officer (to avoid electric-shock treatment), notes that after this trial, "neurologists began to express concern about their accountability to public opinion." Justin Godart, the man who would inaugurate the Musée du Val-de-Grâce, soon issued an official Health Service statement. Marc Roudebush, "A Battle of Nerves: Hysteria and Its Treatment in France During World War I" (PhD diss., University of California, Berkeley, 1995), 209. Because the Musée du Val-de-Grâce opened so soon after the Deschamps verdict, Godart may have viewed the museum as a way to address the public's questions about the medical and psychological treatment of wounded soldiers. For an account of the museum's postwar significance as a public site to "perpetuate scientific learning," see Service de

Santé Militaire, Dr. A. Monéry, Médecin-Major de 1er Classe, *Le Musée du Val-de-Grâce. Archives et documents de guerre du Service de Santé. Guide-Catalogue* (Paris, 1923), 13. In an oddly celebratory text on plastic surgery published in 1934, Dr. Jacques Maliniak reported that the iconographic collection at the Musée du Val-de-Grâce was one of the largest and most impressive collections of documents pertaining to plastic surgery in the world. Maliniak, *Sculpture in the Living* (New York: Romaine Pearson, 1934), 30.

5 Gaumont's footage of the inauguration of the Musée du Val-de-Grâce, including a view of military and civilian museumgoers packed into the museum's chambers (4 July 1916), is in the collection of Forum des Images, Paris (ex-collection Vidéothèque de Paris), "Actualités Gaumont," 4 July–September 1916, catalog no. VDP 2343. The Musée du Val-de-Grâce has its own records of press reaction to the collection's opening: "La Presse et le Service de Santé," August/September 1916–November/December 1917, cartons 271–79, Archives of the Service de Santé. A small, handheld guidebook to the collections was published in 1916 and then revised and updated in 1923. The former, *Eléments constitutifs des archives et documents de la Guerre. Musée du Val-de-Grâce,* was published by the Ministère de la Guerre, Sous-secrétariat d'État du Service de Santé (Paris: Imprimerie de Chaix, 1916). The 1923 guidebook enabled me to reconstruct the experience of viewing the collections, for it described the order in which one entered the rooms of the collection.

6 Jean Bonnerot, *La Bibliothèque Centrale et les Archives du Service de Santé au Musée du Val-de-Grâce* (Paris: E. Champion, 1918), 3.

7 On the varied uses of such colored-pencil drawings, see Delaporte, *Les Gueules Cassés.* These drawings, as well as the painted plaster sculpture in Figures 23 and 27, are both from the collection of the Musée du Val-de-Grâce, Paris.

8 An important parallel to these moulages exists in the sketchbooks in which artists were charged to draw, with colored pencils, the progress and techniques of surgical procedures. A large body of this work exists today in the Documents Weismann Collection, Archives du Musée du Val-de-Grâce. Donated to the archives in 1958, these *carnets de croquis chirurgicaux,* or albums of surgical drawings, offer a two-dimensional record of corporal reconstruction at the temporary hospital of Chaptal in Paris. The artist, Jacques Weismann, wrote in the letter accompanying his donation (on 3 January 1958) that these sketches offered evidence of the diverse forms of "atypical" surgical interventions undergone by soldiers suffering from facial wounds. The albums of drawings, dated from 1917 to 1919, give evidence of a different kind of aestheticizing of the procedures at Val-de-Grâce: the documentation of specific surgical moments in vivid color is signed by the attending artist. Although most of the *carnets* include images of faces with metal tools or plates inserted into the head, they also picture moments of aesthetic rupture in which Weismann, seemingly overwhelmed by the gruesome sights he has had to record, produces images of corporeal wholeness.

9 Bonnerot, the head archivist for the Musée du Val-de-Grâce, listed the names of those who headed the museum project, and he noted that one of the collection's organizers came from the National Museums and was well-known for his work in art history. Bonnerot, *La Bibliothèque Centrale,* 5.

10 Émile Bacelon, "Le Musée du Val-de-Grâce," *Le Figaro,* 3 July 1916: 3. The idea that the sur-

geons were "sculptors modeling in actual flesh" was commonly held, as in "L'oeuvre de notre Service de Santé Militaire. Le Musée du Val-de-Grace," *Excelsior* (8 July 1916): 12.

11 Léo Clarétie, "Le Génie de la Pitié," *L'Évènement* (12 August 1916): 1.

12 Monéry's 1923 guide to the Musée du Val-de-Grâce urged viewers to see the wax and plaster casts sequentially, from left to right, before to after.

13 Indeed, having met in September 1917 at Val-de-Grâce, Aragon and Breton would have been there together (as noted earlier, Breton was at Val-de-Grâce by January 1917) when articles were still appearing in the press about the "new" museum. As doctors with medical and battlefield experience, the two men would have known about war-related injuries, surgery, and postoperative recovery. But the display at Val-de-Grâce was new to them and to the civilian public because it stressed the aesthetic reconstruction of soldiers' bodies rather than their dismemberment or mutilation.

14 J. Ernest-Charles, "Au Musée du Val-de-Grâce," *Annales politiques et littéraires,* no. 1761 (25 March 1917): 284.

15 Clarétie, "Le Génie de la Pitié," 1. A photograph of a mannequin wearing several prosthetic devices illustrated the article on the museum, "L'oeuvre de notre Service de Santé Militaire," 12. This article included other photographs as well. One showed the *"vitrine des moulages de prothèse de la face"* with an inaugural plaque, a shot of a wall of photographs and moulages documenting the treatment of infected wounds, as well as a photograph of an antityphoid vaccination campaign carried out on Russian troops at a French camp.

16 In 1924, the International Labor Federation put on a large international conference to discuss the development of prosthetic apparel and the relation of prosthetics to labor. See Florent Martin, *Les Mutilations et les appareils de prothèse,* Bureau International de Travail, Geneva, February 1924 (Liège: Georges Thone, 1924).

17 Madame Bayliès is quoted in "Pour les Mutilés. M. Justin Godart inaugure une institution de reeducation, due à la générosité américaine," *L'Évènement,* 10 August 1916: 2.

18 Monsieur Carlier, *mutilé de guerre,* quoted in "Pour les Mutilés."

19 *J'ai Vu* conducted a survey in 1920 asking readers what women of marriageable age would do now that the nation had fewer men. The two-part survey appears in "Enquête: Que vont devenir les 1.500.000 jeunes filles à marier?" *J'ai Vu,* no. 237 (15 January 1920), and no. 240 (1 March 1920).

20 On the birthrate in France during the war, see Marie-Monique Huss, "Pronatalism and the Popular Ideology of the Child in Wartime France: The Evidence of the Picture Postcard," in *The Upheaval of War: Family, Work and Welfare in Europe, 1914–1918,* ed. Richard Wall and Jay Winter (Cambridge: Cambridge University Press, 1988), 329–67; and Mary Louise Roberts, *Civilization Without Sexes: Reconstructing Gender in Postwar France, 1917–1927* (Chicago: University of Chicago Press, 1994), 89–148.

21 Figures 31–34 correspond to the following catalog numbers of the photographic collection of the Musée d'Histoire Contemporaine–Bibliothèque de Documentation Internationale Contemporaine (BDIC), Paris: Drawer C-13, "Santé-Hygiène": L856, L857, L858, and L859 (28 June 1916). Each image was stamped *"censuré"* (censored) by military authorities, even though similar images were displayed at Val-de-Grâce after 1916.

22 This title is not mine: the back of the photograph is inscribed "Champfleury (?). le lieutenant———, amputé. deux maris." From the photographic collection of the Musée d'Histoire Contemporaine–BDIC, catalog no. 0899/26 (5 October 1917).

23 André Breton, "Manifeste du surréalisme (1924)," in *Manifestes du surréalisme* (Paris: Gallimard, 1963), 31–32.

24 When Aragon's poem was published in 1974 as part of his complete works, he included the following notation at the end of the piece: "Written on a grey envelope open like a belly, Spring 1920." Louis Aragon, *L'Oeuvre poétique,* vol. 1, *1917–1920* (Paris: Livre Club Diderot, 1974), 196. The original manuscript for this poem, written on the unfolded envelope, is in the collection of the Fonds Louis Aragon, Manuscripts Department, Bibliothèque Nationale de France, Paris (catalog p. 44, notice 29; R° 4505U V° Crayon gris 414U).

25 Louis Aragon, "Réclame d'aucun produit," *L'Oeuvre Poétique,* 195–96.

26 André Breton, *Conversations: The Autobiography of Surrealism* (New York: Paragon, 1993), 21. Hal Foster recalls this story as an "uncanny" account of surrealism's origins. He begins his account of surrealism's traumatic origins with Breton's reminiscence, which resonates with the techniques of bodily reconstruction on view at Val-de-Grâce. Foster, *Compulsive Beauty* (Cambridge, MA: MIT Press, 1993), xi.

27 In addition to Roudebush's dissertation (1995, note 4), see his essay of the same title, "A Battle of Nerves: Hysteria and Its Treatments in France During World War I," in Mark Micale and Paul Lerner, ed., *Traumatic Pasts: History, Psychiatry, and Trauma in the Modern Age, 1870–1930* (Cambridge: Cambridge University Press, 2001), 253–79, especially 261–67, where Roudebush links hysteria and the simulation of illness to gender politics.

28 According to Marcel Fleiss, owner of Galerie 1900–2000 (the gallery that published the two masks in 1986), sculptor René Iché made the masks of Breton and Eluard. Iché's heirs (in an e-mail exchange with author, summer 2005) state that they believe that the sculptor made the masks in about 1930. Henri Béhar, the author of *André Breton* (Paris: Calmann-Lévy, 1990), 216, dates the two masks to 1929, although other scholars date them to 1930 or 1931. Robert Lebel dates them to circa 1930 in "André Breton, initiateur de la peinture surréaliste," in José Pierre, *L'Aventure surréaliste autour d'André Breton* (Paris: Artcurial, 1986). The Marcel Fleiss exhibition catalog, *Continent Abstrait Continent Surréaliste,* gives the date as circa 1931 (Paris: Galerie 1900–2000, 1986): 70. Jean-Michel Goutier, a close friend of Breton's in the last years of his life, believes the masks were done sometime in 1929 or 1930 and remarks that they hung on the walls of Breton's Paris studio for years. According to Goutier, Eluard's mask even sustained a bullet hole during the liberation of Paris in 1945. (Jean-Michel Goutier, interview with author, Paris, June 1994)

29 Ruth Leys, "Death Masks: Kardiner and Ferenczi on Psychic Trauma," *Representations* 53 (Winter 1996): 44–73.

30 Leys, "Death Masks," 60.

31 Jean Paulhan did the same in his repetition of the sights he had seen in the trenches, in his book *Le Guerrier appliqué* (Paris: Sansot, 1919).

32 A few years younger than Breton and Aragon, Desnos met them both in 1921 and attended meetings of the *Littérature* group regularly by 1922.

33 Robert Desnos, "Pénalités de l'Enfer ou Nouvelles Hébrides," in *Nouvelles Hébrides et autres textes, 1922–1930* (Paris: Gallimard, 1978), 25–26.

34 Ibid., 39.

35 Ibid., 45.

36 Ibid., 56.

37 The manuscript for the "cemetery" is now part of the collection in the Manuscripts Department at the Bibliothèque Nationale de France, Paris (Coll. Desnos, catalog p. 231). A typescript version of this original manuscript first appeared in the Gallimard edition of *Nouvelles Hébrides,* 103.

38 Reading from left to right beginning in the upper-left corner of the photographic "frame," the catalog of surrealists reads as follows: (top row) Maxime Alexandre, Louis Aragon, André Breton, Luis Buñuel, and Jean Caupenne; (second row) Salvador Dalí and Paul Eluard; (third row) Max Ernst and Marcel Fourrier; (fourth row) Camille Goemans and René Magritte; (bottom row) Paul Nougé, Georges Sadoul, Yves Tanguy, André Thirion, and Albert Valentin. The photographs are identified by David Sylvester in "La grande icône surréaliste," in *André Breton: La Beauté convulsive,* 192.

39 I. Wallard, "Photomaton recherche son identité," *Le Photographe,* no. 1436 (July–August 1986): 27. First commercialized in England in 1928 and then installed in a few "luxury" locations in Paris during June of the same year, the Photomaton was an automatic cabin that allowed people to make photographic self-portraits. The Photomaton provided a relatively inexpensive way to document oneself while also turning the experience of identity "portraiture" into a form of entertainment. Christian Villetorte, the marketing director of Photomaton (Paris) describes the early Photomatons as being *"très snob"* and notes that the company first placed them mainly in luxury department stores in an effort to attract a rather well-heeled clientele (Christian Villetorte, interview by the author, Paris, 3 March 1994). On the rise of the Photomaton, see *Identités: De Disderi au photomaton* (Centre National de la Photographie, Paris, and Éditions du Chêne, Paris, 1985), 117. On the judicial functions of identity portraiture and the development of the mug shot, see Allan Sekula, "The Body and the Archive," *October* 39 (Winter 1986): 3–64. On the social impact of identity portraiture in particular, and on the relationship between photography in general and state power, see John Tagg, *The Burden of Representation* (Amherst: University of Massachusetts Press, 1988).

40 Louis Tomellini, Laboratory of the Legal Identity Service of the Paris Préfecture of Police, *Metric Photography (Bertillon System), New Apparatus for the Criminal Department. Directions for Use and Considerations of the Applications to Forensic Medicine and Anthropology,* extract from the *Archives of Criminal Anthropology and Forensic Medicine,* no. 170, 15 February 1908 (Lyon: A. Rey et Cie., 1908). Tomellini's text includes a section entitled "Metric Photography Applied to Dead Bodies."

41 Rudolf Kuenzli, "Surrealism's Misogyny," in *Surrealism and Women,* ed. Mary Ann Caws, Rudolf Kuenzli, and Gwen Raaberg (Cambridge, MA: MIT Press, 1990), 17–26.

42 Erich Maria Remarque, *All Quiet on the Western Front,* trans. A. W. Wheen (Boston: Bulfinch/Little, Brown, 1996); Remarque, *À l'oeust rien de nouveau* (Paris: Stock, 1929).

43 *Altar of the Fatherland* was published as Figure 20 in Aragon's "La Peinture au Défi" (Paris:

Librairie José Corti/Galerie Goemans, 1930). The collage was subsequently published in Louis Aragon, *Les Collages* (Paris: Hermann, 1965).

44 Aragon owned *Altar of the Fatherland* for much of his life. For the provenance and publication history of Ernst's *Altar of the Fatherland,* including Aragon's ownership of it, see Werner Spies, ed., *Max Ernst Oeuvre-Katalog,* vol. 1, *Das Graphische Werk,* ed. Helmut R. Leppien (Houston, TX: Menil Foundation/Cologne: M. DuMont Schauberg, 1975), 313, fig. 1402, and Werner Spies, *Max Ernst, Collages,* trans. John William Gabriel (New York: Abrams, 1991), 127.

45 Louis Aragon, "Introduction à 1930," *La Révolution surréaliste* 12 (15 December 1929): 62–64.

46 Romy Golan, *Modernity and Nostalgia: Art and Politics in France between the Wars* (New Haven, CT: Yale University Press, 1995), ix.

Chapter 3. The Advertisement of Emasculation

1 For two accounts of the exposition, see Kenneth Silver, *Esprit de Corps: The Art of the Parisian Avant-Garde and the First World War, 1914–1925* (Princeton, NJ: Princeton University Press, 1989): 362–72; and Nancy Troy, *Modernism and the Decorative Arts in France: From Art Nouveau to Le Corbusier* (New Haven, CT: Yale University Press, 1991).

2 Romy Golan, *Modernity and Nostalgia: Art and Politics in France between the Wars* (New Haven, CT: Yale University Press, 1995), 18–19.

3 Another version of this image, taken from behind and to the left of a seated café patron (a different man, if one can judge from the neater felt hat and suit, although an equally impressive stack of plates is also in evidence in this version), appeared in an auction sales catalog in 1979. The Ovomaltine poster is just visible at the upper left of the image, and another blurred male body (suited, hatted in almost identical fashion as the seated man) walks into the image at the upper right. Christie's London, 19th and 20th Century Photographs, 31 October 1979, #228.

4 Although not an official member of the group around Breton and Aragon, Kertész suggested that his work might be considered surrealist even if he didn't adhere to a specific surrealist program. Sandra Phillips notes that although Kertész often denied any interest in surrealism or an official relationship with the group, "some would like to call" his 1925 photograph of mannequin legs upside down in a sculptor's studio "surrealist." Sandra Phillips, "The Photographic Work of André Kertész in France, 1925–1926: A Critical Essay and Catalogue," vol. 1 (PhD diss., City University of New York, 1985), 357.

5 On the equation of mass culture with women in modernity, see Andreas Huyssen's chapter "Mass Culture as Woman," in his *After the Great Divide: Modernism, Mass Culture, Postmodernism* (Bloomington: University of Indiana Press, 1986), 44–55.

6 Although this photograph is usually entitled "On the Quai near Saint-Michel," its original caption identified the amputee as a war veteran: "Au fil de l'eau, ce robuste ancien combattant regarde défiler les images du 269e de ligne dans le passé et celles du 269e de ligne, dans l'avenir." In its 1934 publication, however, the photograph was cropped so that only the body

of the amputee appeared. See *Paris, vu par André Kertész,* text by Pierre Mac Orlan (Paris: Plon, 1934): 19.

7 My thanks to Don LaCoss for our lively discussion of this material; the suggestion comes from him that this reading of the image is the visual equivalent of a "phantom limb."

8 Susan Buck-Morss, *The Dialectics of Seeing. Walter Benjamin and the Arcades Project* (Cambridge, MA: MIT Press, 1989), 95.

9 Pierre Mac Orlan, "La Photographie et le Fantastique Social," *Les Annales politiques et littéraires* (1 November 1928): 414.

10 See Sandra Phillips, "André Kertész: The Years in Paris," in *André Kertész: Of Paris and New York,* ed. Sandra S. Phillips, David Travis, and Weston Naef (New York: Thames & Hudson/Art Institute of Chicago, 1985), 40–41.

11 Kertész's surrealist identity stems from the repeated publication of this group of distorted female nudes from 1933. Twelve of Kertész's distorted female nudes were published in conjunction with a short (if hyperbolic) poetic text by A.-P. Barancy, "Fenêtre ouverte sur l'au-delà," *Le Sourire* (9 March 1933). (Sandra Phillips and Pierre Borhan both cite the date erroneously as 2 March 1933.) Five of the images appeared in Bertrand Guégan's "Kertész et son miroir," *Arts et Métiers Graphiques* 37 (15 September 1933): 23–24. The major portion of these distorted female nudes was not published until the mid-1970s, in André Kertész, *André Kertész: Distortions* (New York: Knopf, 1976). Finally, Kertész's surrealist persona most recently found a public when some of his works appeared in the important 1985 exhibition catalog: Rosalind Krauss and Jane Livingston, *L'Amour Fou: Photography and Surrealism* (New York: Abrams, 1985), 214.

12 Hilton Kramer, introduction to *André Kertész: Distortions.*

13 Mary Ann Caws, "Ladies Shot and Painted: Female Embodiment in Surrealist Art," in *The Female Body in Western Culture: Contemporary Perspectives,* ed. Susan Rubin Suleiman (Cambridge, MA: Harvard University Press, 1986), 270–71.

14 Ibid., 273–79.

15 Carol Armstrong, "The Reflexive and the Possessive View: Thoughts on Kertész, Brandt and the Photographic Nude," *Representations* 25 (Winter 1989): 57–70.

16 Pierre Borhan published one example of the 1929 male distortions, an image of Carlo Rim, but refrained from close analysis of the work; his account neither discusses the existence of this series of negatives nor links these early distortions of men to the female nudes of 1933. See Pierre Borhan, ed. *André Kertész: His Life and Work* (Boston: Little, Brown, 1994).

17 Armstrong, "The Reflexive and the Possessive View," 60–66.

18 Carlo Rim, "Luna Park ou la clef des songes," *VU* 125 (August 1930): 786–87.

19 Glass negatives at the Fonds Kertész, Paris, show Kertész and Rim sitting at the edges of the room, watching the process of distortion unfold (KRT 284V, KRT 257V, KRT 270V). They appear to be reenacting their own experience with the mirror in 1929 by making the female distortions together in 1933.

20 Bertrand Guégan, "Kertész et son miroir," *Arts et Métiers Graphiques* 37 (15 September 1933): 24.

21 This aspect of Guégan's writing seems to support Carol Armstrong's argument about the female distortions' self-regard in "The Reflexive and the Possessive View." Armstrong argues

that the bodies seem to be in contact with themselves and that they are participating not only as objects of the gaze but as objects of their own gazes down at themselves. This structure, she contends, allows the spectator to identify not only with a phallocentric gaze but with a self-absorbing one, such as the gaze that Sigmund Freud describes in "Instincts and their Vicissitudes," *Standard Edition of the Complete Psychological Works of Sigmund Freud,* trans. James Strachey (London: Hogarth, 1963), vol. 14, 111–40.

22 Freud articulates the relationship between the male child's anxiety about the woman's (his mother's) lack of a penis and the resulting deferral of his anxiety about castration onto another object in "Fetishism," *Standard Edition,* vol. 21, 152–55. Christian Metz's formulation of the photograph as itself a fetish adds an intriguing twist to consideration of Kertész's work. See Christian Metz, "Photography and Fetish," *October* 34 (Fall 1985): 81–90.

23 Desnos, "Pénalités de l'Enfer ou Nouvelles Hébrides," in *Nouvelles Hébrides et autres textes, 1922–1930* (Paris: Gallimard, 1978), 90.

24 Viewed next to its unpublished, full-frame glass-negative source, we can see that the version published in 1976 has been cropped to exclude contextual references to the process of deforming the body, a process that Kertész himself underwent (KRT 856V). This effect is indicative of the marketplace at the time, which largely demanded that female bodies stimulate the viewer's desire for the female body as an object, erasing traces of the image's origins in work that conjures male anxiety.

25 In his response to a *Minotaure* survey, Carlo Rim remembered the experiment with Kertész's camera at Luna Park fondly and remarked that seeing himself before the distorting mirror elicited feelings of shock and liberation. "Pouvez-vous dire quelle a été la rencontre capitale de votre vie?" (Can you say what has been the most important meeting of your life?) *Minotaure* 3–4 (December 1933): 113.

26 Sarah Greenough explores the idea that Kertész described the series of female distortions alternatively as "Grotesques" in "To Become a Virgin Again, 1925–1936," in *André Kertész,* ed. Sarah Greenough, Robert Gurbo, and Sarah Kennel (Princeton, NJ: Princeton University Press, 2005), 82.

27 In referencing the *missions héliographiques* that took place in Haussmann's Paris of the 1860s, I want to draw attention to the similarities between the *missions'* efforts to document both the new city and its recently destroyed past and the post–World War I efforts to record the mutilated male body even as it was being reconstructed. On the *missions héliographiques,* see Elizabeth McCauley, *Industrial Madness: Commercial Photography in Paris* (New Haven, CT: Yale University Press, 1994).

28 The surrealists considered Paris to be the quintessential catalyst of surreal experience. Thus, Atget, because of his interest in representing the city as a mix of up-to-date and outmoded elements, became an honorary member of the collective. Three texts that explore surrealism's interest in Atget are Robert Desnos, "Emile Atdget [*sic*]," in *Merle* 3 (3 May 1929), reprinted in *Nouvelles Hébrides et autres textes, 1922–1930,* 434–35; Thomas Michael Gunther, "Les photographies d'Atget achetées par Man Ray," in *Colloque Atget,* proceedings of the meeting at the Collège de France, 14–15 June 1985 (Paris: Photographies, March 1986), 70–73; and Ian Walker, "A Surrealist Atget," in *City Gorged with Dreams: Surrealism and Docu-*

mentary Photography in Interwar Paris (Manchester, England: Manchester University Press, 2002), 88–113.

29 This idea of a fusion of document and fantasy draws on Ian Walker's reading of surrealist documentary photography in *City Gorged with Dreams*, 22–23.

Chapter 4. Man Ray, Lee Miller, and the Photography of Surrealist Sexuality

1 Pierre Drieu la Rochelle, *La Suite dans Les Idées* (Paris: Au Sans Pareil, 1927), 125.

2 Carolyn Dean, "History, Pornography and the Social Body," in *Surrealism: Desire Unbound*, ed. Jennifer Mundy (New Haven, CT: Yale University Press, 2001), 230.

3 Miller reported on her retrieval and printing of the negative during a conversation with David Hurn at Arles in 1976. Hurn in turn reported the conversation to Antony Penrose in June 1984. Penrose, *The Lives of Lee Miller* (London: Thames & Hudson, 1985), 30.

4 Ernst Kris and Otto Kurz's book *Legend, Myth, and Magic in the Image of the Artist* (New Haven, CT: Yale University, 1979), was a key early twentieth-century text that documented the conventions of artistic biography. For a discussion of the heterosexual artistic couple in the modern period, see Whitney Chadwick and Isabelle de Courtivron, eds., *Significant Others: Creativity and Intimate Partnership* (London: Thames & Hudson, 1993).

5 Lee Miller with Mario Amaya, "My Man Ray," *Art in America* 63 (May/June 1975): 54–61.

6 Among the key biographical works that laid the groundwork for subsequent discussions of Miller's relationship to surrealism are Penrose, *Lives of Lee Miller*; Jane Livingston, *Lee Miller: Photographer* (New York: Thames & Hudson; Los Angeles: California/International Arts Foundation, 1989); Rosalind Krauss and Jane Livingston, *L'Amour Fou: Photography and Surrealism* (New York: Abbeville, 1985); Amy Lyford, "Lee Miller's Photographic Impersonations: Conversing with Surrealism, 1930–1945," *History of Photography* 18 (Autumn 1994): 230–41; and the documentary film written and directed by Sylvain Roumette, *Lee Miller: Through the Mirror* (Paris: Terra Luna Films, 1995).

7 "My Man Ray," 56.

8 Ibid., 57.

9 Antony Penrose describes their attitude toward their collaboration as follows: "A measure of Lee's and Man Ray's mutual respect was that neither of them was seriously concerned when their credits were wrongly ascribed. Man Ray passed quite a lot of his own work over to Lee to free himself for painting." Penrose, *Lives of Lee Miller*, 30.

10 Antony Penrose, interview with the author, East Sussex, England, June 1990.

11 Jane Livingston, *Lee Miller: Photographer*, 1989. Livingston organized the exhibition for the Corcoran Gallery in Washington, D.C., and the show then traveled to the San Francisco Museum of Modern Art.

12 Susan Rubin Suleiman, "A Double Margin: Women Writers and the Avant-Garde in France," in *Subversive Intent: Gender, Politics, and the Avant-Garde* (Cambridge, MA: Harvard University Press, 1990), 11–32.

13 For Miller's statement about Man Ray's violent response to her work, see Penrose, *Lives of Lee Miller*, 30.

14 Ibid.

15 *Arts et Métiers Graphiques* 16 (15 March 1930): 97 (fashion portrait) and 107 (Miller's neck).

16 Rrose Sélavy, "Men Before the Mirror," in *Photographs by Man Ray 105 Works, 1920–1934* (Hartford, CT: James Thrall Soby, 1934), 66.

17 Mikhail Bakhtin's conception of language's dialogical structure has shaped my thinking about Miller's incorporation (and critique) of Man Ray's photographic language, as has Susan Rubin Suleiman's work on women artists and the avant-garde. Mikhail Bakhtin, "Discourse in the Novel," in *The Dialogic Imagination* (Austin: University of Texas Press, 1981), 282; Susan Rubin Suleiman, "A Double Margin," 11–32.

18 André Breton and Louis Aragon, "Le Cinquantenaire de l'hystérie," *La Révolution surréaliste* 11 (15 March 1928): 22.

19 A print of *La Prière* at the Musée National d'Art Moderne (MNAM), Paris, includes a hand-drawn set of pencil markings on the print that emphasize the toes, buttocks, and fingers of the figure; each of these elements is outlined in pencil by, apparently, Man Ray's hand. MNAM accession number AM 1994–394–1494.

20 Man Ray's sense of being under Miller's power is evident in a letter that he wrote to her sometime during their relationship as well as in a note he wrote on 11 October 1932 on the reverse of a cut-out photograph of her eye that he affixed to a metronome: "With an eye always in reserve. Material indestructible. . . . Forever being put away. Taken for a ride. . . . Put on the spot. . . . The racket must go on—I am always in reserve. MR." Penrose, *Lives of Lee Miller,* 39, 40.

21 On the surrealist exploitation of hysteria as an expressly feminine affliction, see Gloria Feman Orenstein, "*Nadja* Revisited: A Feminist Approach," *Dada/Surrealism* 8 (1978): 91–106; Susan Rubin Suleiman, *Subversive Intent,* 88–118; David Lomas, "Seductions of Hysteria," chapter 2 in *The Haunted Self: Surrealism, Psychoanalysis, Subjectivity* (New Haven, CT: Yale University Press, 2000), 52–93; Roger Shattuck, "The Nadja File," *Cahiers Dada/Surréalisme* 1 (1966): 49–56.

22 André Breton, *Nadja,* trans. Richard Howard (New York: Grove Press, 1960), 143.

23 Breton and Aragon, "Le Cinquantenaire de l'hystérie," 22.

24 "Nadja (fragment)," *La Révolution surréaliste* 11 (15 March 1928): 9–11.

25 Man Ray made two versions of the image, the second of which surfaced in a sale at Sotheby's, New York, 23 April 1994, fig. 338. The Sotheby's announcement gives the date of the photograph as 1929, and the stamp "8, rue du Val-de-Grâce, Paris" on the back of the photograph indicates that it was, indeed, likely taken in 1929 or 1930, when Man Ray had a studio on the rue du Val-de-Grâce. Lucien Treillard corroborates the dating of the image to 1929 or 1930.

26 André Breton, "Second Manifesto of Surrealism (1929)," in *Manifestoes of Surrealism,* trans. Richard Seaver and Helen R. Lane (Ann Arbor: University of Michigan, 1972), 177. Dawn Ades reinforces this reading of Breton, insisting that the surrealists pulled back from their public audience during the late 1920s and early 1930s so that they could continue to work without making the kinds of concessions (political, ideological, or otherwise) that might dilute their revolutionary mission. Dawn Ades, *Dada and Surrealism Reviewed* (London: Hayward Art Gallery/Arts Council of Great Britain, 1978), 251.

27 Sigmund Freud, "The Sexual Aberrations," in *Three Essays on the Theory of Sexuality,* trans. James Strachey (New York: Basic Books, 1975): 7.

28 Ibid., 7.

29 Ibid., 14.

30 Freud believed that in a second pregenital phase, "passive" and "active" currents operate simultaneously within the child's psyche. He suggested that arresting ambivalence at that stage could, in certain cases, prompt the emergence of neurotic behavior. Sigmund Freud, "Infantile Sexuality," in *Three Essays on the Theory of Sexuality* , 63–65.

31 Sigmund Freud, "On Narcissism: An Introduction," *Standard Edition of the Complete Psychological Works of Sigmund Freud,* trans. James Strachey (London: Hogarth, 1963), vol. 14, 88–89.

32 Ibid., 89.

33 Man Ray revealed his jealousy and anxiety about Miller's self-sufficiency in a letter to her reproduced in Penrose, *Lives of Lee Miller,* 38.

34 My thanks to Anne Wagner for pointing out the visual similarities between Man Ray's form and the Rodin sculpture.

35 Lee Miller is quoted in Julia Blanshard, "Other Faces Are Her Fortune," *The Poughkeepsie Evening Star* (1 November 1932). Special thanks to Carolyn Burke for generously providing me with a copy of this article.

36 Benjamin Péret commented on reticence about male bodily display (especially to other men) at the third session of the "Recherches sur la Sexualité" (1–14 February 1928). After a discussion about the roots of shame and Breton's insistence that shame has its roots in one's sexuality, Péret answered the question "What is shame?" as follows: "It's a feeling of embarrassment which I have felt and now feel less and less, for example in being seen naked. I have a certain shame about showing myself naked in front of men, but far less in front of women." José Pierre, ed., *Investigating Sex,* trans. Malcolm Imrie (New York: Verso, 1992), 40.

37 The growing literature on the so-called third sex in France at the time included the work of Willy (Prof. Dr. Lery-Lenz), such as *Le Troisième Sexe* (Paris: Paris-Édition, 1927) and *Encyclopédie de la Vie Sexuelle* (Paris: Aldor, 1934).

38 Pierre Klossowski argues that we must understand Sade's male pervert in just this way—as a perversion of the rationality of mind that is assumed to be natural in men. Thus, the identification with the "monstrous" feminine, as he calls it, reflects the perversion of imagination typical of the Sadeian male pervert. Pierre Klossowski, *Sade My Neighbor,* trans. Alphonso Lingis (Evanston, IL: Northwestern University Press, 1991), 34–37.

39 Carolyn Dean, "History, Pornography and the Social Body," 228.

40 Carolyn Dean, *The Frail Social Body* (Berkeley: University of California Press, 2000), 64–68.

41 For a complete chronology of Freud's work published in French translation, see Alain de Mijolla, "Freud en français jusqu'en 1940," *Revue Internationale d'Histoire de la Psychanalyse* 4 (1991): 267–68, 283–89. Many literary journals of the 1920s—such as *Mercure de France, Nouvelle Revue française,* and *Les Marges*—reference Freud's notion of the *inconscient* or otherwise discuss the relationship between sexuality and creativity. Exemplary articles include Georges Dubujadoux, "Les Lettres françaises et l'Inconscient," *Mercure de France* (1 February

1924): 577–611; and Marcel Boll, "Le Système du Docteur Freud," *Mercure de France* (1 July 1924): 5–54.

42 "L'Homosexualité en Littérature," *Les Marges* (15 March 1926): 176–216, and (15 April 1926): 242–45.

43 *Les Marges* continued its interrogation of the literary scene later on in 1926 with an *enquête* that sought to find the sources of a perceived "sickness" in French literature. Respondents determined that the sickness was now not only in individual authors' works but also in the publishing industry. Publicity-hungry authors were suffusing their works with images that some observers categorized as perverse, "inverted," or sexually deviant, simply to gain commercial success. "Enquête sur les maladies de la littérature actuelle," *Les Marges* (September-October 1926): 5–139. One "malady" enumerated by the survey was the "commercial exploitation of the most abject vices or movements of conscience that should be the most secret" (6). The editors at *Les Marges* were clearly concerned that commercializing and marketing homosexuality (or perversion) would be detrimental to the great traditions of French literature. Thus, we can imagine how the surrealists' coupling of sexual ambiguity and narcissism with the mechanics and techniques of publicity must have rankled the editors of *Les Marges*.

44 Gerard Bauer, response to the survey "L'Homosexualité en Littérature," *Les Marges* (15 March 1926): 181.

45 Under the heading "The Primary Instinctual Processes of Homosexuality," Hesnard summarized the idea as follows: "We can say that the affective biography of homosexuals reveals . . . from the beginning an exclusive maternal identification, at times complicated by a tender and passive attitude to the father. . . . This maternal identification, attached above all to sexual characteristics, had been intimate enough to make the infant a feminine individual with respect to the problem of the sexes." Angelo Hesnard, *Psychologie homosexuelle* (Paris: Stock, 1929), 65–66. Hesnard, with Dr. Régis, first published Freud's ideas in French, beginning with the fundamental *La Psychanalyse des Névroses et des Psychoses* (Paris: Alcan, 1914). Freud's works were published in translation in France during the 1920s: *Three Essays on the Theory of Sexuality* appeared in 1923; *A General Introduction to Psychoanalysis,* in 1921; *the Interpretation of Dreams,* in 1925; and *Group Psychology and the Analysis of the Ego,* in 1924.

46 Camille Mauclair, response to the survey "L'Homosexualité en Littérature," *Les Marges* (15 March 1926): 202.

47 The full texts of the *Recherches sur la Sexualité* were first edited and published by José Pierre as part of the Archives du Surréalisme series (Paris: Gallimard, 1990). Malcolm Imrie translated them into English in 1992: Pierre, *Investigating Sex.* Dawn Ades helpfully contextualizes the *Recherches* in her afterword to this English translation, 185–206.

48 Apparently, women participated only in the eighth (early November 1930), ninth (24 November 1930), and tenth (26 November 1930) sessions. José Pierre suggests that a woman may have participated in the seventh (6 May 1928) session, although he admits to some speculation about this early inclusion of a female voice in the dialogue. For a complete list of participants in each session, see Pierre, *Investigating Sex.*

49 Dawn Ades emphasizes this use of the *Recherches* at the time as the basis for a critique of the

return to order and its nomination of conventional or so-called normal sexualities and practices. Ades, afterword to Pierre, *Investigating Sex,* 185–206.

50 Louis Aragon, "Recherches sur la Sexualité," *La Révolution surréaliste* 11 (15 March 1928): 37.

51 Man Ray in the second session in Pierre, *Investigating Sex,* 28–29

52 Ibid., 27. Following closely on the heels of Man Ray's statement, Louis Aragon presented an exceptionally open way of thinking about homosexuality when he said, "Homosexuality seems to me to be a sexual inclination like any other. I don't see it as a matter for any kind of moral condemnation."

53 Ibid., 33.

54 Benjamin Péret, Louis Aragon, and Man Ray, *1929* (Paris, 1929).

55 Although a recent reprint of *1929* is now available (Paris: Allia, 1993), when I first viewed this book in Paris in 1992, it remained cataloged in the *enfer* section of the Bibliothèque Nationale de France, Imprimés, a section conventionally reserved for politically or sexually subversive works.

56 Freud's account of "sexual aberrations"—particularly that of "inversion"—appears in *Three Essays on the Theory of Sexuality,* trans. James Strachey (New York: Basic Books, 1962), 2–16. At the beginning of his discussion on bisexuality, Freud wrote, "It is popularly believed that a human being is either a man or a woman. Science, however, knows of cases in which the sexual characters are obscured, and in which it is consequently difficult to determine the sex. . . . The importance of these abnormalities lies in the unexpected fact that they facilitate our understanding of normal development. For it appears that a certain degree of anatomical hermaphroditism occurs normally. . . . These long-familiar facts of anatomy lead us to suppose that an originally bisexual physical disposition has, in the course of evolution, become modified into a unisexual one, leaving behind only a few traces of the sex that has become atrophied" (7). Later in this account of bisexuality, Freud analyzes the psychical hermaphroditism of the bisexual individual as another part of the equation that leads to inversion. Freud used popular notions of male homosexuality to drive home his claim: "The theory of bisexuality has been expressed in its crudest form by a spokesman of the male inverts: 'a feminine brain in a masculine body'" (8). Even in this abbreviated account of inversion, Freud puts forth the popular idea of male homosexuality as the feminization of the male psyche.

57 Maurice Heine, "Note sur un Classement Psycho-Biologique des Paresthésies sexuelles," *Minotaure* 3–4 (1933): 36. Heine's *Receuil des confessions et observations psycho-sexuelles* (Paris: Édition Jean Crès, 1936) joins patient narratives of male masochism and sadomasochism to a Freudian account of the subject's fundamental bisexuality.

58 On Sade's relation to surrealism, see Neil Cox, "Critique of Pure Desire, or When the Surrealists Were Right," in *Surrealism: Desire Unbound,* ed. Jennifer Mundy (New Haven, CT: Yale University Press, 2001), 245–73.

59 Ades, *Dada and Surrealism Reviewed,* 255.

60 In his autobiography *Self Portrait,* Man Ray claimed to derive pleasure from seeing his wife Donna in pain: "I was trembling with rage. This would be final, I decided—passing the shaving mirror I saw a distorted face with disheveled hair . . . then ran up three steps at a time and without knocking put my shoulder against the door. It flew open; Donna was sitting on the

couch. In a choked voice I asked her what she wanted, before she could answer, I pulled out my belt and began lashing her. She fell on her face moaning; I continued striking her back a number of times, then stopped and told her to explain the marks to Luis. I'd be waiting for him if he wanted further explanation." Man Ray, *Self Portrait* (Boston: Little, Brown, 1963), 94.

61 Man Ray discusses his interests in Sade and Sadeian projects as well as his relationship to Maurice Heine in Pierre Bourgeade, *Bonsoir, Man Ray* (Paris: Belfont, 1972), 75–85.

62 Man Ray, "L'Age de la Lumière," *Minotaure* 3–4 (1933): 1.

63 Man Ray's *Hommage to D.A.F. de Sade* and *Monument à D.A.F. de Sade* appeared in *Le Surréalisme au Service de la Révolution* 2 (October 1930) and 5 (May 1933), respectively.

64 Published in *Le Surréalisme au Service de la Révolution* 1 (July 1930). The photograph of Miller by Man Ray is the sixth image (unpaginated) between pages 16 and 17.

65 André Breton, "Il y'aura une fois," *Le Surréalisme au Service de la Révolution* 1 (July 1930): 2–5.

66 Seabrook lived in Paris off and on from the mid-1920s until 1934 and maintained a relationship with both Man Ray and Lee Miller during the early 1930s. Seabrook was well-known in Paris circles, particularly among the surrealists, as a practitioner of sadomasochism. Man Ray discusses Seabrook and his sexual proclivities in *Self Portrait,* 192–93. Not only did Man Ray help Seabrook procure contacts in the fashion and design worlds to help him construct costumes for his sexual play, but Miller and Man Ray apparently also participated in his activities, at least on one evening at Seabrook's. See an undated letter from Seabrook to Man Ray, Fonds Man Ray 9809, Feuille 1178, Musée National d'Art Moderne, Paris, Bibliothèque Kandinsky; also, a note from Seabrook to Man Ray asking the latter to "bring Miss Miller" to dinner if she is around, Fonds Man Ray 9808, Feuille 1175, Musée National d'Art Moderne, Paris, Bibliothèque Kandinsky.

67 Man Ray notes that Seabrook asked him to design a "high silver collar" for his wife, Marjorie: "Measurements were taken of Marjorie's neck; the collar was to follow the line of her chin so that she had to keep her head up high and not be able to turn it. My silversmith made a very pretty job of it: two hinged pieces of dull silver studded with shiny knobs, that snapped into place, giving the wearer a very regal appearance. . . . She was to wear the bauble at home to please Seabrook's penchant for fetishism, and because it became quite uncomfortable after a while. She also wore it at a social function once; it was a sensation, few suspecting its real function. He made her wear the collar thereafter whenever they went out to dinner and took a certain pleasure in watching her at the table eating and drinking with difficulty." Man Ray, *Self Portrait,* 193–94.

Chapter 5. The Lessons of Barbette

1 Lucien Treillard made this analogy in an interview with the author in Paris, June 1994. Cocteau mentions Man Ray's interest in photographing Barbette in "Le numéro Barbette," *Nouvelle Revue française* 27 (1926): 33–38.

2 My thanks to Darcy Grigsby for pointing out this linguistic play with the word *barbe.* Barbette's act repeated this gender play in its structure and its deployment of a feminized mascu-

line object. A second reference point for her name may have been the famous singer and music-hall performer Mistinguett, who was popular during the 1920s.

3 *Variétés* 7 (15 November 1929). The double portrait of Barbette–Van der Clyde appears on the fifth page of images following page 534. That year, a spread on Barbette also appeared in Michel Georges-Michel, "Barbette," *VU* 48 (February 1929): 115.

4 Georges-Michel, "Barbette," 115.

5 Pierre Bost, *Le Cirque et le Music-Hall* (Paris: Au Sans Pareil, 1931), 41.

6 Ibid., 196.

7 Maurice Verne, *Musées de Voluptés. Le secret des nuits électriques* (Paris: Éditions des Portiques, 1930), 221.

8 Legrand-Chabrier, "Barbette avant et après son numéro," *L'Entr'acte* (December 1925): 13–14.

9 Legrand-Chabrier, "Comment Barbette se métamorphose," *Le Petit Parisien*, 17 February 1935: n.p.

10 Ibid.

11 James Thrall Soby, ed., *Photographs by Man Ray 1920 Paris 1934* (Hartford, CT: James Thrall Soby, 1934).

12 Jean Cocteau described Barbette as a "bandage-maker's Apollo" in "Le numéro Barbette," 34.

13 Ibid., 37.

14 Verne, *Musées de Voluptés*, 223.

15 On 1920s advertising, mannequins, and commercialization, see Tag Gronberg, "Beware Beautiful Women: The 1920s Shopwindow Mannequin and a Physiognomy of Effacement," *Art History* 20 (September 1997): 375–96.

16 Soby, *Photographs by Man Ray.*

17 Ibid., 84. One reason for this omission might have been the degree of Barbette's popularity: Man Ray and his publisher may have presumed that Barbette needed no introduction to her publics in Europe and the United States. However, both her pose and her appearance as an unidentified figure could also have been efforts to differentiate her body from those of the images of men that preceded hers. Because Barbette was an oddly feminine mix of the signs of the feminine and the masculine, both in her physicality and her indeterminate gender, perhaps this image's lack of a caption or name bespeaks its relationship to the more traditionally "nameless" image of the female nude. On masculinity and the text "Men Before the Mirror" in Man Ray's (and Duchamp's) work, see David Hopkins, "Men Before the Mirror: Duchamp, Man Ray and Masculinity," *Art History* 21 (September 1998): 303–23.

18 Gertrude Stein's portrait appears on page 66 of Soby, *Photographs by Man Ray;* Barbette's, on page 84. The comparison of the two images' gender indeterminacy would, of course, have accrued meaning as the reader turned the pages of the sections "Women" and "Men" to find that the final images in each group speak of gender's fluidity.

19 Pierre Drieu la Rochelle, *Mesure de la France* (Paris: Grasset, 1922), 113–14.

20 On *L'Homme couvert de femmes* and Drieu's depiction of a man who slips between sexual obsession and impotence, see Frédéric J. Grover, *Drieu la Rochelle and the Fiction of Testimony* (Berkeley: University of California Press, 1958), 95–98. On the question of pleasure seeking

and male extinction in Drieu's writing, see Marie Balvet, "Decadence et restauration du corps chez Drieu la Rochelle," *Les Temps modernes* 39 (November 1982): 1184–86.

21 Drieu la Rochelle, *Mesure de la France,* 113.

22 Pierre Drieu la Rochelle, "Chronique des Spectacles," *Nouvelle Revue française* 22 (1 January 1924): 97–98.

23 Ibid., 98. In 1927 Drieu returned to Barbette in a chapter on the music hall in *La Suite dans les idées* (Paris: Au Sans Pareil, 1927). Rima Drell Reck sees Drieu's review of Barbette through a much more negative lens than do I. She implies that his review of Barbette is in some ways an attack on his surrealist friends' celebration of popular culture. I respectfully disagree. Rima Drell Reck, *Drieu la Rochelle and the Picture Gallery Novel* (Baton Rouge: Louisiana State University Press, 1990), 11–26.

24 Pierre Drieu la Rochelle, *Socialisme fasciste* (Paris: Gallimard, 1934).

25 Pierre Drieu la Rochelle, "La véritable erreur des surréalistes," *Nouvelle Revue française* 25 (1925): 166–71.

26 On Drieu's extranationalist bent, see David Carroll, *French Literary Fascism: Nationalism, Anti-Semitism, and the Ideology of Culture* (Princeton, NJ: Princeton University Press, 1995), 127.

27 George Mosse, *Nationalism and Sexuality* (New York: Howard Fertig, 1985), 153.

28 Drieu la Rochelle, *Socialisme fasciste,* 102.

29 On Drieu's notions of the body, gender, and fascism, see Marie Balvet, "Decadence et restauration du corps chez Drieu la Rochelle," *Les Temps modernes* 39 (November 1982): 1182–97; David Carroll, "Literary Fascism and the Problem of Gender: The Aesthetics of the Body in Drieu la Rochelle," in *French Literary Fascism,* 147–70; and Thomas M. Hines, "Myth, Misogyny, and Fascism in the Works of Drieu la Rochelle," *Modern Fiction Studies* 24 (1978): 197–207.

30 On Drieu's links to (and criticisms of) surrealism, see Dominique Desanti, *Drieu la Rochelle. Du dandy au nazi* (Paris: Flammarion, 1978); Michel Winock, "Une parabole fasciste: *Gilles* de Drieu la Rochelle," *Le Mouvement social* 80 (July 1972): 29–47; Julien Hervier, "Drieu et l'image des surréalistes dans *Gilles,*" *Roman 20/50* 24 (December 1997): 93–109.

31 Pierre Drieu la Rochelle, *Gilles* (Paris: Gallimard, 1939), 182.

32 Ibid., 182.

33 Ibid., 183.

34 Ibid., 349–50.

35 Hal Foster, *Compulsive Beauty* (Cambridge, MA: MIT Press, 1993), 119. Foster's argument, too elaborate to discuss in detail here, also turns on the notion that the fascist male is compelled to attack his "social others"—Jews, communists, homosexuals—because they appear as the fantasmatic symbols of his own dissolution (physical as well as psychic). Yet, in such attacks, the fascist male also acknowledges the essentially "fragmentary, fluid, feminine" nature of his own desires and sexuality. Foster's analysis, like mine, depends on Klaus Theweleit's *Male Fantasies,* trans. Stephen Conway, (Minneapolis: University of Minnesota, 1987), particularly volume 1, *Women, Floods, Bodies, History.* See also Amelia Jones's analysis of combat, masculinity, and anxiety about femininity in *Irrational Modernism: A Neurasthenic History of New York Dada* (Cambridge, MA: MIT Press, 2004), 47.

36 This reading of German fascism's integral connection to a masculine-feminine dynamic is Klaus Theweleit's, in *Male Fantasies.*

37 Drieu la Rochelle, *Socialisme fasciste,* 38–40.

38 Ibid., 41–42.

39 Drieu la Rochelle, *Socialisme fasciste* , 102.

40 Therese Lichtenstein, *Behind Closed Doors: The Art of Hans Bellmer* (Berkeley: University of California Press, 2001).

41 See Mark Antliff, "Fascism, Modernism, and Modernity," *The Art Bulletin* 84 (March 2002): 148–69; and Matthew Affron and Mark Antliff, eds., *Fascist Visions: Art and Ideology in France and Italy* (Princeton, NJ: Princeton University Press, 1997).

42 Alice Kaplan's work on fascism and French culture, including *Reproductions of Banality: Fascism, Literature, and French Intellectual Life* (Minneapolis: University of Minnesota Press, 1986) and *The Collaborator: The Trial and Execution of Robert Brasillach* (Chicago: University of Chicago Press, 2000), has been an inspiration to me. She has pushed hard to reevaluate the links—often avoided, discredited, or disavowed—between ideologies and practices that many scholars have considered to be in essential opposition to one another.

43 On Drieu's fascism as a critique of nationalism, see Carroll, *French Literary Fascism,* 125–46.

Conclusion. On Masculinity and Reconstruction

1 Louis Aragon, "Introduction à 1930," *La Révolution surréaliste* 12 (15 December 1929): 64.

2 Timothy J. Clark, "Jackson Pollock's Abstraction," in *Reconstructing Modernism: Art in Paris, New York, and Montreal, 1945–1964,* ed. Serge Guilbaut (Cambridge, MA: MIT Press, 1990), 178–79.

SELECTED BIBLIOGRAPHY

Archival Sources and Private Collections

Fonds Louis Aragon, Centre National de la Récherche Scientifique, Paris, and Department of Manuscripts, Bibliothèque Nationale de France, Paris

Fonds André Kertész, Mission de la Patrimoine Photographique, Paris

Fonds Man Ray, Bibliothèque Kandinsky, Musée National d'Art Moderne/Centre Georges Pompidou, Paris

Lee Miller Archive, East Sussex, England

Collection Lucien Treillard, Paris

Don André Vigneau, Bibliothèque Historique de la Ville de Paris

Primary Sources

"*L'Âge d'Or.* Correspondance Luis Buñuel–Charles de Noailles. Lettres et Documents (1929–1976)." *Les Cahiers du Musée National d'Art Moderne* (Hors-Série/Archives, 1993).

Aragon, Louis. "Au bout du quai, les Art Décoratifs!" *La Révolution surréaliste* 5 (15 October 1925): 26–27.

———. "Fragments d'une conférence." *La Révolution surréaliste* 4 (15 July 1925): 25.

———. "Introduction à 1930." *La Révolution surréaliste* 12 (15 December 1929): 57–64.

———. "Lautréamont et nous." 1er partie. *Les Lettres françaises* (1–7 June 1967): 5–9.

———. *L'Oeuvre poètique.* Vol. 1, *1917–1920*. Paris: Livre Club Diderot, 1974.

———. *Le Paysan de Paris*. Paris: Gallimard, 1953.
———. "La Peinture au Défi." In *Les Collages*. Paris: Hermann, 1965. Originally published as part of an exhibition catalog, Paris: José Corti/Galerie Goemans, 1930.
———. "Project for a History of Contemporary Literature." In *The Dada Painters and Poets*, edited by Robert Motherwell, 230. Cambridge, MA: Harvard University Press, 1981.
———. "Texte surréaliste." *La Révolution surréaliste* 7 (15 June 1926): 20.
Aragon, Louis, and André Breton. "Le Cinquantenaire de l'hystérie." *La Révolution surréaliste* 11 (15 March 1928): 20–23.
Bacelon, Émile. "Le Musée du Val-de-Grâce." *Le Figaro* (3 July 1916): 3.
Barancy, A.-P. "Fenêtre ouverte sur l'au-delà." *Le Sourire* (9 March 1933): n.p.
Bernheim, Dr. Hippolyte. *Automatisme et Suggestion*. Paris: Alcan, 1917.
Bonnerot, Jean. *La Bibliothèque Centrale et les Archives du Service de Santé au Musée du Val-de-Grâce*. Paris: E. Champion, 1918.
Bost, Pierre. *Le Cirque et le Music-Hall*. Paris: Au Sans Pareil, 1931.
Boularan-Deval, Dr. A. "Le Service de Santé à travers les âges." *Le Monde Illustré* (4 November 1916): 280.
Breton, André. "Avis au Lecteur." Preface to *La Femme 100 Têtes*, by Max Ernst. Paris: Éditions de l'Oeil, 1956.
———. "Caractères de l'évolution moderne." In *Les pas perdus*, 141–65. Paris: Gallimard, 1924.
———. *Entretiens*. Paris: Gallimard, 1952. Also published in English as *Conversations: The Autobiography of Surrealism*, translated by Mark Polizzotti. New York: Paragon, 1993.
———. "The Exquisite Corpse, Its Exaltation." In *Surrealism and Painting*, translated by Simon Watson Taylor, 288–90. London: Macdonald, 1972.
———. "Manifeste du surréalisme (1924)." In *Manifestes du surréalisme*, 11–64. Paris: Gallimard, 1963.
———. *Manifestoes of Surrealism*. Translated by Richard Seaver and Helen Weaver. Ann Arbor: University of Michigan Press, 1972.
———. *Nadja*. Translated by Richard Howard. New York: Grove, 1960.
———. *Les Pas Perdus*. Paris: Gallimard, 1990.
———. "Second Manifeste du Surréalisme." *La Révolution surréaliste* 12 (15 December 1929): 1–17.
———. "Le Surréalisme et la peinture." *La Révolution surréaliste* 4 (15 July 1925), 6 (1 March 1926), 7 (15 June 1926), 9–10 (1 October 1927).
Breton, André, and Paul Eluard. "Notes sur la poésie." *La Révolution surréaliste* 12 (15 December 1929): 53.
Breton, André, and Philippe Soupault. *Les Champs magnétiques*. Paris: Gallimard, 1968.
Cahuet, Albéric. "Le Château des faces massacrées." *L'Illustration* 169, no. 2 (11 June 1927): 626.
Chéronnet, Louis. "Affiches du mois." *L'Art Vivant* (1 June 1926): 429.
———. "L'Art dans la Rue." *L'Art Vivant* (1 January 1926): 25.
Clarétie, Léo. "Le Génie de la Pitié." *L'Évènement* (12 August 1916): 1.
Crevel, René. *Mon Corps et Moi*. Paris: Éditions Pauvert, 1979.
Desnos, Robert. "Emile Atdget" [*sic*]. In *Merle* 3 (3 May 1929). Reprinted in *Nouvelles Hébrides et autres textes, 1922–1930*, 434–35. Paris: Gallimard, 1978.

———. *La Liberté ou L'Amour.* Paris: Gallimard, 1962.
———. *Nouvelles Hébrides et autres textes, 1922–1930.* Paris: Gallimard, 1978.
Drieu la Rochelle, Pierre. "Chronique des Spectacles." *Nouvelle Revue française* (1 January 1924): 97–98.
———. *Gilles.* Paris: Gallimard, 1939.
———. *L'Homme Couvert des Femmes.* Paris: Gallimard, 1925.
———. *Mesure de la France.* Paris: Grasset, 1922.
———. *Socialisme fasciste.* Paris: Gallimard, 1934.
———. *La Suite dans les idées.* Paris: Au Sans Pareil, 1927.
Ducasse, Isidore, Comte de Lautréamont. *Oeuvres complètes.* Paris: Gallimard, 1973.
"Enquête: Que vont devenir les 1.500.000 jeunes filles à marier?" *J'ai Vu,* no. 237 (15 January 1920), and no. 240 (1 March 1920).
Ernest-Charles, J. "Au Musée du Val-de-Grâce." *Annales politiques et littéraires,* no. 1761 (25 March 1917): 284.
Freud, Sigmund. "Fetishism." Translated by James Strachey. *Standard Edition of the Complete Psychological Works of Sigmund Freud.* Vol. 21, 149–57. London: Hogarth, 1963.
———. "Instincts and their Vicissitudes." Translated by James Strachey. *Standard Edition.* Vol. 14, 111–40. London: Hogarth, 1963.
———. "On Narcissism: An Introduction." Translated by James Strachey. *Standard Edition.* Vol. 14, 67–104. London: Hogarth, 1963.
———. *Three Essays on the Theory of Sexuality.* Translated by James Strachey. New York: Basic Books, 1962.
Georges-Michel, Michel. "Barbette." *VU* 48 (February 1929): 115.
Gide, André. *Corydon.* Paris: Gallimard, 1924.
Guégan, Bertrand. "Kertész et son miroir." *Arts et Métiers Graphiques* 37 (15 September 1933): 23–24.
Heine, Maurice. "Note sur un Classement Psycho-Biologique des Paresthésies sexuelles." *Minotaure* 3–4 (1933): 36.
———. *Receuil des confessions et observations psycho-sexuelles.* Paris: Éditions Jean Crès, 1936.
Hesnard, Angelo. *L'Individu et le Sexe. Psychologie du Narcissisme.* Paris: Stock, 1927.
———. *La Psychanalyse. Théorie sexuelle de Freud.* Paris: Stock, 1924.
———. *Psychologie homosexuelle.* Paris: Stock, 1929.
Hesnard, Angelo, and Dr. Régis. *La Psychanalyse des Névroses et des Psychoses.* Paris: Alcan, 1914.
"L'Homosexualité en Littérature." *Les Marges* (15 March 1926): 176–216; and (April 1926): 242–45.
Janet, Pierre. *L'Automatisme psychologique.* Paris: Alcan, 1913.
Legrand-Chabrier. "Barbette avant et après son numéro." *L'Entr'acte* (December 1925): 13–14.
———. "Comment Barbette se métamorphose." *Le Petit Parisien,* 17 February 1935.
Maas, Walter S. "Subconscient et Publicité." *Arts et Métiers Graphiques* 1 (15 September 1927): 56–57.
Mac Orlan, Pierre. "La Photographie et le Fantastique Social." *Les Annales politiques et littéraires* (1 November 1928): 413–14.
Maliniak, Dr. Jacques. *Sculpture in the Living.* New York: Romaine Pearson, 1934.

Martin, Dr. Florent. *Les Mutilations et les appareils de prothèse.* Liège: Georges Thone, 1924.

Ministère de la Guerre, Sous-secrétariat d'État du Service de Santé. *Eléments constitutifs des archives et documents de la Guerre. Musée du Val-de-Grâce.* Paris: Imprimerie de Chaix, 1916.

Monéry, Dr. A., Médecin-Major de 1er Classe. *Le Musée du Val-de-Grâce. Archives et documents de guerre du Service de Santé. Guide-Catalogue.* Paris, 1923.

Myers, F. W. H. *The Human Personality and Its Survival of Bodily Death.* London: Longmans, Green, 1907.

"L'Oeuvre de notre Service de Santé militaire. Le Musée du Val-de-Grace." *Excelsior* 8 (July 1916): 12.

Paris, vu par André Kertész. Text by Pierre Mac Orlan. Paris: Plon, 1934.

Paulhan, Jean. *Le Guerrier appliqué.* Paris: Sansot, 1919.

Peignot, Charles. "Mannequins." *Arts et Métiers Graphiques* 10 (15 March 1929): 595.

Péret, Benjamin, and Louis Aragon. *1929.* Paris, 1929.

Pierre, José, ed. *Tracts surréalistes et déclarations collectives, 1922–1939.* Vol. 1. Paris: Terrain Vague, 1980.

"Pour les Mutilés. M. Justin Godart inaugure une institution de réeducation, due à la générosité américaine." *L'Évènement* (10 August 1916): 2.

Ray, Man. "The Age of Light." In *Photographs by Man Ray 1920 Paris 1934,* edited by James Thrall Soby. Hartford, CT: James Thrall Soby, 1934. Reprint, New York: Dover, 1979.

———. *Self Portrait.* Boston: Little, Brown, 1963.

———. *This Quarter* (1932): 55.

"Recherches sur la Sexualité." *La Révolution surréaliste* 11 (15 March 1928): 32–40.

Remarque, Erich Maria. *All Quiet on the Western Front.* Boston: Little, Brown, 1930.

Rim, Carlo. "Luna Park ou la clef des songes." *VU* (August 1930): 786–87.

Science et Dévouement. Paris: Aristide Quillet, 1918.

Sélavy, Rrose. "Men Before the Mirror." In *Photographs by Man Ray 1920 Paris 1934,* 66. Hartford, CT: James Thrall Soby, 1934.

Soby, James Thrall, ed. *Photographs by Man Ray 1920 Paris 1934.* Hartford, CT: James Thrall Soby, 1934.

Strehly, Georges. *L'Acrobatie et les acrobates.* Paris: C. Delagrave, n.d.

Tomellini, Dr. Louis. Laboratory of the Legal Identity Service of the Paris Préfecture of Police. *Metric Photography (Bertillon System), New Apparatus for the Criminal Department. Directions for Use and Considerations of the Applications to Forensic Medicine and Anthropology.* Lyon: A. Rey et Cie., 1908. Extract from the *Archives of Criminal Anthropology and Forensic Medicine,* no. 170 (15 February 1908).

Verne, Maurice. *Musées de Voluptés. Le secret des nuits électriques.* Paris: Éditions des Portiques, 1930.

Secondary Sources

Ades, Dawn. *Dada and Surrealism Reviewed.* London: Hayward Gallery, 1978.

———. "Duchamp's Masquerades." In *The Portrait in Photography,* edited by Graham Clarke, 94–114. London: Reaktion, 1992.

———. "Photography and the Surrealist Text." In *L'Amour Fou: Photography and Surrealism,* edited by Rosalind Krauss and Jane Livingston, 155–89. New York: Abbeville, 1985.
———. *Photomontage.* New York: Pantheon, 1976.
Affron, Matthew, and Mark Antliff, eds. *Fascist Visions: Art and Ideology in France and Italy.* Princeton, NJ: Princeton University Press, 1997.
Althusser, Louis. "Ideology and Ideological State Apparatuses." In *Lenin and Philosophy and Other Essays.* Translated by Ben Brewster, 127–86. New York: Monthly Review Press, 1971.
André Breton: La Beauté convulsive. Paris: Musée National d'Art Moderne/Centre Georges Pompidou, 1991.
André Kertész: Distortions. London: Thames & Hudson, 1977.
Antliff, Mark. "Fascism, Modernism, and Modernity." *The Art Bulletin* 84 (March 2002): 148–69.
Aragon parle avec Dominique Arban. Paris: Seghers, 1968.
Armstrong, Carol. "The Reflexive and the Possessive View: Thoughts on Kertész, Brandt and the Photographic Nude." *Representations* 25 (Winter 1989): 57–70.
Bakhtin, Mikhail. "Discourse in the Novel." In *The Dialogic Imagination,* translated by Caryl Emerson and Michael Holquist and edited by Michael Holquist, 259–422. Austin: University of Texas Press, 1981.
Balibar, Étienne. "The Nation Form: History and Ideology." In *Race, Nation, Class: Ambiguous Identities,* edited by Étienne Balibar and Immanuel Wallerstein. London: Verso, 1991.
Barbedette, Gilles, and Michel Carassou. *Paris Gay 1925.* Paris: Presses de la Renaissance, 1981.
Beale, Marjorie. "Advertising and the Politics of Public Persuasion in France, 1900–1939." PhD diss., University of California, Berkeley, 1991.
———. *The Modernist Enterprise: French Elites and the Threat of Modernity, 1900–1940.* Stanford, CA: Stanford University Press, 1999.
Beauvoir, Simone de. *The Ethics of Ambiguity.* Translated by Bernard Frechtman. New York: Citadel Press, 1965.
Becker, Jean-Jacques, and Serge Berstein. *Victoire et frustrations, 1914–1929.* Paris: Seuil, 1999.
Béhar, Henri. *André Breton.* Paris: Calmann-Lévy, 1990.
Benjamin, Walter. *Paris, Capitale du XIXe Siècle. Le Livre des Passages.* Paris: Les Éditions du Cerf, 1993.
Billeter, Erika, ed. *La Femme et le surréalisme.* Lausanne: Musée Cantonal des Beaux-Arts, 1987.
Blanchot, Maurice. *Lautréamont et Sade.* Paris: Éditions de Minuit, 1949.
Bonnet, Marguerite. *André Breton. Naissance de l'aventure surréaliste.* Paris: José Corti, 1975.
Borch-Jacobsen, Mikkel. *The Freudian Subject.* Translated by Catherine Porter. Stanford, CA: Stanford University Press, 1988.
Borhan, Pierre, ed. *André Kertész: His Life and Work.* Boston: Little, Brown, 1994.
Bourgeade, Pierre. *Bonsoir, Man Ray.* Paris: Belfont, 1972.
Bourke, Joanna. *Dismembering the Male: Men's Bodies, Britain, and the Great War.* Chicago: University of Chicago Press, 1995.
Brassaï, *The Secret Paris of the 1930s.* Translated by Richard Miller. New York: Pantheon, 1976.
Broude, Norma, and Mary Garrard, eds. *Reclaiming Female Agency: Feminist Art History after Postmodernism.* Berkeley: University of California Press, 2005.

Buck-Morss, Susan. "The City as Dreamworld and Catastrophe." *October* 73 (Summer 1995): 3–26.
———. *The Dialectics of Seeing: Walter Benjamin and the Arcades Project*. Cambridge, MA: MIT Press, 1991.
Butler, Judith. *Gender Trouble: Feminism and the Subversion of Identity*. London: Routledge, 1990.
Carassou, Michel. *René Crevel*. Paris: Fayard, 1989.
Carroll, David. *French Literary Fascism: Nationalism, Anti-Semitism, and the Ideology of Culture*. Princeton, NJ: Princeton University Press, 1995.
Caws, Mary Ann. "Ladies Shot and Painted: Female Embodiment in Surrealist Art." In *The Female Body in Western Culture: Contemporary Perspectives*, edited by Susan Rubin Suleiman, 262–87. Cambridge, MA: Harvard University Press, 1986.
———. "Seeing the Surrealist Woman: We Are a Problem." In *Surrealism and Women*, edited by Mary Ann Caws, Rudolf E. Kuenzli, and Gwen Raaberg, 11–16. Cambridge, MA: MIT Press, 1991.
Chadwick, Whitney. *Women Artists and the Surrealist Movement*. Boston: Little, Brown, 1985.
Chadwick, Whitney, and Tirza True Latimer, eds. *The Modern Woman Revisited: Paris Between the Wars*. New Brunswick, NJ: Rutgers University Press, 2003.
Chessel, Marie-Emanuelle. *La Publicité. Naissance d'une profession, 1900–1940*. Paris: CNRS Éditions, 1998.
Chevrefils-Desbiolles, Yves. "Les Revues d'art de l'entre-deux-guerres à Paris." Doctoral thesis, Paris 01, Université de Lille III, 1992.
Conley, Katharine. "La Femme automatique du Surréalisme." *Pleine Marge* 17 (June 1993): 69–80.
Courouve, Claude. *Bibliographie des homosexualités II (1882–1924)*. 3rd ed. Paris: C. Courove, 1981.
La Course au Moderne. France et Allemagne dans l'Europe des Années Vingt 1919–1933. Paris: Musée d'Histoire Contemporaine–Bibliothèque de Documentation International Contemporain, 1993.
David-Ménard, Monique. *Hysteria from Freud to Lacan*. Translated by Catherine Porter. Ithaca, NY: Cornell University Press, 1989.
de Lauretis, Teresa. *Technologies of Gender: Essays on Theory, Film, and Fiction*. Bloomington: Indiana University Press, 1987.
Dean, Carolyn J. *The Frail Social Body: Pornography, Homosexuality, and Other Fantasies in Interwar France*. Berkeley: University of California Press, 2000.
———. *The Self and Its Pleasures: Bataille, Lacan and the History of the Decentered Subject*. Ithaca, NY: Cornell University Press, 1992.
Delaporte, Sophie. *Les Gueules Cassées. Les blessés de la face de la Grande Guerre*. Paris: Éditions Noêsis, 1996.
Doherty, Brigid. "Figures of the Pseudorevolution." *October* 84 (Spring 1998): 65–89.
———. "'See, We Are All Neurasthenics!' or, the Trauma of Dada Montage." *Critical Inquiry* 24 (Autumn 1997): 82–132.
Dumas, Marie-Claire. *Robert Desnos ou l'exploration des limites*. Paris: Klincksieck, 1980.
L'Ecotais, Emmanuelle de, and Alain Sayag. *Man Ray, La Photographie à l'Envers*. Paris: Centre Georges Pompidou/Seuil, 1998.
"La Femme surréaliste." Special issue, *Obliques* 14–15 (1977).

Foresta, Merry, Francis Naumann, Billy Klüver, Julie Martin, Elizabeth Hutton Turner, Sandra S. Phillips, Stephen C. Foster, and Roger Shattuck. *Perpetual Motif: The Art of Man Ray.* Washington, DC: National Museum of American Art, Smithsonian Institution/New York: Abbeville, 1988.
Foster, Hal. "L'Amour Faux." *Art in America* (January 1986): 116–29.
———. "Armor Fou." *October* 56 (Spring 1991): 64–97.
———. *Compulsive Beauty.* Cambridge, MA: MIT Press, 1992.
Foucault, Michel. *The Birth of the Clinic: An Archaeology of Medical Perception.* Translated by A.M. Sheridan Smith. New York: Vintage, 1973.
———. *The History of Sexuality.* Vol. 1, *An Introduction.* Translated by Robert Hurley. New York: Vintage, 1978/1990.
Galerie 1900–2000. *Continent Abstrait, Continent Surréaliste.* Paris, 1986.
Gauthier, Xavière. *Surréalisme et sexualité.* Paris: Gallimard, 1971.
Gilbert, Sandra M., and Susan Gubar, eds. *No Man's Land.* Vol. 2, *Sexchanges.* New Haven, CT: Yale University Press, 1989.
Gilman, Sander L. "The Image of the Hysteric." In *Hysteria Beyond Freud,* edited by Gilman, Helen King, Roy Porter, G.S. Rousseau, and Elaine Showalter, 345–452. Berkeley: University of California Press, 1993.
Golan, Romy. *Modernity and Nostalgia: Art and Politics in France between the Wars.* New Haven, CT: Yale University Press, 1995.
Goldstein, Jan. *Console and Classify: The French Psychiatric Profession in the Nineteenth Century.* New York: Cambridge University Press, 1987.
———. "The Uses of Male Hysteria: Medical and Literary Discourse in Nineteenth-Century France." *Representations* 34 (Spring 1991): 134–65.
Gramsci, Antonio. *Selections from the Prison Notebooks.* Edited and translated by Quintin Hoare and Geoffrey Nowell Smith. New York: International Publishers, 1971.
Greeley, Robin Adèle. "Image, Text and the Female Body: René Magritte and the Surrealist Publications." *Oxford Art Journal* 15 (1992): 48–57.
———. *Surrealism and the Spanish Civil War.* New Haven, CT: Yale University Press, 2006.
Greenough, Sarah, Robert Gurbo, and Sarah Kennel, eds. *André Kertész.* Princeton, NJ: Princeton University Press, 2005.
Griffin, Roger. *The Nature of Fascism.* New York: St. Martin's Press, 1991.
Gronberg, Tag. "Beware Beautiful Women: The 1920s Shopwindow Mannequin and the Physiognomy of Effacement." *Art History* 20:3 (September 1997): 375–96.
Gubar, Susan. "Representing Pornography: Feminism, Criticism, and Depictions of Female Violation." *Critical Inquiry* 13 (1987): 712–41.
Gunther, Thomas Michael. "Les photographies d'Atget achetées par Man Ray." In *Colloque Atget* (held at the Collège de France, 14–15 June 1985). *Photographies* (Paris, March 1986): 70–73.
Haiken, Beth. "Plastic Surgery and Beauty at 1921." *Bulletin of the History of Medicine* 68 (1994): 429–53.
Hall, Lesley. *Hidden Anxieties: Male Sexuality, 1900–1950.* Cambridge: Polity, 1991.
Hammond, Paul. *L'Âge d'Or.* London: British Film Institute, 1997.

———. "Lost and Found: Buñuel, *L'Âge d'Or* and Surrealism." In *Luis Buñuel: New Readings,* edited by Peter William Evans and Isabel Santaolalla, 13–26. London: British Film Institute, 2004.

Heymann, Claude. "Sur le tournage de *L'Âge d'Or.*" *Jeune cinéma* 134 (April–May 1981): 6–11.

Higonnet, Margaret R., Jane Jenson, Sonya Michel, and Margaret Collins Weitz. *Behind the Lines: Gender and the Two World Wars.* New Haven, CT: Yale University Press, 1987.

Hopkins, David. "Men Before the Mirror: Marcel Duchamp, Man Ray and Masculinity." *Art History* 21: 3 (September 1998): 303–23.

Huss, Marie-Monique. "Pronatalism and the Popular Ideology of the Child in Wartime France: The Evidence of the Picture Postcard." In *The Upheaval of War: Family, Work and Welfare in Europe, 1914–1918,* edited by Richard Wall and Jay Winter, 329–67. Cambridge: Cambridge University Press, 1988.

Identités: De Disderi au photomaton. Paris: Centre National de la Photographie / Éditions du Chêne, 1985.

Irigaray, Luce. "Any Theory of the 'Subject' Has Always Been Appropriated by the 'Masculine.'" In *Speculum of the Other Woman,* translated by Gillian C. Gill, 133–46. Ithaca, NY: Cornell University Press, 1985.

Jones, Amelia. *Irrational Modernism: A Neurasthenic History of New York Dada.* Cambridge, MA: MIT Press, 2004.

Kaplan, Alice. *Reproductions of Banality: Fascism, Literature, and French Intellectual Life.* Minneapolis: University of Minnesota Press, 1986.

Klossowski, Pierre. *Sade My Neighbor.* Translated by Alphonso Lingis. Evanston, IL: Northwestern University Press, 1991.

Koven, Seth. "Remembering and Dismemberment: Crippled Children, Wounded Soldiers, and the Great War in Great Britain." *American Historical Review* (October 1994): 1167–1202.

Kracauer, Siegfried. *The Mass Ornament: Weimar Essays.* Translated by Thomas Y. Levin. Cambridge, MA: Harvard University Press, 1995.

Kral, Petr. "*L'Âge d'Or* aujourd'hui." *Positif* 247 (October 1981): 44–50.

Krauss, Rosalind. "Corpus Delicti." In *L'Amour Fou: Photography and Surrealism,* edited by Rosalind Krauss and Jane Livingston, 57–100. New York: Abbeville, 1985.

———. "Nightwalkers." *Art Journal* 41 (Spring 1981): 33–38.

———. "The Photographic Conditions of Surrealism." In *The Originality of the Avant-Garde and Other Modernist Myths,* 87–118. Cambridge, MA: MIT Press, 1986.

———. "Photography in the Service of Surrealism." In *L'Amour Fou: Photography and Surrealism,* edited by Rosalind Krauss and Jane Livingston, 14–42. New York: Abbeville, 1985.

Kris, Ernst, and Otto Kurz. *Legend, Myth, and Magic in the Image of the Artist: A Historical Experiment.* New Haven, CT: Yale University Press, 1979.

Kuenzli, Rudolf. "Surrealism's Misogyny." In *Surrealism and Women,* edited by Mary Ann Caws, Rudolf Kuenzli, and Gwen Raaberg, 17–26. Cambridge, MA: MIT Press, 1990.

Leys, Ruth. "Death Masks: Kardiner and Ferenczi on Psychic Trauma." *Representations* 53 (Winter 1996): 44–73.

———. "Traumatic Cures: Shell Shock, Janet and the Question of Memory." *Critical Inquiry* 20 (Summer 1994): 630–34.

Livingston, Jane. *Lee Miller: Photographer.* New York: Thames & Hudson; Los Angeles: California/International Arts Foundation, 1989.
———. "Man Ray and Surrealist Photography." In *L'Amour Fou: Photography and Surrealism,* edited by Rosalind Krauss and Jane Livingston, 115–47. New York: Abbeville, 1985.
Lomas, David. *The Haunted Self: Surrealism, Psychoanalysis, Subjectivity.* New Haven, CT: Yale University Press, 2000.
Lyford, Amy J. "Lee Miller's Photographic Impersonations, 1930–1945: Conversing with Surrealism." *History of Photography* 18 (Autumn 1994): 230–41.
MacGregor, William B. "Advertising Individuality: Rrose Sélavy and the Making of Duchamp's Reputation." Master's thesis, University of California, Berkeley, 1991.
MacMillan, James. *Housewife or Harlot: The Position of Women in French Society.* New York: St. Martin's Press, 1980.
Mangan, J.A., and James Walvin, eds. *Manliness and Morality: Middle Class Masculinity in England and America, 1800–1940.* New York: St. Martin's Press, 1987.
Martin, Jean-Hubert. *Man Ray Photographe.* Paris: Philippe Sers, 1982.
Matlock, Jann. "Masquerading Women, Pathologized Men: Cross-Dressing, Fetishism, and the Theory of Perversion, 1882–1935." In *Fetishism as Cultural Discourse,* edited by Emily Apter and William Pietz, 31–61. Ithaca, NY: Cornell University Press, 1993.
Maugue, Annelise. *L'Identité Masculine en Crise.* Paris: Rivages, 1987.
McCauley, Elizabeth. *Industrial Madness: Commercial Photography in Paris.* New Haven, CT: Yale University Press, 1994.
Metz, Christian. "Photography and Fetish." *October* 34 (Fall 1985): 81–90.
Micale, Mark S. "Charcot and the Idea of Hysteria in the Male: Gender, Medical Science, and Medical Diagnostics in Late Nineteenth Century France." *Medical History* 34 (October 1990): 363–411.
———. "Hysteria Male/Hysteria Female: Reflections on Comparative Gender Construction in Nineteenth-Century France and Britain." In *Science and Sensibility: Gender and Scientific Enquiry 1780–1945,* edited by Marina Benjamin, 200–39. Oxford: Basil Blackwell, 1991.
Micale, Mark S., and Paul Lerner, eds. *Traumatic Pasts: History, Psychiatry, and Trauma in the Modern Age, 1870–1930.* Cambridge: Cambridge University Press, 2001.
Mijolla, Alain de. "Freud en Français jusqu'en 1940." *Revue Internationale d'Histoire de la Psychanalyse* 4 (1991): 283–89.
Mileaf, Janine. "Between You and Me: Man Ray's *Object to Be Destroyed.*" *Art Journal* 63 (Spring 2004): 4–23.
Miller, Lee. "I Worked with Man Ray." *Lilliput* 9 (October 1941): 315–19.
Miller, Lee, with Mario Amaya. "My Man Ray." *Art in America* 63 (May/June 1975): 54–61.
Mosse, George L. *Fallen Soldiers: Reshaping the Memory of the World Wars.* Oxford: Oxford University Press, 1990.
———. *The Image of Man: The Creation of Modern Masculinity.* Oxford: Oxford University Press, 1996.
———. *Nationalism and Sexuality: Respectability and Abnormal Sexuality in Modern Europe.* New York: Howard Fertig, 1985.

Mundy, Jennifer, ed. *Surrealism: Desire Unbound.* Princeton, NJ: Princeton University Press, 2001.

Nadeau, Maurice. *The History of Surrealism.* Translated by Richard Howard. Cambridge, MA: Harvard University Press, 1989.

Nesbit, Molly. *Atget's Seven Albums.* New Haven, CT: Yale University Press, 1992.

Le numéro Barbette. Paris: Jacques Damase, 1980.

Nye, Robert A. *Masculinity and Male Codes of Honor in Modern France.* New York: Oxford University Press, 1993.

Orenstein, Gloria Feman. "*Nadja* Revisited: A Feminist Approach." *Dada/Surrealism* 8 (1978): 91–106.

Panchasi, Roxanne. "Reconstructions: Prosthetics and the Rehabilitation of the Male Body in World War I France." *Differences* 7.3 (1995): 109–40.

Penrose, Antony. *The Lives of Lee Miller.* London: Thames & Hudson, 1985.

Penrose, Roland. *Man Ray.* London: Thames & Hudson, 1975.

Phillips, Sandra. "André Kertész: The Years in Paris." In *André Kertész: Of Paris and New York,* edited by Sandra Phillips, David Travis, and Weston J. Naef, 50–51. Chicago: The Art Institute of Chicago, 1985.

———. "The Photographic Work of André Kertész in France, 1925–1936: A Critical Essay and Catalogue." 2 vols. PhD diss., City University of New York, 1985.

Pierre, José, ed. *Investigating Sex.* Translated by Malcolm Imrie. New York: Verso, 1992.

Recherches sur la Sexualité (January 1928–August 1932). Archives du surréalisme 4. Edited by José Pierre. Paris: Gallimard, 1990.

Roberts, Mary Louise. *Civilization Without Sexes: Reconstructing Gender in Postwar France, 1917–1927.* Chicago: University of Chicago Press, 1994.

Roudebush, Marc. "A Battle of Nerves: Hysteria and Its Treatment in France During World War I." PhD diss., University of California, Berkeley, 1995.

Roudinesco, Elisabeth. *La Bataille de Cent Ans: Histoire de la Psychanalyse en France.* Vols. 1 and 2. Paris: Seuil, 1986.

Rubin, Gayle. "The Traffic in Women: Notes on the Political Economy of Sex." In *Toward an Anthropology of Women,* edited by Rayna B. Reiter, 157–210. New York: Monthly Review Press, 1975.

Sanouillet, Michel. *Dada à Paris.* Paris: J.-J. Pauvert, 1965.

Scepi, Henri, and Jean-Luc Steinmetz, eds. *Lautréamont: Retour au Texte.* Poitiers: La Licorne, 2001.

Sekula, Allan. "The Body and the Archive." *October* 39 (Winter 1986): 3–64.

Shattuck, Roger. "Candor and Perversion in No-Man's Land." In *Perpetual Motif: The Art of Man Ray,* Edited by Merry Foresta. Washington, DC: National Museum of American Art, 1988.

———. "The Nadja File." *Cahiers Dada/Surréalisme* 1 (1966): 49–56.

"Shell-Shock." Special issue, *Journal of Contemporary History* 35: 1 (2000).

Sherman, Daniel J. *The Construction of Memory in Interwar France.* Chicago: University of Chicago Press, 1999.

Short, Robert. *Dada and Surrealism.* London: Octopus Books, 1980.

———. "Paris Dada and Surrealism." *Journal of European Studies* 9 (1979): 75–98.

Silver, Kenneth. *Esprit de Corps: The Art of the Parisian Avant-Garde and the First World War, 1914–1925*. Princeton, NJ: Princeton University Press, 1989.
Silverman, Kaja. *Male Subjectivity at the Margins*. New York: Routledge, 1992.
Soucy, Robert. *Fascist Intellectual: Drieu la Rochelle*. Berkeley: University of California Press, 1979.
Soupault, Philippe. *Lautréamont*. Paris: Seghers, 1946.
Spiteri, Raymond, and Donald LaCoss, eds. *Surrealism, Politics, Culture*. Aldershot, England: Ashgate, 2003.
Sternhell, Zeev. *Neither Right Nor Left: Fascist Ideology in France*. Translated by David Maisel. Berkeley: University of California Press, 1986.
Stich, Sidra, ed. *Anxious Visions: Surrealist Art*. Berkeley: University Art Museum, 1990.
Stovall, Tyler. "Paris in the Age of Anxiety, 1919–39." In *Anxious Visions: Surrealist Art*, edited by Sidra Stich, 201–21. Berkeley: University Art Museum, 1990.
Suleiman, Susan Rubin. *Subversive Intent: Gender, Politics, and the Avant-Garde*. Cambridge, MA: Harvard University Press, 1990.
Sylvester, David. "La grande icône surréaliste." In *André Breton: La Beauté convulsive*. Paris: Musée National d'Art Moderne, 1991.
Tagg, John. *The Burden of Representation*. Amherst: University of Massachusetts Press, 1988.
Theweleit, Klaus. *Male Fantasies*. Vols. 1 and 2. Translated by Stephen Conway. Minneapolis: University of Minnesota Press, 1987–89.
Walker, Ian. *City Gorged with Dreams: Surrealism and Documentary Photography in Interwar Paris*. Manchester: Manchester University Press, 2002.
Walz, Robin. *Pulp Surrealism: Insolent Popular Culture in Early Twentieth-Century Paris*. Berkeley: University of California Press, 2000.

INDEX

Designer:	Barbara Jellow
Text:	9.5/13.5 Scala
Display:	Scala and Fenwick families
Compositor:	BookMatters, Berkeley
Indexer:	Andrew Joron
Printer and Binder:	Asia Pacific